PUBLIC AUTHORITIES

of

First published in 1992 by
Earlsgate Press,
Earlsgate House, 11 West End,
Winteringham, South Humberside. DN15 9NR
Tel: 0724 733517   Fax: 0724 732676

British Library Cataloguing - in - Publication Data:

A Catalogue record for this book is available from the British Library

ISBN   1-873439-80-6.

Printed by Europress (Hull)

DEDICATION

FOR PETER

Preface

The aim of this book is to describe and evaluate the rules which govern liability claims by and against public authorities. There seemed a pressing need for a book dealing with this subject in relation to the law of England and Wales: the last to treat the subject comprehensively was Street's *Governmental Liability* back in 1953, and there have, of course, been significant developments since then. This is not to say, however, that much valuable work has not been done on the subject since that time, and for many parts of the book I have been fortunate in being able to draw on the writings of a large number of distinguished scholars who have made contributions in this field.The book covers liability claims in contract, tort and restitution, and also claims for payments due under statute. As well as dealing with domestic law it considers the law relating to claims against our government for breach of European Community rules, a subject which is becoming of increasing practical importance.

A number of people assisted me in this project in various different ways. I am very grateful to Peter Cane, Jack Beatson, Nuala O'Loan, Barry Hough, Richard Kidner and Christopher Harding, all of whom kindly read portions of the manuscript; to David Lambert of the Welsh Office, who discussed various aspects of the work with me and provided me with some interesting material; and to Ann Sherlock for her help with matters relating to Community law. I would also like to thank Kiew Lai Wah for her work in checking citations; Carol Parry and Cath Bean for typing the final manuscript; and Lillian Stevenson and Meirion Derrick in the UCW law library, who have always been cheerful and patient in dealing with my (numerous) requests and queries.

Much of the material in chapter 11, on restitution, is based on research I did for the Law Commission whilst acting as a consultant for its recent project on payments made under mistake of law. I would like to express my thanks to the Commission for allowing me to use the material.

The manuscript was substantially completed in October 1991. However, I was able to make some amendments to take account of more recent developments, including the European Court decision in Francovich in November, and the Public Works Contracts Regulations and Public Supply Contracts Regulations which were enacted in December.

Sue Arrowsmith
Aberystwyth, March 21 1991

List of Abbreviations

The works listed below are referred to in this book by the following abbreviations:

P. Hogg, *Liability of the Crown* (1989).   Hogg

P.P. Craig, *Administrative Law* (2nd ed. 1989).   Craig

H.W.R. Wade, *Administrative Law* 5th ed.1988).   Wade

M.A. Jones, *Text book on Torts* (3rd ed.1991).   Jones

W.V.H. Rogers, *Winfield and Jolowicz on Tort*
(13th ed. 1989)....   Winfield and
                                                             Jolowicz

R. Goff & G.Jones, *The Law of Restitution*
(3rd ed. 1986)   Goff and
                                                             Jones

Glanville Williams, *Crown Proceedings* (1947)   Glanville
                                                             Williams

M. Aronson and H. Whitmore, *Public Contracts and Torts*
(1982)   Aronson and
                                                             Whitmore

Street. *Governmental Liability* (1953)   Street

Table of Contents

Detailed Table of Contents

Chapter 3

Public Procurement

Chapter 4

Public Employment

Chapter 7

Breach of Statutory Duty

Chapter 8

Nuisance and Rylands v Fletcher

Chapter 9

Compensation Outside the Private Law

Chapter 10

Compensation for Breach of European Community Law

Chapter 11

Restitution

Chapter 12

Payments Due Under Legislation

Table of Cases

ENGLISH AND COMMONWEALTH

EUROPEAN COMMUNITY - NUMERICAL LIST

TABLE OF LEGISLATION

ENGLISH AND COMMONWEALTH

<u>Statutes</u>

Secondary Legislation

European Community

1

Introduction

1.1. The Public Law-Private Distinction

In principle it is the ordinary private law, applied by the ordinary courts, which governs the liability of public authorities. In this respect English law can be contrasted with that of some other jurisdictions, such as France, where most matters of governmental liability are dealt with by a special body of public law rules, adjudicated by a separate system of courts. Although there is no single distinct body of public law rules in English law, however, there are substantial modifications, exceptions, and additions to the general law in the way in which it applies to public authorities, which reflect the special position and characteristics of these authorities. It is with these special rules that this book is concerned.

The fact that there is no distinct single body of "public law" adjudicated by a separate court does not, however, mean that it is never necessary to draw a distinction between the public and private law spheres. (For general discussion see Harlow, (1980) 43 MLR 241; Samuel, (1983) 46 MLR 558; Beatson, (1987) 103 LQR 34; Cane, "Public Law and Private Law - a study of the analysis and use of a legal concept" in *Oxford Essays in Jurisprudence 3rd Series* (1987), eds. Eekelaar and Bell).

Some of the special liability rules discussed in the following pages are not, in fact, framed in terms of any distinction between public and private law: they are rules of more general application, but which have a particular importance for public authorities. For example, the immunity which such authorities often enjoy from liability in nuisance arises from the fact that powers have been conferred on them by statute, and it may also apply to private bodies which have comparable statutory powers (see 8.1.2), and the rule that estoppel may not operate contrary to statute, whilst in practice usually arising in a public law context, is also a rule of general application (on this see in particular 2.3.2.1). There are also many special rules which are peculiar to the Crown, and their scope is defined by considering who acts for the Crown. All these may be thought of as rules of public law, but determining their scope does not require us to define exactly what is meant by public or private.

In other cases, however, special rules have been formulated by reference to a distinction between the public and private spheres, or the governmental and non-governmental. Thus, the tort of misfeasance in public office applies only where there is an exercise of a "public" power (see 9.1.3), and the availability of exemplary damages in tort may depend on whether there has been an exercise of "governmental" authority (see 5.5.2.2). In the area of restitution there has recently been held to be a special "public law" rule which applies to allow recovery of overpayments made to "public" bodies, and the Law Commission has also suggested the creation of a special statutory rule of "public law" in this area (see 11.2.2.2 and 11.2.5). Further, the important European Community directives on the award of public works and supplies contracts, discussed in chapter 3, are also defined as applicable in the field of "public law". There are also many general doctrines, not concerned with liability alone, the scope of which depends on a public-private distinction. One is the principle which determines whether an individual can obtain a remedy for non-compliance with a directly effective European Community Directive, where the member state responsible has failed to implement it: a remedy may be obtained only against "the State" and entities with a certain type of connection with "the State", since the reason for allowing a remedy is that the State which has responsibility for implementing the Directive should not be able to take advantage of its own failure to do so (see case 8/81, *Becker v Finanzarnt Munster-Innenstadt* [1982] ECR 53; case 152/84, *Marshall v Southampton and South West Hampshire Area Health Authority (Teaching)* [1986] ECR 723). The scope of many of the substantive principles of judicial review under the common law is also generally explained in terms of "public" and "private"; and in Canada the question has also arisen in relation to the scope of judicial review under the Canadian Charter of Rights and Freedoms, which is confined to "government" action (on this see *McKinney v University of Guelph,* Dec. 6 1990 (SCC); *Retail, Wholesale and Department Store Union v Dolphin Delivery Ltd* [1987] 33 DLR (4th) 174; Otis [1987] PL 516; Gibson, (1983) 13 Man LJ 505).

Finally, the question of the public-private divide may arise not only in deciding the scope of substantive rules but in determining which rules are to be treated as public law rules for remedial or procedural purposes. English law has recently developed a distinction between public law and private law in relation to the special procedure in Order 53 which applies to public law actions (see 1.3 below). It is also interesting that a division of rules into public and private under the Common Law has been needed to determine the legal regime applicable to disputes in the Canadian province of Quebec. Following the subjection of the province to the English Crown, it was decided that matters of public law were to be governed by the Common Law, whilst matters of private law were to be determined by the French based Civil Law, which applied at the time of conquest. (On the application of the distinction in the context of liability see, in particular, *Laurentide Motels Ltd v Beauport* [1989] 1 SCR 705 and Arrowsmith, [1990] PL 481). Generally the problem which arises is deciding which *bodies* should be regarded as within the scope of particular public law rules. The formulation of clear principles is not easy: the structure of the institutions set up in the United Kingdom to deal with social, economic and regulatory matters has become increasingly diverse, and any sort of public-private line increasingly difficult to draw (see Lewis, "Regulating Non-Government Bodies: Privatization, Accountability, and the Public-Private Divide" in *The Changing Constitution* (2nd ed. 1989) eds. Jowell and Oliver, ch. 9). In some cases the concept of "public" has been given a wide definition. Thus it has been held that judicial review under Order 53 is available in relation to bodies which have no statutory or common law powers, but exercise a public regulatory or disciplinary function *(R v Panel on Take Overs and mergers ex parte Datafin plc* [1987] QB 815; *R. v Advertising Standards Authority, ex parte Insurance Services plc* [1989] 133 Sol Jo 1545; *R. v F.I.M.B.R.A., ex parte Cochrane* [1990] COD 33; though for the limitations on review see *R. v Disciplinary Committee of the Jockey Club, ex parte Massingberd-Munday* The Times Jan 3 1991; *Law v National Greyhound Racing Club Ltd* [1983] 1 WLR 1302). A wide view was also taken by the European Court in considering the direct effect of Directives in *Foster v British Gas* (case C-188/89, [1991] QB 405). Here it was held that an action could be available against "a body, whatever its legal form, which has been made responsible, pursuant to a measure adopted by the state, for providing a service under the control of the state and which has for that purpose special powers". This was subsequently held by the House of Lords to cover the predecessor of British Gas, the British Gas Corporation ([1991] 2 All ER 705). It was not necessary to determine whether the newly privatised British Gas plc would be covered also, but it may be that this body and the other newly privatised utilities will be held within the scope of the decision.

In addition, even with *bodies* clearly recognised as public authorities, there has been debate as to whether certain of their functions are to be treated as "public" functions. In particular, there has been argument over whether the government is subject to public law in carrying out functions such as procurement and employment, and in exercising the powers which it possesses as a landowner-activities which are not of an inherently governmental nature, and which could be carried out by private persons without any special powers. The tendency has been to expand public law doctrines to cover such activities. Thus it has been held that the tort of misfeasance in public office applies to the exercise of any power of a local authority, including an authority's powers as landlord under a lease of commercial premises (see 9.1.3); that the special category of governmental action in relation to exemplary damages may apply to conduct in making a contract of employment (see 5.5.2.2); and that there is no distinction between the Crown's special powers and its actions as landowner, in applying the rule that the Crown is not bound by the burden of statutes (see 1.2.1.6). There has also been a trend towards increased judicial review of contractual activities, though in the past it has been asserted that these activities are immune from scrutiny because they are "private" in nature and, thus it was reasoned, a matter for the private law alone (on this see 2.9 and 4.4 below; and also *McKinney v University of Guelph,* above, and *Committee of the Commonwealth of Canada v Canada* (Jan 25, 1991 (SCC) as regards the application of the Canadian Charter). It has also been made clear that directly effective provisions of European Community directives can be relied upon to give enforceable rights against the government in relation to all its activities, not just those of a peculiarly governmental nature *(Marshall v Southampton and South West Hampshire Area Health Authority,* above). On the other hand, the distinction between ordinary, or private, and governmental activities continues to have some relevance - for example, it appears to be influential in determining the scope of the public law immunity from negligence liability (see 6.2 below).

The English approach to public liability, and indeed public law rules generally, is flexible: the courts can choose to draw the public-private line at different points, according to the context. It is clear that in some contexts a different definition of "public" is required from that adopted in others. For example, the operation of certain rules, such as the special rule on restitution mentioned above, or the tort of misfeasance in public office, are properly framed in terms of public power, or public law; but it is not appropriate that all disputes relating to these rules should be required, or even permitted, to be determined under the "public law" procedure of Order 53 (on this see further 1.3 below). However, it is desirable in all cases to bear in mind the other contexts in which the public-private line is drawn: very often it may be that the same "public" characteristics are relevant in a number of different areas of law, and consideration of relevant analogy is likely to lead to a more consistent and coherent body of law. Thus, for example, it may be argued that the application of both judicial review principles and the tort of misfeasance in public office, and also the availability of exemplary damages in public law cases, are all justified by the obligation which public officials have to act for the benefit of others, and that the scope of these rules should be similar, and perhaps identical.

Writing in the nineteenth century the famous jurist A.V. Dicey made much of the fact that English law did not recognise any separate body of public law liability rules (see, in particular, *Introduction to The Law of the Constitution* (10th ed. 1959)). The application of the ordinary law he considered a desirable state of affairs which provided the best possible protection for individuals against potential state tyranny. Dicey has been much criticised, however, for placing undue emphasis on the *principle* of the application of the ordinary private law - the fact that the applicable rules were not regarded as a distinct and separate body of law. It is argued that he gave insufficient attention to the reality - which was that there were at that time many exceptions and qualifications to the principle, and many gaps in the protection given to individuals, particularly because of the special privilages and immunities which were then enjoyed by the Crown.

The accuracy of Dicey's assessment of the respective merits of the French and English public liability rules in the nineteenth century is now of purely historical interest. However, the respective merits of the different approaches adopted by the two systems have remained a matter for debate today. This debate has generally proceeded on the basis that the recognition of a distinct body of law applying to public authorities is likely to produce *more* substantive differences in the law between public and private than one which does not - although a system which starts from the principle that the ordinary private law applies may also adopt many special rules of liability, as English law clearly has done. Those who have favoured the English approach have generally done so because of a belief that the tendency of a special public law system is to produce too many special rules which unduly favour the state (see, for example, Hogg, at pp. 1-3; Harlow, above). However, "special" rules do not necessarily grant immunities and exemptions to the administration. Many of the special rules mentioned above provide additional rights for citizens against the state, beyond those which are they enjoy against their fellow citizens; and modern writers who have favoured the adoption of the French approach in the United Kingdom have done so largely because they believe, contrary to Dicey, that it offers, on balance, better protection for citizens than the existing approach, as well as being more sensitive to the needs of the administration (see, for example, Mitchell, *The Contracts of Public Authorities* (1954), at pp. 6-7; Street, at pp. 185-186; Friedmann, *Law in a Changing Society* (Pelican ed., 1964), at p. 303).

Probably the best starting point in considering public liability problems is the application of the ordinary law: this represents an important political ideal, and in the vast majority of cases it is clear that liability problems should be resolved by applying this ordinary law. However, it is possible generally to resolve problems in this way in a system which also recognises public law as a distinct body of rules: the strong presumption would be that the ordinary law applies, but at the same time the fact that the case is one of "public law" would require the courts to give attention to the question of whether any special rules should apply. Such an approach may well produce a body of law which is more sensitive to both the special needs and the special obligations of the state. However, the main disadvantage may be a less flexible approach to the definition of "public", which may need to vary according to the particular context. As for the question of separate courts to adjudicate public liability cases there seems no pressing need for such a major reform, which would probably have only marginal advantages. There is probably little to choose between the French and English approaches, and certainly no strong case for an overhaul of our present system.

1.2. The Administration

An understanding of the legal structure of the state and, in particular, of the position of the Crown within it, is essential to understanding many of the cases on governmental liability. This section will examine the position of the Crown and its agents, and the various special rules and privileges applicable to the Crown, which may be relevant to civil liability actions. The position and nature of other public authorities will then be noted briefly.

1.2.1.   The Crown and it's Agents

1.2.1.1. The nature and powers of the Crown

Many of the legal powers of central government are vested in a legal entity referred to as the Crown. There has long been debate as to the precise nature of this entity, which indeed goes back to the Middle Ages, though the debate then took a rather different form (see Maitland, (1901) 17 LQR 131; Kantorowicz, *The King's Two Bodies : a Study in Medieval Theology* (1957)). The modern debate over the nature of the Crown can only be understood in the light of the historical evolution of the British constitution. At one time the powers of government were vested in the monarch personally, both in law and in practice. Only gradually did a distinction develop between his powers in public affairs, which came by convention to be exercisable in most cases only on the advice of government officials, and of his own private powers which, like any other individual, he could exercise of his own accord. One view of the Crown today is that in law it is still not possible (except where provided for by statute) to make a distinction between the public and private capacities of the monarch, and that those powers exercised on the advice of public officials are still, in law, the powers of the individual who is the reigning monarch. In other words, it is considered that "the Crown", as a legal term of art, means simply that individual who is King or Queen at the time - a natural legal person. The alternative view is that the term "the Crown", as it is used in relation to public affairs, refers to an artificial legal person, probably a common law corporation, which is distinct from the human person of the monarch. Thus, for example, when Parliament gives a power to requisition property to be used for the public good to "the Crown", it is conferring this power not on the Queen personally, but on the common law corporation of the Crown, a public body.

A number of cases have proceeded on the basis of the first view set out above, that the Crown is to be equated with the monarch. Thus in *The Bankers Case* in 1695 ((1700) 90 ER 270) it was held that the King acting in governmental matters had a power to contract to borrow money without the need for Parliamentary approval, on the basis that he was a natural person, and this power is possessed by natural persons (see p. 271 per Coke C.J.). This view was also adopted as recently as 1977 by the Supreme Court of Canada in *J.E. Verrault & Fils v Quebec* ([1977] 1 SCR 41). The case, which clearly concerned the Crown's powers in the public sphere, raised the question of the scope of a Minster's power to bind the Crown in contract, which was governed by certain articles in the Quebec Civil Code. Different principles of agency applied according to whether the principal was a natural person or corporation. The court, stating that "Her Majesty is clearly a physical person" (at 47 per Pigeon J) held that the article governing the liability of natural persons applied (and see also *Quebec v Labreque* [1980] 2 SCR 1057). The historical immunity of the Crown from tort liability (see 1.2.1.4) also seems to be premised on similar reasoning - the King as an individual could not be held to have acted wrongly, and hence the Crown could not be liable for damage caused in the course of government business. This time the natural personality of the monarch had the consequence of producing *special* rules for the government, since the King as a natural person was treated in this respect in a different way from other natural persons.

On the other hand, some *dicta* in English cases reject this view of the nature of the Crown. In *Re Mason* ([1928] 1 Ch 385) Romer J, whilst deciding the case on other grounds, took the view that, under the common law, obligations incurred by the King can be enforced by his successors, since the Crown is a common law corporation and thus has a continuous existence. (The matter is now expressly dealt with by s.32 Crown Proceedings Act 1947). The view that the Crown is a corporation has also been expressed, obiter, by Lord Simon in the House of Lords *(Town Investments v Department of the Environment* [1978] AC 359 at 401). The idea of the Crown as a natural person is also difficult to square with the idea of the Crown as "divisible" between the different Commonwealth jurisdictions (as to which see generally Hogg, at pp. 10-12). Thus the Court of Appeal has held that obligations incurred by the Crown in right of

Canada or the Canadian provinces may not be enforced against the British Crown (*R. v Foreign Secretary, ex parte Indian Association of Alberta* [1982] Q.B. 892 - although it could be argued that this and similar decisions turn on the construction of specific statutory provisions).

This second view, that the Crown in public affairs is a corporation, is preferred by most modern writers (see, for example, Marshall, *Constitutional Theory* (1971) at pp. 17-24; Hogg, at p. 13; Turpin, *Government Procurement and Contracts* (1989), at p. 82; though Maitland, above, preferred the view that the Crown was a natural person, and this view is also accepted by Street, at p.3 and Mundell, [1960] 2 OHLJ 56). It is clear that it is the better view: to equate the state with the person of the monarch is an anachronism and can only detract from a proper consideration of the problems of modern public law. It may be that rules applicable to natural persons should also be applied to the Crown in many cases, but this should be done only after proper consideration of the question, and not by logical deduction from what is in reality a fiction. The view that the Crown is a natural person might have seemed unarguable but for the recent pronouncements of the Canadian Supreme Court; our own courts are not bound to follow them and should not do so.

There has been some debate over whether, if the Crown is indeed a corporation, it is a corporation sole or a corporation aggregate; Lord Simon in *Town Investments,* above, suggested the latter (and see also Maitland, above) but others have generally assumed it is a corporation sole.

Whatever the nature of the Crown it is clear that in it are vested many of the important powers of government. First, the Crown has many important power under the common law. These include powers of type snared by private individuals, such as the power to contract (see 2.3.1.1) and to give gifts, as well as special powers which individuals do not have under the common law. These latter powers have traditionally been termed "prerogative" powers, though this term is not without ambiguity since it has sometimes been used to refer to all the powers which the Crown possesses under the common law, including those which are not unique to the Crown.

In addition to its common law powers, the Crown also has some powers conferred on it under statute. It is today the practice to confer statutory powers on named Ministers rather than in the name of the Crown itself. Powers are generally given in the name of the Crown itself only when it is intended that the power shall be exercisable by the Prime Minister. The power is not, in this case, given in the name of the Prime Minister because of the curious convention that the office of Prime Minister is not generally mentioned expressly in legislation. In those few cases where the power is given in the Crown's name it is clear that the power is legally that of the Crown itself. Where powers are conferred in the name of a

Minister the position is less straightforward, and is considered at 1.2.1.2 below. As indicated above, the Crown's powers in relation to public affairs are not exercised by the monarch personally, but by government officials acting on behalf of the Crown.

1.2.1.2. The independent powers of Crown agents

The most rational legal framework for government and, it is submitted, the most desirable, would be obtained by recognising the Crown as possessing the legal powers of central government. Ministers of the Crown and other authorities set up to exercise central government powers (as to which see 1.2.1.5) would not be regarded as having any separate public powers. However, a reason for not adopting this approach is that the Crown enjoys many privileges and immunities which are considered to be unwarranted at the present day (see, in particular, 1.2.1.5 and 1.2.1.6 below). This fact has tempted the courts to find ways to avoid the conclusion that a particular power or act is that of "the Crown"; and to do this they have sometimes chosen to attribute the powers of central government to specific Crown agents instead of the Crown itself.

The main group of decisions taking this approach is that in which the courts have considered the availability of prerogative relief. Such relief is not available against the Crown itself. However, in a line of cases concerned with judicial review of statutory powers conferred on Ministers in their own names, the courts have held that such relief is available, on the basis that such powers are conferred on Ministers as *persona designata,* and not as agents for the Crown. Hence, it is argued, any remedy for a breach of public law in exercising the power is being given against the Minister and not the Crown (see Wade, at pp. 662-663. This is also implicitly recognised by s.40 (5) of the Crown Proceedings Act 1947). However, these cases sit uneasily with the approach of the courts to the grant of injunctions. Injunctions are also generally unavailable against the Crown, and further cannot be granted against a servant or agent of the Crown where the effect would be to give relief against the Crown (see 1.2.1.5 below). It has been held that this prohibition means that no injunction may be granted against a Minister even when exercising functions conferred on him in his own name (*Merricks v Heathcote-Amory* [1955] Ch 567; *R. v Secretary of State for Transport, ex parte Factortame* [1990] 2 AC 85). Hence the extent to which the Minister is to be considered to be acting in a separate public capacity, so that he cannot be equated for immunity purposes with the Crown, remains unclear.

A similar uncertainty is found in the cases which have considered whether a public authority which is a Crown agent may be held liable in tort or may undertake liability in contract in a separate capacity. It has recently been held that where a duty is placed by statute on a named Minister it is the Minister and not the Crown who is liable, thus allowing the court to evade restrictions on the liability of the Crown itself for breach of statutory duty (see 5.4.4.3). This is in line with the courts' approach to the grant of the prerogative orders. It also seems that corporate Crown agents may in principle be directly liable for their torts (see 5.4.7.2). The cases concerning the existence of an independent capacity to contract in Ministers and other Crown agents, on the other hand, are somewhat conflicting. There is no need to recognise such a capacity since these bodies may rely on the Crown's common law capacity to contract to make the contracts needed to carry out their functions; but there are several decisions which have suggested that an independent capacity exists. Here also the concern has been to avoid the special privileges and immunities which would apply if the contract in question were made by the Crown itself. These decisions are analysed at 2.3.1.2 below.

Some writers, notably Professor Wade, have supported enthusiastically this move towards recognising a separate capacity (see in particular Wade, at pp. 51-52, and also (1991) 107 LQR 4). Obviously this approach produces anomalies - for example, there is no reason why the availability of the prerogative orders should differ according to whether a statutory power is intended to be exercisable by the Prime Minister (in which case it is conferred on the Crown), or some other Minister; but it might well be suggested that arguments of justice should prevail over those of logic and principle. However, there is some difficulty in applying and developing any doctrine which does not rest on sound principle, and this tends to create further anomalies and uncertainty in the law, as is amply illustrated by the conflicting decisions concerning the separate capacity of Crown agents. Probably it would be better for the courts to adopt a presumption that an act of a Crown agent is an act of the Crown itself; and to the extent that Crown immunities are considered anomalous, these should be attacked more directly, at least insofar as this is not precluded by legislation.

1.2.1.3. Crown proceedings

At common law the Crown could not be sued in the courts in the same manner as other legal persons, a rule which seemed to have evolved from the principle that a feudal lord could not be sued in this own courts. However, a number of methods of obtaining redress against the Crown were developed over the centuries. By the end of the nineteenth century by far the most important was the petition of right procedure. (For further detail see Clode, *Petition of Right* (1887); Robertson, *Civil Proceedings by and against the Crown* (1908); Morgan, "Remedies Against the Crown", in Robinson, *Public Authorities and Legal Liability* (1925), xvii). Under this procedure a petition requesting redress could be brought to the monarch (in practice, the government of the day), and if it revealed questions suitable for resolution by the ordinary courts, the government could hand the matter over to the courts for the issues raised in the petition to be adjudicated. Once the issues were before the court in this way they would be determined according to the ordinary private law.

The petition could, in theory, only be considered by the courts if the Crown gave its "fiat", or permission, though by the end of the nineteenth century it appears that this was given as a matter of course. The procedure for bringing a claim under the petition of right procedure was much more cumbersome than that which applied in an ordinary action, though the position was improved by reforms in 1860 in the Petitions of Right Act, which considerably increased the popularity and importance of the petition of right. The petition could not be used, however, in all cases in which a civil action could be brought against a subject. It was established by the end of the nineteenth century that it was available for claims in contract (see 2.7); for most, if not all, claims in restitution (see 11.1); and for the recovery of sums due under statute (see 12.1). It could not, on the other hand, be used to hold the Crown liable in tort, although claims in tort could effectively be brought before the court in other ways, provided the Crown was prepared to cooperate, so that in practice the position in relation to tort claims was not much different from other types of action (on this see 5.4.1). In addition, the difficulties in bringing proceedings against the Crown were to an extent avoided by statutory provisions allowing a subject to bring in some circumstances an action against a Minister, instead of against the Crown itself.

Major reform of the system of crown proceedings did not occur until the Crown Proceedings Act in 1947 (for the background see 5.4.1 below). Section 1 deals with those claims which had in the past been brought to court by means of the petition of right procedure. It provides that where a claim might previously have been enforced by petition of right, it may be enforced as of right, and without the fiat of the Crown, in proceedings taken under the Act. The section also makes the same provision for proceedings previously enforceable by virtue of some statutory provision which is repealed by the Act. With very limited exceptions the Act does not make any other provision for actions in contract or restitution, or for recovery of a sum due under statute. This means that the scope of modern liability of the Crown in these areas depends on the scope of the old petition of right (or statutory) procedures. It does not, however, seem that there are any gaps in the scope of the Crown's liability.

In relation to claims in tort the Act had not only to provide a procedure for bringing an action, but also to reform the substantive law, which had been held not to apply at all to the Crown. The effect of the provisions in the Act on tort liability is to place the Crown substantially, though not entirely, in the same position as a private individual. The details of the reforms of these are examined at 5.4 below.

It is provided in section 40 (1) of the Act that nothing in the Act "shall apply to proceedings by or against, or authorise proceedings in tort to be brought against, His Majesty in His private capacity". It follows from this that a tort claim cannot be brought against the Queen personally. It is less clear, on the other hand, what is the position in relation to contract. This provision means that the Act does not positively authorise an ordinary action to be brought. However, it may be that a claim is still available under the petition of right procedure. Historically, this was available against the Crown in relation to private matters (see Clode, above, at p. 189), and it can be argued that the procedure is abolished only to the extent that proceedings under section 1 have replaced it, and not for claims - such as those against the Crown personally - which are not within the scope of section 1 (see Wade, at pp. 831-832, who points out that although the petition of right is listed in Schedule 1 as amongst procedures abolished by the Act, there is no express provision for its abolition elsewhere).

The form of proceedings under the Act is laid out in section 17 and is somewhat curious. The Crown itself is not made a party to the proceedings, but proceedings must be instituted against the "appropriate" department, which clearly means the department responsible for the matter which is the subject of the litigation (s.17 (3)). Under section 17 (1) the Minister for the Civil Service is required to maintain a list of "authorised departments" which may be sued under the Act. Where none of the authorised departments is "appropriate", or the plaintiff has reasonable doubts which is appropriate, the action must be instituted against the Attorney General (s.17 (3)). There is provision for the court to substitute an authorised authority for the Attorney General or *vice versa,* on application by the wrongly named party (s.17 (4)). Where proceedings are brought by the Crown they may, under the Act, be brought in the name of an "authorised department" or the Attorney General instead of the Crown itself. Section 32 of the Crown Proceedings Act expressly provides that no claim by or against the Crown, nor any proceedings for the enforcement of such a claim, shall "abate or be affected" by the demise of the Crown. It had once been considered, on the theory that the Crown is a natural person, that all claims against the Crown must abate when the monarch died (indeed this once applied to all litigation in the King's Courts, not just litigation against the Crown). In fact, this view appears to be rejected by the common law (*Re Mason* [1928] Ch 385).

1.2.1.4 Enforcement of judgements against the Crown

Under section 25 (3) of the Crown Proceedings Act money ordered to be paid in civil proceedings against the Crown must be paid out by the "appropriate government department". Section 35 (1) provides generally that any expenditure incurred under the 1947 Act shall be defrayed out of moneys provided by Parliament. It is not stated anywhere that payment under section 25 (3) shall be subject to the existence of a Parliamentary appropriation, and it thus seems that these provisions operate to provide a permanent statutory appropriation for sums ordered to be paid by the court in liability suits under the Act (see Hogg, at p. 49; and for further discussion of this point in the context of contractual claims see 2.6 below).

It is arguable that an order of mandamus would lie to compel the responsible Minister to pay out any sum ordered, since under section 25 (3) there is duty for payment to be made by the "department", not the Crown. Mandamus, though not available against the Crown, is available in respect of a duty cast on the Minister himself, and this section can be argued to create such a duty, though it speaks in terms of the department and not the Minister.

If the government refuses to comply, however, there can be no execution against the Crown nor attachment of the debt owed. This was the rule at common law and it has been put on a statutory footing by section 25(4) of the 1947 Act. It has been suggested by Hogg that this is one of the very few immunities of the Crown which can still be justified under the modern law: "... it is not appropriate that public property be vulnerable to seizure and sale at the instance of a private party" (p. 51).

1.2.1.5 Immunity of the Crown from coercive remedies

The Crown is generally immune from the remedies of specific performance and injunction, an immunity which obviously may be important in the context of liability claims. (See further, Matthews, (1988) 8 OJLS 154; Smythe, (1989) 139 NLJ 1236; Wade, (1990) 107 LQR 4; Oliver, (1991) 54 MLR 442; Barav, (1989) 26 CML Rev 369).

At common law neither an injunction nor an order of specific performance could be obtained against the Crown. In relation to civil proceedings the common law rules have been enacted in section 21 of the Crown Proceedings Act, which provides in section 21(1) that in civil proceedings against the Crown the court "shall not grant an injunction or make an order of specific performance". In addition it is provided in section 21(2) as follows:

"The court shall not in any civil proceedings grant any injunction or make any order against an officer of the Crown if the effect of granting the injunction or making the order would be to give any relief against the Crown which could not have been obtained in proceedings against the Crown".

"Officer" of the Crown is defined to include any servant of the Crown, including a Minister. It does not, however, include a public authority, such as a health authority, which is a Crown agent (*British Medical Association v Glasgow Health Board* [1989] AC 1211).

These provisions apply, as indicated, to "civil proceedings" which obviously will include claims in contract and tort (and also includes proceedings in the High and county courts for the recovery of fines and penalties: see s.38(2)). The effect of the provisions in relation to claims in contract and tort is noted below (see 2.6 and 5.4.6-7). The main difficulties arise in determining when relief against a government officer can be considered as giving relief against "the Crown".

It is expressly provided in section 21(1) that in lieu of an order of specific performance or an injunction the court may make an order "declaratory of the rights of the parties". The main drawback of the fact that only a declaration is available is that an interim declaration may not be granted, and hence a plaintiff is unable to obtain interim relief against the Crown pending trial of an action by writ in contract or tort (*R. v Secretary of State for Trade ex parte Factortame Ltd.* [1990] 2 AC 85). The absence of the possibility of interim relief is widely regarded as an unfortunate gap in the law, and most writers have favoured the view that at the very least the court ought to recognise the possibility of an interim declaration (see, for example, Craig, at pp. 527-8; Wade, at pp. 588-589; Hogg, at p.28).

An injunction is also unavailable in proceedings for judicial review, either against the Crown, or against a Minister exercising powers conferred on him in his own name (*Factortame,* above. The principle in this context derives from the common law since judicial review proceedings are not "civil proceedings" for the purpose of the rule in s.21 of the CPA). As indicated above the prerogative orders are also unavailable against the Crown, though these remedies may be obtained against Ministers exercising powers conferred on them in their own name (see 1.2.1.2). The court may grant a stay of a decision challenged in judicial review proceedings, under Rule 10 (a) of Order 53, including where the effect is to give relief against the Crown (*R. v Secretary of State for Education and Science, ex parte Avon County Council* [1991] 1 QB 558). This means interim relief is effectively available in some cases. However, a stay will not avail the applicant where interim relief requires some positive action by the government, and also may only be used to prevent the continuation of "proceedings", not to prevent implementation of a decision already taken (*Minister of Foreign Affairs v Vehicles and Supplies Ltd.* [1991] All ER 66). A party with a private law claim may be able to use the judicial review procedure to obtain an interim remedy in those limited cases where his private law claim depends on showing some breach of public law - for example, where he contends that his contract has been terminated in breach of public law, or he brings a claim for misfeasance in public office. In these cases he may bring a judicial review action and attach to it a claim for damages (see 1.3 below).

There is now an exception to the principle that an injunction is not available against the Crown or its officers. This applies where there is an issue of breach of European Community law, and no remedy other than an injunction would effectively protect Community law rights arising from the alleged breach. In this case an injunction will be made available against the Crown to protect those rights. This issue is considered further at 1.6.2.2 below. Probably this will override both the prohibition in section 21 of the Crown Proceedings Act and the common law rule which applies to judicial review proceedings.

In addition to conferring immunity in respect of the remedies of specific performance and injunction, section 21(1) of the Crown Proceedings Act 1947 also provides that no order may be made against the Crown for the recovery of land or other property, but that instead the plaintiff may obtain a declaration that he is entitled, as against the Crown, to the property in question.

1.2.1.6. Immunity from the burden of statutes

One of the most important privileges of the Crown is its immunity from the burden of statutes. The Crown is not subject to any burden imposed by a statute "unless the statute says so expressly or by necessary implication" (*B.B.C. v Johns* [1965] Ch 32 at 79 per Diplock L.J. See generally Hogg, Ch. 10; Wade, at pp. 827-829; Craig, at pp. 524-526; Street, at pp. 143-154 and (1948) U of TLJ 537; Glaville Williams, at pp. 48-58; Woolfe [1990] PL 14). This rule has been much criticised but was recently affirmed by the House of Lords in *Lord Advocate v Dumbarton D.C.* ([1990] AC 521). It was held that the legal basis of the "immunity" is a presumption of legislative interpretation that Parliament does not intend to bind the Crown by general words in a statute. (For the other leading decisions see *B.B.C. v Johns,* above; *Province of Bombay v Municipal Corporation of the City of Bombay* [1947] AC 58; *Madras Electric Supply Co. v Boarland* [1955] AC.667 In *Bropho v State of Western Australia* (1990) 171 CLR 1 (noted by Kneebone, [1991] PL 361) the High Court of Australia took a slightly different view of the immunity to that taken by the House of Lords). It is expressly provided in the Crown Proceedings Act 1947 in section 40(2)(f) that, except as otherwise provided for in the Act, nothing in the Act is to affect this immunity.

It was said in *Province of Bombay* that the Crown would be bound by necessary implication when to hold otherwise would wholly frustrate the purpose of the legislation. However, a test slightly less generous to the Crown was put forward by Lord Keith in *Lord Advocate v Dumbarton D.C.* where he suggested that the Crown will be bound if the legislation would otherwise be frustrated "in a material respect".

It was made clear in *Dumbarton* that the Crown will not be considered to be bound simply because other provisions in the same legislation are expressly stated not to bind the Crown. From this there cannot be inferred an intention that the other provisions in the legislation are intended to be binding. It was also made clear that the special presumption applies in relation to the Crown's "ordinary" activities as a landowner - its application is not limited to cases where the Crown's special powers or privileges are in issue.

1.2.1.7. Crown agents

The phrase "Crown agents", has no precise legal meaning, but is generally used to refer to public bodies which carry out all or most of their functions on behalf of the Crown and enjoy the benefit of certain general Crown immunities, such as the Crown's immunity from the burden of statutes (see 1.2.1.6 above). At one time it was easy to determine which bodies should be entitled to this status. The business of central government was generally carried on through government departments headed by a Minister, or by bodies which, though not called government departments, were very similar to departments in their structure and other characteristics, and these were always regarded as Crown agents for general immunity purposes. However, as government activity extended into new fields, and the entities set up to carry out these activities became increasingly diverse in form, disputes sometimes arose about which of these bodies were so closely associated with central government that they should be regarded as agents of the Crown (see further Wade, at pp. 169-171; Hogg, at pp. 245-256; Griffith, (1952) 9 U of TLJ 169; Flanagan, (1988) 67 Can Bar Rev 229; McNairn, (1973) 6 Ottawa L Rev 1).

Today it is the practice to make clear in the statute setting up a public authority whether or not it is to be treated as an agent of the Crown. For example, in the Education Reform Act 1988 which set up the National Curriculum Council and the Curriculum Council for Wales, it is expressly provided that these bodies shall not be regarded as servants or agents of the Crown "or as enjoying any status, immunity or privilege of the Crown", nor may their property be considered that of the Crown or held on behalf of the Crown (Sch.2 paras. 1 and 2). However, express provisions are not always included and in such a case the existence or not of Crown status will have to be determined by the courts (see, in particular, *Mersey Docks and Harbour Board Trustees v Cameron* (1861) 11 HLC 443; *The Bank voor Handel en Scheepvaart v Administrator of Hungarian Property* [1954] AC 584; *Tamlin v Hannaford* [1950] 1 KB 18); *Forestry Commissioners v Argyll County Council* [1950] SLT 264; *British Broadcasting Corporation v Johns* [1965] Ch. 32; *Pfizer Corp. v Minister of Health* [1965] AC 512; *Nottingham Hospital Management Committee v Owen* [1959] 1 QB 50)).

One factor often mentioned is whether the function carried out by the authority is within the traditional sphere of government: if so, the body set up to carry it out is more likely to be treated as a Crown agent. Thus in *Tamlin v Hannaford* the British Transport Commission was held not to be a Crown agent for the purpose of immunity from the burden of statutes, one factor being that it was set up to take over an activity formerly carried out by the private sector. In *Johns*, above, the British Broadcasting Corporation was also held not to be a Crown agent for the purpose of the Crown's immunity from taxation, because the function of broadcasting was entirely new. In *Argyll*, on the other hand, the authority, which had taken over functions traditionally exercised by the Crown in relation to woodlands and forest, was held to be a Crown agent.

This test, however, can be criticised on the basis that the government may have deliberately taken over an activity from the private sector in order that the commercial element be subordinated to matters of public interest. It is also difficult to see why an activity should be treated as non-governmental simply because it is new. Probably the nature of the activity and whether it is one traditionally carried on by government would be regarded as much less important today. Instead, it seems that the most important factor is the degree of control over the authority which is exercised by Ministers of the Crown. The fact that there is some supervision by a Minister, however, or that the Minister has the power to give directions on certain matters, does not necessarily mean that the body is a Crown agent: it is a matter of degree (see, for example, *Tamlin v Hannaford*, above), Indications in the statute itself may also help to determine the issue, even if the body's status is not stated expressly: for example, the fact that it was provided that the B.B.C. may have its stations taken over in an emergency "on behalf of her Majesty" was held in *Johns* to be an indicator that the B.B.C. was not intended to be a Crown agent itself (see 62 per Willmer LJ).

A body which is a Crown agent for general purposes such as the immunity of the Crown from the burden of statutes will not necessarily be equated with the Crown for all purposes. There has been much debate, for example, concerning the extent to which bodies of this kind can, and do, act, or undertake liability, in an independent capacity, and the extent to which they are entitled to the benefit of Crown immunities in such circumstances. This issue was considered generally at 1.2.1.2 above. In some cases statute will make clear that bodies which are agents of the Crown for some purposes are not be treated as such for others. Thus Health Authorities in the National Health Service generally exercise their functions on behalf of the Crown and are generally entitled to enjoy Crown immunities (*Pfizer*, above, holding the NHS to be part of "the services of the Crown" for the purpose of the Crown's right to use patents; *Owen*, above), but it is expressly provided that they are to have the same legal rights and liabilities as if they were acting as principals, and their servants are not Crown servants in law (see National Health Service Act 1977, Sch. 5, para. 15).

As indicated above, Ministers are obviously entitled to Crown status. They often have a distinct legal identity in a capacity which is separate from that of the individual holding the office of Minister, being incorporated as corporations sole (though this is not invariably done). Whether or not there has been incorporation, it appears that a Minister may, as with other entities which enjoy Crown status for general purposes, also act in an independent capacity for some purposes (see 1.2.1.2). Ministers of the Crown are thus in a legal position very similar to that of other authorities acting for the Crown, but in some respects they may be treated differently. In particular, Ministers are categorised as "officers" or "servants" of the Crown in some contexts, whereas other entities acting as agents for the Crown would not be, and this may have some legal consequences. An illustration of this was noted at 1.2.1.5 above, where it was explained that Crown agents who are not Ministers of the Crown are not "servants" for the purpose of the immunity of Crown servants from injunctions under section 21(2) of the Crown Proceedings Act. Another is mentioned below at 5.4.3.4, where the importance of who is a servant is considered in the context of the vicarious liability of the Crown.

1.2.2.   *Other public authorities*

Much of the business of government is carried on by public bodies which are not agents of the Crown. Many are local, such as the general local authorities, and fire authorities. The central government has also created many other, diverse, legal authorities which are not Crown agents to carry on specific aspects of its work: the National Curriculum Council and the British Broadcasting Corporation were mentioned at 1.2.1.7 above as two bodies which do not enjoy Crown agency status. Most of these governmental bodies are created by statute and are given corporate form, and are generally referred to as "statutory corporations". They have a legal identity and capacity which is quite separate from that of the Crown, as has a private corporation which is created either directly under statute or under the Companies Acts.

These statutory corporations possess only those powers which have been conferred upon them by statute. This doctrine was initially developed mainly in relation to private corporations created by statute but was also applied in a similar way to statutory public authorities (*Attorney General v Manchester Corporation* [1906] 1 Ch 643; *Attorney General v Fulham Corporation* [1921] Ch 44). Under this principle public bodies must look to statute not only for any extraordinary powers which they wish to exercise, such as any power to tax or impose fines or sanctions, but also for the power to do those things which a natural person could do without special authority. Unlike the Crown they do not share the powers of natural persons. Thus statutory authority is needed, for example, if a public body wishes lawfully to carry on a business, or make gifts, or contracts. If it has not been given the requisite power by statute then it can be restrained from engaging in such activities. The scope of the authority's powers is a matter to be determined by the construction of the statute in each case (on this see further Cross and Bailey, *Local Government Law* (7th ed., 1986), at pp. 3-14; in relation to contractual powers 2.3.3 below).

Anything done by such an authority which is outside the scope of its statutory powers is said to be *ultra vires*. The extent to which civil liability may attach to such bodies with respect to acts which are *ultra vires* is an important question which has given rise to much debate and is discussed at 1.4.1 below.

Of course, government activities have not only been carried out by the Crown and through corporations specifically created under statute, but have taken an increasingly diverse form. For example, the government may leave the task of regulating a particular activity to an existing self-regulatory body, sometimes stepping in to confer special statutory powers, or to provide funding; and activities are sometimes carried on by companies incorporated under the general Companies Acts, but owned by the government. Important recent developments have included the privatisation of a substantial part of industries such as gas, water and electricity, formerly carried on by public authorities of the traditional type, or by companies based on a private law model but subject to public ownership. It is obviously not possible here to consider the legal structure of all the different types of bodies which may be regarded, for some purposes at least, as within the public sphere, and, hence, within some of the special public law rules covered in this work. (For a discussion of the diverse forms which government activity has taken in recent years, and the difficulties of ensuring appropriate control and accountability see Lewis, "Regulating Non-Government Bodies: Privatisation, Accountability and the Public Private Divide", in *The Changing Constitution* (2nd ed. 1989), eds. Jowell and Oliver, ch. 9, and also the works cited there). The extent to which public law rules of civil liability apply to bodies taking a form different from the traditional statutory corporation funded with public money is touched on in discussing the various specific rules (and see also 1.1 above).

1.3. Financial Claims and Order 53

1.3.1.   Introduction

There is a special procedure for public law actions, contained in section 31 of the Supreme Court Act 1981 and Order 53 of the Rules of the Supreme Court. The main features which differentiate this procedure from the ordinary writ procedures are the very short limitation period which applies (a claim must normally be brought within three months); the need to obtain leave of the court before bringing a claim; the fact that discovery, cross examination and the use of interrogatories are much more rarely permitted than under the writ procedure; and the fact that remedies are discretionary. (For details of the procedure see further Wade, Ch. 18; Craig, at pp. 410-429). Judges who hear claims under Order 53 are taken from a special list of judges, who, by virtue of their position on this list, have become experienced in administrative law matters (see Blom-Cooper, [1982] PL 250).

In determining the extent to which this procedure is relevant to financial claims against government two questions arise. First, in what circumstances may a litigant choose to use the procedure for such a claim? Second, in certain cases, the procedure *must* be used instead of the ordinary writ procedure, and it is necessary to consider when, if ever, this is the case with liability claims.

1.3.2   When may Order 53 be used?

The procedure applies where the applicant seeks certiorari, prohibition or mandamus (s.31(1) of the Supreme Court Act 1981). These are remedies which have always been available only in public law cases - for example, where a decision is challenged as *ultra vires* or there is an alleged failure to perform a public duty. They may not be used to challenge a decision which is wrongful merely because it is a breach of contract, a private law matter (*R. v Post Office, ex parte Byrne* [1975] ICR 221; and see Craig, at p. 383). The procedure may also be used to seek a declaration or injunction, but only where the matter is one of "public law" (see s.31(1) and 31(2)). The provisions themselves do not use the phrase "public law", but it is used universally by the courts and writers to indicate the scope of the procedure.

In addition, where the applicant seeks in a judicial review action one of the five remedies mentioned above he may join a claim for "damages", provided that this claim arises "from any matter to which the application relates" (s.31(4)). He may not use the procedure where the *only* remedy he seeks is damages. It is expressly provided that damages may only be awarded where they could also have been awarded in an action begun by writ (Supreme Court Act 1981 s.31(4)). It is thus clear that the relevant provisions do not create any new right to damages, but simply allow a claim for damages under one of the existing principles of law to be joined to the application (see *Calveley v Chief Constable of Merseyside* [1989] AC 1228).

It does not seem possible to make a claim in restitution under Order 53 since a sum claimed in a restitutionary action does not fall within the concept of "damages" (see *Wandsworth L.B.C. v Winder* [1985] AC 461, at 484 per Parker L.J. and 480 per Robert Goff L.J.). This is unfortunate, since it is equally useful for an individual to be able to combine a claim for a public law remedy with one for financial redress in a restitutionary action as in an action for tort or breach of contract. Probably mandamus cannot be brought to compel payment, since the action would simply be one to recover a debt owed in private law (although once judgement has been given there is a statutory duty to pay and mandamus thus probably becomes available to compel payment : see 1.2.1.4 above). Thus to recover the sum a claim probably must be brought by writ. There is also no provision for obtaining other remedies, such as specific performance, though an applicant might find it useful to obtain this remedy following a finding of invalid action - for example, an invalid attempt to terminate his contact of employment (see further 4.4.3 below). In relation to the recovery of a grant or subsidy due under statute, there is likewise no specific provision for allowing recovery of the sum due and this also would seem to be outside the concept of "damages". In this case, though, there may clearly be an action for mandamus to compel payment since the duty to pay the sum is a statutory duty in public law (see 12.1 below), and any such action for mandamus will of course be brought under the section.

An important question is whether interest is available in an application for review. Interest on the amount of a claim will generally be awarded in an action begun by writ, under the court's power to do so in proceedings for "the recovery of a debt or damages" (see s.35A of the Supreme Court Act 1981). Probably this will also apply to damages awarded in an application for review (though cf. Bradley [1989] PL 197). It seems, however, that no interest can be awarded on the amount of a sum wrongly withheld in an application for mandamus to compel payment of the sum. In *R. v Secretary of State for Transport ex parte Sherriff & Sons Ltd.* (The Independent, 12 Jan. 1988; Lexis) it was held that section 35A of the Supreme Court Act only applied to "private law" claims, and an action for mandamus was an action in the field of public law. Thus a person wishing to recover such a sum may prefer to bring a claim by writ where available (see 12.1 below).

For what type of damages claim may the procedure be used? First, such a claim sometimes depends on whether a decision is *ultra vires*, or whether the government has breached a public law duty (see further 1.4.2 below). These are clearly "public law" issues which may be resolved under Order 53. An applicant may in such a case use the procedure to obtain compensation, by attaching a damages claim to his application for a remedy to challenge the decision (or omission) in question. Alternatively he may challenge the decision under the procedure and then bring a separate action for damages by writ.

It is less clear whether certain other issues on which liability depends, which relate particularly to public bodies, could be said to be issues of "public law", so that they may be the subject of an application for judicial review. For example, could it be argued that the question of whether a public body is liable in negligence for omissions in a situation where a private person would not be is an issue of public law for this purpose? (On this issue see 6.4 below). If so, a declaration could be sought under Order 53 to answer this question, and a claim for damages attached to the application. The advantage of this would be to allow litigants to take advantage of the expertise of the High Court judges specialising in administrative matters, even in relation to smaller claims which would normally be required to be brought in the county court. The better view, however, is that such issues are not issues of "public law" for this purpose: it is better to leave such cases to the county court.

It is quite clear that where the ordinary law applies, in the sense that the fact that the defendant is a public body does not affect the applicable rules in any way, the issue of liability is quite clearly not a "public law" issue and the Order 53 procedure can have no application (*R. v Secretary of State for the Home Department, ex parte Dew* [1987] 2 All ER 1049).

It is provided in Rule 9(5) of Order 53 as follows:

"Where the relief sought is a declaration, an injunction or damages and the Court considers that it should not be granted on an application for judicial review but might have been granted if it had been sought in an action begun by writ by the applicant at the time of making his application, the Court may, instead of refusing the application, order the proceedings to continue as if they had begun by writ".

This means that where the applicant brings his claim under Order 53 believing that it raises an issue of public law, but the Court finds that it does not, the Court can simply permit the action to continue by a different procedure.

It is not clear whether this provision also gives the Court a discretion to order the action to proceed as if begun by writ not only where the matter cannot be within Order 53 because there is no issue of "public law", but also because it considers that Order 53 is inappropriate for other reasons. In other words, it is not clear whether the court could conclude "that the Order should not be granted on an application for judicial review" even though the matter *could* have been dealt with in that way.

1.3.3. When must Order 53 be used?

A litigant whose liability claim depends on an issue of public law may frequently prefer not to use Order 53. This may be because he cannot obtain all the relief he requires through judicial review, and wishes to avoid the inconvenience of two separate sets of proceedings, or because he wishes to avoid some of the special features of the Order 53 procedure such as the short time limits for making an application, or the restrictions on cross examination.

It was held in *O'Reilly v Mackman* ([1983] 2 AC 237) that, as a general principle, where the Order 53 procedure is available that procedure *must* be used. Where one of the prerogative orders is sought this is the only procedure which exists, as is clear from section 31 of the Supreme Court Act 1981. As far as the declaration and injunction are concerned, however, the section states only that they *may* be sought in an application for review. When the new procedure was implemented it was assumed that a party would have the choice of seeking these remedies in a public law case either in a review action or under the ordinary writ procedure (which had applied to these remedies prior to the Order 53 reforms), and also that any damages claim which depended on showing a breach of public law could likewise be brought under the ordinary procedure. However, in *O'Reilly* it was held that as a general rule the procedure *must* be used where available even though the legislation does not expressly state this: if a claim which could be brought under the procedure is brought by writ, the claim will be struck out as an abuse of the process of court. The reason given was that the special procedure provides a number of safeguards for public bodies, and it is an abuse of process to avoid these by proceeding by writ. This "exclusivity" rule has been condemned by most writers who have argued, first, that even if special protection is desirable, the need for this is greatly outweighed by the practical problems of distinguishing between public and private law, and, second, that there is in any case no need for the sort of protection given by the special procedure (see, for example, Wade, at pp. 680-681, Craig, at pp. 421-426; though cf. Woolf, [1986] PL 220 and *Protection of the Public: a New Challenge* (Hamlyn Lectures 1990)). However, the exclusivity principle is firmly established: it could be overturned only by statute or by another decision of the House of Lords.

If all issues of "public law" affecting liability claims were required to be determined under Order 53 this would have serious adverse consequences for many litigants. In particular, the right to claim would be lost if an action were not brought within the very short time period for Order 53 applications. However, an exception to the exclusivity principle, for some of these cases at least, was envisaged by Lord Diplock in *O'Reilly*: he suggested that possibly Order 53 need not be used where the invalidity of a decision arises "as a collateral issue in a claim for infringement of a right of a plaintiff arising under private law" (at 1134). He did not elaborate, but subsequent cases have developed further an exception for public law issues arising in the context of private law claims. It is now clear, as a result of the recent decision of the House of Lords in *Roy v Kensington and Chelsea and Westminster Family Practitioner Committee* ((1992) 1 All ER 705) (1992) 1 ALL ER 705 that private law claims, though raising issues of public law, may as a general principle be pursued by writ or summons in the ordinary way.

This has generally been taken to be the law since the decision of the House of Lords in *Wandsworth v Winder* ([1985] AC 461). In this case Winder refused to pay a rent increase purportedly imposed by the Council, claiming that it was invalid and ineffective because it was unreasonable under public law principles. The Council brought an action for the amount which it claimed was owed. The Council argued that the reasonableness of its decision to raise the rent could, as a public law issue, be raised only in proceedings for judicial review, and could not be put forward as a defence to the recovery action by the Council. Lord Fraser, who gave the only reasoned judgement, gave two reasons for making an exception to the exclusivity principle. The first was that the public law issue was raised by way of defence, so that the applicant had not chosen the procedure; the second was that a private law contractual right was at issue. He did not make it clear whether each of these circumstances would be sufficient alone to bring the case within the exception to the exclusivity principle.

However, it has now been stated by the House of Lords in *Roy*, above, that where a litigant asserts his rights in private law the fact that this may involve the examination of a public law issue does not require him to bring an action under Order 53, whether the issue is raised by way of defence (as in *Winder*) or whether it is he who initiates proceedings. The case concerned a General Practitioner entitled to a certain allowance under statute. The Committee had decided to abate the allowance on the basis that Roy had not fulfilled one of the necessary conditions of devoting a substantial amount of time to his private practice. Roy claimed the amount by writ, and the Committee sought to have the action struck out on the basis that he should have proceeded to challenge their decision under Order 53. The House refused to strike out the claim. It was held that the right to be paid was a private law right, whether it arose directly under the statute or under a contract between the two parties, and as such could be contested in an action brought by writ or summons, even though the matter might require an adjudication on matters of public law. This decision confirmed the approach which appeared to be endorsed by the Court of Appeal in *An Bord Bainne Co-operative Ltd v Milk Marketing Board* ([1984] 2 CMLR 584) and *Ettridge v Morrell* ([1981] 85 LGR 100) (and for discussion of the other case law, which was not entirely consistent, see Cane, [1983] PL 202; Beatson (1987) 103 LQR 34).

It is clear that the concept of a private right for this purpose covers at least claims in contract, tort and restitution, as well as claims for a sum due under legislation, such as was in issue in *Roy* itself.

A qualification to the view that public law issues may generally be adjudicated in an ordinary action was mooted recently in the Court of Appeal in *Woolwich Equitable Building Society v I.R.C.* ([1991] 3 WLR 790). In that case the Court held that the plaintiff had a right to recover a payment which had been made pursuant to an *ultra vires* demand by the Inland Revenue Commissioners, because of a special principle of "public law", applicable only to public bodies, which allows the recovery of payments made in such circumstances (see further 11.2.2.2 below). Woolwich had in this case challenged the validity of the demand for payment in a judicial review action, before bringing its claim for recovery (a claim for interest owed only, since the Revenue has voluntarily repaid the capital). There is some suggestion in the judgements of both Glidewell and Ralph Gibson LJJ that this might be necessary before a recovery action based on the special, public law principle can be brought, although neither expressed a firm view on the matter. The basis of this seems to be that the principle of recovery itself is one which is special to public authorities. This would suggest that misfeasance claims also, for example, cannot be brought until the invalidity of the authority's action has been challenged by judicial review. There is no reason at all, however, why liability claims based on a special principle should be treated less favourably than claims which are not based on a special principle, and it is submitted that it was unnecessary for Woolwich to have brought a review action: the validity of the demand could have been challenged in the recovery proceedings. It would be particularly unfortunate if an initial challenge under Order 53 were required in the context of restitutionary claims, since a claim for a sum due in restitution cannot be made on an application for judicial review (see 1.3.2.1). To require a challenge by judicial review as a condition precedent for recovery would thus mean that two separate sets of proceedings would be required whenever a claim is made on the basis of the *Woolwich* principle, and presumably also where there is an exercise of special statutory rights to recover (as to which see 11.2.3 below). Certainly the suggestion that Order 53 proceedings might be required in this type of case seems inconsistent with the general statement of principle subsequently made in *Roy*.

In *Cocks v Thanet D.C.* ([1983] 2 AC 286) the House of Lords considered further what constituted a private right for the purpose of the exception to the exclusivity rule. In that case the plaintiff brought an action by writ claiming damages for an alleged breach of the Council's duties to provide accommodation to homeless persons, and also sought a mandatory injunction to force the Council to provide accommodation, and a declaration that the Council was in breach. The duties were stated by the statute to apply only on certain conditions: in particular, the duty to provide permanent accommodation did not apply if the applicant was intentionally homeless. The House of Lords held that whether the requisite conditions were satisfied was a matter to be determined by the Council in its discretion - subject, of course, to the usual principles of judicial review. Any private law rights, the Court held, did not arise until this discretion had been exercised positively in the claimant's favour. Hence the only option prior to a favourable determination was to seek a remedy under Order 53 to require the authority to make this determination. In so far as the House is correct to assert that no private right can arise until the authority has exercised its discretion in the plaintiff's favour, it is true that no action brought by writ should be permitted. This is, in fact, an unfortunate view of the law: where a public authority's executive duty to act depends on the exercise of a discretion, a right to damages for non-performance should be held to exist even though no determination has yet been made (see 7.2 below). To hold otherwise has the unfortunate effect of depriving a plaintiff of damages for loss suffered during the period in which the authority wrongly refuses to determine his case according to law. However, it does seem to provide the basis for the decision see *Cocks* (see further below) and it seems that it represents the law.

Whatever the position with damages for breach of statutory duty it seems clear that where there is a right to a sum under statute which depends on the exercise of some discretion, the right to payment does not arise until the discretion is exercised in the claimants favour (see 12.2). Until this is done the only right of the claimant is to challenge the authority's exercise of, or refusal to exercise, its discretion, under Order 53.

Another factor mentioned by Lord Diplock in *Cocks v Thanet* was that to give a right to damages without first remitting the matter would require the court to exercise the authority's discretion for it. This is because in order to show damage the plaintiff will have to show that the authority would have exercised its discretion in his favour: if they had not found the requisite conditions to be satisfied the claimant would not have been provided with housing anyway, and so cannot be said to have suffered any loss. This second factor may have influenced the House's conclusion that no right arose until the discretionary determination had actually been made, since to hold that the private right exists until this point avoids any need for the court to second-guess, in a damages action, the exercise of discretion. However, as will be explained at 1.4.2 below, this problem of second guessing the exercise of discretion may arise in many contexts in relation to governmental liability claims, and cannot always be dealt with in this way. For example, in an action for misfeasance for wrongful refusal of a licence, it can only be shown that loss was suffered if the licence would have been awarded if the authority had acted properly. Here the tort is shown by proof of conduct known to be wrongful: how the authority's discretion would have been exercised goes only to proof of damage. If this problem is the real reason for the court's decision that Order 53 should have been used in *Cocks,* then the refusal to award damages before a determination of the matter has been made by the authority should extend to all cases where the result depends on the exercise of a discretion by the authority itself, including the example of misfeasance just given.

If *Cocks* could be explained in this way, instead of on the basis that there was no private right, statements that no private right exists in such a case could be dismissed as dicta. However, subsequent cases, including *Wandsworth v Winder, Davy v Spelthorne B.C.* (1984) AC 262 and *Roy v Kensington etc Family Practitioner Committee* above, have taken the view that Cocks is explained by the absence of any existing private law right in the case and it seems that this must thus be considered as the true basis of the decision. In any case, it would be undesirable to force all cases which depend on the authority's discretion to be heard under Order 53, since this has the effect of dramatically reducing the time limit for challenge and foisting upon the applicant the other disadvantages of the special procedure, something which the court has recognised in principle should not be done with private law claims. The advantages to the court of requiring an applicant to challenge the decision directly in these cases would, it is submitted, be outweighed by these other considerations. This second factor mentioned by Lord Diplock should, then, be disregarded as an explanation for the decision in *Cocks v Thanet.*

1.4. Civil Liability and Ultra Vires

1.4.1. Can liability arise from ultra vires action?

Bodies created by statute may engage only in those limited activities which are expressly or impliedly permitted by legislation (see further 1.2.2 above). The Crown has all the powers of a natural person, but these may expressly be restricted; and it only has other powers to the extent that they have been conferred by Parliament, or are within the narrow limits of its remaining prerogative powers (see 1.2.1 above). Where an authority acts outside the limits permitted under these rules it is usual to speak of the act or activity in question as being "ultra vires", "invalid" or "void".

This terminology tends to suggest that unauthorised acts are devoid of all legal effect. If this is the case, it can then be argued that such acts cannot give rise to civil liability, where general principles require the attribution of some act to the defendant for liability to arise (on this see further Warren, (1926) 2 CLJ 180; Goodhart, (1926) 2 CLJ 350). Thus it might be concluded that an unauthorised contract cannot be enforced; or that no liability in tort can result from an *ultra vires* act because the act cannot be attributed to an authority which lacks the legal capacity to perform such an act. Similar arguments might apply to some restitutionary claims. Thus, to succeed in a claim in restitution it is necessary to show the defendant has received a benefit, and one way of showing that goods and services received are a benefit is to show that the defendant ordered them knowing payment was intended - as where goods are requested under a contract which turns out to be invalid. Where the authority has no power to order the goods it might be thought that the request could not have legal effect in this way.

An argument of this kind, based on the premise that an unauthorised act must be a legal nullity, was used by the House of Lords in the famous case of *Ashbury Railway Carriage and Iron Co. v Riche* ((1875) LR 7 HL 653) as reason to deny the enforceability of an unauthorised contract made by a private corporation. However, there is no logical reason why an act which is not permitted may not have legal consequences if carried out. This is seen in the fact that a number of public law rules - particularly certain procedural requirements laid down in statute - are treated as non-invalidating: although a remedy may be given to prevent an authority acting in contravention of them, a contravention has no impact on the effectiveness of action taken in breach (see Wade, at pp. 245-247). Even acts which are generally categorised as "invalid", are recognised as capable of giving rise to some legal consequences : the general label of "invalid" is simply a convenient shorthand for indicating that certain legal consequences are excluded (see Craig, at pp. 320-323). The formal argument that an *ultra vires* act is a "nullity" should not allowed to determine the question of civil liability.

However, in some cases there may be policy arguments against liability. For example, where a public body undertakes an *ultra vires* business, it may be argued that it is contrary to the policy of the *ultra vires* rule to hold it liable for torts committed in the course of the business, since one purpose of the rule is to prevent the authority risking public funds on unauthorised activities. Similarly, it appears contrary to the same policy to enforce contracts made in the course of such a business; or to allow a restitutionary claim for the value of goods or services supplied to a public body under such a contract.

In these cases it is necessary to weigh the policy of the *ultra vires* rule against the interests reflected in the general rules of private law, under which a liability claim would ordinarily be allowed. It is submitted that as a general principle the law should give priority to the ordinary private law, and should not allow the fact that an act is in breach of public law to affect the position. However, the courts have not always adopted this view. The current law concerning the effect of a breach of public law in relation to particular areas of liability is considered below. (See 2.3.1.3 (contract); 5.3 (tort); 11.4 (restitution)).

1.4.2   *Liability and the ultra vires exercise of discretion*

Sometimes the success of a claim will depend on whether or not a particular action or decision is *ultra vires*. This often arises in tort cases. Thus, a claim for interference with the plaintiff's goods or with his physical person or his liberty, or an action in nuisance for interference of his enjoyment of property, will fail if interference is authorised by statute (see 5.2.4); but there will often be no defence where the action taken is outside the scope of any special powers given by the statute. A claim for misfeasance in public office will generally depend on showing *ultra vires* conduct by the defendant authority (see 9.1 below); and a claim may be available in negligence where it can be shown that the authority acted *ultra vires* because of a lack of care in ensuring compliance with its statutory mandate (see 6.3.1). A restitutionary claim may also depend on showing *ultra vires*. For example, where there has been a lawful demand for payment of a tax there can obviously be no recovery of any tax paid pursuant to the demand; but where the demand was not lawful, the tax may be recovered in some circumstances (see 11.2).

Sometimes there is a blatant absence of jurisdiction - for example, where a public body pulls down a house, but has no powers to pull down houses at all. In many cases, however, the authority does have a power to carry out actions of that type, but is in breach of some principle regulating the manner in which that power must be exercised. These may be common law principles, such as the principles of natural justice, or the proper purposes rule; or rules laid down in statute - for example, a requirement of consultation, or a rule requiring a decision to be made only following the approval of a particular individual. In such a case it may be that although decision was in fact invalid, the same decision would have been made even if the authority had acted lawfully. Applying private law principles of liability, in some cases this may mean that a claim which would otherwise succeed should be defeated, or, with torts actionable *per se,* that the plaintiff should be limited to nominal damages. For example, with a claim based on misfeasance or negligent excess of power, the plaintiff's loss will normally lie in the fact that the government has refused, *ultra vires,* to confer on him some benefit, such as a grant or a licence. To show loss it will be necessary to show that the benefit in question would have been conferred if the government had acted lawfully: if it would have been refused anyway there is no substantial damage suffered. With a restitutionary claim for the recovery of some invalid tax, it can be argued that the government is never *unjustly* enriched (this being an essential element of any claim) where the tax would have been levied anyway.

There may, of course, be difficulty in knowing what decision the authority would have made if it had acted properly. This kind of problem arises in many other contexts. In judicial review actions a court will normally grant a remedy regardless of whether it believes a reconsideration would make a difference. In some natural justice cases the courts have refused to intervene, when they have taken the view that a hearing would have made no difference, but they have been severely criticised for this. (On this see the discussion in Craig, at pp. 212-213). However, although the ordinary inconvenience of requiring an administrator to reconsider an issue will not lead the courts to refuse judicial review because it thinks the outcome is likely to be the same, the technical nature of a breach seems sometimes to be taken into account in exercising the courts' discretion to refuse a remedy in exceptional cases, such as where the grant of a remedy would cause particular inconvenience to the public (see, for example, *R. v Secretary for Social Services, ex parte Association of Metropolitan Authorities* ([1986] WLR 1). In addition, the fact that breach of particular procedural provision will frequently not affect the outcome may lead the legislature to state, or the court to conclude, that the provision should be treated as non-invalidating (on this see Wade, at pp. 245-247). In criminal matters the basic approach is the same as with judicial review : in *DPP v Hutchinson* ([1990] 3 WLR 196) the House of Lords held that where there is a prosecution under an *ultra vires* bye-law, the court should not attempt to determine whether the authority would still have enacted a bye-law which would have caught the defendant's conduct, if the authority had known that the bye-law in its existing form was unlawful. Rather, the invalidity of the legislation generally means that no conviction is possible.

What should the approach be in liability cases? The need to predict what the decision would have been can sometimes be avoided, because there is still a "live" issue, and any award of damages can be postponed until the authority itself has reconsidered. For example, an applicant for a licence may seek to have an unlawful refusal reconsidered and also to claim for business lost in the period before this occurs. In such a case the question of damages for business lost can be left until the application has been reheard. (For a recent example see the various reported decisions culminating in that of the Court of Appeal in *R. v Petch, ex parte H.M. Treasury,* Jan. 15 1991; Lexis, discussed below at 6.4). However, redetermination is sometimes not apposite - for example, where an applicant has become insolvent and no longer seeks a licence. In determining liability, it is submitted that here the starting point should be to require proof of the way in which discretion would have been exercised, according to the ordinary rules of private law which apply to that type of case. In a judicial review action it is desirable that the matter should be remitted for rehearing by the proper authority; and in a criminal case the defendant should be given the benefit of any doubt, which can best be achieved by a general rule which prevents the court from examining at all what it thinks the administration would have done. However, in a case of civil liability the best approach is to deal with the issue on a case by case basis.

Some writers have seen constitutional objections to this, on the basis that it involves the courts adjudicating on matters which have been entrusted by the legislature to administrative authorities (see Hogg, at p.114, who says that the court would be "usurping" the function of the legislature; Harlow, *Compensation and Government Torts* (1982), at p.94; Craig, (1980) 96 LQR 413 at 439). However, the objections are not constitutional but practical - the court is not deciding what should be done but what the administrator would have done, and if there is evidence that this would have been different from the courts' own choice the courts will take account of it. The best way of assessing what the administrator would have done may in some cases be for the court to say what it would have done itself, but this does not change the nature of the exercise. It is better for the court to attempt this in exercising its own constitutional function of adjudicating on liability claims according to the usual general principles, than to decline to deal with claims altogether. ˙

In many cases there may be no practical difficulties. Thus, where a licence has been refused it may easily be shown that it would have been granted where, for example, it is the practice to grant licences in every case where certain objective conditions are satisfied, or where past practice of granting a licence to the particular applicant indicates clearly that it would have been given in the future (as was the case in *Roncarelli v Duplessis* [1959] 16 DLR 2d 689, discussed below at 9.1). In more difficult cases the courts must determine the matter as best they can, applying the usual tests (which in tort means the plaintiff must prove his loss on the balance of prohabilities). Sometimes this may involve issues very similar to those which are adjudicated in purely private law cases, which supports the argument that no special rule is needed to deal with the issue of public law *ultra vires.* For example, one situation in which it may be necessary to determine how a public authority would have exercised its discretion is in awarding damages to a contractor who claims he was denied a contract because of some breach of public law. This may occur where there has been breach of European Community tendering rules, or of the rules under the Local Government Act forbidding evaluation on the basis of non-commercial considerations, damages being available under statute in both these cases (see further 3.2.4 and 3.1.3). In awarding damages the court may have to decide whether the contractor would have succeeded in obtaining the contract but for the unlawful conduct of the authority. This may be difficult; but a similar assessment is required in private law where a tenderer sues for breach of the implied contract under the authority promises to give consideration to the bid (see *Blackpool and Fylde Aero Club v Blackpool District Council* [1990] 3 All ER 25).

In some limited contexts it may be useful, however, to use a different approach. For example, it is suggested below that with a claim for misfeasance in public office - which involves either malice or deliberate wrongdoing - the best approach would be to place on the authority the burden of showing that its discretion would not have been exercised in the plaintiff's favour, rather than requiring the plaintiff to show that it would (see 9.1.5). Another useful approach to some "discretion" problems where it is difficult for the court to assess the plaintiff's prospects of a favourable decision might be to apply the principle of *Chaplin v Hicks* ([1911] 2 K.B. 786), used in some contract cases, whereby the plaintiff is awarded a proportion of what he would have gained if successful, to represent the "loss of his chance". Whether this approach may ever be used in tort cases was left open by the House of Lords in *Hotson v East Berkshire Health Authority* ([1987] 1 All E.R. 210). It could be used, for example, where there is a breach of public law relating to a design contest for a building, or where an authority has a wide discretion in granting licences, which are given on artistic grounds. Yet another possible approach might be to award damages on proof of a reasonable prospect of success. However, whilst an attractive idea, this last possibility does not seem to find any precedent in private law cases, and it seems difficult to justify a wholly novel approach simply because the issue which the court must decide depends on how a public law discretion would have been exercised.

An existing rule which appears directed at the same problem is the rule applying to cases of malicious prosecution and other torts concerned with abuse of legal process, which requires that the defendant acted without reasonable and probable cause, as well as maliciously (see Winfield and Jolowicz, at pp. 547-550). The effect of this rule is to preclude any liability towards an individual who may well have been subjected to legal process even apart from the defendant's malice. The rule cannot be evaded by suing for misfeasance in public office (see 9.1.4 below).

1.4.3   Causation

Another issue which has been raised in relation to liability for *ultra vires*
decisions is whether a plaintiff who acts in reliance on such a decision may
be said to have caused his own loss. It has been suggested in some cases
that, since he is free to ignore an *ultra vires* decision without penalty, it is
his own action and not the decision to which the loss is attributable (see
further McBride, [1990] CLJ 323, at pp. 337-40; *Administrative Justice :
Some Necessary Reforms*, Report of the Committee of the Justice - All
Souls Review of Administrative Law in the United Kingdom (1988)). Most
recently, this view was stated, *obiter,* by Lord Diplock in the Privy Council
in *Dunlop v Woollahra Municipal Council* ([1982] AC 158). In this case
the plaintiff sought damages for loss suffered from *(inter alia),* his acting on
a resolution passed by the Council to fix a building line for his property. It
was contended that the resolution was invalid for breach of procedural
requirements. Lord Diplock commented as follows: "The effect of the
failure (to give a hearing) is to render the exercise of the power void and the
person complaining of the failure is in as good a position as the public
authority to know that is so. He can ignore the purported exercise of the
power. It is incapable of affecting his legal rights".

The statement is, however, purely *obiter* since the claims failed for
other reasons. In fact, it is submitted that it is almost always reasonable for
a person to act on an *ultra vires* decision (and given that the difficulty of the
legal issues in *Dunlop* led the Judicial Committee to conclude that the
authority itself had not failed to take reasonable care though it had erred in
determining the scope of its powers, it is difficult to see how the plaintiff's
act in reliance could have been unreasonable!). Where a plaintiff does an act
which is a necessary cause of his loss, but which is reasonable, this is
generally held not to "break the chain of causation" - that is, the plaintiff's
act does not prevent the defendant's own act from being a cause of the
damage (see Jones, at p.146). Thus, it should have been possible for the
authority to be held liable in *Dunlop*, if the other requisites of liability were
present. This was the view preferred also in the Justice - All Souls Report,
above (see pp.347-348).

1.5.   Privileges of Public Authorities in Civil Litigation

The Crown enjoys a number of privileges in litigation, which are exclusive
to the Crown and do not apply to public authorities generally. The most
significant were noted at 1.2 above. Another important immunity, enjoyed
not only by the Crown but also by other public authorities is an immunity

from being required to produce documents in litigation, in some cases where to order their production would be contrary to the public interest. This is generally referred to as public interest immunity. The inability of a party seeking to establish the liability of a public body to obtain relevant documents may often mean that a good case cannot be proven in court. A detailed consideration of this problem is outside the scope of this book. For an outline of the rules governing this issue the reader is referred to Craig, at pp.514-523; Wade, at pp.833-843; and Hogg, ch 4.

1.6. Liability under European Community Law

1.6.1. Introduction

A civil claim against the United Kingdom government may sometimes arise out of a breach of European Community law.

The United Kingdom became a member of the European Community on 1 January 1973. The Community comprises three separate Communities - the European Economic Community (EEC) and the European Atomic Energy Community (Euratom), which were both set up by the Treaty of Rome in 1957; and the European Coal and Steel Community (ECSC), established earlier in 1951, under the Treaty of Paris. The European Communities Act 1972 provides, in section 2(1), that all: "rights, powers, liabilities, obligations and restrictions from time to time created or arising by or under the Treaties, and all such remedies and procedures from time to time provided for by or under the Treaties, as in accordance with the Treaties are without further enactment to be given legal effect or used in the United Kingdom, shall be recognised and available in law, and be enforced, allowed and followed accordingly."

Certain of the measures "created or arising by or under the Treaties" have "direct effect"; that is, they confer rights directly on individuals in the Community, without any need for the member states to enact specific legislation to give effect to these rights (see further Steiner, *Textbook on EC Law* (2nd ed. 1990) ch.2). Where there is a breach of some directly effective provision, an individual whose rights have been affected may seek a remedy to redress the breach and this may include a liability claim. For example, where the government has levied a charge which contravenes a directly effective rule of Community law, an individual may seek to recover the amount which he has paid; or he may, to give another illustration, seek damages for loss of profits where, in breach of Community provisions, he has been refused a licence to trade.

Many of the cases have concerned domestic governments themselves implementing measures which contravene Community law - for example, by levying taxes or charges which are discriminatory as between persons in the different member states. In addition, domestic governments may be liable for actions which they take on behalf of the Community. The Community does not have any significant administrative machinery in the member states, and thus relies on the governmental machinery of those states to implement its own policies. For example, all customs duties are now under the control of the Community, but are collected on its behalf by the authorities of the member states. Domestic bodies are also responsible for making and collecting the payments required under the Community's Common Agricultural Policy. Member states may sometimes incur civil liability in the course of administering these policies, either because the Community measures are themselves invalid, or because the domestic authorities misinterpret and wrongly apply the Community provisions.

In principle, liability for breach of European Community law is determined by applying the ordinary domestic rules on governmental liability (see 1.6.2 below), but the question demands separate treatment since Community law itself imposes important qualifications to this principle, which means that liability cannot be considered solely in terms of the application of the relevant heads of domestic law. It is convenient to set out briefly here the general principles relating to liability under Community law (and see further Gravells, [1991] PL 180; Ward, (1990) 19 Anglo Am L Rev; Barav, ch. 11 in Schermers, Heukels and Mead eds., *Non-Contractual Liability of the European Communities* (1988); Steiner, (1987) 12 EL Rev 102; Oliver, (1987) 50 MLR 881; Green, (1984) 48 Rabels Zeitschrift 509). Specific problems of liability are dealt with at appropriate points later in the book (see below ch.10 (compensation); 11.2.7 (restitution); and 12.3 (withholding of subsidies and grants). The discussion will be confined to questions of liability under the law of the European Economic Community.

1.6.2.   Remedies for Enforcing European Community Law

1.6.2.1. The basic principle : application of national law

Responsibility for enforcing individual rights which arise under Community law lies with the member states. Where an individual wishes to sue an authority of a member state for breach of a directly effective provision of Community law, the action must be brought against the offending government body in the domestic courts; there is no provision for individuals to enforce their rights against the government in the European Court of Justice ("the European Court"). In such an action it is, in principle, the law of the member state which determines the relevant forum and procedure for the action, as well as the procedural conditions, such as the limitation period (case 33/76 *REWE v Landwirtschaftskammer Saarland* [1976] ECR 1989; case 45/76 *Comet BV v Produktschap voor Siergevassen* [1976] ECR 2943; case 101/78 *Granaria v Hoofdproduktschap voor Akkerbouwprodukten* [1979] ECR 623). National law will also, in principle, govern the nature and scope of the remedy (case 68/79 *Hans Just v Danish Ministry of Fiscal Affairs* [1980] ECR 501).

In some cases Community measures lay down express rules on the remedy to be given for particular breaches, or the procedural conditions to be followed. Where remedies are provided in a regulation, they are applicable automatically in each member state. Where remedies are specified in a directive, member states must take steps to provide the remedy which has been stipulated. Where this is not done by the date for implementation, an individual may be able to obtain the stipulated remedy anyway, but only where the "remedy" provision itself has direct effect (case 79/83 *(Dorit Harz v Deutsche Tradax Ambit* (1984) ECR 1921 at 1924; case 14/83 *Von Colson and Kamann v Land of North Rhine-Westphalia* [1984] ECR 1891 at 1909). Illustrations of remedies expressly stipulated in Community provisions are considered below (see 3.2.4 for remedies for breach of the Community rules on procurement; and 11.2.7.2 on the recovery of charges). Even where express remedies are given, however, the nature of the remedy and the procedural conditions are generally not spelt out in any detail; and to the extent that they are not comprehensive, matters will still be left to national law.

1.6.2.2. Limitations : effectiveness, non-discrimination and deterrence

Although remedies are in principle matters of national law, the domestic authorities do not, however, have an entirely free hand; the European Court has held that national remedies and procedures must comply with certain conditions. The power to lay down these conditions has been held by the European Court to derive from Article 5 of the Treaty of Rome, which states that member governments must take all possible steps to ensure the fulfilment of obligations arising under the Treaty (case 213/89,*R.v Secretary of State for Transport ex parte Factortame Ltd* [1990] 3 WLR 818 (ECJ)).

First, the rules governing recovery must not be "less favourable than those governing the same right of action on an internal matter" (case 33/76 *REWE v Landwirtschaftskammer Saarland* [1976] ECR 1989). This means, for example, that damages must be awarded for loss caused by action which is invalid under Community law where damages would be awarded for a comparable breach of domestic law, and that procedural restrictions such as time limits cannot be more stringent than those applied to comparable domestic actions. This can be referred to as the "principle of non-discrimination". There may, of course, be room for debate as to what is a comparable domestic action, and there may also be problems where domestic law treats two cases which are apparently alike in a different manner.

Second, the European Court has said that remedies must be direct and effective - the "principle of effectiveness" (e.g. *REWE* above; case 45/76 *Comet BV v Produktschap voor Siergevassen* [1976] ECR 2043; case 179/84 *Bozetti v Invernizzi* [1985] ECR 2301). What precisely this principle requires is an important question. Fundamentally, the issue is the extent to which the European Court will be prepared to intervene in the details of national legal systems to ensure effective protection of Community rights in a manner which is uniform between the member states.

What is clear, at least, is that where domestic law recognises a particular remedy, that remedy must be made available in an *effective* manner for the protection of Community rights. It is not sufficient that the remedy is available under the same conditions as in domestic actions, if this alone renders the right given by domestic law ineffective. An aspect of this is that national law may not impose conditions on the grant of the remedy which make Community rights "impossible in practice or unduly difficult to exercise". Thus it has been held that evidential requirements which make the exercise of the right virtually impossible are to be disallowed, even though the same requirements apply to actions brought under domestic law as well (case 199/82, *Amminstrazione Delle Finanze Dello Stato v San Giorgio SpA* [1983] ECR 3595, discussed below at 11.2.71). Similarly, other conditions for the exercise of the remedy, such as limitation periods, must be reasonable (*REWE and Comet,* above).

The effectiveness principle was taken further by the European Court in its decision in *Factortame (R. v Secretary of State for Transport, ex parte Factortame* [1990] 3 WLR 818 (ECJ)). The case concerned legislation which effectively precluded corporate-owned vessels from using United Kingdom fishing quotas unless at least seventy-five per cent of the owner company's shares were held by British citizens, by refusing other vessels the registration which was necessary to enable them to take advantage of UK quotas. The applicants were companies incorporated in the UK, whose directors and shareholders were mainly Spanish, and whose vessels were affected by the provisions. They contended that the provisions contravened Community law, and brought an application for judicial review to compel the Minister of Transport to register their vessels. They sought an interim remedy pending determination of the question, since there would be considerable delay before the legality of the government's action could be determined, during which time the applicant's business would suffer serious losses if the government continued to enforce the challenged measures. However, under domestic law no interim relief is generally available to

compel action on the part of a Minister of the Crown (see 1.2.1.5 above). A
reference was made by the House of Lords to the European Court concerning
the question of whether interim relief was required to be made available
where a breach of Community law is in issue. The Court ruled that where
the national court would grant interim relief "if it were not for a rule of
national law", and such relief is necessary "to ensure the full effectiveness of
the judgement to be given" on the existence of Community rights, the
national court must disapply the restrictive rule of national law and make
available the relief requested. In its subsequent judgement in *R.v Secretary
of State for Trade v Factortame Ltd ((No. 2)* [1990] 3 WLR 856), the House
of Lords interpreted this ruling as requiring the English courts to make
available against the Crown an interim injunction, in cases where
Community rights are in dispute. The basis for this is that interim relief is
available in national law through an injunction, but is precluded in certain
cases by the rule of national law that no such relief is available against the
Crown. This restriction the courts are bound to disapply where necessary to
make effective the rules of domestic law for protecting Community rights.

It is not clear whether the principle of effectiveness may be taken even
further, to require national courts to create entirely new remedies where this
is necessary to protect Community rights effectively. The European Court
has sometimes stated that there can be no obligation to create a remedy
which is not already available in national law (see in particular, case 158/80,
REWE v Hauptzollampt Kiel [1981] ECR 1805). Thus if, for example,
there had been no provision at all for interim relief in English law, then
arguably no such relief could have been required under the principle of
effectiveness. The point might have been considered in *Factortame*, since the
question actually posed by the House of Lords was simply whether interim
relief was a requirement of the effectiveness principle. However, the
European Court avoided giving an answer, and considered only the issue as
reformulated by the court itself, which was whether, *given the existence of
relief*, any obstacle to the grant of relief must be disapplied.

Even though the case law has not gone so far, logic suggests that the
general principle of effectiveness should be held to require the creation of
new remedies; once it is accepted that effective protection must be secured
by the adaption of existing remedies beyond the circumstances in which they
would apply in domestic law, it is anomalous not to require new ones where
effective protection would otherwise be denied. That the national courts have
a   general obligation to give effective remedies for the protection of
Community rights, and must create new remedies if none are available, was
the position argued by the Commission in *Factortame*. It is to be expected
that the European Court will move in this direction in the future and indeed
some writers have asserted that this is already the position (Steiner, (1987)
12 ELR 102 at p.103; Ross, (1990) 15 ELR 476, arguing that this

probably follows from the decision in *Factortame;* and see also Gravells [1991] PL 181 at pp. 107-191). This view is, arguably, supported by those cases in which the European Court has refused to admit a claim for recovery of overpaid charges collected by the member states against the Community itself. These cases appear to be based on an assumption that a remedy will always be made available under national law (see 11.2.7 below), as do some similar cases concerning the non-payment of subsidies (see ch.12). Even if the creation of new remedies cannot be required, this is rarely likely to provide a barrier to the creation of effective protection, since the appropriate remedies will usually be available somewhere in the system, and can be adapted to most circumstances by a broad interpretation of what is an "available remedy" (see further Chapter 10 and 11.2.7.1). In particular, it has been made clear in the recent decision in joined cases C-6/90 and C-9/90, *Francovich v Italian Republic* (The Times November 21 1991) that the national courts may, in some circumstances at least, be required to make available damages as a remedy for breach of Community law, even though damages may not be available in that situation under ordinary principles of domestic law. (The case is discussed in detail in Chapter 10). Whether this is justified on the basis that damages are a remedy available in some circumstances in all states, and thus must be made available to protect Community rights, or whether the case can be regarded as an illustration of a principle that "new" remedies must be created to protect Community rights, is unimportant.

In addition to the requirement that any remedy be non-discriminatory and effective, it has also been said that remedies must "have a real deterrent effect" (*Dorit Harz*, above, at 1941). It probably does not matter whether this is seen as an aspect of the principle of effectiveness or as a separate principle.

1.6.2.3. Claims based on invalid Community measures : the move to harmonisation

In relation to the specific case where the invalidity of a Community measure is in issue, an important further limitation on the remedial discretion of the national courts has been developed by the European Court in the case of *Zuckerfabrik* (cases C-143/88, C-92/89, The Times, March 28, 1991). As will be explained further in the sections on Community law in relation to damages (ch. 10) and restitution (ch. 12), actions in the national court against a member state may be brought either because of a measure taken on national initiative which infringes Community law, or because of a national measure based on a Community measure which is invalid. The *Zuckerfabrik* case concerned an application for an interim remedy in the national courts to prevent the German government acting on what was alleged to be an invalid

Community measure. The European Court ruled that in deciding whether to grant interim relief against the German government the national courts must apply the same principles as would be applied by the European Court if an interim remedy were sought in that Court with respect to the same measure. This might be sought, for example, in an action by an individual to impugn the validity of the Community measure itself, which would be brought in the European Court. The reason given was that it is unsatisfactory that the interim protection given to individuals should vary according whether the individual disputes the national act implementing a Community measure, or the measure itself. It should be emphasised that this principle will *only* apply where interim relief is sought in relation to a challenge to an act on the basis that it is based on an invalid Community measure. It does not apply where the act of a member state is challenged on the basis that it is incompatible with some valid provision of Community law, such as a provision of the Treaty of Rome or valid Community legislation. This was made clear in *Factortame*, above, in which it was stated clearly that it is for member states to decide the principles on which interim relief are to be granted in such cases (though it is always possible that this discretion may be restricted by the requirements of the general principle of effectiveness).

1.6.2.4. The future?

It is obviously important for the functioning of the common market that the remedies for enforcing Community law should be as similar as possible in each state, and there is much support amongst academic writers for the adoption of a uniform approach as far as possible (e.g. Bridge, [1984] 9 ELR 37; Weatherill (1990) 10 YEL 1). The Treaty of Rome in fact gives express powers to the legislative authorities to pass harmonising legislation where the discrepancies between the available remedies in different states are likely to harm or distort the common market (see Articles 100-103 and Article 205) and, as has been explained, this power has been exercised to a limited extent. In addition, the European Court has taken an important step towards harmonisation of remedies relating to invalid community measures in its decision in Zuckerfabriken.

In relation to other breaches of Community law the Court has also, in *Factortame* and *Francovich,* extended the effectiveness principle so as to reduce potential discrepancies between states in the provision of effective redress. It is clear that this effectiveness principle also provides further scope for reducing discrepancies between states : the more stringent the conditions it lays down - for example, on limitation periods - the less is the scope for divergence.

As Community law continues to develop it may be that the weapon of effectiveness will be used increasingly to fashion a truly "European" structure of remedies. Whilst earlier there was a tendency to speak in terms of remedies as a matter for national law subject to limits imposed by the European Court, there are signs that the emphasis is being reversed. Thus in *San Giorgio*, above, Advocate General Mancini spoke of the right of recovery of charges levied by member states in contravention of Community law as a "Community right", and of the states as exercising a "*residual* and *temporary* power to regulate actions for the recovery of undue payments" (emphasis added). However, for the present there remain some significant differences in the remedies systems of different states, particularly in relation to procedure, and there are many who would see further legislative harmonisation of remedies as an important ultimate objective.

1.6.3. Claims by government

The above discussion concerned actions by individuals for breach of their rights under Community law, but a claim by a government might also arise from its *own* breach of Community law. This problem has arisen in practice, for example, in relation to payments made by government in breach of community provisions on State Aids. Claims by the government which are based on a breach of Community law, like claims by individuals, must also be brought in the national courts and are determined according to national law and procedure where there is no Community legislation dealing specifically with the question of remedies (case 265/78 *H. Ferwerda v Produktschap voor Vee en Vlees* [1980] ECR 617; case 54/81 *Firma Wilhelm Fromme v Bundesanstalt* [1982] ECR 1449; cases 205-215/82 *Deutsche Milchkontor v Germany* [1983] ECR 2633). Although no question arises as to the enforcement of individual rights, it has been said that the principle of effectiveness applies here also (*Ferweda*, above, which, although concerned with legislative provisions, seemed to assume the same principle would apply under general principles of law). This is justifiable to protect the policy of Community law which might be prejudiced if no remedy were given - for example, for the recovery of unlawful State Aids. The principle of non-discrimination also applies (*Ferwerda, Deutsche Milchknotor* and *firma Wilhelm Fromme*, above). The requirements of these principles in relation to payments made by governments in breach of Community law is considered at 11.3.2 below.

1.6.4. The influence of Community law on domestic liability rules

Quite apart from the fact that remedies may be required to be provided in our courts for breaches of Community law by the United Kingdom government, accession to the European Community may ultimately have an impact on the law of governmental liability in more indirect ways.

First, the use of national remedies as the starting point for redress of breaches of Community law presents the courts with more opportunities for developing and refining the rules of domestic law on governmental liability. A notable example is *Bourgoin SA v Minister of Agriculture Food and Fisheries* [1986] QB 716, which is now the leading authority on the tort of misfeasance in public office in English law (see 9.1.2 below).

Second, Community law principles may directly influence the content of domestic law. An illustration of this is found in the area of restitution of unlawfully levied taxes. Under the domestic common law, and in some of the statutes dealing with this issue, overpaid taxes are not generally recoverable (see further 11.2.4), but it is likely that our national courts must provide a remedy for the recovery of any tax levied in contravention of Community law (see 11.2.7). The perceived need to provide such a remedy, and the desire to avoid any anomaly between Community and domestic law, prompted the enactment of sections 24 and 29 of the Finance Act 1989, which give a wide right to recover car tax, excise duty and value added tax, not only where these taxes are levied contrary to Community law, but also in other cases (for details see 11.2.3). This was also one factor which prompted the examination of the whole area of the recovery of invalid taxes by the Law Commission (see 11.2.5).

Finally, domestic law might in the future be increasingly subject to the influences of the liability regimes which apply in other member states, and in determining the responsibility of the Community institutions themselves, simply because of the increased exposure to those systems which has resulted from Community membership. This can already be seen in other areas of the law as, for example, in *Brind v Secretary of State for the Home Office* ([1991] 1 WLR 720), where the "Civil Law" doctrine of proportionality was accepted as a potential ground of judicial review.

2

Contracts: General Principles

2.1   Introduction

Government contracts are subject to the ordinary private law: in English law there is no concept of an "administrative contract" subject to a distinct body of public law rules. There is, nevertheless, a substantial body of special rules which apply only, or mainly, to the contracts of government. These derive from a number of sources.

First, the fact that one party is a public authority may affect the way in which the courts interpret the parties' intentions, in deciding whether a contract has come into being, or in construing its terms. Sometimes this is a device for applying rules of policy rather than a genuine attempt to ascertain intentions. Thus, the courts have sometimes suggested that there is no intention to create legal relations, though such an intention would have been held to exist had the parties been private individuals, apparently for policy reasons. One illustration is found in the cases indicating that there may not be any contractual relationship between the Crown and its civil servants, and another in the rule that Crown servants may not be liable for breach of warranty of authority, on the basis that no such warranty is intended (see 4.2.2 and 2.4.3). Other examples are considered in 2.2 below. It is much more rare, on the other hand, for the public nature of a contracting party to be invoked to find a contractual liability where it would *not* normally exist. An example is the approach of Lord Ormrod in the Court of Appeal *Gibson v Manchester C C* ([1978] 1 WLR 520), where he emphasised the fact that the vendor was a local authority selling council houses pursuant to a general government policy, in concluding (with Lord Denning, in a majority decision) that a binding agreement to sell had been reached at a relatively early stage in an exchange of correspondence. The decision was, however, overturned by the House of Lords ([1979] 1 WLR 294). In other cases the public nature of the authority has been cited as a justification for the court's conclusion, where, however, it seems the court would have reached the same result in a private case (see, for example, *Great Northern Railway v Witham* ((1873) LR 9 CP 16). Any rules based on the intentions of the parties may always, of course, be expressly excluded.

The common law has also developed special rules for government contracts which are not based on intention, some of which cannot be excluded. Thus the rule that Crown servants are dismissible at pleasure is generally regarded in this way. Another example is the rule requiring a parliamentary appropriation of payments under a contract (see 2.6). Alongside these rules of public law concerned specifically with contract, the general body of administrative law - the principles of reasonableness, procedural fairness and so on, as well as the general *ultra vires* doctrine - is becoming of increasing importance in the context of government contracts; and failure to comply with these rules may have consequences for contractual liability (see 2.10 below).

A further source of special government contract law is legislation - this is important, for example, in the area of procurement (see chapter 3). As with a breach of common law rules, failure to comply with legislative requirements might have an impact on private law liability. Legislation may also be important in determining the content of a contract: it may stipulate terms which must be included, or are deemed to be included in certain contracts, or the manner in which the terms are to be set (for examples, see the discussion of public employment at 3.1 below).

Finally, another important source of the "law of government contracts" is the terms agreed between the parties, insofar as the law has left them free to do this. These clauses and any interpretation put on them by the courts are a source of the "special" law of government contracts to the extent that clauses found differ from those commonly found in the private sector. Procurement contracts, for example, are often made on standard terms drawn up by the government (see Turpin, *Government Procurement and Contracts* (1989) at pp. 105-111). Many are modelled on clauses found in standard private sector procurement contracts, but others "are designed to give effect to specific public policies or reflect the unique status of the government as a contracting party" (Turpin, at p.107) - for example, "termination for convenience" clauses, allowing the government to terminate the agreement at any time on payment of compensation (see Turpin, at pp. 245-246) and terms designed to ensure that contractors comply with social and economic policies laid down by the government (see 2.2.1 below).

This first chapter on contract deals with the general common law and legislative framework applicable to government contracting, and the relationship between legislative prescriptions and contractual liability. Chapters 3 and 4 examine the main legal provisions in two important areas of contracting - public procurement and employment.

2.2. The Scope of Contract

2.2.1. *The use of contract*

The government today makes considerable use of contract in carrying out its policies and activities. First, contract is used in many situations in which it is also used in the private sphere. Thus the government employs many servants to carry out its business, and the relationship between the government and these individuals is often contractual, though there are also important cases where it may not be (see 4.2.2 and 4.3). Public bodies also make contracts to obtain goods and services from outside suppliers - office equipment, weapons for the army, and advertising and construction services are just a few examples of the huge range of products and services normally obtained from independent contractors. These contracts, called contracts of procurement, are of enormous economic significance: in 1984 the central government market was estimated to be worth close to #15000 million (Turpin, *Government Procurement and Contracts* (1989) at p.x). They have become more important in recent years at both central and local level, as there has been increased emphasis on "contracting out" as the best method of obtaining value for money, both at central level (see Turpin at pp. 206-207 and 257) and at local government level, where obligations to contract out many functions have been imposed by legislation (see 3.1.2 below). Obviously the scope of modern government's activity makes its contractual activities as employer and as purchaser of considerable importance, both to the large number of individuals engaged by the government, or who seek government business or employment, and to the public generally, who pay for these contracts and stand to benefit from their performance.

Most contracts of employment and procurement are freely negotiated in that, first, there is no legal requirement to deal with the government at all, and, second, terms are set by negotiation, although, of course, the government, like some powerful private persons, may often have considerable bargaining power in practice. Thus, the terms of employment contracts, for example, are often determined through collective bargaining (see below at 4.1). Procurement contracts are generally made on standard forms drawn up by the government after consultation with suppliers' representatives, and the price and some other terms determined by competitive procedures or negotiation with individual suppliers (Turpin, at p.105; ch.5). It has often been pointed out that, for the central government, at least, there is no need to use the market or even the contractual method to obtain the services of employees and independent contractors, since it has legislative powers at its disposal. Contract is chosen, however, as a device which generally enables government needs to be met, whilst also providing a useful framework to ensure that those dealing with the government receive fair treatment. The only case where the government's legislative powers are regularly invoked in peacetime to obtain its needs is in relation to the acquisition of land; clearly this is necessary because of the relatively unique nature of land, which means that needs cannot be adequately met through the market. Legislative powers are, of course, invoked in war time, providing both for military conscription and an adequate supply of other goods and services from the private sector (as to the latter see the former Ministry of Supply Act 1939 s.7 (3)). As indicated in 2.1 above, there is also some legislative direction on how the terms of certain types of contracts are to be determined.

As well as purchasing, the government frequently makes contracts to sell or supply goods or services. For example, contract governs its relationship with its tenants, whether of council houses or business premises. There is also often a contract between the government and the user of a public service - for example, of public recreation facilities. Public utilities such as gas, water or electricity, whether in public hands, or in private hands as at present, have since the nineteenth century generally been subject to statutory obligations to supply their products to certain persons, with the terms of supply often regulated (for a summary of the modern position see Foulkes, *Administrative Law* (7th ed. 1990) at pp. 436-438). However, the courts have tended, in these cases, to say that the supply relationship is not a contractual one (see 2.2.2 below).

A rather different use of contract in the public sphere is as a method for regulating behaviour, a use which has attracted attention for the important constitutional issues which it raises (see, for example, Daintith, "The Executive Power Today; Bargaining and Economic Control", *The Changing Constitution* (2nd ed. 1989) eds. Jowell and Oliver, Ch.8; Turpin, *British Government and the Constitution* (2nd ed. 1990) at pp. 409-414; Ganz, *Quasi - Legislation* (1987) *passim*). The traditional method of regulation is by direct legislative prescription backed by legislative sanctions : for example, a fine, imprisonment or loss of benefits such as a right to trade. The government may also, however, use its contractual powers to control behaviour in various ways. We may distinguish between contracts of which the main object is regulation of subject behaviour, and the use of contract bargaining power to regulate matters which are not connected with the main object of the contract.

Illustrations of the first category are licensing agreements which create a contractual relationship between the government and a trader, in which rules for the protection of the public are laid out in the licence as contractual conditions. In such cases legal sanctions for enforcement derive from the legal force of the contract. An example is the case of contracts awarded to companies wishing to operate on the independent television network.

Formerly, these were awarded by the Independent Broadcasting Authority which was directed by section 13 of the Independent Broadcasting Authority Act 1973 to include in the contracts with the companies such provisions as the Authority thought necessary or expedient to enforce compliance with requirements imposed under the Act, which covered matters such as the showing of violence, and the standard of advertising (for discussion see Lewis, [1975] PL 317). Under the provisions of the Broadcasting Act 1990 control over independent television is now given to the Independent Television Commission, which is responsible for issuing licences to television companies. Control is, under this Act, also to be exercised through the inclusion of conditions in the licences. The Commission is required to include conditions relating to some matters (see ss. 6 and 8) and has a general power to include other conditions as appear to the Commission appropriate to enable it to fulfil its regulatory duties under the Act. Local authorities have also used the method of the contractual licence to regulate the conduct of market traders, with sanctions for non-compliance being, for example, the termination or suspension of the licence under the terms of the contract.

Another type of "regulatory" contract is where an individual or body agrees to certain conditions in return for financial aid. Contracts of this type have been made in federal states between the federal governments and private institutions involved in areas which the federal government has no constitutional power to regulate directly. Thus in Canada the federal government cannot regulate directly in the areas of health care and education, but has made "regulatory contracts" with institutions involved in these spheres, since its contractual powers are generally considered free from any constitutional restraints. In this way the federal government obtains a degree of control over the activity whilst the bodies concerned enjoy the advantages of federal funding. Even more significantly, agreements are also made between the federal governments and provincial or state governments to similar effect (see Petter (1989) 68 Can Bar Rev 64), although being between different governments these agreements probably do not constitute legally binding contracts (see Mundell, (1960) 2 OHLJ 56). In the United Kingdom similar agreements have sometimes been made although there is no legal objection to legislation, simply because the government prefers a consensual approach. An example given by Turpin (*British Government and the Constitution*, above, at p.411) is an agreement which was made between the central government, Port of London Authority and the Trade Unions. Under this agreement financial assistance was given to the Authority by central government in return for various promises, including changes in working practices and a commitment not to close the Royal Docks. It is not always clear in this sort of case, where agreements are concerned predominantly with matters of social or economic policy, whether there is a legally binding contract : even if there is consideration, the court may take the view that there is no intention to create legal relations (see 2.2.2 below). The government also uses its contract power to further policies which have nothing to do with the main object of the contract in question. An illustration is the use the government has made of its enormous influence as a purchaser of goods and services from the private sector to induce compliance with government policy (for a modern overview see Turpin, *Government Procurement and Contracts* (1989) at pp. 73-79; Morris, (1990) 19 Anglo Am Law Rev 87; and on policies relating to labour issues Fredman and Morris, *The State as Employer: Labour Law in the Public Services* (1989), ch. 12). Perhaps the most famous example was the government's use of procurement power between 1975 and 1979 in relation to its anti-inflation policy - firms paying wages regarded as excessive were refused government business (see Ferguson and Page, (1978) 128 NLJ 515; Ganz, [1978] PL 333, Daintith (1979) 32 CLP 41). Compliance with government policies may be enforced not only by refusing contract awards but also by imposing conditions in contracts which are awarded. For example, compliance with existing statutory obligations to refrain from racial discrimination has been made a term of many government contracts (Turpin, *Government Procurement and Contracts*, above, at p.78). Procurement power is used also to achieve "secondary" policies in ways which are not aimed at changing individual behaviour - so that they cannot really be classified as "regulatory" - but which forward some secondary policy simply by their implementation. For example, awards have in the past been made to domestic suppliers to maintain a domestic capability, or to prison or sheltered workshops to maintain the viability of these institutions (see Turpin, *Government Procurement and Contracts*, above, at pp. 75-79).

The importance of procurement as an instrument for achieving secondary policies has declined recently as the United Kingdom government has increasingly chosen to emphasise value for money as the main objective of procurement. In addition some (though not all) secondary policies are now precluded by European Community law (see further 3.2), and, in international law, by the General Agreement on Trade and Tarrifs. Domestic legislation, as well as common law developments, have also placed restrictions on local government's powers to take account of non-commercial considerations (see 3.1 and 2.8 below).

Finally, it may be observed that "contractual type" arrangements have been used increasingly in recent years in the UK to regulate and formalise the relationship between certain government agencies, notably in relation to the "next steps" programme. In some of these cases the contractual analogy has an important symbolic function as an expression of the formality of the relationship and of the independence of the entities concerned. Since these relationships do not, however, give rise to private law contractual relationships, they are noted at the end of the next section, "Exclusion of the contractual relationship."

2.2.2. *Exclusion of the contractual relationship*

In some circumstances the law holds that an agreement to which a public body is party does not amount to a legal contract, though a comparable agreement between private parties would be binding.

Crown Service. One example may be the area of Crown service. It has, in the past, generally been considered that the relationship between the Crown and its servants is not contractual (for discussion see 4.2.2). However, the rule, if it still exists, appears to be based on the absence of an intention to create legal relations, rather than any incapacity of the Crown. In reality, of course, the supposed rule developed as a product of a judicial view that it was not appropriate for the relationship to be governed by a legally binding contract.

Supply of services to the public. Similarly, arguments that the relationship is contractual have also been rejected in some cases concerned with the supply of services by public bodies. Thus it has long been held that no contract generally exists between the Post Office and a person using the mail (*Lane v Cotton* (1701) 91 ER 1332; *Whitfield v Le Despencer* (1778) 98 ER 1344; *Treifus and Co. Ltd. v Post Office* [1957] 2 QB 352; though cf. *John Fairfax & Sons Pty. v Australian Telecommunications Commission* (1977) 30 FLR 444 (N.S.W. C.A.)). A charge is, however, recoverable in the courts by the Post Office "as if" it were a simple contract debt (s.28(5) Post Office Act 1969). Liability in tort for the Post Office and its servants and agents, is also precluded, under section 29 of the Post Office Act 1969, though a statutory cause of action is given in certain cases by section 30 (see 5.2.3 below). However, the Post Office frequently negotiates individual agreements with major users of the mail and it is arguable that a contract does exist in these cases, the general rule to the contrary resting on the absence of an intent to create legal relations (the precise basis of the rule was not made clear in *Treifus*). There is no reason to suppose that the position has changed since the Post Office became a statutory corporation in 1969, particularly in view of the fact that the previously existing provisions negating liability in tort and imposing a special statutory liability were expressly retained (see 5.2.3).

Contractual liability in the provision of public services has also been precluded in cases where there is a statutory duty to supply a product on terms regulated by statute. Thus it was held *Willmore v South Eastern Electricity Board* ([1957] 2 Lloyds Rep 375) that the only remedy for a failure to supply electricity, which caused the plaintiff's chicks to die, was recovery of the sum expressly provided by statute: the reasoning of Glyn Jones J (at 380) was that the supply was made because of the statutory duty to supply, and not by way of acceptance of any contractual offer by the plaintiff to take and pay for electricity. Further, express representations by the supplier as to the nature of the supply were held not to be intended to have contractual effect. In *Clegg, Parkinson & Co. v Earby Gas Co.* ([1896] 1 QB 592) it was held that there was no contractual obligation with respect to the nature and quantity of gas supplied under a statutory duty; and in *Read v Croydon Corp.* ([1938] 4 All ER 631) there was held to be no contractual promise to supply water of a particular quality, where the supply was provided under a statutory duty. In these cases it may not be so much the existence of the duty to supply as the fear of imposing widespread liability on utilities, particularly for economic losses, which has led the courts to the conclusion that there is no contract: for the same reasons the courts have circumscribed carefully any cause of action against utilities in negligence (see ch.6) or for breach of statutory duty (see ch.7). The position is probably the same today: gas, water and electricity are still generally supplied under a statutory duty (see Gas Act 1986, s.9; Electricity Act 1989, s.16; Water Act 1989 ss. 46-48)) on prescribed, or regulated, terms and there is nothing specifically to suggest that consumers generally have a contract. However, utilities are given power to make "special agreements" with some customers in which some terms of supply are privately agreed (see, for example, Gas Act 1986 s.14 (3); Electricity Act 1989, s.22), and it might be argued that these, at least to some extent, create a contractual relationship, though the supply is provided under a duty (and see also s.10 (7) of the Gas Act). The provision of telephone services on the other hand, does occur under a contract (see Telecommunications Act 1984; Sch. 5, para. 12), with compensation for failure to supply being provided on a contractual basis. Agreements made by British Telecom generally describe themselves as contractual. However, it is interesting that here damages for economic losses are carefully limited by express terms (see Conditions for Telephone Service (1991), 21.3.2; 21.4).

It seems also that there is no contract between a National Health Service patient to whom drugs are supplied for a fee under regulation, either with the chemist or the Health Service (*Pfizer Corporation v Ministry of Health* [1965] AC 512, where the House of Lords emphasised the existence of the legislative duty to supply in reaching this conclusion; *Re Medicaments Reference* [1971] 1 All ER 12; *R. v The Pharmaceutical Society of Great Britain, ex parte The Association of Pharmaceutical Importers* [1987] 3 CMLR 951).

Grants and subsidies. Another situation in which the courts have rejected the argument that there is a contractual relationship is where a grant or subsidy is promised to individuals who comply with certain conditions.

In *R. v Secretary of State for Transport, ex parte Sherriff* (The Independent, Jan 12 1988; noted by Bradley [1989] PL 197) the applicant was promised a grant towards the cost of certain works. These were being carried out to provide access from the applicant's industrial site to British Rail facilities, under a scheme which was designed to encourage the use of rail, as opposed to road, haulage. Taylor J rejected the submission that the promise was an offer, accepted by the performance of the works, so as to bring into effect a unilateral contract to pay the grant: "There was no intention to create contractual relations. The respondent was simply exercising a statutory power to grant money out of public funds upon conditions over which he had discretionary control". This clearly suggests there will generally be no contract where a grant is promised. In the later case of *Cato v Minister of Agriculture, Fisheries and Food* ([1989] 3 CMLR 513) the Court of Appeal considered an agreement whereby the Ministry promised a grant to the plaintiff if his fishing vessel were decommissioned, in pursuit of a common market policy to reduce fishing capacity. It was said by Purchas LJ (at 533) to be "unarguable" that there was an intention to create contractual relations. In several Australian cases involving grants and subsidies there has also been held to be no intention to create legal relations (see, for example, *Australian Woollen Mills Pty Ltd v Commonwealth* (1955) 93 CLR 546 (P.C.) (promise to pay subsidy on wool used for manufacture locally); *Logan Downs v Commissioner for Railways* ([1960] Qd R 191) (promise to pay rebate on freight charge for livestock used to replace drought losses); *Administration of Papua New Guinea v Leahy* ((1961) 105 CLR 6 (High Ct. Aus.; arrangement to provide assistance to eradicate ticks from cattle). And see the discussion in Rose, "The Government and Contract", in *Essays on Contract* (1987) ed. Finn, Ch.9; Allard, (1989) 12 UNSW LJ 114 at 118-121; Aronson and Whitmore, at pp. 204-205)).

Although in the Australian cases (at least in the first two mentioned) the courts' conclusion may have been correct on the basis that there was simply a general statement of government policy, in the English cases, which concerned detailed agreements with specific individuals, it is difficult to see why there could be no intention to contract. There seems in addition no problem with the requirement of consideration since the grants were being paid in order to secure from the applicant a specific benefit to the public interest. In *Sherriff* the judge said that no contract should be found because the Minister retained a discretion to decide if the relevant conditions had been met, and might wish to change his mind about payment if this were not done. However, the terms of the contract would include the conditions known to the applicant; and public law rules would render ineffective any contractual promise which was contrary to statute or fettered the legislative discretion given to the Minister (see 2.5 below). An intention to contract should held to exist in this sort of situation, unless the contrary is made clear.

Relationship between public agencies. Finally, in this context, it is interesting to note that a contractual-type framework has increasingly been utilised to provide the basis for dealings between different organisations in the public sector.

In particular, this development can be seen in the "next steps" programme. (On this see further Goldsworthy, *Setting up Next Steps* (1991), an HMSO publication). The aim of this programme is to separate the policy making functions of central government from the function of implementing, or administering, decided policies, its objective being to increase efficiency in management: it is expected that the separation will produce better monitoring and accountability in relation to the management function, will raise the status of civil service managers and will give managers greater autonomy in their sphere of expertise. To this end in the last three years a number of separate agencies have been set up within government departments, each headed by a Chief Executive, to be responsible for the administration of policies set at the political level. The most famous example is the Benefits Agency, set up from 1991 to administer benefits which come under the auspices of the Department of Social Security. The relationship between the minister and agency is governed by a "framework document", similar to a contract: the contractual analogy is seen as a suitable basis for the governance of the relationship. However, it seems clear that there is no private law contractual relationship between a Minister and the "next step" agencies, since these agencies have no legal identity which is separate from that of the Minister. As indicated earlier, the framework document serves primarily as a symbol of the intended formality of the relationship and of the perceived independence of the parties to it; their position is intended as far as possible to be analogous to that of parties to a private law commercial contract, even though there do not exist parallel methods of legal enforcement.

A similar sort of relationship exists between a District Health Authority in its capacity as a "purchaser" of health services for its patients, and its own Direct Management Units which act as a provider of such services (see Langley, [1900] PL 527), - again the relationship cannot be contractual since the Management Unit has no legal identity separate from that of the District Health Authority.

As was noted at 2.2.1 above, contracts between federal and provincial governments in the federal states of the Commonwealth may well be unenforceable for the same reason - the lack of distinct legal identity of the parties.

A final interesting example of a contractual-type relationship which does not create contractual rights enforceable in private law is that which is created between certain health service authorities involved in health care under section 4(1) of the National Health Service and Community Care Act 1990. This creates a special type of agreement, an "NHS contract", which is defined as an arrangement by which one health service body arranges to receive health services from another (s.4(1)). Such an agreement exists, for example, where health services are purchased by a general practitioner or by a District Health Authority from a Hospital Trust, which is a legal entity entirely separate from the District Health Authority. There is no NHS contract, however, where services are purchased by a District Health Authority from its own Direct Management Unit, which, as indicated, does not have a separate legal identity.

Although designated a contract, the agreement is stated, however, not to give rise to any contractual rights or liabilities, even though it would otherwise do so (s.4(3)). Instead, it is provided that disputes under such an agreement are to be resolved by the Secretary of State who may appoint a person to resolve them on his behalf (s.4(3)). In practice, such contracts include arbitration clauses, and disputes are resolved by an arbitrator named by the parties. The National Health Service contract is a particularly interesting example of the way in which the private law contractual model is adopted in a public law context, but is specifically altered to suit the particular context of public law. It has been useful to divide this discussion of the scope of contract in public law into two sections - one dealing with the uses of contract, and the other with cases in which the contractual relationship is excluded. The example of the national health service contract, however, straddles the boundary between the "contractual" and the "non-contractual"; and it illustrates nicely the flexibility of the basic contract model as a tool of government.

2.3.   Capacity

For a contract to bind a public body it is necessary, first, that the body has capacity to make that contract and, second, that the human agent who has purported to conclude the contract on behalf of the public body has the authority to do so. Capacity is considered in this section, and authority at 2.4 below.

2.3.1.   The Crown

As explained earlier (see 1.2.1.1) the Crown is considered to possess all the legal powers of a natural person, including the power to make contracts. This was originally deduced from the premise that the Crown for purposes of government is to be equated with the person of the reigning monarch. The leading authority is *The Bankers Case* ((1700) 90 ER 270) in which it was held by the Barons of the Exchequer that the King had authority to borrow money and charge the revenue of the hereditary excise with the interest payments, without the need for the contract to be authorised by Act of Parliament: "to refrain the King from such a power," reasoned Chief Justice Coke, "is absurd ... absurd because by this he would have less power than any of his subjects, or than he himself had when he was a subject" (at 271). The decision was approved by the House of Lords, though no reasons were given, as was then the practice. The principle which it established has been confirmed in modern decisions in other Commonwealth jurisdictions (see *J.E. Verrault v Quebec* [1977] 1 SCR 41; *Quebec v Labrecque* [1980] 2 SCR 1057; *New South Wales v Bardolph* (1934) 52 CLR 455 per Evatt J at pp. 474-475). It was suggested by Rich J in *New South Wales v Bardolph,* above, that the Crown may make only such contracts as are "incidental to the ordinary and well recognised functions of government" (at 496); but this limitation has never been applied, and is generally rejected by writers (see Aronson and Whitmore, at p.197; Campbell, (1970) 44 ALJ 14).

The reasoning on which the rule of general common law capacity has been based was criticised at 1.2.1.1 above. It was suggested that the Crown in its public capacity is at common law a corporate legal entity which is quite distinct from the legal person of the reigning monarch, and the policy arguments in favour of this approach apply with equal force to contract (see further below). However, the rule that the Crown in its public capacity possesses a general and unlimited power to contract is probably too well entrenched for judicial alteration and its existence seems to be universally accepted by modern commentators (see, for example, Turpin, *Government Procurement and Contracts* (1989), at pp. 83-84; Hogg, at pp. 163-164; Puri, *Australian Government Contracts* (1978), at p.45; Aronson and Whitmore, at pp. 187-188).

Although in principle the Crown shares with natural persons a general power to contract, it is arguable that the general public law principle against the fettering of discretion imposes a restriction on the capacity of the Crown (see 2.5). Further, although the courts have now accepted that the Crown is legally capable of making a contract with its servants (see 4.2.2), it may still be incompetent to restrict its freedom to dismiss its servants at will (see 4.2.3). Constraints on the contract-making process, arising from the operation of other common law principles of judicial review such as natural justice, may also, arguably, affect the validity of Crown contracts (see 2.9 and 2.10 below). Thus, the courts have not been entirely consistent in applying the view that the Crown is to be equated with a natural person, but have allowed for special governmental rules.

Parliament exercises a limited legal control over expenditure made under contracts, by virtue of the general rule that there must be a Parliamentary appropriation for all expenditure (on this see 2.6). However, the recognition of the Crown's general capacity to contract, means that other matters relating to contracts are not legally subject to Parliamentary approval. For example, secondary policies carried out through procurement (as to which see 2.2.1) do not require Parliamentary sanction. The government can thus avoid scrutiny of important policy issues. Parliamentary scrutiny and debate of such policies is desirable in principle, to ensure both the interests of affected individuals and the merits of the policies are properly considered. It has been suggested by Daintith, for example, that the way in which procurement power was used to induce compliance with the government's anti-inflation policy in the 1970s, whereby those not complying with the government's expectations were refused access to government contracts, would never have been approved by Parliament, because of the arbitrary and secret way in which it was administered ("The Executive Today: Bargaining and Economic Control" in *The Changing Constitution*, eds. Jowell and Oliver (2nd ed. 1989) Ch.8). Of course, the significance of Parliamentary approval should not be exaggerated - the realities of Executive control of Parliament, the use of delegated legislation and other features of the constitution, mean that controls over administrative activity other than the legal requirement of Parliamentary approval are often more important. In any case, the government often chooses to submit its policies to Parliament though it is not required to do so; and contractual activity is scrutinised by Select Committees (see Turpin, above, at pp. 261-263). Nevertheless, the legal requirement of Parliamentary authorisation has some significance, and the importance of this gap in relation to contract is heightened by the fact that such activities are not within the jurisdiction of the Ombudsman (see 2.11), and by doubts over the availability of judicial review (see 2.9). If the courts were to develop a rule limiting the power of the Crown to make contracts it would not be necessary to hold a contract made in breach of the restrictions to be void : a remedy could be made available to restrain the making of a contract, but once made it could be treated as enforceable. This is the general rule applied to the contracts of common law corporations which exceed their powers (*Sutton's Hospital Case* (1612) 77 ER 937; *Riche v Ashbury Railway Carriage and Iron Co.* (1874) LR 9 Ex 224 at p.263).

Parliament may restrict the scope of the Crown's common law powers by statute (*Attorney General v de Keyser's Royal Hotel Ltd.* [1920] AC 508) and may, of course, choose to restrict the power to contract in this way. A statutory power to contract given to the Crown will generally overlap with that existing under the common law, and even if the common law power is not expressly restricted it will by implication be subsumed in the statutory one (*de Keyser's Royal Hotel,* above), and any conditions or limitations on the statutory power must be observed. Such a principle was stated by Rich J in *New South Wales v Bardolph,* above (at p.496): "Where the administration of particular functions of government is regulated by statute and the regulation expressly or impliedly touches the power of contracting, all statutory conditions must be observed and the power is no doubt no wider than the statute contemplates."

2.3.2.   Crown agents

Public authorities which are Crown agents, such as Ministers of the Crown and Crown corporations, have general *authority* to make contracts on behalf of the Crown in connection with their functions and activities (see 2.4.2 below). It is also necessary to consider whether such bodies have in addition any independent *capacity* to make contracts - that is, may they undertake contractual liability in their own name? (see further Arrowsmith, [1990] 28 OHLJ 571).

There are three main possibilities:

1) Crown agents have no independent capacity to contract, and cannot thus be sued on any contract which they negotiate: the Crown is the only government entity which is a party to the contract.

2) Crown agents have a capacity to make themselves party to a contract vis-a-vis the other party, who may thus sue the agent for breach when the agent has chosen to contract in its own name; but agents may not undertake primary liability, which always rests on the Crown.

3) Crown agents have a capacity to contract on matters within their area of responsibility in the same way as any other artificial legal entity - for example, a municipal authority. Thus, though they have authority to contract on behalf of the Crown should they choose to do so, they may alternatively make contracts to which the Crown is not a party, and for which the Crown bears no legal liability towards the "agent".

To the extent that a body has authority to make contracts for the Crown, it has no need of any capacity to contract in its own name, whether under 2) above (that is, as agent only) or under 3) (as principal): to make the contracts which it needs in carrying out its functions it may utilise the authority which it possesses as a Crown agent. However, several cases suggests that some Crown agents do have a capacity to contract in their own name, at least where they have corporate status conferred upon them by statute.

This suggestion was first made in *Graham v Public Works Commissioners* ([1901] 2 KB 781). The plaintiff, who had contracted to build a post office for the government alleged a breach of the agreement. In order to avoid the petition of right procedure he sued the Commissioners, an incorporated body, in their own name, rather than the Crown itself. It was held that he was entitled to do so. Phillimore J considered that incorporation simply allowed an action against the Commissioners as "nominal" defendants for the Crown, so avoiding the need for the petition of right procedure. If this is the basis for the decision, it probably has no modern significance. Ridley J, however, took a different approach, holding that the Commissioners were liable since they had chosen to contract in their own name. Clearly he accepted that they had an independent capacity to contract, although it is not clear whether he thought that they could undertake primary liability, or could contract only as agents of the Crown. This approach of Ridley J was followed by the Privy Council in *International Railway Co v Niagara Parks Commission* ([1941] AC 328). Here also it was held that the plaintiff could sue the corporate agent which had negotiated the contract rather than the Crown itself, to avoid the petition of right procedure. Luxmoore J, tendering the advice of the Committee, expressly rejected the view that "the Commission has no other capacity than that of Crown agent or servant" (at 342). The Commissioners had, he concluded, power to undertake liability, and had exercised it here: both the Crown and its agent, it concluded, had made themselves party to the agreement. Again, it was not necessary to consider the question of whether the authority could undertake primary liability : the contract was quite clearly made on behalf of the Crown, and it was assumed the Crown would be primarily liable.

Ridley J and Luxmoore J thus appear to accept that Crown agents, at least those which are incorporated, may contract in their own name in connection with their authorised functions, even though these functions are carried out on behalf of the Crown, and that in determining the capacity in which the contract was actually made the courts must look to the intentions of the parties. The Crown and its agent are treated as distinct entities, and the relationship between them determined by the ordinary private law rules of principal and agent. As indicated, however, there is no need to recognise this separate capacity to contract. The motivation for these decisions was clearly to permit the plaintiff to sue without using the petition of right procedure, regarded as unsatisfactory long before its abolition. This reason for holding that there is a separate capacity to contract has long since disappeared. However, the approach could still be used to avoid the application of other Crown immunities. This development of the idea of a separate contractual capacity can be compared with the development of the *persona designata* doctrine, which allows the courts to grant prerogative relief against unlawful acts of the central executive (see 1.2.1.2; and see also the discussion of breach of statutory duty at 5.4.4.3). Most recently, the view that a corporate Crown agent has a capacity to contract was taken by Dillon LJ in *McLaren v Home Office* ([1990] IRLR 338). It was used here to support his view that the alleged rule that the Crown cannot contract with its servants had no application to the Home Office, which had taken over the statutory powers to contract of the Prison Commissioners, an incorporated body. However, this was not necessary for the decision, since it is now recognised that the Crown itself does have a capacity to contract with its servants (see 4.2.2 below).

A different approach to the question of a separate capacity was adopted by the House of Lords in *Town Investments v Department of the Environment* ([1978] AC 359) which was not referred to in *McLaren*. The issue was whether a certain lease was within the scope of legislation giving protection from rent increases, which applied only where the "tenant" and "occupier" were the same person. The Department of the Environment had responsibility for providing accommodation for other Departments and had negotiated the lease of the premises. They were then occupied by the officials of a different Department. The landlord argued that the Minister of the Environment was himself the tenant, and thus tenant and occupier were not one and the same. The landlord's main argument was based on the approach in *Niagara Parks*, treating the agent and the Crown as separate legal entities with a separate capacity, and the relationship between them as determined by the general law of principal and agent. The Minister of the Environment, it was argued, had the power to enter a lease in his own name by virtue of the fact of incorporation; the capacity in which the lease was made was to be determined by the ordinary rules of construction; and applying these principles here the Minister and not the Crown was the "tenant".

This approach was accepted by Lord Morris in his dissenting judgement. It was rejected, however, by the majority, which found the Crown to be both tenant and occupier. It should be pointed out that it is not made expressly clear whether their Lordships considered that the questions of who was the party to the contract, and who held the interest in the lease, were necessarily to be answered in the same way : if not, the case might be regarded as of limited authority in relation to contract. However, an assumption that the two are the same does seem to underlie the judgements, and many of the passages refer only to the question of liability on the contract.

Lord Diplock, with whom Lord Edmund Davies agreed, considered it inappropriate to determine the relationship between the Ministers and the Crown according to the general private law of agency: "it is not private law but public law that governs the relationships between Her Majesty acting in her political capacity, the government departments among which the work of Her Majesty's government is distributed, the ministers of the Crown in charge of the various departments and civil servants." (at 380). He concluded that "acts of government that are done by any ministers are acts done by the Crown" (at 381). Hence the "tenant" of a lease made under the "designation" of a Minister is the Crown. However, the precise basis for this conclusion is not clear. He may have thought that the Minister did not possess an independent capacity to contract at all. Alternatively, he may have considered that an independent capacity existed, but that there is a strong presumption that a Minister acts only on behalf of the Crown (as to which see p.364) - in other words that "public law" governs the interpretation of intention, but does not affect the existence of capacity. Lord Kilbrandon is similarly ambiguous : "I do not", he said "find the concepts of agency or trust, even as analogues, relevant in this context" (at p.402); but he did not state whether a Minister could ever undertake liability in an independent capacity. Either approach would also fit with a statement of MacKinnon L.J. in *Minister of Supply v British Thomson Houston* ([1943] 1 All ER 615 at 617), where he stated that it is a "well known" principle of common law that a Minister may not be sued in his own name. Lord Simon more clearly took the view that Ministers do not possess an independent capacity to act, comparing the relationship between the Minister and the Crown to that of a hand with a body (at p.400): the acts of the hands must always be the acts of the body. Whichever of the two interpretations is adopted, it is difficult to reconcile the approach of their Lordships with that of the Privy Council in *Niagara Parks,* where the Crown and Ministers were treated as ordinary legal persons. Though cited by counsel *Niagara Parks* was not referred to in the judgments.

Town Investments has attracted some criticism (see, for example, Harlow, (1980) 43 MLR 241 at pp. 244-248; Wade, (1991) 107 LQR 5). The main argument in favour of the approach in *Niagara Parks* is that recognition of an independent capacity to contract in Crown agents provides a device to avoid Crown immunities: it can be argued that where the agent undertakes liability in his own name (or at least where the agent is primarily liable) such immunities do not apply. However, this is an unsatisfactory and artificial device. It means that the application of an immunity may depend on the capacity in which the agent has chosen to act in the particular case and, possibly, on the capacity in which the agent is sued or chooses to sue (see Arrowsmith, above); and it introduces complexity and uncertainty. It is also strange to hold agents liable to suit since many do not have any independent assets with which to satisfy a judgement against them (a point stressed in the course of argument in *Graham* (at pp. 784-785); and see Glanville Williams (at p.21)).

The better approach is to treat Ministers and other Crown agents as possessing no independent capacity to make contracts, unless such a capacity is clearly conferred by statute. Powers to enter into a specific type of contract given to a named Minister should not normally be considered to confer such a capacity : these provisions are probably concerned with authority to contract on behalf of the Crown, and not with the capacity of Crown agents (see 2.4.2). The decisions in *Niagara Parks* and *Graham* should be explained as turning on the fact that incorporation allows Crown agents to be sued in their own names, but only as nominal defendants for the Crown, so allowing the petition of right procedure to be avoided but leaving all other consequences of Crown status unaffected. This, as indicated above, seemed to be the view of Phillimore J in *Graham.*

It is always possible, of course, for statute to make clear that it is intended to confer a separate contractual capacity on a Crown agent; and the fact that this has been done in some cases seems to support the view that a separate capacity is not intended to arise from the mere fact of incorporation. Thus, for example, the Health Authorities have a separate capacity to contract : the National Health Service Act 1977 (Sch. 5 para. 15(1)) provides that an authority may enforce rights and incur liability "in all respects as if it were acting as principal", even when exercising functions on behalf of the Secretary of State or some other authority.

2.3.3   *Public bodies which are not Crown agents*

2.3.2.1. *Scope of the power to contract*

As explained at 1.2.2., most public bodies which are not Crown agents, including most local authorities, have been created by statute and most are incorporated. Such bodies are often referred to as "statutory corporations". These statutory corporations have only those powers specifically conferred upon them : in contrast with the Crown they do not share the powers of natural persons. Acts done outside the scope of their statutory powers are said to be *ultra vires.* This doctrine has been applied both to private corporations (*Ashbury Railway Carriage and Iron Co. v Riche* (1875) LR 7 HL 653) and to statutory public authorities (*Attorney General v Manchester Corporation* [1906] 1 Ch 643; *Attorney General v Fulham Corporation* [1921] 1 Ch 44; and for a general discussion of the *ultra vires* principle in relation to local authorities; see Cross and Bailey, *Local Government Law* (7th ed 1986), at pp. 3-14).

The principle applies equally to contract as to other functions or activities: in *Ashbury* the House of Lords held that the company had no power to contract for the construction of a railway, the construction of railways falling outside the company's authorised objects. The rule was invoked in relation to contracts of a public authority in *Hazell v Hammersmith and Fulham L.B.C.* ([1991] 1 All ER 545). The authority had entered into a number of "interest rate swap" transactions. These were, essentially, speculative transactions which meant that the authority would make profits if interest rates moved in one way - as expected by the Council - but would result in losses if movements went the other way. Rates moved against the authority, and, on the assumption that the transactions could be enforced against the authority (as to which see 2.3.3.2), it stood to suffer losses of perhaps several times its annual budget (see the figures given by Lord Templeman at p.552). The auditor sought a declaration that all the swap contracts were unlawful as the authority had no statutory power to make them, and was successful before the House of Lords.

The scope of contractual authority depends on the precise details of the statute. Sometimes a power to make a contract for a specific purpose is conferred by statute : for example the Local Authorities (Goods and Services) Act 1970 authorises agreements between certain public bodies for the procurement of goods and services from each other. It is not necessary, however, for every type of contract, or other act, to be expressly and precisely authorised : it has been said that "whatever may be fairly regarded as incidental to, or consequential upon, those things which the legislature has authorised ought not (unless expressly prohibited) to be held by judicial construction, to be *ultra vires.*" (*Attorney General v Great Eastern Railway* (1880) 5 App Cas 473 at p.478; and on this principle generally see Wade, at pp. 240-241). Under this principle if a particular object or activity is authorised - for example, the building of a sports stadium - the authority will have the power to make contracts for the purpose of that activity, though no express power to contract is given in the statute. Whether this power to contract should be regarded as expressly authorised by the provision authorising the relevant activity, or authorised as incidental to it under the *Great Eastern Railway* rule, is probably immaterial. With respect to local authorities section 111 Local Government Act 1972 confers a power to do anything which is calculated to facilitate, or is conducive or incidental to, the discharge of any of its functions. It has been said that this is a statutory embodiment of the rule in *Great Eastern Railway (Hazell,* above, per Lord Templeman at 554).

A contract which is not for the furtherance of some authorised activity will, applying the above principles, be unlawful, as illustrated by *Hazell,* above. In that case it was held that a "swap" transaction could never be lawful. Many transactions, however, are of a type which are capable of being lawful, but are unlawful because of the purpose for which they are made. The legality of a contract to borrow money, for example, will depend on the legitimacy of the purpose for which it is borrowed. A contract may also be unlawful if it is unreasonable (*Municipal Mutual Insurance v Pontefract Corporation* ((1917) 116 L.T. 671; though here the contract was held to be a reasonable one).

Some corporate public bodies have been created by an exercise of the Crown's prerogative power to create corporations. The jurisdiction of these bodies is governed by the terms of their Charter of incorporation. Contracts made outside the terms of the Charter are unlawful and may be restrained by an injunction. Other bodies, including a number of London boroughs, have been incorporated under a statutory power given to the Crown to create corporate authorities. In this case, the scope of their powers depends on the intention of the statute in each case (*Hazell*, above). Thus it was held in *Hazell* that the power to incorporate London Boroughs by charter in section 1 London Government Act 1963 only permitted the creation of boroughs with the same limited powers as those created by statute. Hence the contracts of those boroughs were lawful only if made within the terms of the relevant statutes.

2.3.3.2. Effect of an unlawful contract

A party with standing may restrain the authority from entering into an unlawful agreement, as with any other act which is a breach of public law. It has not been expressly determined, however, what is the effect of a breach on the validity of a concluded contract. This issue was not addressed in *Hazell v Hammersmith and Fulham L.B.C.* ([1991] 1 All ER 545) which involved an action by the auditor for a declaration that the transactions were unlawful, and did not require consideration of their enforceability.

In private law the common law rule was that a contract for an unlawful object concluded by a statutory corporation could not be enforced against the corporation. This was established by the famous House of Lords decision in *Ashbury Carriage and Iron Co. v Riche* (1875) LR 7 HL 653). As explained at 1.4.1 above, this conclusion was explained as a logical necessity where the transaction was not authorised by the legislation. It was reinforced by the court's belief that the rule of non-enforceability was desirable in order to protect those for whose benefits the restrictions on contractual power were imposed - in the case of a private company, the shareholders and creditors of the company - by preventing any funds being expended on unauthorised purposes. The courts in Canada applied the same rule to contracts made for unlawful purposes by statutory public authorities (*Sydney v Chappel Bros. & Co.* [1910] 43 SCR 478); and held that where terms were unlawful they would be severed from the contract and only lawful terms enforced (*Burnaby v B.C. Electric Railway Co.* (1913) 12 SLR 320). Although the English cases have not considered the problem of unlawful objects, they have held that contracts which are unlawful as a fetter on discretion are void (see 2.5.3 below). They have also refused to enforce against the public authority contracts made following a breach of procedural requirements (see 2.10). These cases tend to suggest that a contract for an unlawful object also could not be enforced against the authority; and it has sometimes been assumed that the invalidity of the "swaps" contracts follows from the ruling in *Hazell* that these are transactions which the authorities are not permitted to make (see *Barclays Bank plc v Hammersmith and Fulham L.B.C.*, The Times Nov 27 1991).

If this approach is followed, and the contract is held unenforceable against the authority, further questions may arise if the other party has executed all or part of the obligations before *ultra vires* is raised. If anything has purportedly been transferred to the authority under the invalid agreement, it seems that the property will pass to the authority (*Ayers v South Australian Banking Co.* (1871) LR 3 PC 548 *(ultra vires* contract of private company); *Breckenridge Speedway ltd. v The Queen* [1970] SCR 175 *(ultra vires* contract of public authority); *Stocks v Wilson* [1913] 2 KB 235 (contract vitiated by the incapacity of a minor) - although some dicta in *Sinclair v Brougham* ([1914] A.C. 398) appear to suggest the contrary :see p.414 per Viscount Haldane, p.435 per Lord Dunedin, p.441 per Lord Parker). Where the other party's performance has conferred a benefit on the authority, however, whether by way of money, goods or services, or in some other form, there may be a remedy in restitution to recover the value of the benefit. An objection may be that, like a claim in contract, a claim in restitution may prejudice the interests which the *ultra vires* rule is designed to protect; but it is submitted that a claim should be allowed nevertheless. This question is discussed further at 11.4 below.

If the contract is unenforceable against the authority, it seems clear that where it is still executory, it also cannot be enforced *by* the authority, since there will be no consideration for the other party's promise. More difficult questions arise, however, where the authority has executed its own obligations. Certainly at the very least the authority will have a remedy in restitution for the value of any benefit which it has conferred on the other party by its performance (see further 11.4.3). It is also arguable that the authority should be able to enforce the contract itself (see further Furmston (1961) 24 MLR 715; Arrowsmith, *Government Procurement and Judicial Review* (1988) at pp. 242-235). In *Bell Houses v City Wall Properties* ([1966] 1 QB 207), in the context of a claim against a private company, Mocatta J held that the only claim available was one in restitution; but the point was left open by the Court of Appeal (see [1966] 2 QB 656 at pp. 693-694 per Salmon L.J.; and for the Canadian authority which is inconclusive on the point, see Arrowsmith, above, and Maddaugh and McCamus, *The Law of Restitution* (1990), at pp. 333-337). However, if a contractual claim is allowed, it should be available only where the authority has fully executed its obligations, and there is no possibility of further liability, since it is unfair to allow the contract to be enforced against the other party when it has not received the whole of the consideration promised. For example, if the authority has delivered goods to the third party, it should not be able to sue on the contract, since the third party will not be able to sue for damages for breach of any terms relating to the quality or fitness of the goods.

It is submitted that property purportedly transferred should pass from the authority as well as to it. There is no clear authority on the point. Such authority as exists with respect to the analagous case of property handed over by a minor under an agreement vitiated by his incapacity is inconclusive: see Goff and Jones, *The Law of Restitution* (3rd ed. 1986) at pp. 426-427; Treitel, *The Law of Contract* (10th ed. 1987) at p. 427).

A principle that unlawful contracts may not be enforced against a public authority is open to criticism, because of the hardship this may cause to the other party. He is deprived not only of any expectations of a profit which are generally protected by contract law, but may have incurred expense commencing, or preparing for, performance (although, as indicated, a remedy in restitution may be available where he has provided a benefit to the authority). It is arguable that these interests outweigh those protected by the *ultra vires* rule.

With private companies the common law has been reformed by statute, the effect of which is generally to allow the other party to enforce the agreement (35(1) Companies Act 1985, as amended by s.108 Companies Act 1989), subject to an exception where he is in bad faith (though even knowledge that the company has exceeded its powers does not amount to bad faith : s.35(2)b) Companies Act 1985, as amended by s.108 Companies Act 1989)). There are also special rules applicable to those connected with the company (s.122 A Companies Act 1985, as inserted by s.109 Companies Act 1989). In addition, statutes laying down procedural requirements in relation to public contracts have sometimes stated expressly that the contract is not to be invalidated by a breach, and none has stated that it should be invalidated (see 2.10 below).

Should the question of the validity of contracts for an unlawful object arise today the courts might choose not to apply *Ashbury* to public law, and to hold the contract enforceable. The old public law cases concerned with procedural requirements could be explained as turning on the particular intention of the statute by which they were imposed. It was reasoned in *Ashbury Carriage Co.* that an act outside the corporation's authority was incapable of having legal effect. However, as was explained at 1.4.1 above, this reasoning is flawed : because an act is not permitted does not mean it cannot have legal consequences. It is submitted that *Ashbury* should not be applied in the public law context. Contracts which are unlawful for a breach of public law should generally be enforceable at least where the contractor is not aware that the contract is unlawful: the *prima facie* right of the contractor should prevail over the public interest. This should be apply even if, as in *Hazell*, the contract is one which on its face could not have been lawfully made: the onus should be on the authority itself to ensure compliance with its legislative mandate, and not on the contractor. Alternatively, however, the courts might wish to hold that the contract is enforceable only where it is one which might have been lawful if made for a proper purpose, and the other party does not know of the improper purpose.

In some cases it may be that the main object of the contract is lawful, but there is some objection to its terms (as in *Roberts v Hopwood* [1925] AC 578, holding that a local authority could not promise to pay its employees wages above the market rate). If unlawful contracts generally are enforceable, then contracts with unlawful terms clearly ought to be enforceable as well. If not, the contract would arguably be enforceable to the extent that the unlawful terms can be severed.

Where a corporation is created under the Crown's common law powers, it is clear that its contractual capacity is the same as that of a natural person. It may be restrained from making a contract which is outside the terms of its charter, and the revocation of the charter is a sanction which may be invoked where it acts unlawfully, but any contract actually concluded will be fully enforceable (*Sutton's Hospital Case* (1612) 77 ER 937). Where a body is created by the Crown under a specific statutory power to create a corporation the width of its lawful activities will depend on the particular statute. It seems likely that in a case where an authority is limited to those powers conferred by statute, the effect of a breach will be the same as a breach by an authority which is created by statute.

2.3.4. *Compromises of ultra vires contracts*

Where a contract is *ultra vires* and unenforceable, any compromise of a dispute under the contract which is based on the assumption that the contract is valid, will itself be invalid (Re *Jon Beauforte* [1953] Ch 131). However, it is open to the parties to make a compromise over the very issue of the contract's legality (Re *Jon Beauforte; Binder v Alachouzos* [1972] 2 QB 151, holding effective a compromise of an illegal agreement, where the question of illegality had itself been in dispute). If, however, an unlawful contract is itself enforceable, as was argued above should be the case in public law, there can be no objection to any compromise of the obligations arising under it, even though the parties did not know of its unlawful nature.

2.4.   Authority

2.4.1.   General principles

In deciding who has the authority to act for a public body the same problems arise as in deciding who has authority to bind any artificial entity. In private law it is now accepted that the starting point is that the ordinary rules of agency operate (*Freeman and Lockyer v Buckhurst Park Properties (Mangel)* [1964] 2 QB 480), and the courts have applied the same principles in public law (*Attorney General for Ceylon v A.D. Silva* [1953] AC 461; *North West Leicestershire D.C. v East Midlands Association* [1981] 1 WLR 1396). Applying these general rules, a public body is bound, first, if the agent has actual authority. This may be express - that is, expressly given by some individual or organ which has the power to confer that authority. Actual authority may also be implied : where a person is properly appointed to an office it is implied that he has all the authority which normally goes with that office, unless the contrary is stated. An agent may also bind a principal under the doctrine of ostensible authority, which applies where the agent is represented to the third party as having authority. (For a further outline see Treitel, *The Law of Contract* (7th Ed. 1987) Ch 17; and for a more detailed account, Reynolds, *Bowtead's Law of Agency* (15th ed 1985)).

Officials or organs of a public body have express authority to contract to the extent that authority is conferred on them by statute. Express authority also exists where authority has been expressly delegated to other organs or individuals by those who have a power to make the delegation. Implied actual authority exists where persons have been properly appointed to an office, or an organ of the authority properly constituted, and that person or organ exercises functions normally associated with it, provided that such authority is not specifically negatived by superior instructions (see *North West Leicestershire D.C. v East Midlands Housing Association*, above). In both cases, actual authority will be precluded where statute provides that the person or organ in question is not authorised to bind the authority to a particular act or class of acts : this must make it legally impossible for the requisite actual authority to be created. Thus, for example, if statute lays down that a specified function is to be carried out by the Council of a local authority, then an individual officer cannot have actual authority to do that act, even though the Council has purported to delegate such authority to him. It is possible, however, that a requirement that a contract be concluded by a certain person or body might be treated as non-invalidating.

Ostensible authority exists where a representation of authority is made by a person concerned with the management of the relevant part of the business (*Freeman and Lockyer*, above, at 506 per Lord Diplock). There is considerable overlap between this doctrine and that of actual authority: for example, ostensible authority, as well as implied actual authority, may be invoked where a person is appointed to an office which usually carries such authority, since permitting the appointee to act in the office amounts to a representation that the person appointed has that authority. Where actual authority exists there is no need to rely on this doctrine. It will be invoked, however, where usual authority has been negatived by superior instructions that the officer may not engage in a particular type of transaction, and these instructions have not been communicated to the person dealing with the officer. It will also apply where the officer has been held out to have authority which he has not actually been given, in some way other than by appointment to a particular office: for example, where the officer is specifically represented to have authority with respect to a certain class of transaction.

It was explained that actual authority cannot exist where statute precludes a particular official from acting. In some cases of this type third parties have therefore tried to invoke the doctrine of ostensible authority. However, the accepted view is that the doctrine of ostensible authority cannot operate to hold the authority bound contrary to the statutory restriction. The rule is seen as an illustration of the general principle (not confined to public law, but most frequently invoked in this context) that an estoppel cannot operate to hold a party to a representation of a state of affairs which is contrary to statute. On the basis of this rule, a public body cannot be estopped by a representation that it has the capacity to do an act, when it has no such capacity (see generally Wade, at pp. 264-266; Craig, ch.16 and (1977) 93 LQR 398; Bradley, [1981] CLP 1; Fazal [1972] PL 143; Ganz, [1965] PL 237; and for an example in the context of a restitutionary claim see 11.3.1 below). Likewise it cannot be held to a representation that authority has been delegated to a party when delegation is expressly or impliedly forbidden. It is an interesting question whether, if a statutory requirement is treated as non-invalidating for the purpose of the actual authority rule, it is also possible to be bound by a representation which is contrary to the requirement.

The above principle on ostensible authority is illustrated by the case of *Western Fish Products v Penwith District Council* ([1981] 2 All ER 204). In this case a planning officer represented to the plaintiff in a letter that planning permission would not be required for the plaintiff to use a factory which it had bought in the manner which the plaintiff proposed, on the basis that it was covered by an established user right. The plaintiff then began work renovating the factory so that it could be used for the proposed business. However, the Council to whom the decision on planning permission was entrusted by statute, concluded that permission was necessary, refused permission, and served enforcement notices. The plaintiff alleged that the representation of the officer estopped the Council from refusing permission. This argument was, however, rejected by the Court of Appeal: it was held that by statute the decision was for the Council and the decision of the officer could not therefore be binding, even if the Council had represented that such authority existed. The case was not actually concerned with a contract, but the same principles would apply in a contractual context (see Hilliard, (1976) 54 Can Bar Rev 401).

The operation of the general rule on estoppel and statute can be criticised (see Craig, ch.16 and (1977) 93 LQR 398; Bradley, (1981) CLP 1). The effect of the rule is that the public interest protected by the statutory restriction is always permitted to outweigh the interest of the individual who relies on the representation. However, it is by no means always clear that the public interest in enforcing the statute is indeed greater, and Craig has convincingly argued that the courts ought to be permitted to balance the competing interests in each case to decide if the authority should be held to its representation (Craig, pp. 480-487). If injustice to the individual by denying effect to the representation would be greater than the detriment to the public in holding it binding, it should, he argues, be given effect. Even where this is not so, so that enforcing the representation is not justified, he argues that compensation should be payable for any loss the individual has suffered (pp. 481-482). Similar arguments lie behind the case for enforcing *ultra vires* contracts: the individual should be afforded those rights given by the ordinary private law, which should not be denied because the government has failed to adhere to statutory restrictions designed to protect the public (see 2.3.3.2 above). In the present context it is submitted that these arguments generally lead to the conclusion that any contract which would be binding, but for the restrictions, should be enforced. If there is a particular reason why this should not be so, the problem should be dealt with by limiting the plaintiff to damages.

2.4.2.   Servants and agents of the Crown

Some special consideration is required of the position of servants and agents of the Crown.

First, it is necessary to consider how agency rules apply in relation to Ministers of the Crown. A ministerial office may be created at common law or by statute (see further Wade, at pp. 53-54). Whatever the manner of creation, the Minister will generally have a number of powers and functions conferred on him by statute in his own name. It is not entirely clear to what extent Ministers may bind the Crown in contract. A wide view might be that any contract made by a Minister in his public capacity will bind the Crown. On one interpretation, the decision of the House of Lords in *Town*

Investments v *Department of the Environment* ([1978] AC 359), discussed at 2.3.2 above, could be cited in support of this wide view. It was been suggested that the case is authority for the proposition that Ministers, and also other Crown agents, do not have an independent *capacity* to contract. It is also arguable that the *dicta* in the case cited at 2.3.1.2 above can be read as putting forward a wider theory that a Minister has no separate legal identity at all expect to the extent that this is specifically conferred by statute, and that for "authority" purposes also the Minister is merged in the Crown. However, this approach has not been adopted in other jurisdictions (see *J.E. Verrault & Fils* v *Quebec* ([1971] SCR 41 and *R.* v *C.A.E. Industries* (1985) 5 WWR 481 (Canada); *Meates* v *Attorney General* ([1979] 1 NZLR 415 (New Zealand)) and seems unlikely to be applied in the United Kingdom to the question of authority. Probably ordinary agency principles apply and it is necessary to look for actual or ostensible authority on the part of a Minister for any particular contract to bind the Crown. These ordinary principles of agency certainly apply to servants of the Crown who are not Ministers (*A.G. for Ceylon* v *A.D. Silva*, above).

Applying these ordinary principles, it is clear that express actual authority exists where the contract relates to functions and activities entrusted to the agent or servant by statute (*A.D. Silvas*, above). It was suggested at 2.3.2 above that such provisions do not confer any independent capacity to contract. It is submitted that their effect is in fact to confer an authority to contract on behalf of the Crown. Although these statutes may confer powers on Ministers to carry out functions as *persona designata* rather than as agents of the Crown (see 1.2.1.2 above), the *capacity* to make contracts in connection with these functions remains that of the Crown at common law, and the effect of the statute insofar as contract is concerned is simply to give the power to the agent to exercise that common law capacity on the Crown's behalf.

It is unclear whether there is room for any concept of usual authority in relation to Crown agents, at least those whose functions are generally defined by statute. It seems, from the decision in *A.D. Silva*, above, that where an agent's functions are set out in statute, then, *prima facie*, the statute will be regarded as laying down exhaustively the scope of the matters in relation to which that person may contract on behalf of the Crown. *A.D. Silva* concerned a sale by a Customs Officer, who was an agent of the Crown, of some silver plate which, unknown to him, belonged to the Crown. Under the Customs legislation he had power to sell certain property, but this did not extend to property belonging to the Crown itself. It was held that the purported sale did not bind the Crown: there was no authority to bind the Crown to this sale from the legislation, since it did not confer on the officer the function of selling the Crown's property, and there was no ostensible authority. The Privy Council rejected the contention, which seems to have been based on an idea of usual authority, that the officer had authority to bind the Crown by virtue of his position as a Customs Officer. On the other hand, in the New Zealand case of *Meates v Attorney General*, above, it was suggested, though without any discussion, that a Minister of the Crown could enjoy usual authority. It is submitted that the approach in *A.D. Silva* is to be preferred: the concept of usual authority is generally inappropriate in relation to the sort of unique offices and jurisdiction given by the government to its agents, and where the jurisdiction of those agents has been set out in a statute, it seems reasonable to assume that this *prima facie* defines the scope of their intended activities.

However, although relevant statutory provisions should be regarded prima facie as exhaustive of the scope of the matters on which the agent has authority to contract, the contractual authority of Crown agents may surely be extended without the need for any statute, if this is done expressly by the Crown. The authority conferred by statute need not be regarded as exhaustive and restrictive. This seemed to be contemplated in *A.D. Silva*, above, where it was said that authority could be conferred by statute "or otherwise" (at 479). Indeed, this seems to follow from the fact that the Crown can generally appoint any person its agent for a limited purpose - there is no reason why it should not also be able to extend the authority of those who have already been made its agents for some purposes by statute. The question may arise as to whether an Order in Council is necessary to confer such authority or whether the Cabinet - or even perhaps the Prime Minister - might confer additional authority to act. In *R. v C.A.E. Industries*, above, the majority of the Federal Court of Canada held that authority could be conferred on a Crown agent (here, Ministers of the Crown) by the Cabinet, and no Order in Council was required.

Crown agents, like other public officials, may make arrangements which bind their employer under the doctrine of ostensible authority. This was accepted in *A.D. Silva*. Where there is a representation that a person has authority beyond that given by statute, this will be binding only if made by those with the responsibility for the area in question. In a case like *A.D. Silva* it is submitted that a representation that the Customs Officer had authority to sell the Crown property could have been binding, though such a sale was outside the scope of the statute, provided it was made by the Cabinet, or, say, a Minister responsible for the sale of Crown property (in the same way as actual authority might have been conferred on the Customs Officer beyond the scope of the statute). In other words, insofar as the power to contract is concerned, the statutory provisions merely empower the agent; they are not restrictive in the sense that they limit the authority which may be conferred.

2.4.3. Breach of warranty of authority

Normally where a servant purports to contract for a principal but exceeds the scope of his authority to do so, he will be liable to the other party to the purported agreement, for breach of an implied warranty that he has the authority to bind the principal to the contract. In the case of *Dunn v MacDonald* ([1897] 1 QB 555) it was held by the Court of Appeal that this rule did not apply to a servant of the Crown. There was no implication of such a warranty in the case of a Crown servant, although the servant could expressly make himself liable if he wished. The language of the court suggests that the rule is one of general application, applying wherever a Crown servant purports to contract for the Crown. The justification given for rejecting the usual implication was one of public policy - that otherwise people would not be willing to act on behalf of the Crown. The supposed rule has, however, been criticised by many writers, on the basis that there is no reason why the Crown should be treated differently from any other public body (see for example, Craig, at p.496; Wade, at p.823; Hogg, at pp. 173-174). The case can, in fact, be explained on narrower grounds, in that the reason the agent could not bind the principal in this case was that the principal was incapable of making such an agreement in law: it concerned an agreement for a fixed term of service, and the Crown cannot bind itself to keep its servants on for a fixed term (see 4.3.2 below). Where the reason for the want of authority is a rule of law, it is not generally covered by any implied warranty, even in private law (see Reynolds, *Bowstead on Agency* (15th ed. 1985) at pp. 461-462).

2.4.4. Personal liability

Where an agent makes a contract on behalf of a principal, there is a presumption that the agent does not normally undertake personal liability. Not surprisingly, this applies to public servants also (*MacBeath v Haldimand* (1786) 99 ER 1036; *Gidley v Lord Palmerston* (1822) 129 ER 1290). Although, in theory, a public servant could contract in his own name when acting on behalf of the Crown, there is no reported case in which this has occurred.

2.5.   Fettering of Discretion by Contract

2.5.1.   Introduction

It is a general principle of public law that a public authority must retain the
freedom to exercise its discretionary powers as is required from time to time
in the public interest. An aspect of this is a rule that a public body may not
fetter its discretion by making a rigid rule on how it will exercise its
discretion in future cases: it must consider each case on its merits as it
arises, although it may develop guidelines to assist it (on this rule see
Craig, at pp. 311-313; Wade, at pp. 370-375). Another aspect of the general
principle is a rule which limits the extent to which a public authority may
bind itself by contract (or by grant) to limit its future freedom of action. In
fact, every contract limits future freedom of action in some way. However,
it is clear that not every contract by a public body can be prohibited, since
such a body needs contractual powers in order to carry out many of its
functions effectively. Thus, for example, it is useful for an authority to be
able to make covenants restricting the way in which it will use land, in
order to persuade the landowner to sell, or to sell at a reasonable price. The
courts have therefore attempted to devise a rule which allows public bodies,
as far as possible, to make those contracts which are useful to them, whilst
prohibiting those which unduly interfere with their freedom to act in the
public interest. (On this area see further Mitchell, *The Contracts of Public
Authorities* (1954); Street, ch.3; Aronson and Whitmore, *Public Torts and
Contracts* (1982), at pp. 194-203; Turpin, *Government Procurement Law
and Contracts* (1989) at pp. 85-90; Craig, at pp. 502-511; Wade, at pp. 375-
381; Hogg, at pp. 169-172; Rogerson, [1971] PL 288).

2.5.2.   Scope of the doctrine

The basic rule is that a contract is an unlawful fetter on discretion where
it is "incompatible" with the exercise of some other power possessed by the
authority (*Birkdale District Electricity Supply Co. v Southport Corporation*
[1926] AC 355; *British Transport Commission v Westmoreland C.C.*
[1958] AC 126).
Always within this category is a contract which binds the authority to
do something in contravention of what is required by statute. Such contracts
are clearly incompatible with the exercise of the statutory discretion which
they purport to restrict and are never enforceable. An example is the case of
an agreement to decide future planning applications in a particular way: this
cannot be enforced because the planning statutes require that such decisions
be taken according to the statutory procedure, at the time of the application

(*Stringer v Minister of Housing and Local Government* [1970] 1 WLR 1281).

More problematic, is the case where the contract does not conflict with something which the authority is required to do, but is inconsistent with something which the authority may wish to do in the future. The courts will not strike down every contract which limits the *possible* exercise of a discretionary power in the future, since this would be unduly restrictive of the power to make contracts. As indicated above, the court must balance the need for the authority to make contracts in connection with its present activities against the need for it to retain freedom of action.

It may first be noted that it was held by the House of Lords in *British Transport Commission v Westmoreland C.C.*, above, that a contract or grant can only fail if it is reasonably foreseeable that a conflict will arise between that contract or grant and the exercise of a future power. The concept of "reasonably foreseeable" was in fact used interchangeably with "probable" or "likely" in the leading speech of Lord Sumner, suggesting a test favourable to upholding contracts. In *Westmoreland* itself it was held that a footpath across a bridge could be validly dedicated to the public even though this would prevent the authority from exercising in the future a statutory power which it possessed to discontinue the bridge.

Even if a conflict is foreseeable, or probable, however, it appears a contract may still not constitute a fetter : thus in the *Birkdale* case, discussed below, it can be argued that, although the contract was upheld, a conflict was reasonably foreseeable. Other factors must also be considered, such as the nature and importance of the power which has been "fettered" by the contract or grant, and the advantages of permitting the authority to make a binding agreement in the particular case.

The early leading case where an agreement was held to be an unlawful fetter on discretion is *Ayr Harbour Trustees v Oswald* ([1883] 8 App Cas 623). In this case the harbour trustees, who had been incorporated for the purpose of acquiring land to develop and improve a harbour, covenanted with the former owner of some land which they acquired not to obstruct his access to the harbour from the land which he still retained. The agreement, which obviously limited the way in which they could in the future exercise their statutory power to build on the land acquired, was held to be an unlawful fetter. A significant factor was that development of the land was the very purpose for which the trustees were established (see *Birkdale District Electricity Supply Co. v Southport Corporation* at 372 and 375 per Lord Sumner), and that the covenant fettered in advance their discretion in respect of the redevelopment. It has been suggested, on the other hand, that a similar covenant might have been upheld if made after the main lines of development had been set (see Rogerson, [1971] PL 288 at p.291). Another example of an unlawful fetter on discretion is found in *Triggs v Staines*

U.D.C. ([1969] 1 Ch 10). The Council was considering designating a piece of land as a public space. The owner convenanted with the authority to grant to it an option to purchase; but a condition was included that if the option were not exercised within a certain period the land would be freed for development. The whole agreement was held void since a substantial part of the authority's consideration was a promise not to exercise its powers to make the land into a public space, and this was void as a fetter on its discretion. Similarly, in *Ransom and Luck Ltd v Surbiton B.C.* ([1949] Ch 180) a promise not to revoke a planning permission in the future was held to be unlawful; and in *William Cory and Son v London Corporation* ([1951] 2 KB 476) it was said that the corporation could not bind itself not to legislate health and safety conditions relating to the carriage of refuse in barges, which would make Cory's contract, for the disposal of the corporation's refuse, more onerous to perform.

Most of the cases have concerned statutory authorities, but a similar principle was applied to the Crown in *The Amphitrite (Rederiaktiebolaget Amphitrite v R.* [1921] 3 KB 500), in which it was held that the Crown could not be bound by a wartime assurance to a foreign shipowner that his ship would not be seized if certain conditions were complied with (and see also *Commissioners of Crown Lands v Page* [1960] 2 QB 274, and *Board of Trade v Temperley Steam Shipping Co.* (1926) 26 Lloyds Rep 76, aff'd (1927) 27 Lloyds Rep 230, discussed below, cases which also concerned the Crown). The cases on statutory authority were not referred to, and there are some later dicta which suggest that any fettering rule applied to the Crown rests on a presumption that the Crown does not intend to make agreements which fetter its discretion, rather than on the absence of any common law capacity in the Crown to make such agreements (*Robertson v Minister of Pensions* [1949] 1 KB 227 at 231 per Lord Denning; *Page*, above, at 292 per Lord Devlin). However, the better view is that the fettering rule is a rule of public policy which applies in the same way to the Crown as to other statutory authorities. In relation to the Crown the doctrine will preclude contracts which are a fetter either on the exercise of the statutory powers which it possesses or, as in *The Amphitrite* itself, on the exercise of its general common law powers. (See generally Turpin, *Government Procurement Law and Contracts* (1989) at pp. 87-90).

In a number of other cases the argument that a contract is a fetter has been rejected. One such case, *British Transport Corporation v Westmoreland*, has already been considered above : it appears that the argument that there was an invalid fetter failed because a conflict between the contract and the authority's future exercise of discretion was not probable. Likewise in *Blake v Hendon Corporation* ([1962] 1 QB 283) it was held that land could be dedicated as a public park though this would preclude other uses of land which the authority was empowered to make under statute. The courts have also upheld restrictive covenants which have the effect of limiting the authority's future use of land, on the basis that it is useful for the authority to be able to make such covenants and grants in order to acquire land for its current purposes, and thus they should not automatically be struck down because they conflict with possible future uses of its land. Thus in *Stourcliffe Estates Co. v Bournemouth Corporation* ([1910] 2 Ch 12) a covenant to use land as a pleasure ground and not to erect any building was upheld, though it prevented the corporation from using its statutory powers to build lavatories in the park; in *Leicester (Earl) v Wells-next-the-sea U.D.C.* ([1973] Ch 110) a covenant to use land only for allotments was held binding; and in *Dowty Boulton Paul v Wolverhampton Corporation* ([1971] 1 WLR 204; decided differently on other grounds in (No. 2) [1976] Ch 13) it was held that a covenant to allow another the use of a municipal airfield was not an unlawful fetter though this would prevent use of the airfield for other purposes.

The question of fettering in relation to a restrictive covenant also arose recently in *R. v. Hammersmith and Fulham L.B.C., ex parte Beddowes* ([1987] QB 1050). In pursuance of a policy to sell off its local authority housing to provide homes for private ownership, the Council contracted to sell one block of flats to a developer, and convenanted not to let on short term tenancies in the future any vacant flats nearby which were still in Council ownership. The object of this was to ensure that the general area was established as one of private ownership. The covenant was challenged as a fetter on the Council's future discretion to revert to a policy of local authority housing with its remaining accommodation; but it was upheld by a majority of the Court of Appeal.

It thus seems clear that as a general rule covenants which restrict land use will be upheld, though there will be exceptional cases, as illustrated by *Ayr Harbour,* when the authority is legally required to retain the discretion to use certain land in a particular way.

It may be noted that Fox L.J. stated in *Beddowes* (at 1065) that whenever the exercise of a power "can reasonably be regarded as in furtherance of the statutory object" (here, the selling of Council homes to private ownership), the exercise of that power will be upheld, though it conflicts with the possible future exercise of other powers; and a similar approach was adopted at first instance in *Dowty Boulton Paul,* above. This approach, however, would deprive the fettering doctrine of any effect, and is inconsistent with cases like *Ayr Harbour* and *Triggs v Staines* where the contracts in question were in furtherance of some statutory purpose but were still struck down. If they were not in furtherance of some statutory power they would anyway be unlawful quite apart from the fettering rule: see 2.3.3 above. Although this reasoning cannot be correct, however, the decisions themselves are probably correct on their facts.

Another important decision of a different type, is *Birkdale and District Electricity Supply Co. v Southport Corporation,* above. In this case the House of Lords upheld a promise by the Electricity Company that it would not increase its prices beyond those charged by Southport Corporation, although the company had an express statutory discretion to fix its prices. The agreement was held to be an exercise of the discretion rather than a fetter on it; and it was suggested by Lord Sumner (at 371-372) that the fettering doctrine would not invalidate contracts made in the course of the "business management" of an undertaking. The advantages to the authority of being able to make binding agreements was emphasised by the court; and this can explain why the stipulation was valid even though a desire to change the pricing policy might arguably have been said to be foreseeable. It was also stated by Rowlatt J in *The Amphitrite* that the doctrine has no application to a "commercial contract", as opposed to "an assurance as to what its executive action would be in the future" (at 503). This might suggest that the doctrine does not apply to procurement contracts, as well as not applying to contracts in the course of management of a business undertaking. In fact, contracts of procurement may well fetter the government's power to act on important matters of public interest - for example, the power to cancel an order for a weapons system which has become obsolete before completion. However, it may be appropriate to treat such contracts as valid in accordance with general principles, either because a conflict with the public interest is not probable with any given contract, or because, even if it is, the considerable advantages in allowing legally binding agreements of this type outweigh the disadvantages. In practice, the central government normally includes in its supply contracts clauses, called "termination for convenience" clauses, which allow it to cancel a contract at any time, on payment of compensation (see Turpin, above, at pp. 243-246).

The courts will not imply into a contract a term which, if implied, would be an unlawful fetter on discretion in the sense explained above. This is illustrated by *Cory,* above. There was here no express term that the Corporation would not pass legislation which made the contract more onerous, but it was argued that such a term should be implied. The court held that any express term would be invalid as an unlawful fetter (see Lord Asquith at 485), and therefore could not be implied. In two cases concerning the Crown the courts have also refused to imply terms which would restrict freedom of executive action. The first is *Board of Trade v Temperley Steam Shipping Co. Ltd.,* above. Here the company owned a vessel chartered to the Crown. Under general powers to prevent resources being used for works which were not related to the war effort, the government refused to allow proper repairs to the vessel, which was therefore unable to operate. Under the terms of the charterparty the Crown was not bound to pay hire to the company in such an event. The company contended that a term should be implied into the contract that the Crown would do nothing to hinder its performance. A general term of this nature would normally be implied into such an agreement. However, Roche J held that no such term should be implied to the extent that it would preclude the exercise by the Crown of powers "entirely remote from the charterparty". In the similar case of *Commissioners of Crown Lands v Page*, above, it was held that there could be no covenant for quiet enjoyment implied into a lease granted by the Crown, to the extent that this would render it a breach of contract for the Crown to exercise its powers to requisition the land. Lord Devlin said that even an express covenant "must by necessary implication be read to exclude those measures affecting the nation as a whole which the Crown takes for the public good" (at 292). It has already been suggested, at 2.4.1 above, that the application of the fettering principle to the Crown should be treated as rule of public policy rather than one based on the intention of the Crown; and it is submitted that terms of the type contended for would have been invalid if they had been held to be included.

If, on the other hand, the alleged term is not of a type which would fall within the general fettering doctrine, even though it might restrict future executive action, the courts should not "construe" the contract in such a way as to exclude the obligation. If a promise would be included in a contract between two private parties, it should make no difference that one party is a public authority. In other words, the court should not effectively extend the established fettering doctrine through the "backdoor" method of construction of the contract.

2.5.3. *Effect of the doctrine*

Where a substantial part of the consideration provided by a public body under a contract is a promise which is an unlawful fetter on its discretion, in the case of statutory authorities, the whole contract is void. It is unenforceable against the authority (*Ayr Harbour Trustees v Oswald* (1883) 8 AC 623), and is unenforceable by the authority (*Triggs v Staines U.D.C.* [1969] 1 Ch 10). In some cases a term of the contract may be an unlawful fetter, but the term may not be such as to constitute a substantial part of the consideration. For example, in *William Cory and Son v London Corporation* ([1951] 2 KB 476), discussed at 2.5.1 above, the court held that any term that the authority would not exercise its legislative powers to make contractual performance by the other party more onerous would have been an unlawful fetter. Clearly, though, this would have affected only a small part of the authority's consideration. In such a case it seems that if the term can be severed it will be treated as void. This was suggested in *Cory* though the question was not considered expressly, since the court held that no such term was included. This might in some cases cause hardship to the other party to the agreement if it has affected the consideration payable by him, and that consideration cannot also be severed from the contract.

If, as suggested at 2.5.1, the fettering rule applies as a matter of public policy to the Crown, it seems that any contract within the rule should be invalid here also.

2.5.4. Exercise of powers in breach of contract

Where a contract is not within the scope of the fettering doctrine, a public authority might, under public law, decide to exercise its powers in a manner which is a breach of contract. Such an exercise of powers is not *ultra vires*. Thus it was held by Woolf J in *R. v Hillingdon Health Authority, ex parte Goodwin* ([1984] ICR 800) that it was not ultra vires to close a cottage hospital, though this involved a breach of a contractual obligation to the hospital doctors to give three months notice on termination of their employment. However, it was held that the fact that the exercise of power involves a breach of private law contractual obligations was a factor which must be taken into account, under the public law "relevant considerations" rule. If the authority's action is a breach of contract, there will, of course, normally be a right to damages. It is, of course, open to Parliament to take away any common law right to damages if it chooses to do so, by passing legislation which contravenes contractual rights. This option is probably not available to lesser legislative authorities, however.

2.5.5. Critique

The fettering doctrine gives the public interest priority over the private interest of the other party to the contract. Where a contract, or promise, is void as a fetter on discretion, the contractor's expectations are defeated, and he may also have suffered loss commencing or preparing for performance. As with contracts which are unlawful because they are made for unauthorised purposes, it can be argued that the contract ought to be treated as valid, so as to allow the contractor to sue for damages for breach of contract in the usual way. However, the courts should be able to refuse any claim for specific performance. Hogg has argued for this solution (see Hogg, at pp. 172-3). He suggests that there is no need for any special public law rule, since the court may refuse to enforce the promise itself, where appropriate, by relying on its general discretion to refuse specific relief. If in exceptional cases this placed an intolerable damages burden on the government, the matter could be dealt with by legislation.

However, although compensation ought to have been payable in some of the cases which have fallen within the doctrine including, it is submitted, *Ayr Harbour* and *The Amphitrite* (discussed at 2.4.2 above), this seems unwarranted in others (see further Rogerson [1971] PL 288). An example is the case of *Board of Trade v Temperley Steam Shipping Co. Ltd.*, discussed at 2.5.2, where the effect of upholding the usual implied covenant against hindering performance of the contract would have been to allow the company to claim from the Crown the hire lost due to the prohibition on repairs. Other shipowners would have to bear the loss from this general prohibition themselves, and it is difficult to see why a company should be in a better position simply because its commercial contract happened to be with the government. Similarly, in *Cory* and *Page*, discussed at 2.5.2, it is arguable that the risk of the measures which were implemented also should be placed on the contractor. However, the position should differ where the Crown makes a *specific* assurance, whether to its own contractor or someone else, that it will not take the action in question. This arguably places the contractor in a different position from others, so that compensation should be recoverable. It is only where the assurance arises as part of general covenant primarily directed to matters other than the exercise of governmental powers that compensation should be denied.

In conclusion it is submitted that most agreements now struck down as a fetter on discretion ought to be treated as binding and the government required to compensate for any breach. However, in the limited circumstances just outlined, a special rule may be needed to prevent those engaged in commercial deals with public bodies from obtaining a fortuitous dispensation from the burden of general governmental measures.

2.6. The Requirement of an Appropriation

It is a fundamental constitutional principle that all expenditure by the Executive must be authorised by Parliament (*Auckland Harbour Board v R.* [1924] AC 318 at pp. 326-7). Funds are "appropriated" by Parliament to different areas of government activity in the annual Appropriation Act, to cover expenditure in the year ahead, with supplementary Acts in between if necessary. Expenditure made without an appropriation is unlawful and may be recovered by the government in a restitutionary action (*Auckland Harbour Board*, above; and see further below at 11.3). In practice, appropriations are normally voted in general terms to cover broad areas of government activity, rather than for specific projects or items of expenditure. Where expenditure is due under a contract, it is sufficient authorisation of that expenditure if it falls within one of the broad heads in the appropriations; it is not necessary that funds be appropriated specifically for that contract (*New South Wales v Bardolph* (1934) 52 CLR 455). It is arguable that where contractual expenditure is partly attributable to some "secondary" policy (as to which see 2.2.1 above), such expenditure ought to be set off against sums appropriated for the secondary objective, rather than those appropriated for the subject matter of the contract. For example, where the government pays more than would otherwise be necessary in order to award a contract for the purchase of defence supplies to a firm in a less developed region, the extra amount paid should be treated as referable to the appropriation relating to regional development, and not defence. This issue does not appear to have been considered judicially.

The question has been raised as to how appropriation requirements might affect contractual liability. Some *dicta* in early cases seemed to suggest that the absence of an appropriation for the amount needed by the government to perform a contract would render that contract invalid, or null (*Churchward v R.* (1865) LR 1 QB 173 at 209 per Shee J; *Commercial Cable Co. v Newfoundland Government* [1916] 2 AC 610 at 617 per Viscount Haldane). These *dicta* have sometimes been suggested to mean that the contract is invalid if funds have not been authorised in advance of the contract. This would be unfortunate, since the normal practice, as indicated, is to vote appropriations on an annual basis for expenditures falling due in that year, whereas contracts are frequently made which are to be performed by the government in future years. If this were indeed the rule a significant change in constitutional practice would be required. In any case, even if funds exist for the activity in question at the time the contract was made, they may have been spent on other things relating to that activity by the time performance is due. This situation would not be caught by a rule which looks to the availability of funds at the time the contract is made. This matter was carefully considered by the High Court of Australia in *New South Wales v Bardolph,* and it was held - in reliance on some more ambiguous dicta on this point in later Commonwealth cases - that the absence of an appropriation cannot affect the initial validity of a contract entered into by the Crown. (For a full discussion of the authority see Street, at pp. 89-94). This is now widely accepted to be the law in other Commonwealth jurisdictions, including the United Kingdom (Turpin, at pp. 91-94; Craig, at pp. 294-295; Mitchell, *The Contracts of Public Authorities* (1954), at p.73; Street, at p.91; Hogg, at pp. 164-166).

It is still necessary to consider, however, what is the position where at the *time performance falls due* there is no appropriation to cover the required expenditure. In *New South Wales v Bardolph* it was stated that in such an event the contract would be unenforceable, but the court did not explain what was meant by this. It seems clear that if no appropriation does exist, then not only can the judgement not be enforced by the court if the Crown refuses to meet it (which is the case anyway - see 1.2.1.4 above), but it would be unlawful for the Crown to choose to do so without first obtaining a vote of funds. Any sum paid out should be recoverable in a restitutionary action, in accordance with the general rule on recovery of unlawful expenditure (see 11.3). Turpin (at pp. 93-94) has suggested that in such a case the court should give a judgement as to the liability of the Crown in the ordinary way, on the assumption that funds will be made available to meet the judgement, unless there is clear evidence that Parliament does not intend to make such funds available. There seems, in fact, no reason why judgement should not be given even where it *is* clear funds will be denied. The judgement should surely not be affected by the outcome of judicial speculation about the likely future behaviour of Parliament. If there is no appropriation, this may be an empty victory for the other contracting party, but he might still wish to pursue the action to establish the principle of liability.

Hogg has argued that the victory would not, however, be empty. In the United Kingdom section 25 of the Crown Proceedings Act 1947 places an obligation on the Crown to meet all judgement debts. Hogg suggests that the effect of this is to make a continuing statutory appropriation for all such debts (Hogg, pp.164-166). From this it follows that once a judgement has been given that the Crown is liable in contract either to pay a specific sum or damages, an appropriation to satisfy it comes into existence by virtue of section 25. Hence, the position of the other contracting party is not in the end affected by the appropriations rule. This would not, of course, be the case if this interpretation of section 25 is incorrect; nor it is so in jurisdictions where there is clearly no permanent appropriation for payment of judgement debts. (For the position elsewhere in the Commonwealth see Hogg, at pp. 164-166).

In practice the absence of an appropriation is unlikely to be a problem. This is because, first, it is rare that performance of a contract requires expenditure not provided for already, given the broad terms of the appropriations, and, second, even where this is so, Parliament is likely subsequently to vote the necessary sum.

2.7. Crown Proceedings and Immunities

It was explained in chapter 1 that at one time the Crown was not liable to suit in the ordinary way, but that many claims relating to the Crown's liability could be brought to the court by using the petition of right procedure, which, however, required the fiat of the Crown (see 1.2.2). It was established in the nineteenth century that this procedure could be used to hold the Crown liable in contract, both for a liquidated sum due under a contract (*Thomas v The Queen* (1874) CR 10 QB 31) and for damages for breach (*The Windsor and Annapolis Railway Co. v R.* (1886) 11 App Cas

607). The Crown in its public capacity is now generally liable to suit in contract in the courts without the need for a fiat. This arises from the operation of section 1 of the Crown Proceedings Act 1947, which provides that the Crown is liable to suit under the Act where prior to the Act proceedings could have been brought by petition of right. Procedure under the Act is outlined at 1.2.2 above.

The general privileges and immunities of the Crown may of course affect actions in contract. Of particular significance are the rules that the remedies of specific performance and injunction are not available against the Crown (see 1.2.1.5) . Liability may also be affected by the rule that the Crown is not bound by statute except by express mention or necessary implication (see 1.2.1.6). However, in practice many important statutes concerned with contractual liability expressly bind the Crown, including the Sale of Goods Act 1979, the Supply of Goods and Services Act 1982, and the Unfair Contract Terms Act 1977.

Where a Crown agent contracts in an independent capacity, Crown immunities may not apply. For example, in an action against a Crown agent in an independent capacity, the court may be able to grant an injunction or order of specific performance. Where a Minister contracts in such a capacity, however, such relief will probably be precluded by section 2(2) of the Crown Proceedings Act 1947 : as explained earlier this forbids the grant of such an order against a servant or officer of the Crown where the effect would be to give relief against the Crown (see 1.2.1.5). (In any case, it has been argued that Ministers do not possess an independent capacity to contract so the question should not arise: see 2.3.2). Certain other Crown agents are not, on the other hand, covered by this provision (see 1.2.1.5), and so these remedies should be available where an action is brought against them in an independent capacity. It was argued above that such bodies are presumed not to have such a capacity; but such a capacity is sometimes expressly conferred, so that this issue may in fact arise in practice. The courts might also be prepared to accept in these cases that the Crown's immunity from the burden of statutes, for example, would not apply.

2.8.   Immunities and the Crown's Contractors

A question which has been little discussed, and on which there is a surprising dearth of authority, is the extent to which independent contractors share in Crown immunities when they are engaged in work for the Crown (though see Hogg, at pp. 238-239). This is particularly likely to arise in relation to the rule that statutes are presumed not to bind the Crown, which has resulted from the Crown's being exempt from much regulatory legislation (see 1.2.1.6). For example, the Crown is not mentioned in the Control of Pollution Act 1974, which gives it an important exemption, in carrying out public works, from noise control and other restrictions under the Act. In this context the Crown's immunity protects the servants of the Crown from suit or from prosecution in a personal capacity as well as protecting the Crown itself (*Cooper v Hawkins* (1904) 2 KB 164). May independent contractors engaged by the Crown claim similar immunity?

It is submitted that the general principle is that Crown immunity does not extend to individual contractors, and that statutes are generally presumed to bind them when they are engaged in Crown work. The leading authority is the House of Lord decision in *Dixon v London Small Arms Company* ((1875-6) 1 App Cas 632). In this case the Crown had engaged the defendant to manufacture rifles, and in doing so the defendant had infringed the plaintiff's patent. It was assumed that the Crown itself, if it had decided to manufacture these rifles, would not have been restricted by the patent, on the basis that a grant of a patent, like a statute, was presumed under the common law not to bind the Crown. The House held that the defendants did not share the Crown's immunity : they clearly considered that the immunity did not generally extend to independent contractors. This is desirable as a *prima facie* rule, on the basis that the decision whether to take advantage of Crown immunities in particular cases should rest with the Crown itself. Frequently it does not do so, but voluntarily complies with regulatory statutes. Since the Crown has no right to control the way in which a contractor carries out his work, a general rule which allowed the contractor the benefit of Crown immunities would mean that the decision whether to invoke them would be effectively transferred to him and away from the Crown.

It may be argued that the above rule may prejudice the Crown's interests, by making work more difficult or expensive to carry out, and increasing the cost to the Crown. However, it should always be open to the Crown to invest the contractor with the Crown's own immunity if it chooses. This seems to have been accepted in *Dixon,* where there are suggestions that the Crown's immunity would have applied if the Crown had intended to create the contractor its "agent" (at p.641, 642 and 645 per Lord Cairns). The term "agent" is a loose one, used in different contexts to describe a relationship between two parties : for example, the extent to which one party (the agent) may make contracts with a third party which bind another (the principal); or the extent to which one party is vicariously liable to another for the torts of someone (the agent) who is not his servant. There need be no connection between the uses of the term in different contexts, and it is submitted that its use here was intended merely to convey the view that the Crown may designate a contractor as having Crown status for the purpose of Crown immunity. The view that the Crown may do this is further supported by the fact that Lords Cairns, Hatherley and Penzance all emphasised that it was possible for the contractor to have performed the agreement without infringing the patent. The implication here is that if the contract could not have been performed without an infringement, the defendants would have escaped liability. This can be explained on the basis that the contractor would be invested with immunity by the Crown by necessary implication from the terms of the contract (and see also *Re Telephone Apparatus Manufacturers Application* (1963) LR 3 RP 462; *Bradken Construction v Bracken Hill pty.* (1979) 145 CLR 107, which could be explained on the same basis though there are some statements in these cases that a contractor is not bound where application of the statute would "prejudice" the Crown, a formula which might suggest a wider scope for the immunity). This solution, which provides for Crown immunity to extend to contractors only where the Crown so designates, ensures that immunity exists only where the Crown has positively determined that it shall be invoked in relation to the work in question.

The court should, it is submitted, be slow to find, however, that a contractor has been invested with such immunity. This should apply only where it is expressly stated in the contract, or arises by implication from the fact that the performance of the contractual objective would otherwise be frustrated. The question of the Crown's control over the particular activity and other factors relevant to the question of who is a Crown agent (see 1.2.1.7) should not be relevant to this issue. The issue of deciding who is "the Crown" in this sense is quite separate from determining the question of whether a party recognised as an independent contractor is entitled to take advantage of the Crown's immunity under the terms of his contract. (cf. the arguments in *R. v London Waste Regulation Authority ex parte Specialist Waste Management Ltd,* 19 Oct 1988; Lexis).

The position should be no different where immunity arises in relation to a work authorised by statute. If the Crown wishes its contractors to take advantage of its immunities, this ought be specifically provided for by the Crown (or the statute). In some cases a contractor may obtain exemption from regulatory provisions by operation of the defence of statutory immunity : where a party is authorised by statute to carry out some work, and that work inevitably involves some conduct which would normally be a tort, such conduct is considered lawful because of the statutory authorisation (see ch. 7 below). This applies to work done by independent contractors. It may happen that the Crown itself would anyway be exempt from liability because it is immune from the statute by which liability is imposed. But the immunity of the contractor under the statutory authority defence has nothing to do with the more general immunity of the Crown. Where the conduct in issue is not an inevitable result of exercising the statutory powers, the contractor should have immunity only, as indicated, if it is given by the Crown, or by the legislation.

2.9. Judicial Review

There has in the past been some reluctance to subject contractual activities to the usual administrative law principles, such as natural justice. This has extended to steps taken both in the award and allocation of contracts, and to performance of a contract or the exercise of contractual rights, though it is more pronounced in relation to the latter. It has frequently been stated that there can be no review unless there is some special element of "public law" involved, suggesting that it is only in exceptional cases that judicial review is available. This restrictive approach is to some extent the product of policy factors, which are touched on below. However, the courts also appear to have been influenced by more abstract considerations - for example, the concept of freedom of contract, the idea of contract as a consensual relationship, and, perhaps most importantly, the strong perception of contract as a purely "private law" law matter. These influences may have led them to be more cautious in reviewing contractual activities than is warranted by the nature of the interests involved (see further Arrowsmith, *Government Procurement and Judicial Review* (1988) at pp. 10-12).

Recently, there have been signs of a retreat from this restrictive approach. Thus there are a number of cases in which the courts have either ignored or rejected the need for a specific element of public law for review, whilst in others they have been quick to find that some special element of public law does exist. There are also now important legislative provisions regulating the government's contractual powers, notably in the area of procurement (see ch.3), which may give rise to judicial review actions; and the effect of this may be to make judicial review of contract under the common law more acceptable. In addition, the decision of the House of Lords in *Council of Civil Service Unions v Minister for the Civil Service* ([1985] A.C. 374) has now been taken to establish that the common law powers of the Crown are subject in principle to judicial review, opening up the possibility of review of the common law contractual powers of the central executive. However, the law is still unsatisfactory and in a state of some uncertainty. It is best explained by looking at the decisions relating to discrete areas of contractual activity. (For fuller discussion see Arrowsmith, (1990) 106 LQR 277).

First, there are some decisions concerning the use of contract as a regulatory device. The impact of the general restrictive approach has, perhaps surprisingly, been to create a presumption that functions which are essentially regulatory are not generally subject to control by judicial review where carried out through contract. Thus in *R v Independent Broadcasting Association ex parte Rank Organisation* (March 26 1986; Lexis) the Court of Appeal held that decisions made by the IBA under a franchise contract with the television company (as to which see 2.2.1 above) would be reviewable only if there were some specific element of "public law" to the decision. This the court thought would normally be the case only if the power to make the decision in question were specifically given by statute. (For further discussion and criticism see Taggart, *Corporatisation, Privatisation and Public Law* (1990), Legal Research Foundation Pub. No. 3). In relation to the award of these contracts it was also stated by Lord Denning in *Cinnamond v British Airports Authority* ([1980] 1 WLR 582 at 590) that no hearing would be given to a disappointed applicant, although it is true that, quite apart from the contract point, the courts are generally unwilling to give a hearing for the grant of a licence: *McInnes v Onslow Fane* [1978] 1 WLR 1520.

The need for some special public law element for review has also been required in some cases in which market or street traders have sought review of the termination of their contractual licences to trade. However, in these cases the courts have been willing to find the requisite "public law" element, and so to give the relief sought, suggesting that they are uneasy with the restrictive approach to review of contractual powers. In *R v Barnsley Metropolitan District Council ex parte Hook* ([1976] 1 WLR 1052) a trader sought review of a decision to terminate his licence for a market stall, alleging breach of natural justice. The Council argued that since the relationship was contractual it was excluded from the ambit of judicial review. Both Lord Denning MR and Scarman LJ appeared to accept this argument in principle. They found, however, that there was a sufficient element of public law for review in that the council's powers to regulate trade in this market affected powers to trade there which the subject previously had under the common law. In *R v Wear Valley District Council ex parte Binks* ([1985] 2 All ER 699) the same argument was made when a trader sought review of its decision to terminate an informal contractual arrangement under which he had been permitted to operate as a vendor of takeaway food on council property. Taylor J also seemed to accept that a purely contractual power is not generally subject to review. However, he again found that judicial review was available on the facts, because there was an element of public law : although there was here no regulation of common law rights this element was found in the fact that the public had access to the land. It is highly unsatisfactory that the availability of review in these cases should depend on the kind of factors mentioned as sufficient to constitute a "public law" element. The court ought to focus on the nature of the interest of the regulated party. This was the approach of Lord Denning and Templeman LJ in another market trader case, *R v Basildon District Council ex parte Brown* ((1981) 79 LGR 655), in which Lord Denning, contrary to his approach in *Hook*, expressly dismissed the idea that the contractual nature of the power had any relevance for the scope of judicial review. It is a pity that this approach was not followed in the later decision in *Binks*.

Another context in which significance has been attached to the contractual nature of a relationship in relation to judicial review is public employment. Here also the courts have held that administrative law doctrines have no application unless there is a specific "public law" element to the case. The case law in this area is outlined at 4.4 below. Here it is sufficient to note that the particular significance of the contractual relationship is seen by the fact that where there is no contract between the government and its servant, it has been suggested that judicial review will apply in the normal way (*R v Civil Service Appeal Board ex parte Bruce* [1988] 3 All ER 686, discussed at 4.4.2 below; though cf. the approach in later cases, also discussed at 4.4.2).

In the area of leases and tenancies, on the other hand, the courts have not attached importance to the existence of a contract : in several decisions they have accepted, though without addressing the question specifically, that the exercise of a power to terminate a residential tenancy is subject to judicial review on the usual principles (*Cannock Chase D.C. v Kelly* [1978] 1 WLR 1; *Sevenoaks D.C. v Emmett* (1979) 78 LGR 346; and see *Wheeler v Leicester C.C.* [1985] AC 1054 (decision to refuse use of Council rugby ground unreasonable) and *R v Port Talbot B.C., ex parte Jones* [1988] 2 All ER 207). However, the argument that the exercise of a power under a lease is only reviewable if there is some specific element of public law was made in the Court of Appeal in *Jones v Swansea City Council* ([1990] 1 WLR 54; aff'd [1990] 1 WLR 1453). The action was not one for judicial review but for damages for misfeasance in public office. The plaintiff, a tenant of business premises leased from the council, sought damages in respect of the council's refusal to give consent to a change of user of the premises, alleging this had been done with an intent to injure the plaintiff and her husband, a prominent member of the council opposition group. The council argued that the power, since it arose under the lease, was a purely private power, the exercise of which was not subject to judicial review, and which therefore could not give rise to liability for misfeasance. The court found that misfeasance could apply (see 9.1.3 below). However, it found it unnecessary to decide whether there was any connection between the scope of the tort and the scope of the common law principles of judicial review. It is clear that the court inclined towards the view that such a power should generally be subject to public law controls when exercised by a public authority (see in particular the statement of Slade LJ at 70), but felt reluctant to state clearly that the power is subject to judicial review because of the restrictive approach to the review of contractual powers which has been adopted in other contexts.

A final area to consider is procurement. It was assumed for a long time that procurement powers were not subject to administrative law doctrines (see, for example, de Smith, *Judicial Review of Administrative Action* (4th ed. ed J.M. Evans, 1980) at p.163; Cane, *An Introduction to Administrative Law* (1986) at p.218). However, in recent cases the courts have applied these principles to the award of procurement contracts. Thus in *R v Enfield London Borough Council ex parte Unwin* ([1989] COD 466) it was held that a contractor who did most of his business with the government was entitled to a hearing before he was struck off the list of approved council contractors for alleged misconduct, and also before he was refused the chance to bid for the renewal of a contract which he currently held. The courts have also applied the common law proper purposes doctrine to the decision of the choice of contractor (*R v Lewisham London Borough Council ex parte Shell UK Ltd* [1988] 1 All ER 938). It is now forbidden by the Local Government Act 1988 to take account of "non commercial" considerations in procurement, a prohibition which applies not only to the award of contracts but also to the termination of existing contracts (see 3.1.4 below). It would be odd if common law principles were not also to apply to termination and the exercise of other contractual rights: for example, this would mean that a contractor might be given a hearing before a renewal of a contract which has expired but not before a decision is taken to terminate his existing contract.

It can be seen that there has been an increasing tendency to subject contractual powers to review, but it cannot definitively be stated that these powers are reviewable in the same manner as other powers of government: the view that there must be some "special" element of public law is still influential. This is unfortunate: the courts ought to look at the nature of the power and the interests affected and decide in this light what is the appropriate scope of review. There should be no presumption that a contractual power cannot be reviewed and no need to search for a special element of public law. This should apply even where the relationship is one which has a parallel in the private sphere, such as a lease, or a contract of employment or procurement, both because of the public interest which may be affected and because of the special obligations which public bodies have to act fairly towards those with whom they deal. This was recognised recently by La Forest J in the Supreme Court of Canada who stated in *McKinney v University of Guelph* (Dec 6 1990) that the fact that a government decision is made under a contract should not preclude the operation of the Canadian Charter of Rights and Freedoms. The fact that the relationship is governed in principle by the private law does not mean that it is not appropriate to apply in addition the special rules of public law. Where there is a conflict between them - as, for example, where it is argued that the breach of a public law rule should affect the subject's right to enforce the contract - it is quite possible to give priority to the principle of private law liability if this is thought desirable (see 2.10 below). Of course in some cases it will not be appropriate to apply public law principles for specific reasons of policy - where, for example, the legislature has demonstrated an intention that a contracting body should be able to compete with private enterprise on the same terms. In other cases the scope of the principles of judicial review will be limited: for considerations of administrative convenience it might be argued, for example, that a hearing should not be granted to every contractor refused a procurement contract with the government (see Arrowsmith, *Government Procurement and Judicial Review* (1988) Ch.8). But these considerations are not specifically tied to the contractual nature of the relationship.

2.10. The Impact of Judicial Review

2.10.1. Contract awards

Where a contract is affected by a breach of public law a question may arise as to the effect of the breach on the contract. This has already been considered in relation to contracts with an unauthorised object, which are probably invalid (see 2.3.3.2). Contracts which are unlawful as a fetter on discretion have also been held to be invalid (see 2.4).

The courts have also considered the effect on a contract of a breach of procedural requirements, and have tended here also to find that a breach of public law renders any subsequent agreement void. Thus in *Young & Co. v Royal Leamington* ((1883) 8 AC 517) the House of Lords held that failure to comply with a statutory requirement that a seal be affixed to certain works contracts rendered the contract invalid. Moreover, it was held that no restitutionary remedy was available for work done (see further 11.4.2). In *Rhyl U.D.C. & Rhyl Amusements* ([1959] 1 WLR 465) a breach of a requirement to obtain ministerial approval for a lease was also held to be invalidating. Likewise, in *Melliss v Shirley Local Board* ((1885) 16 QBD 446) it was held that where there was a breach of a requirement prohibiting the authority's servants from being concerned or interested in contracts with the authority, the contract could not be enforced against the authority, though this case might perhaps be considered to be in a different class from the others since the other party to the contract, who will be prejudiced by non-enforcement, was himself a party to the breach. Breach of the former common law requirement that a seal must be affixed to corporate contracts, which applied to public as well as private corporations, also prevented a contract from being enforced (see *Lawford v Billericay RDC* [1903] 1 KB 772). Modern provisions, however, sometimes now state that a procedural breach is not to affect a contract. Thus section 135 of the Local Government Act 1972 requires local authorities to make standing orders relating to the award of procurement contracts by competitive procedure, but provides that a breach shall not invalidate a concluded agreement. It is not stated what is the consequence of a breach of the provisions of Local Government Act 1988 prohibiting decisions from being taken on the basis of non-commercial considerations (see 3.1.1). In implementing the European Community Directives on procurement procedures member states are expressly given a choice as to whether or not it should be possible for a contract to be invalidated by a breach; and the implementing legislation in the United Kingdom provides that contracts shall not be invalidated (see 3.2.4).

The problem may also arise in relation to breaches of common law principles of review. Although the courts have accepted in a number of cases that the award of a contract may be subject to judicial review (see 2.9), it has not been necessary in any of these cases to decide what would be the impact of a breach on any contract.

The general presumption should be that the private law applies in the ordinary way, and that the contract is not affected. It was suggested above that this should also generally be the case where a contract is made for an unlawful object (see 2.3.3.2) or where it falls within the fettering doctrine (see 2.5.3). However, there may be a stronger argument for invalidating the contract where the provision breached is designed to protect the "rights" of a particular individual who will be prejudiced if the contract is not set aside. Such public law rights will often be adequately protected through the grant of an interim remedy to prevent the contract going ahead, but this may not be possible - for example, where the contract has already been concluded or where urgency requires that it be concluded straightaway. Perhaps the best approach in such cases would be to recognise a discretion in the courts to invalidate the contract, but with a presumption that it would be allowed to stand. However, it can be argued that most of those affected by unlawful contract awards - for example, procurement contractors - do not have any protected interest in this sense, though they may have standing to enforce the relevant provisions in the public interest.

2.10.2. The exercise of contractual rights

The effect of an action for judicial review may arise also in relation to the exercise of contractual rights. A number of employment cases have been concerned with a purported exercise of a right to terminate the relationship, which has been done in breach of public law. It has been assumed in these cases that the unlawful action is not effective to put an end to the relationship, although it would have been effective but for the breach of public law (see, for example, *Ridge v Baldin* ([1964] AC 40), including in cases where the employment relationship is contractual (*Malloch v Aberdeen Corporation* [1971] 1 WLR 1578). This seems correct, since otherwise the applicant will be deprived of any effective remedy. Similarly, the exercise of any other contractual right in a manner which is in breach of public law should be treated as ineffective.

What will be the contractual consequences of an abortive termination? Where there is an attempt to terminate a contract which is ineffective because the termination is not warranted under the terms of the contract - rather than because of a breach of public law - the attempt may itself constitute a repudiatory breach by the party making it, which means that the other way elect them to terminate the contract. However, if the attempt is made in good faith, with an intention to preserve the contract on foot if it is erroneous, it will probably not be regarded as a repudiation of the agreement (*Woodar Investment Development Ltd v Wimpey Construction (U.K.) Ltd.* ([1980] 1 WLR 277). The same principles should apply where the reason that a purported termination is ineffective is because of a breach of public law. Of course, even if the purported termination is not itself a repudiatory breach, the subsequent conduct of the authority, when it acts on the purported termination, may amount to a breach of contract and even a repudiation - for example, where a contractor is refused access to the premises on which is supposed to work.

Often a contractor will be content to seek damages for any breach of contract which follows from a breach of public law. In other cases, however, he may wish to continue performance of the contract against the wishes of the authority. Under the ordinary law of contract specific relief is exceptional, being granted only where damages are an inadequate remedy; and even then it will frequently be refused on other grounds in the exercise of the court's discretion. There is, however, some suggestion in the cases that a public law remedy may be used to give specific relief in circumstances where the private law would not. This arises from some of the decisions concerned with dismissals from public employment in breach of public law. It has been assumed in several of these cases that the grant of a public law remedy in respect of the dismissal will generally entail reinstatement of the applicant in his employment, even though the circumstances are such that no specific relief would be granted under the private law (for these cases see 4.3.3 below). This might suggest that where there is breach of public law in terminating some other type of contract - say, where a procurement contract is terminated for an improper purpose - the courts would compel the public authority to treat the contract as subsisting, though the authority wishes to regard it as at an end.

However, this seems illogical: there is no reason why the principles governing reinstatement should be different where a termination is invalid for a breach of public law than where it is ineffective because not contractually justified. A litigant should not be able to avoid the restrictions on contractual remedies imposed by the private law, simply because a breach of his contract happens to have been preceded by an invalid attempt to terminate it. This would only be the case if there is something in the nature of the circumstances in which public law applies, which makes specific relief particularly appropriate. In fact, public law originally applied only to employment in the nature of an office, which was seen as a species of property, and the effect of specific relief in these cases could be seen as restoring property to its rightful owner. However, the scope of public law is now much wider (see 4.4.2). In any case, this reasoning suggests that where an office holder has a contract which is terminated in breach of the terms of the contract, specific relief ought to be available to him under private law principles. In general, the application of completely different principles in granting specific relief, just because there happens to have been some breach of public law in the case, cannot be justified. In fact, despite the apparently more generous approach of the public law employment cases, the results of these cases can be reconciled with the principles which now given the grant of specific relief in employment cases in private law; and they should be explained on this basis. This is discussed further at 4.4.3 below.

It is submitted, then, that the question of whether the court will give relief to keep a contract on foot will depend on the application of the ordinary private law principles. The fact that the dispute happens to arise out of a breach of public law should not affect the position.

An action for review of any invalid exercise of contractual rights may, of course, be brought under Order 53. It may be noted that the court does not have power to grant specific performance in such an action - though an injunction may be obtained. This is discussed further at 1.3 above. It might be desirable for the court to have a power to make an order for specific performance under the procedure, as well as to give damages. It is possible, however, for the affected party to have the public law matters on which his contractual claim depends adjudicated in an ordinary action, without the need to bring an action to challenge the termination under Order 53 first (see 1.3), so that only one set of proceedings is required.

2.11. Contract and Ombudsmen

The government's contractual activities are to a large extent excluded from the scrutiny of the Commissioners for Administration or "Ombudsmen".

Excluded from the jurisdiction of the Parliamentary Commissioner for Administration is "action in matters relating to contractual or other commercial transactions" (Parliamentary Commissioner Act 1967, s.5(3) and Sch.3). There is an exception for contracts relating to the compulsory acquisition of land (and also of land which could have been acquired under compulsory purchase powers if this had been necessary). The general exclusion is not well drafted since it seems to assume that all contractual transactions are commercial, but this clearly is not so (see 2.2 above). In practice the Commissioner has in fact investigated some matters involving a contractual relationship which might be said not to be of a "commercial" nature - for example, the services of the Public Trustee, and land registration (see Williams, *Maladministration: Remedies for Injustice* (1976) at p.65). It is clear, though, that commercial contract matters such as procurement are outside the Commissioner's jurisdiction; and he has also said that he may not investigate activities relating to the award of industrial assistance where it takes a contractual form (see Select Commissioner on the Parliamentary Commissioner for Administration, Fourth Report, Minutes of Evidence Session 1979-80, HC 444, para.74). Personnel matters, both civil and military, are also expressly excluded from the Commissioner's jurisdiction (Parliamentary Commissioner Act 1967, s.5 (3) and Sch.3).

The Local Commissioners are also precluded from investigating "action taken in matters relating to contract or other commercial transactions" (Local Government Act 1974, s.26(7) and Sch.5, Para.3). In this case, however, the relevant provisions elaborate further. Expressly stated to be outside the Commissioners' jurisdiction are the operation of passenger transport, the carrying on of a dock or harbour undertaking, the provision of entertainment, the operation and provision of industrial establishments and markets, and procurement. Apart from these cases transactions made under any public general Act of Parliament may be investigated, and specifically included also are transactions relating to the acquisition and disposal of land (see Sch.5, para.3). As with the Parliamentary Commissioner, there is also an express exclusion for personnel matters. Similar exclusions of contractual and, expressly, personnel, matters apply to the jurisdiction of the Health Service Commissioners, except that the Commissioners may investigate matters relating to the provision of services for patients even though they may be "contractual" (National Health Service Reorganisation Act 1973. s.34(5); Sch.3, para.4).

The wide exclusion of contractual activities from the jurisdiction of the Ombudsmen has been influenced by the perception of contract as a private or "non-governmental" matter, which has also led to a reluctance to subject these activities to judicial review (see 2.9 above). The exclusion has been repeatedly criticised by the Commissioners themselves, by the Select Committee on the Parliamentary Commissioner, and by many review bodies and Commissions (for these criticisms see Arrowsmith, (1990) 10 LS 231 at pp. 240-243). The exclusion is clearly unwarranted, even so far as it relates to "commercial" transactions such as procurement. It is difficult to see why matters such as allegations of corruption in the award of contracts or the unfair blacklisting of certain firms are inherently unsuitable for investigation. In particular, questions of this type can be, and are, raised in the House of Commons by M.P.s, and it seems anomalous that they should not be able to call upon the Parliamentary Commissioner to assist them in any investigation. Such activities are within the jurisdiction of the Ombudsman in a number of other countries. (For an account of Ombudsman investigation in the area of public procurement in Australia, for example, see Allard [1989] 12 UNSW LJ 114 at 127-129). They ought also to be brought within his jurisdiction in the United Kingdom.

3

Public Procurement

The importance of the government's activities as a purchaser of goods and services from the private sector has been indicated above (see 2.2). Until recently procurement in the United Kingdom was largely free from legal regulation, being carried on within the framework of the private law of contract and a few constitutional constraints. However, the position has begun to change dramatically. One recent development is the application of the common law principles of judicial review to procurement (see 2.9 and 2.10). In addition, important legislation has been enacted, first, on the domestic front, to regulate aspects of the contracting of local government, and, second, at a European level, to open the European public procurement market to competition. These provisions are considered in the following sections. They are complex and detailed and the following is an outline only: for more detail readers are referred to the more specialist works cited in the text below.

3.1. Local Authority Procurement

3.1.1. Standing orders on competitive procedures

Under section 135 Local Government Act 1972 local authorities must make standing orders providing for competitive procedures to be used in the award of their contracts. Since, however, with smaller contracts any savings through opening up the process to competition may be outweighed by the administrative costs, thresholds may be set, below which competitive procedures are not required. The object of the section is to ensure that procedures are followed which allow the authority to obtain the best value for money. There is no requirement to award the contract to the party offering the best value, but it is probable that if an authority does not award the contract either on this basis or on the basis of some lawful "secondary" consideration, its decision could be challenged as made for an improper purpose or unreasonable (see 2.8 above). The power to take into account secondary considerations has also now been severely curtailed by the Local Government Act 1988 (see 3.1.4 below), so that it seems that "best value" will normally be the sole lawful factor to consider.

If the standing orders are breached, a contractor may have an action for judicial review to prevent the authority from going ahead with the award process (*R. v Hereford Corporation ex parte Harrower* [1970] 1 WLR 1424; *McKee v Belfast Corporation* [1954] NI 122). The question of *locus standi* is unclear: in *Harrower* it was held that an aggrieved contractor had standing to obtain certiorari in his capacity as ratepayer, but no standing, either for certiorari or mandamus, as an interested contractor *per se*. However, *Harrower* was decided before the introduction of the new test of standing of "sufficient interest" under the Order 53 procedure (see Craig, ch.12). Standing for all the remedies is now the same, and might be given to contractors, though the issue has not been expressly decided. Failure to comply with the standing orders does not invalidate any concluded contact (Local Government Act 1972 s.135(4)).

3.1.2.   *Compulsory competitive tendering and the "contracting out" policy*

To obtain goods and services needed for delivering services to the public, government bodies in the United Kingdom have traditionally (though not invariably) tended to look to the private sector rather, than, for example, manufacturing the necessary goods and equipment "in-house". As regards the actual delivery of public services, on the other hand, it has been usual for public bodies to do this themselves, rather than relying on independent contractors. In the 1980s, however, the central government adopted a "contracting out" policy, which was manifested by moves to increased contracting out of its own work (see Turpin, *Government Procurement and Contracts* (1989) at pp. 206-207) and in the National Health Service, as well as its policy of promoting contracting out by local authorities. Under Part III of the Local Government Planning and Land Act 1980 the government provided for compulsory tendering by local authorities with respect to construction and maintenance work, but on the whole in the early 1980s relied on a policy of exhortation and encouragement to persuade local authorities to contract out the provision of services. This policy met with considerable resistance, and, following the 1985 Green paper, *Competition in the Provision of Local Authority Services*, extensive compulsory provisions were introduced by the Local Government Act 1988. A detailed account is found in Cirrell and Bennett, *Compulsory Competitive Tendering: Law and Practice* (looseleaf).

The 1980 and 1988 Acts essentially require that, with respect to the functions covered, competitive procedures must be followed wherever the authority is considering performing the function through its own employees. The purpose of this is to ascertain whether the "in-house" approach will give best value for money, or whether the function would be more economically performed by using outside contractors. It should be emphasised that there is no requirement for competitive procedures where the authority has already taken a decision to contract out the function. In this case, the selection of the contractor will be subject to the competition requirements in the authority's standing orders (see 3.1.1 above) and to requirements imposed by European Community law, and any other legislation (see 3.1.3). There will be no need, however, to adhere to the procedures set out immediately below, which are designed solely to ensure that a decision to contract out is taken where appropriate.

The primary justification for the contracting out policy has been to obtain better value for money. However, it has been said that tendering has other attractions also: "businesses in the (increasingly important) service sector of the economy could be encouraged, public expenditure and manpower reduced, national pay bargaining undermined, and the position of public service trade unions threatened" (Radford, (1988) 51 MLR 747 at p.749). On the other hand, fears have been expressed that contracting out results inevitably in a diminished quality of service which, though cheaper, may be worse "value". In particular, it may be difficult to ensure that outside contractors meet certain minimum standards, including in sensitive areas - for example, that those engaged in the care or instruction of children are suitable for the task.

The 1988 Local Government Act imposes contracting out obligations with respect to a range of functions listed in section 2, including refuse collection, cleaning of buildings and streets, some catering, ground maintenance and the maintenance of vehicles. The Secretary of State is given a power to add further functions to the list and has already added management of sports and leisure facilities (Local Government Act 1988 (Competition in Sports and Leisure Facilities) Order 1989, S.I. 1989/2488, amending section 2(2) and para.8, Sch.1 of the Act). The timetable for the commencement of contracting out of these activities is contained in statutory instruments (Local Government Act 1988 (Defined Activities) (Competition) (England) Regulations, S.I. 1988/137 as amended by S.I. 1991/2 32; separate regulations apply to Wales). Where the authority is contemplating giving work to its own labour organisation, it must first make a call for competition by placing a notice in a local newspaper and also a "publication circulating among persons who carry out work of the kind concerned", describing the work and inviting persons to express interest in bidding (s.7). At least three persons (or all those interested if there are fewer than three) must be invited to submit bids, and the authority itself must submit a written bid if it wishes its own organisation to carry out the work (s.7(4)). Under section 7(5) the Secretary of State is given a power to vary the number of bids required. In reaching a decision that the authority itself should carry out the work, it is required that the authority should not act in such a way as to restrict, distort or prevent competition (s.7(7)).

The Secretary of State is given, by section 8, power to make regulations relating to the administration of the tendering process under these provisions.

The above provisions apply only where the work is "functional work" which means essentially work carried out by the authority in connection with its own activities, or those of certain other public authorities, including Ministers of the Crown (see s.3 and Department of Environment Circular 19/88). With work which is not functional work, special provisions apply (see ss.4 and 5).

The contracting out provisions on construction and maintenance are still contained in the 1980 Local Government Planning and Land Act, with some amendments made by the 1988 Act, and are broadly similar to those in that Act, with the same objectives. For "functional" work (see s.8) tenders must be sought from at least three parties who are not other local authorities, and certain other conditions complied with (s.9). (For the conditions applying to non-functional work see s.6). The general prohibition on anti-competitive behaviour has been applied to this area by the 1988 Act (see ss.7 1A and 9(4)(aaaa) of the 1980 Act, as inserted by s.32 Sch.6, paras.2 and 3 of the 1988 Act).

3.1.3. Competitive tendering under European Community and other provisions

Competitive procedures are now widely required for the award of major contracts under European Community Directives adopted to open up the public procurement market to Europe wide competition. These Directives and the United Kingdom legislation implementing the Directives are discussed at 3.2. These obligations are often incorporated into local authorities standing orders on tendering (see 3.1.1 above).

An authority may also be obliged to comply with other statutory tendering obligations relating to particular functions (see, for example, Transport Act 1985, s.89, concerning required tendering procedures for subsidised public transport services).

3.1.4. Prohibition of "non-commercial considerations"

Local authorities, like other governmental bodies, have a long history of using procurement to promote secondary policies - that is, they have used their discretion in selecting a contractor or laying down the terms of the contract for purposes other than the procurement of goods and services on the best possible terms (see 2.2 above). Thus, for example, until recently a number of authorities refused to award contracts to firms having connections with South Africa in order to discourage such connections, and thereby to put pressure on the South African government to end apartheid. Recent legal developments, however, mean that the use of contract in pursuit of such policies is now generally forbidden. First, recent cases have made it clear that the general administrative law principle that powers may be exercised only for the limited purposes contemplated by the statute applies to procurement, and it appears that, *prima facie*, only factors relating to the goal of obtaining necessary goods and services as efficiently as possible may be taken into account in exercising procurement functions. This development was considered at 2.9 above. Second, authorities are now substantially barred from taking secondary considerations into account by provisions in the Local Government Act 1988.

The key provision is section 17(1). This provides that with respect to public works and supplies contracts (which are defined by section 17(3) to include contracts for the provision of services), authorities listed in Schedule 2 must exercise specified procurement functions "without reference to matters which are non-commercial matters for the purpose of this section. Matters which are "non-commercial" for this purpose are defined in section 17(5). They include, *inter alia*, terms on which contractors employ their workers, and other specified matters relating to opportunities and conditions for employees; involvement of contractors with "irrelevant fields of government policy"; contractors' conduct in industrial disputes; the origin of contractors' supplies, and the territory of their business activities; and any "political, industrial or sectarian affiliations". (For elaboration of the meaning of some of these matters see further s.17(8)). The authority is prohibited from taking account of non-commercial matters not only in so far as they relate to the contractor, but also the contractor's suppliers and customers; any subcontractor and his suppliers or customers; and bodies associated with any of these (s.17(7)). The Secretary of State has a power to add other matters to this list of prohibited considerations, where a matter "appears to him irrelevant to the commercial purposes" of procurement contracts (s.19(1)). If a non-commercial consideration is not within the list it is not prescribed by the Act. Thus, for example, an authority may stipulate for compliance with general health and safety laws so long as this does not impose requirements on the contractor in relation to his contracts with his own work force (*R v London Borough of Islington, ex parte Building Employers Confederation* [1989] IRLR 382). Matters not caught by the Act may still, however, be caught by the common law proper purposes rule (see 2.9 above).

Although section 17 purports to be concerned with the prohibition of "non-commercial" considerations - and such an intention is borne out by the fact that the Secretary of State's power to add matters to the list is defined in terms of matters appearing to be irrelevant to commercial purposes - it seems that some of the matters specified in the statute could relate to the "commercial" interests of the contract. For example, the conditions under which a contractor's employees are employed may affect the stability of his workforce and hence his reliability in performing the contract. Likewise the territorial origin of the contractor's business interests may be relevant to the predicted reliability of his performance. Arguably, the provisions might be interpreted as precluding these considerations only where taken into account for non-commercial reasons.

As indicated, section 17 only applies to decisions taken in the exercise of specified functions relating to procurement. However, these are widely stated. They are not confined to acts carried out in the course of award procedure but extend to acts in the course of contract administration. They include, *inter alia*, the inclusion of persons on approved lists; acceptance of tender submissions; selection of the contractor; the approval or nomination of sub-contractors; and the termination of the contract (s.17(4)).

The Act expressly preserves any other rights of judicial review in relation to the functions controlled by it. Thus if the authority were to take into account some non-commercial consideration which is not listed in the Act, a review action might still be available, by virtue of the general principles of administrative law outlined in 2.9 above. However, the more favourable conditions applying to actions under the Act - such as the general right to damages, and the presumptions in section 19(10) (both discussed immediately below) - would not apply where the contractor relies on such general principles.

Section 19(7) provides that non-compliance is not to be a criminal offence, but that an action for judicial review is available. Standing is given to any potential contractor, or (where an award has already been made) any former potential contractor, and in addition to any body representing contractors (s.19(7)(a)). It was suggested at 2.10 above that a breach of the section should not invalidate any concluded contract.

It is also provided that a failure to comply with section 17 is actionable in damages "by any person who, in consequence, suffers loss or damage" (s.19(7)b)). This seems to require that any person claiming should be able to prove that but for the breach he would have been awarded the contract: otherwise he cannot be said to have suffered loss "in consequence of" the breach. The amount which can be claimed by a party who has submitted a tender is limited to "damages in respect of expenditure reasonably incurred by him for the purpose of submitting a tender" (s.19(8)). This is a maximum, and less should be awarded where less is suffered. Illogically, this restriction applies only where a person has submitted a tender so that, for example, where the authority has negotiated informally with two parties and decided in favour of one on the basis of prohibited considerations, there is no limit. Presumably damages may then be recovered on the ordinary tortious measure, which may include a claim for lost profits. The "tendering costs" limitation for bidders appears to apply even where there has been a deliberate or malicious breach of the rules on non-commercial considerations, although under general principles full tort damages are available in such a case (see 9.1 below). This is because the "tendering costs" limitation is stated to apply in *any* action under section 17(1). However, it would be possible to claim full damages for misfeasance to the extent that the authority's action also constitutes a breach of the general "proper purposes" rule.

To bolster enforcement of these rules it is provided that, for certain procurement decisions, an authority must give to an affected party a written statement of reasons for the decision, within fifteen days of receipt of a written request from that person (s.20). The decisions covered are defined in section 20(2). This is designed to help contractors determine whether there is any ground for judicial review.

In certain circumstances an authority is deemed to have acted on the basis of non-commercial considerations: no actual proof of the authority's motive is required. This is so where the authority asks a contractor a question relating to a non-commercial matter or where it submits a draft contract or draft tender containing provisions relating to a non-commercial matter, except in so far as permitted by section 18 (s.19(10)).

Section 71 Race Relations Act 1976 requires local authorities, in exercising their functions, to have regard to the need to eliminate unlawful discrimination, to promote equality of opportunity, and to promote good relations between different racial groups. It has been held that, under the general law, this section allows an authority to take into account "race relations" matters in awarding procurement contracts (*R v Lewisham L.B.C., ex parte Shell U.K. Ltd.* [1988] 1 All ER 938). Section 18 of the 1988 Act now specifically regulates the extent to which this duty may be taken into account in the exercise of procurement functions; this may be done only to the extent permitted by the section (s.18(1)). The section permits an authority to ask in writing of a contractor questions approved by the Secretary of State, and request evidence as permitted by the Secretary of State, to the extent that this is reasonably necessary to ensure compliance with the authority's own duty on race relations matters under section 71. It also empowers the authority to include terms to secure this end. The section does not expressly permit the refusal of contracts (as opposed to the inclusion of relevant terms in the contract) because of the response, though this might be implied (Radford, above, at p.760). It expressly precludes the authority from terminating a contract where a contractor does not comply with the stated terms (s.18(3)). Through Ministerial control and limits on termination, the section thus reduces the previous freedom of authorities to use their procurement powers to enforce policies on race relations.

There has been some debate over the justification for the "non-commercial considerations" prohibition. The expressed rationale of section 17 is to require local authorities to act only by reference to commercial matters in procurement. It seems logical to preclude reference to "secondary" considerations where they relate to matters over which local authorities generally have no jurisdiction: if authorities cannot regulate behaviour, or implement some policy, through other methods, there is no reason they should be able to do so through contract. Even if the area in question is under local authorities' control, where there is a regulatory scheme in force which provides safeguards for those regulated, it would be anomalous to allow those safeguards to be avoided by allowing regulation through contract. On the other hand, if policy making or implementation on a matter is generally within the authority's jurisdiction (as with race relations matters) there seem to be no logical reason to forbid the use of procurement, as opposed to other methods, as a tool of implementation (see further, Arrowsmith, *Government Procurement and Judicial Review* (1988) ch.12). It would seem more satisfactory to leave the question of the legitimacy of secondary considerations to the courts, which could take into account the factors referred to. However, it is arguable that the legislation is not merely concerned with involvement of local authorities in irrelevant policy matters, but that it is "a determined attempt to drive down the cost of providing local services, with little regard for the consequences" (Radford, (1988) 51 MLR 747 at 758). In other words, it is designed to reduce authorities' discretion in trading off quality and expense, with the aim of reducing overall expenditure. On this view, it may be considered intentional that matters such as working conditions of contractors' employees should not be taken into account, even though it might affect the quality of service: cost, rather than general "value for money" is considered paramount. This could also explain the strategy of refusing to let authorities take account of concerns which are generally within their jurisdiction: it is not their involvement *per se* which is objectionable, but the financial costs of implementing such policies through contract.

Certain non-commercial matters are in addition precluded from consideration by local authorities by virtue of their obligations under European Community law. These are discussed next.

3.2   European Community Law

3.2.1.   Introduction

The government procurement market is of enormous economic significance in the European Community. It has been estimated that it is worth about 530 billion ECUs a year and the Commission has said that it accounts for 15% of the Gross Domestic Product of the Community (European Commission, *Completing the Internal Market* (1985) (White Paper to the European Council), COM (85) 310). Only a tiny fraction of government work (estimated at less than 2% by the Commission) is awarded to firms outside the awarding state. The Commission considers that an important factor in explaining the low level of awards to non-domestic suppliers is that member states have discriminated in favour of home suppliers, either because of deliberate policies of domestic preference, or simply because of undue caution or apathy in widening their supplier base. It is the Commission's conviction that there would be enormous savings made by opening up the procurement market to free competition. Savings may arise both directly, through the savings to government entities which obtain better value for money, and indirectly, through the effect which opening up of the market will have in promoting efficient enterprise. A policy of opening up the public market to Europe wide competition has thus now become an important aspect of the drive towards completion of the internal market by 1992. This policy is being put into effect mainly through a series of Directives requiring governments to take positive steps to open up their markets, the mainstay of which is a requirement that competitive procedures be used to award contracts. Some Directives have already been adopted, but a number are still under consideration, and this is an area of rapid development. In addition, discrimination in procurement is prohibited under the EC treaties themselves. The open procurement policy has also been advanced by requiring open competition for contracts which relate to projects funded by grants or loans from the Community.
    Some argue that, whatever the legal remedies, the Directives will not be effective if governments are determined to discriminate. It has also been suggested that, even if the Directives are properly implemented, there may be little impact on the market. Many complaints have been made that the administrative costs of the policy are excessive and will outweigh any benefits, or, at least, that the current provisions are too burdensome. The extent to which these fears and criticisms are well founded is difficult to judge, and remains to be seen.
    The Treaties and Directives do not generally preclude discrimination against firms which are not established in the Community or individuals

who are not Community nationals, but are concerned only with opening up markets to Community suppliers. However, such discrimination will be permitted only if allowed under domestic law, and with local authorities will normally be precluded either by the Local Government Act 1988 (see 3.1.2) or by the common law principles of judicial review (see 2.9). In addition, discrimination in relation to non-member states may be contrary to the United Kingdom's Treaty obligations. In particular the government must adhere to the Agreement on Government Procurement which applies to signatories of the General Agreement on Trade and Tarrifs, and this includes many countries which are not members of the European Community. This requires the use of non-discriminatory procedures for the award of many supply contracts let by the central government (although local authorities are not yet covered by the provisions). Further, an accord negotiated in late 1991 between the Community and the States of the European Free Trade Association envisages the extension of the Community procurement regime to cover those states as well.

3.2.2. The Treaty of Rome

Although public procurement is not expressly mentioned in the Treaty of Rome, some of the general provisions of the Treaty impose obligations in relation to the procurement function (see further Weiss, (1988) 18 EL Rev 318 at pp. 319-321). One important provision, for example, is Article 30, which prohibits quantitative restrictions on imports or measures having equivalent effect. This was invoked in relation to a procurement matter in *EC Commission v Ireland* (the "Dundalk water case", case 45/87R [1989] 1 CMLR 225). In this case the water company had called for tenders for pipes to be used in a construction project, and had included a requirement for compliance with an Irish National Standard of construction, which was currently met by the products of only one company, an Irish firm. The procurement was not covered by any Directive at that time, since the Directives in force did not extent to the water sector. It was held by the European Court of Justice that the use of such a standard in specifications to preclude tenders based on different specifications - which might be just as acceptable for the purposes of the project - was *prima facie* a breach of Article 30 as an obstacle to trade (and see also case 21/88 *Du Pont de Nemours Italiana SpA v Local Health Authority No. 2, Carrara* [1991] 3 CMLR 25). Other Articles of the Treaty which could be relied upon include those on the right to establish (Article 52 *et seq)* and those on the freedom to provide services (Article 59 *et seq)* (see C-3/88 E.C. *Commission v Italy* [1991] 2 CMLR 115).

The Treaty provisions may usefully be invoked (as in *Dundalk*) in relation to those areas which have not at the time of the action been covered by Directives; for example, at the time of writing there is no Directive in force relating to services contracts, but obligations under the Treaty still apply. (For details of a Commission proposal on services see 3.2.5 below). The Treaty may also be relied upon to impose obligations with respect to contracts which relate to sectors which are excluded from the scope of the Directives for some particular reason, for example, because they are of an amount which is too low to be caught by the Directives. Thus, although such contracts need not be advertised in accordance with the Directives, it may be argued that discriminatory provisions included in contracts which are advertised will be unlawful under the Treaty. Where the relevant article of the Treaty has direct effect, it may be invoked by aggrieved suppliers to obtain a remedy in the national courts (see 1.6.1).

3.2.3. The general Directives on works and supplies

As indicated above, a series of Directives have been adopted in relation to procurement, which reinforce and supplement the basic principles set out in the Treaty of Rome. Some Directives were adopted long before the 1985 White Paper, with a Directive on public works contracts in 1971 (71/305/EEC 1971 OJ L185 - "the Works Directive"), and one on public supplies contracts in 1977 (77/62 EEC, 1977 OJ L13 - "the Supplies Directive"). However, these provisions were largely ignored in practice and it was concluded by the Commission in its 1985 White Paper that they had proved largely ineffective. Substantial amendments were made to both Directives, introducing more stringent and detailed controls, along with various provisions to ensure that the Directives could not be evaded by contracting authorities, as had occurred previously. These changes were introduced by Directive 89/440/EEC (1989 OJ L210) amending the Works Directive, and Directive 88/295/EEC 1988 (OJ L127) amending the Supplies Directive. (See O'Loan (1992) 1 PPLR 40; Sohrab, (1990) 10 OJLS 523; Boncompagni (1990) 7 ICLR 255; von Bael, (1989) 1 LIEL 21; Marks (1990) 6 ICLR 424; Weiss, 7 (1988) 10 EL Rev 318). In addition, a separate Directive lays down certain requirements relating to the remedies which member states must make available to suppliers who allege a breach of Community law in relation to contracts falling within the Works or Supplies Directives (see further 3.2.4). These three Directives have now been implemented in the UK by the Public Works Contracts Regulations 1991 (S.I. 1991 No. 2680) (the "Works Regulations") and the Public Supply Contracts Regulations 1991 (S.I. 1991 No. 2679) ("The Supplies Regulations"), which were enacted under the powers contained in s.2(2) European Communities Act 1972.

The Supplies Regulations apply to contracts for purchase and hire (including hire purchase) where the contract is for a pecuniary interest and is made in writing (Supplies Regs. 2(1) and 5). The Works Regulations also apply only to works contracts for a pecuniary consideration and made in writing (Works Reg. 2(1)).

The authorities to which the Regulations apply are listed in Supplies Regulation 3 and Works Regulation 3. They apply, of course, to ministers of the Crown and central government departments, and to general local authorities and also, *inter alia*, to fire and police authorities. There is also provision for the Regulations to apply to certain bodies established to meet "needs in the general interest" and "not having an industrial or commercial character" which are financed, supervised or appointed by an authority subject to the Regulations.   Excluded from the scope of both the Directives and the Regulations are most contracts relating to transport, water, energy and telecommunications (see Supplies Reg. 6; Works Reg. 6). These sectors were originally excluded from the EC Directives mainly because of the enormous variations in the degree of public ownership and control of such activities between the different states of the Community. A special regime is now being established to deal with procurement in these sectors, which is considered at 3.2.6 and 3.2.7. The Regulations, as permitted by the relevant Directives, also contain exemptions relating to national security (Supplies Reg. 6(d); Works Reg. 6(d)).

Obviously, compliance with advertising and other requirements involves administrative costs which cannot be justified where potential savings are small, and the Directives, and the implementing Regulations, therefore apply only to major contracts. For supplies, the general threshold is 200,000 ECUs or more, or 130,000 ECUs for contracts which are also subject to the General Agreement on Trade and Tariffs, which covers contracts of this lesser amount (Supplies Reg. 7). The Works Directive applies to contracts valued at 5 million ECUs upwards (Works Reg. 7). Both Directives, and both sets of Regulations, contain provisions which forbid avoidance by splitting up contracts to bring the amount below the threshold, something which many authorities allegedly had been doing before the 1988-1989 reforms.

The basis of the Community's policy for opening up the market is to require contracts falling under the Directives to be awarded by competitive procedures, in such a manner as to give equal opportunities to bidders from all member states. For supply contracts the rules on this are laid down in Supplies Regulations 10-13. According to these Regulations contracts must generally be awarded by what are designated "open" procedures. This means that the contract must be advertised in the *Official Journal of the Communities,* and all interested persons be permitted to submit a tender. In "justified cases" an authority is permitted, alternatively, to use what are designated "restricted" procedures. This means that the contract is advertised in the *Official Journal* so that parties who may want to bid can express interest, and formal tenders are then invited from a limited number only of those who respond, selected by the authority. In selecting bidders the authority must not discriminate against suppliers from other member states (Article 19). Restricted procedures are envisaged as applying, *inter alia,* where the costs of an open procedure (which may, of course, involve the assessment of a very large number of tenders) are likely to be disproportionate to the value of the contract. This restricted procedure, however, is regarded as exceptional, and authorities must draw up a report justifying its use in each case, which the European Commission may require to be produced. In a limited number of specified, exceptional, cases, an authority may dispense with these procedures and simply negotiate the contract with a selected supplier or suppliers, a process referred to as the "negotiated" procedure. This is permitted, for example, in cases of "extreme urgency" (provided the emergency was unforeseeable and not engineered by the authority), or where there is only one possible supplier. Again records must be kept to enable the authority to justify a decision to use this procedure.

Under the Works Regulations in contrast with the Supplies Regulations, where open procedures are stipulated as the norm, an authority is given a free choice between open and restricted procedures. Where the latter is chosen, five is stipulated as a minimum number to invite, twenty the maximum (Reg. 12(6)). There is also provision for negotiated procedures in specified exceptional cases. The circumstances in which negotiated procedures may be used and the applicable conditions are similar to, though not identical with, those specified in the Supplies Regulations.

One of the problems with the Directives before amendment was that, even where contracts were advertised in accordance with the requirements set out, bidders from other member states who might wish to respond might have more difficulty in doing so than those in the domestic market, and thus need more time to prepare their bids. The Directives as amended set out generous time limits for the preparation of bids, as well as other matters relating to the award process, which authorities are required to adhere to, and these have been implemented in the Supplies and Works Regulations. (See Works Regulations 11, 12 and 13 and also Regulation 2(3) on calculation of time periods; Supplies Regulations 11, 12 and 13 and 2(3)).

The Directives expressly state that contractors may be excluded from participation in an award procedure on a number of specified grounds, such as bankruptcy or proven professional misconduct (Supplies Directive Article 26; Works Directive, Article 23). These are laid out in Supplies Regulation 13 and Works Regulation 13.

It is now clear that other conditions of eligibility, including those arising from the use of procurement to promote more general social and economic policies (see 2.2 above), may be imposed, provided they are compatible with the Treaty. This question arose in *Gebroeder Beentjes RV v Netherlands* (case 31/87 [1985] ECR 4635), in which the European Court held that it would be permissible to require compliance with a condition relating to the engagement of the long-term unemployed provided the condition was compatible with the Treaty provisions. The Directives specifically provide for the continuation of existing national provisions to reduce regional disparities and to create jobs in underdeveloped or declining areas, until 31 December 1992, when such policies must be eliminated (Supplies Directive Article 35; Works Directive Article 29a). However, such measures are permitted only to the extent that they are consistent with the Treaty, and it appears that such provisions are in fact generally incompatible with the Treaty (case C-21/88, *Du Point de Nemours Italiane SpA v United Sanitaria Locale No. 2 Di Carrara* [1991] 3 CMLR 25).

The Works and Supplies Regulations do not specifically limit the freedom of authorities to pursue secondary policies, which will thus be lawful where otherwise permitted by UK and Community law. In relation to local authorities in the United Kingdom such policies are, however, generally forbidden by the Local Government Act 1988 (see 3.1.4). In addition, such policies may be precluded by the administrative law rule that only relevant considerations may be taken into account in awarding a contract, a rule which applies both to local authorities and to other statutory bodies (see 2.9 above).

Limitations are imposed on the critieria which may be used for the selection of the successful contractor from those responding. Relevant criteria are set out in Works Regulations 20 and Supplies Regulation 20. Essentially, there are only two bases on which selection may be made; the contract must be awarded either to the contractor offering the lowest price, or to the contractor who submits the "economically most advantageous tender" - which means that commercial factors other than price, such as the quality of the goods or the proposed delivery date, may also be taken into account. Where the latter basis is chosen, authorities must state this in the tender documents, and must also state what the relevant commercial criteria will be, in order of importance where possible (Works Reg. 20(3); Supplies Reg. 20(3)). This seems primarily intended to make it easier for a review body to assess whether an authority has taken account only of legitimate criteria in making the award, should a complaint be made. It also has the effect of making the process fairer for bidding contractors, who know better how to frame their bids.

Under the Works Directive, once an award has been made, an authority must, on the request of any unsuccessful party, supply a statement of reasons for the rejection of his application or tender, within fifteen days of the request, and this is provided for in Works Regulation 22. Obviously this provision, as with the comparable requirement of domestic law under the

Local Government Act 1988 (see 3.1.4), is designed to assist contractors in challenging an award alleged to be in breach of the rules regulating the award process. There is, anomalously, no similar requirement under the Supplies Directive, and none has been included in the Supplies Regulations.

Other important provisions in the Directives are those designed to ensure that the product or works required are specified in such a way as not to favour, in practice, an individual contractor or contractors in a particular state or group. If specifications are given by reference to national standards, for example, this clearly favours contractors already producing products for the domestic market, who are likely to be domestic contractors. As has been seen (see 3.2.2) such practices have been held by the European Court to be *prima facie* in breach of the Treaty. The Directives deal specifically with this potential difficulty by requiring that - where they exist - either "national standards implementing European standards" or "European technical approvals or common technical specifications" should be used. (Supplies Directive Article 7; Works Directive Article 10). These Articles make further detailed provision to ensure that non-discriminatory specifications are used where these particular standards are not available for the product in question. Limited exceptions are provided for. An example is where use of such standards would lead to purchases being incompatible with existing equipment, provided that the authority can demonstrate a clear strategy for changeover to Europe-wide standards in the future. These Community rule relating to specifications have been implemented in Supplies Regulation 8 and Works Regulation 8.

3.2.4. *Remedies for breach of the Community procurement rules*

Where there is a breach of Community procurement rules, the Commission may bring the state concerned before the European Court under the procedure provided for in Article 169 of the Treaty of Rome. The primary method for ensuring the rules are effectively implemented is likely, however, to be actions by individual contractors.

The question of remedies for aggrieved contractors is now governed in many cases by Directive 89/665/EEC (1989 OJ L 395). This Directive places on member states an express obligation to provide certain remedies to contractors. The Directive, which is normally referred to as the Remedies, or Compliance, Directive, requires states to provide for decisions to be reviewed "effectively", and in particular "as rapidly as possible" (Article 1(1)). Article 1(2) appears to provide that remedies must be as favourable as those available for comparable breaches of domestic law. (The Article is not free from ambiguity, but if this is not its meaning, the same requirement would still apply because of the general Community law principle of non-discrimination; see 1.6 above).

Specifically, the Directive requires remedies be provided to set aside unlawful decisions (Article 1(b)), and that interim measures be made available for the suspension of proceedings pending trial (Article 1(a)). The Remedies Directive applies to actions for a breach of the Works and Supplies Directives, and also to actions for a breach of other Community rules (which would include rules in the Treaty of Rome), in the case of award procedures which fall within the scope of the Works and Supplies Directives. It also applies to breaches of domestic measures which implement the relevant Community rules.

The question of remedies is dealt with specifically by Supply Regulation 26 and Works Regulation 31. (For a detailed examination see Arrowsmith, (1992) 1 PPLR 92). These Regulations make specific provision for an action in the High Court by a contractor to obtain a) a set-aside of a decision made in breach of the rules in the Regulations or EC Treaties and b) an order from the court for the contracting authority to amend any contract documents. The latter might be used, for example, when discriminatory specifications are included in a call for tenders, to order these to be amended, without any need to strike down the whole call for tenders. In addition, it seems that an unlawful decision may be challenged by means of an application for judicial review, since the Regulations expressly provide that the above provision is without prejudice to the existing powers of the court. In relation to judicial review, it is expressly provided in the above Regulations that the court shall have the power to award an injunction against the Crown.

Although, as explained above, the Remedies Directive requires that national courts be given a power to set aside unlawful decisions, the Directive does provide that where a contract has actually been concluded, member states may limit contractors to a remedy in damages (Article 2(6)). In other words, it is open to national law to refuse to invalidate contracts even though made in breach of Community law. The UK Regulations expressly provide that the courts shall not award any remedy other than damages once the contract has been concluded. (Regs 26(6) and 31(7)). (For the effect of a breach of other public law provisions on concluded contracts in English law see 2.10 above).

It is provided that the review proceedings should be required to be brought promptly, and in any event within three months from the time when grounds for proceeding first arose, though with a discretion in the court to extend the period (Regs. 26(4)(b) and 31(5)(b)).

Standing to challenge procurement decisions must, under the Directive, be given to contractors who had, or have, an interest in obtaining a contract; and who have risked, or risk, being harmed by an infringement (Article 1(3)). This is implicitly confined to those contractors with rights under Community law. The UK Regulations limit standing to such contractors -

that is, those who are nationals of, or established in, one of the member states. (See Works Reg 4 and 31(1); Supplies Reg 4 and 31(1)).

The Remedies Directive also requires that member states provide for a power to award damages to persons harmed by an infringement. The basis on which damages are to be awarded is not specified, and the objective of the requirement - whether it is designed primarily as a method of compensation for contractors, or to deter breaches of Community law - is not clear. If it is desired to provide compensation for affected contractors, two main difficulties arise. First, there is the problem of proving that any particular contractor would have succeeded with his tender (those who would have failed even if the authority had complied with the law will, of course, have lost nothing). Second, there may be difficulty in proving the amount of profits which would have been made following a successful bid. If a contractor has to prove his loss in both respects, this may sometimes make it difficult to succeed - although in other cases there may be no problem. It is likely, in fact, that some states will adopt an approach to awarding damages which does not simply require the contractor to prove on the balance of probabilities that he has suffered loss.

With respect to the problem of proving the contract would have been won, one possibility is to award damages to all those who would have had a reasonable possibility of obtaining the contract, rather than requiring proof that any specific contractor would have been successful. However, the law might prefer not to award damages for all profits which might have been made from a successful tender, since several contractors may be able to claim a "reasonable possibility" of success, and to pay damages to all of them would be too burdensome on the authority. Thus damages might be limited to tender costs, or to a percentage value of the contract. A variant on this approach would be allow those who would have had a reasonable prospect of success to recover a proportion of the likely profit, according to the number of contenders; thus, if there were four contenders each could sue for one quarter of the likely profit. This approach is used in English contract law to deal with some cases of uncertain losses (*Chaplin v Hicks* [1911] 2 KB 786). The House of Lords recently left open the question of whether it may also be used in tort: *Hotson v East Berkshire Health Authority* [1987] 1 AC 750.

The Supplies and Works Regulations do not specify how damages are to be assessed but simply provide for damages to suppliers who have "suffered loss or damage as a consequence of the breach". This might suggest an ordinary tortious measure according to which it is for the contractor to prove both that the contract would have been won, and what profits would have been made. However, since the measure is one which is designed to give effect to obligations under EC Directives, it is open to the court to adopt the interpretation which best accords with the requirements of EC law.

It has been said that there must be "effective" review, and it is arguable that this requires that the remedies system must be dissuasive of breaches and that adequate remedies must be given for aggrieved contractors. Probably a system of review which provides for frequent interim relief will satisfy this requirement from both perspectives, even though such relief might sometimes be refused in the courts' discretion. On the other hand, if the courts are not normally willing to exercise their discretion to grant interim relief, because of the disruption it would cause to the procurement process, it may be that damages will have an important role in making the system effective (Article 2(4) specifically provides that review bodies may take account of the public and other interests in deciding whether to grant interim relief). Damages will be important since the courts are not permitted to invalidate contracts already awarded: if no interim relief is given, a contract is likely to have been concluded before the trial, and damages will then be the only remedy available. If it is difficult to obtain damages because of problems of proof, then arguably the system as a whole will not be effective. It remains to be seen whether the British courts will be willing to award interim relief readily; hostility to frequent court interference in the procurement process was expressed by both the government and groups representative of contractors when the question of remedies for breach of the procurement Directives was examined by the House of Lords (House of Lords Select Committee on the European Procurement Report, Session 1987-88: "Compliance with Public Procurement Directives", summary of evidence, at p.7). If not, then it may be that an interpretation of the Regulations is required which would make it easier to claim damages that would be the case if the ordinary tort principles were to be applied.

Apart from the possibility of an action by an aggrieved contractor to enforce Community law rules, the Commission may intervene to ensure compliance with the Directives, though it does not have sufficient resources to police their enforcement adequately - and, indeed, the Remedies Directive was introduced with the objective of making aggrieved contractors, through actions in the national courts, the primary policing mechanism. Article 3 of the Remedies Directive now provides a special procedure for Commission intervention, providing that where the Commission has evidence of a clear infringement of the Works or Supplies Directive by a member state, it may demand an explanation or correction. Where it considers that some authority in a member state is not complying with its obligations under the Directives, it may take proceedings against the relevant state in the European Court under Article 169 of the Treaty of Rome.

As indicated, the Remedies Directive does not apply to a breach of Community law in respect of an award procedure outside the Directives - for example, one which relates to a contract of a value below the relevant thresholds. Remedies in this case are the ordinary remedies provided by UK law in respect of unlawful contract awards, though subject to the Community law principles of non-discrimination and effectiveness (see 1.6 above).

3.2.5.   The Commission proposal on services contracts

There is, at the time of writing, no Directive on contracts for services, though it may be possible to rely on provisions in the Treaty of Rome to prevent discriminatory practices (see 3.2.2.2). The Commission produced a proposal for a general Services Directive in 1990 (COM (90) 372) and in August 1991 produced an amended proposal (COM 91 322 Fina 1, Aug 30 1991). It is expected that a Directive will be adopted some time in 1992.

Under the current proposal, contracts for certain services (designated "priority services") will be subjected to a regime very similar to that which applies to works and supplies contracts, as outlined above, and will contain similar exclusions and exemptions. In particular, major contracts will be required to be advertised in the *Official Journal;* competitive procedures will have to be followed; and there will be detailed rules governing specifications. With other types of services, designated "residual", as opposed to "priority", most of the rules, in particular those relating to the use of competitive procedures, will not apply (though the position on this is to be reviewed at a later date). However, provisions on the use of non-discriminatory specifications will be applicable. The proposal is discussed further by Arrowsmith, (1992) 1 PPLR 3.

If a Services Directive is enacted, it is proposed by the Commission that the Remedies Directive, discussed above, will be extended to provide the same remedies system as currently applies to enforcement of the rules on works and supplies.

3.2.6.   Directives relating to the utilities sector

As explained, the water, transport, energy and telecommunications sectors - generally now referred to as the "utilities" sector - are largely excluded from the general Works and Supplies Directives. This exclusion arose from the fact that activities in these sectors are carried on by entities which differ considerably in their legal nature between the different member states, existing at various degrees along the public-private spectrum. It was not thought appropriate to regulate these activities only when carried out by "public" bodies. This would have meant that the market in that sector would have been opened in some states, but not in others.

The Commission, however, in its 1985 White Paper considered it important to regulate this area in the drive towards 1992, because of its enormous significance; over half of total public procurement by value was estimated to arise in these sectors of activity. The Commission thus proposed to introduce regulation of this area, which would extend beyond the public sector. However, it was accepted that the general works and supplies schemes could not be applied without considerable modification to take into account the "commercial" character of many entities operating in this sector. A Directive which reflects this, differing in important ways from the general Directives, has now been enacted to regulate the award of works and supplies contracts in these utilities sectors (Directive 90/531/EEC, 1990 OJ L297). This is generally referred to as the Utilities Directive. Measures to implement the Directive are required to be put into effect in the United Kingdom by 1 July 1992, though it may be provided that the measures shall not be in effect domestically until 1 January 1993 (Article 37). There is currently a Commission Proposal for a "remedies" Directive which will set out remedies required to be given for enforcement.

The Utilities Directive applies only to contracts for works and supplies (Article 4(1)). The Directive applies (Article 2) to public authorities (which are defined in Article 1(1) in the same way as under the Works Directive). In addition it applies (Article 2) to "public undertakings". These are defined (Article 1(1)) as bodies over which public authorities may exercise a dominant influence, by virtue of ownership, financial participation, or the rules which govern the alleged public undertaking (Article 1(2)). It also includes bodies which (Article 2), in relation to the activities covered by the Directive, "operate on the basis of special or exclusive rights" conferred by the government (which are further defined in Article 2(3)). Article 6(1) provides that the Directive is to apply to contracts relating to the activities specified in Article 2; that is, the provision of drinking water, electricity, gas, heat, public transport services, public telecommunications services, terminal facilities for transport, and exploration for fuels. The provision of bus transport (Article 2(4)) and telecommunications networks (Article 8(1)) are both excluded where competitors are free to operate under the same conditions, the idea being that open competition in the award of contracts should be stimulated sufficiently by the competitive environment. Under Article 9 contracts for the purchase of water and fuels for the provision of energy are also exempt. With respect to exploration for fuels, Article 3 allows member states to apply to the Commission for an exemption from compliance where alternative arrangements in the form of non-discriminatory licensing arrangements exist for the award of contracts.

As with the other Directives the provisions govern only major contracts. The thresholds (in Article 12) are 5 million ECUs for works contracts - as with the Works Directive - and 400,000 ECUs, or 600,000 in relation to telecommunications, for supplies contracts - a higher figure than in the general Supplies Directive.

One significant difference between the Utilities Directive and the more general Directives on works and supplies is that procedures for competition are much more flexible under the former. Under the Utilities Directive open, restricted or negotiated procedures (explained at 3.2.3) may be chosen provided there is a "call for competition" published - that is, a notice of the contract requirements, inviting responses (see Article 15(1)). Detailed requirements relating to publication of the notice are set out in Article 16 and in the Annexes. In selecting contractors to participate in negotiated or restricted procedures, objective criteria must be used, which must be made available to contractors on request. As with the other Directives there are time limits for various stages of the award procedure, designed to ensure that bidders from other member states have sufficient time to respond (Articles 20 and 22). The list of exceptions, where no call for competition need be made, is fairly wide (see Article 15(2)).

As with the other Directives, there is a requirement for entities covered to publish annually a notice outlining their intended purchases over the next twelve months, to give contractors time to prepare to win the orders (see Article 17). Provided this general indicative notice is sufficiently specific and meets certain other conditions, it may serve as an actual call for competition, as well as a general notice (see Article 16).

The Directive makes specific provision for the operation of a "qualification" system (Articles 24 and 16). Qualification must be operated on the basis of "objective rules and criteria", to be made available to suppliers on request (Article 24). Under the general Works and Supplies Directives, it is not open to authorities to restrict themselves to considering only contractors on their qualifications lists.

Article 27 governs the criteria by which the award of any contract covered by the Directive must be made. It lays down terms similar, though not identical, to those in the general Works and Supplies Directive, that the award must be made on the basis of either lowest price, or "most economically advantageous" tender, with authorities being required to state in the contract documents any intention to award on the latter basis, and to list the criteria to be used.

As with the general Directives, there are detailed provisions (though not exactly the same as those in the other Directives) designed to ensure that non-discriminatory specifications are used (see Article 13).

There are also requirements that authorities keep records of contract awards which are sufficient to enable them to justify individual decisions to the Commission on request (Article 33). There is also a requirement to make certain statistical reports (Article 34).

Finally, there are, in Article 29, provisions relating to discrimination against goods originating outside the Community, which have no parallel in the general Directives. Generally, the relevant provisions of the Treaty and Directives provide rights of equal access to all firms established within the Community, and governments may not discriminate against the bids of those firms, even though the goods which are to be used in fulfilling the contract originate from third countries. Article 29, however, permits the utilities, should they wish, to reject tenders for supply contracts where more than 50% of the value of the products constituting the tender originate in third countries (Article 29(1) and (2)). In addition, it is *required* that where two or more tenders are "equivalent", and one contains more than 50% "third country products", the one which does not must be accepted (Article 29(2)). Where the price difference is not more than 3%, the tenders are "equivalent". This effectively means that entities may be required to pay more in order to buy products originating within the Community. These provisions are intended to be used as a bargaining tool in negotiating access for Community firms to the markets of third countries. They apply to the extent that the third country has concluded with the Community a Treaty providing for Community access to that third country's market, and is without prejudice to the international and other obligations of the Community and its members to third countries. Thus, it has no application to products originating in states which are signatories of the GATT Agreement on Government Purchasing.

The Utilities Directive does not at present apply generally to contracts for services. However, the Commission has recently produced a proposal for a new Directive which will extend the existing Utilities Directive to the services sector, though with certain exceptions and modifications to take account of the special nature of Services contracts (COM(91) 347, 30 Sept 1991, discussed by Arrowsmith, (1992) 1 PPLR 3).

3.2.7.   *Proposal for remedies for breach of the Utilities Directive*

In 1990 the Commission produced a Proposal (COM(90) 298) for a Directive on the remedies to be available for breach of the Utilities Directive, and it has recently issued a modified proposal (COM(91) 158 Final). On 16 September 1991 the Council adopted a Common Position on this, and this is now before the European Parliament. A Directive is expected to be adopted early in 1992.

The proposed provisions differ in some important respects from the Directive governing remedies in the non-utilities sector (discussed at 3.2.4). As with the general Remedies Directive on Works and Supplies, there is a general requirement to provide remedies which are effective and conform to the general Community principle of non-discrimination. One way in which this may be done is a system of remedies similar to that provided for breaches of the general Works and Supplies Directives; in other words, set-aside orders, damages and interim relief must be made available in an independent national forum. However, for a number of reasons it was considered inappropriate that a scheme of this kind, which involves judicial intervention in the actual procurement process, should be applied across the whole of the utilities sector, in all the member states. This is because of the commercial and/or industrial character of some entities subject to the Utilities Directive, and because of the particular need for many of the services covered to be supplied to the public without the sort of disruption which might arise from judicial interference with the procurement process. In addition, some states felt there were constitutional difficulties in granting some of the measures provided for in the "classic" remedies scheme (see Commission of the European Communities, Bulletin of the European Communities, Supp. 3/90, at pp.6-7). For these reasons, the proposal allows member states to provide that some or all of the utilities within their jurisdictions shall be exempt from the operation of the classic remedies system, and instead be subjected to a special system designed to ensure compliance. Under such a system, provision must be made for review of procurement decisions, but the review body need not be given any power actually to interfere with those decisions. Instead "other measures" must be put into effect to ensure infringements are corrected and further damage from such infringements prevented. Specifically, member states who choose this alternative approach, must provide for financial penalties to be imposed on entities which act in breach of the rules; the penalties must be capable of being imposed at an interim stage and of being conditional on an infringement's not being corrected or avoided. Damages must also be provided as a remedy for aggrieved contractors in the same way as under the "classic" remedies alternative.

As with the general Remedies Directive, the utilities remedies proposal includes a provision for action by the Commission where there is perceived to be a "clear and manifest" breach of the rules. The proposal also provides for two new enforcement concepts which have no parallel in the general Works and Supplies Directives, though arguably they would be just as usefully adopted outside the utilities sector. The first is for a conciliation procedure at Community level for which it is hoped will provide a simpler and more amicable method of dispute settlement than resort to the legal remedies provided for in the Directive. Second, the Common Position provides for a system of "attestation" (or audit) to be made available to contracting entities at their option, so that they may demonstrate to the market that their practices comply with Community law.

4

Public Employment

4.1. Introduction

Public sector employment is governed to a large extent by the same legal framework - both under statute and the common law - as employment in the private sector. Thus, for example, the regulation of industrial action in Britain takes place within the same framework in both public and private sectors; and general employment protection legislation applies to public sector workers. However, there are many important modifications relating to public employment and a number of special rules and principles apply. It is not, of course, possible to examine here all the issues relating to public employment: a detailed examination of the law, practice and policy in this area is found in Fredman and Morris, *The State as Employer: Labour Law in the Public Services* (1989).

As in the private sector, a contract of employment generally forms the foundation of the relationship between government and its employees. However, there are many important cases in public law where no contract exists, and it is unclear whether or not there is any contract between the Crown and its servants. These issues are examined below at 4.2 and 4.3.

Terms and conditions of public employment, contractual or otherwise, are normally negotiated in the ordinary way through collective bargaining. This applies to most civil servants, to workers in the National Health Service, in respect of conditions other than pay; to local government employees; and to those in the fire service and police. Because of the involvement of the central government in funding certain branches of the public service, ministerial approval is sometimes required of terms agreed through a collective bargaining process: this is the case, for example, with the terms of service of the police. In the case of National Health Service workers, though their employer is usually the Regional or Area Health Authority acting in an independent capacity (see 4.2.1), the terms of their employment are subject to any regulations or directions given by the Secretary of State for Social Services (National Health Service Act 1977, Sch.5, para. 10(1)). In a limited class of cases conditions of employment are set following the recommendations of independent non-statutory "review bodies", rather than through a collective bargaining process: such a procedure applies, for example, to judges, to senior civil servants and military officers. (For further details see Fredman and Morris, above, at pp. 142-186). In the, currently unique, case of teachers most terms are actually imposed by the Secretary of State (Teachers Pay and Conditions Act 1987, discussed by Fredman and Morris, at pp. 186-190).

In other cases statute may require certain terms to be included in a contract, once they have been fixed under a specified procedure. Where an employer fails expressly to incorporate terms which he is required by statute to include they will sometimes be considered to be included as contractual terms by operation of the statute; but whether this is so depends on the construction of the particular statute. In *Gutsell v Reeve* ([1936] 1 KB 272) it was held that an agricultural worker could sue in a contractual action for a prescribed minimum wage, though a lower amount was stated to be due in the contract. On the other hand, in *Mulland v William Sanders & Sons* ([1944] KB 78) the Court of Appeal held that legislation requiring industry generally to employ on conditions agreed through collective negotiation, or the equivalent, did not confer on employees a contractual right to sue where payment was not made accordingly. The main factors which the court seemed to regard as distinguishing the case from *Gutsell v Reeve* were the difficulty of establishing with certainty what were acceptable conditions under the legislative formula, and the fact that in *Reeve* the legislation expressly provided that terms which did not comply with it were to be invalidated, which was taken to indicate that the statutory "terms" must replace them.

In other cases, the terms themselves may be directly embodied in Regulations, as are terms applying to the police, for example (see the Police Regulations 1987, SI 1987/851). It would seem to follow from *Gutsell* that an action for breach of contract would be available for non-compliance in such a case if the relationship were generally contractual - though in the case of the police it is not (see 4.3 below). In *Roy v Kensington and Chelsea and Westminster Family Practitioner Committee* (The Times, March 27 1990) it was indicated by the Court of Appeal that Regulations governing the relationship of the parties, the Committee and General Practitioner, constituted terms of a contract between them, but this was doubted by the House of Lords (1992) 1 ALL ER 705).

Where there is failure to comply with a statutory obligation relating to employment, this will be treated as a public law case for the purpose of allowing an action for judicial review, and public law remedies, to enforce the provision. This applies even though the provision relates to a relationship which is a contractual one (*R v East Berkshire Health Authority, ex parte Walsh* ([1985] 1 QB 152).

4.2.   Crown Servants

4.2.1. Introduction

Those working in government departments, and for bodies which, though
not government departments, are Crown agents for the purpose of sharing
the general immunities of the Crown, are presumed unless otherwise shown
to be servants of the Crown itself: they are not in law servants of the body
under whose auspices they work (*Bainbridge v Postmaster-General* [1906] 1
KB 178). This means, for example, that it is the Crown which is
vicariously liable for their torts, and that they are within the scope of
section 21(2) of the Crown Proceedings Act giving immunity in certain
cases from the grant of injunctions (see 1.2.1.4).

However, not all those employed by bodies classified as Crown agents
are Crown servants: sometimes Crown agents have a power to engage
servants in their own right, so that these persons become servants of the
authority itself. A notable example is the National Health Service. It has
been held that the authorities which make up the Service are agents of the
Crown for the purpose of its general immunities (*Pfizer v Ministry of
Health* [1965] AC 512), but those working as servants (as opposed to
contractors) in the Service are the employees of the relevant Health Service
body, usually the Regional Health Authority or the Area Health Authority
(see National Health Service Act 1977 Sch.5, para.15).

Those employed by the Crown are generally engaged under the Crown's
common law powers to employ servants. In some cases an express statutory
power to employ servants is given. In *McLaren v The Home Office* ([1990]
IRLR 338) Dillon LJ expressed the view that those employed by the Home
Office under a power specifically given by section 3 of the Prison Act 1952
to employ prison officers, were in law engaged by the Home Office under
the provision and not under the common law power of the Crown. It was
clearly accepted that the Home Office acted on behalf of the Crown and the
persons so employed were Crown servants (so it is clear, for example, the
Crown would still be vicariously liable for their torts). However, Dillon LJ
expressed the view that other special rules relating to Crown employment,
such as the right to dismiss at will and possibly any presumption that the
Crown was not liable in contract (see 4.2.2 and 4.2.3 below), attached to the
fact of appointment under the common law (or "prerogative"), and not to the
status of Crown servant, so that they would not apply to prison officers. It
was suggested above, however, that such provisions should not be
considered to confer any separate contractual *capacity* on the agent, whether
as agent or otherwise, but merely to confer *authority* to contract on behalf of
the Crown (see 2.3.2). Even if they did confer a capacity to contract, it is

hard to see why it should make any difference to the application of the special Crown rules. Doubtless the judge regarded the rules as anomalous and wished to narrow their scope, but it would have been better to attack the rules more directly (as to which see 4.2.2 and 4.2.3 below), than by introducing such an anomalous distinction. These remarks were *obiter* only, and should not be followed.

The relationship between the Crown and its servants in the civil sector is governed by a detailed set of terms (see further Fredman and Morris, *The State as Employer: Labour Law in the Public Services* (1989) at pp. 21-25). The basic terms are set out in the Civil Service Pay and Conditions Code, which applies to civil servants with appropriate modifications and additions according to the nature of the job. The Code is made up of a combination of regulations which have been promulgated by Order in Council, and less formally promulgated conditions laid down as standard by the government (usually by the Treasury or the Minister for the Civil Service).

One alleged rule special to Crown servants states that they will not be liable under a warranty of authority: this was considered at 2.4.3 above. There are also some further special rules relating to Crown service, which are considered next.

4.2.2. Do Crown servants have a contract?

Servants of most public authorities have a contractual relationship with the employing authority, but there is some uncertainty as to the extent to which Crown servants are engaged under a contract (and for other public law cases where there may be no contract see 4.3 below).

One view, which appeared arguable until very recently, was that, by virtue of a restriction on the Crown's capacity to bind itself to its servants, the relationship can never be contractual. This view of the law was based mainly on cases holding that the Crown may dismiss servants at pleasure, and cannot exclude this right by contract (see 4.2.3). However, even if this particular right cannot be excluded, it does not follow that the Crown cannot be competent to contract with its servants at all. The view that the Crown cannot enter a contractual relationship with its servants was denied by the Divisional Court in *R v Civil Service Appeal Board, ex parte Bruce* ([1988] 3 All ER 686; aff'd [1989] 2 All ER 907, where this issue was not considered) - although the court found that no contract had been concluded. This view seems to have been confirmed by the Court of Appeal in *McLaren v The Home Office* ([1990] IRLR 338 (and see also *Quebec v Labrecque* [1980] 2 SCR 1057). In *McLaren* a prison officer complained that the Home Office had not adhered to the shift system agreed in the course of collective bargaining. He claimed that his relationship with the government was contractual, and that the agreed shift system had been incorporated into his contract. He sought a declaration that there had been a breach of contract, and also claimed for the amount of salary which had been withheld from him for his refusal to work the new system. The Home Office sought to have the action struck out as disclosing no reasonable cause of action, arguing that the parties' relationship was not a contractual one. The argument was successful at first instance; but the Court of Appeal allowed an appeal by McLaren, holding it to be arguable that a contractual relationship existed. It may be noted that Dillon LJ put some emphasis in reaching this conclusion on the fact that a statutory provision conferred on the Home Office the power to engage prison officers (see para.19), and this part of his judgement might seem to suggest that the fact that the employment is under statute rather than the prerogative is relevant to the existence of the power to contract. However, it has been suggested above (see 4.2.1) that such a provision is only concerned with authority, and that any contract is made under common law powers. Further, the *Bruce* case, the statements in which seem to be accepted by Dillon, was clearly concerned with common law powers; and Woolf LJ in *McLaren* does not seem to consider the existence of the statute to be of any relevance. More recently, in *R v Lord Chancellor's Department, ex parte Nangle* ([1991] IRLR 343) the Divisional Court has affirmed the view in *Bruce* that the Crown possesses a general capacity to contract with its servants at common law. This can probably now be taken as established.

An important question which still remains, however, is exactly when the parties will be considered to have an intention to create legal relations: even though the Crown may have the capacity to make a contract with its servants, it is arguable that there is a presumption that it does not normally intend to do so. Old decisions which suggest that there is no contract could arguably be accepted as still valid, but explicable on the basis that no contract was intended rather than that no contract was possible.

One such decision is that of Lord Goddard in *I.R.C. v Hambrook* ((1956) 2 QB 641), in which the Crown attempted to recover the amount of sickness payments made to an injured servant, in an action *per quod servitium amisit*. It was held that no such action lay, since it lay only for a contractual servant and a Crown servant has no contract. This view was based on some earlier cases holding that there is no contractual right to remuneration for work done in the service of the Crown (discussed below), as well as on the cases concerning dismissal at will (discussed at 4.3 below). *Hambrook* is not, however, compelling authority: the decision is one at first instance (it failed in the Court of Appeal on other grounds); as Lord Goddard himself acknowledged, the prior authorities did not compel the conclusion that the relationship is not contractual at all; and an alternative ground (that no damages could be recovered since the payments made were *ex gratia*) was also given for the decision.

The cases relied on in *Hambrook* on dismissal at will are considered at 4.3; suffice it here to repeat that the right to dismiss at will need not preclude the existence of contractual obligations covering other matters. Those cases concerning the right to recover for arrears of pay are more equivocal, but on balance favour recognition of a contractual right to recover. Older authorities had accepted the right to recover pay under the petition of right procedure, without making clear whether the right was based on contract or restitution see Logan, (1945) 61 LQR 260). However, in *Lucas v Lucas* ([1943] P.68), a first instance decision, a contractual right to recovery was denied. In *Hambrook* Lord Goddard suggested a right to recover exists but is based on restitution and not contract. Since *Hambrook* the matter has come before the Privy Council in *Kodeeswaran v Attorney General of Ceylon* ([1970] AC 1111). In this case the Judicial Committee took the view that there was a right in contract to recover arrears of wages against the Crown in right of Ceylon. The applicable law was held to be Roman Dutch, and not English, law; but Lord Diplock stated that the same conclusion would have been reached under English law, preferring the older line of authority, overlooked in *Lucas,* to later decisions. Also in support of the view that the ordinary law generally applies is an *obiter dictum* of Lord Atkin in the Privy Council in *Reilly v The King* ([1934] AC 176 at 179), that "in some offices at least, it is difficult to negative some contractual relations."

The position is complicated by the fact that the current Civil Service Pay and Conditions Code was drafted on the assumption that a contractual relationship does not generally exist under the common law, and contains an express statement, included to reflect this belief, that an appointment is not contractual in nature (on this see further Fredman and Morris, *The State as Employer: Labour Law in the Public Services* (1989) at p.68). Given this, it is arguable that even if the ordinary private law applies, and there is no presumption against an intention to contract, there will not normally be a contract since this statement overrides the presumption that a contract is intended with a master-servant relationship. It is against this background that the most recent decisions must be examined.

The first is that in *Bruce,* above, which concerned an action for judicial review by a civil servant against the Civil Service Appeals Board, to compel the Board to give reasons for a decision. The Divisional Court felt it necessary to decide if the relationship between the servant and the Crown was contractual for the purpose of determining the availability of judicial review (an aspect of the case criticised below at 4.4). Having held, as indicated above, that the Crown was *competent* to make a contract in this case, the Court held, however, that it had not done so in this case. A relevant factor was said to be the statement in the Code - which was drawn to the attention of those engaged - that no contractual relationship existed.

However, the precise significance of this factor was not explained; nor does the court make it clear whether or not a special rule or presumption applies to the Crown. The decision in *Bruce* is consistent with both 1) the view that there is a presumption against a contract, or 2) the view that the ordinary private law applies so there is *prima facie* a contract in a service relationship, the intention to contract being negatived in this case by the express statement in the Code. The later decision in *McLaren*, above, is equally ambiguous. The court did not deal expressly with the question of whether a special rule applies to the Crown, but merely confirmed that a contract was not constitutionally impossible, and held that the matter should therefore go to trial so that the judge could ascertain whether the requisite intention to contract existed.

The most recent decision is that in *R v Lord Chancellor's Department, ex parte Nangle*, above. As in *Bruce*, the question arose in considering whether a civil servant had a right to judicial review. The court held that a contract did exist, expressly declining to follow *Bruce*. The view expressed was that the ordinary private law applied, and that there was thus a strong presumption in favour of an intention to create legal relations, as in other master and servant cases. The old cases were considered to be based on a belief in the Crown's lack of capacity to contract, and now this was rejected, the court thought those cases should be disregarded. It went on to state the view that the statement in the Civil Service Code that there is no contract is intended to be purely "descriptive" of the believed position, and insufficient to override the strong presumption in favour of a contract.

Given the ambiguity of *Bruce* and *McLaren,* and the clear conflict between *Bruce* and *Nangle*, the position remains uncertain. There seems no reason why Crown civil servants should not generally be engaged under contracts, so that contractual remedies are available to both parties and other consequences attached by the law to contractual relationships may ensue without the need for special provision. It is submitted that it is the approach in *Nangle* which should be followed.

One of the main reasons the position has remained unresolved is that it has been of little importance in practice (see further Fredman and Morris, above, at pp. 63-66, and [1988] PL 480). Detailed machinery is provided for resolving employment disputes between the Crown and its servants, and on the whole works well since the Crown in practice acts as a fair employer. Further, certain issues which have depended on the existence of a contract of employment have been dealt with expressly by statute. Thus, for example, under the Employment Act 1988 a Crown servant is deemed to have a contract of service for the purpose of the economic torts (s.30), so that a person may be liable in damages for inducing a Crown servant to breach his service agreement whether or not it is a contract. Crown servants are also expressly given protection from discrimination under the Race Relations

Act 1976 (ss.75 and 76) and the Sex Discrimination Act 1975 (s.85(2)), and also are expressly entitled to the benefits of the Equal Pay Act 1970 (s.1(8)), the scope of protection of employment under these Acts being otherwise generally defined by reference to the existence of a contract of employment.

Even if the ordinary private law now applies to civil servants, it might still be argued that there is no contract with those engaged in military service. It was stated clearly by Lord Esher in *Mitchell v R.* ((1890), noted in [1896] 1 QB 12) that such a relationship is "voluntary" only on the part of the Crown, and that there may be no action for breach of contract. Even if there is normally no contract, however, there seems no reason to deprive the Crown of any capacity to make a contract should it wish expressly to do so.

4.2.3. *Dismissal of Crown servants*

Whether or not the Crown's relationship with a servant is contractual it is clear that at common law the Crown retains the right to dismiss its servants "at will" - that is, there is no cause of action in contract for a servant dismissed without notice and without cause. This was first established in cases concerning dismissal in the military service ([1877] 2 CPD 445; *De Dohse v R.* noted in (1886) 3 TLR 114), and was applied to civil servants in English law by the famous case of *Dunn v The Queen* ([1896] 1 QB 116; and see also the earlier Privy Council case of *Shenton v Smith* [1895] AC 229). It has also been said that the principle applies to preclude any restrictions on the manner in which employment is terminated - for example, through procedures for a hearing before dismissal - since this effectively fetters the right to dismiss at will (*Rodwell v Thomas* [1944] 1 KB 596).

The legal basis of the rule is not entirely certain. In many cases it has been stated that it is a rule of public policy which can only be excluded "by law" and not by any contractual term (*Dunn v The Queen*, above, per Lord Esher; *Gould v Stuart* [1896] AC 575; *Terrell v Secretary of State for the Colonies* [1953] 2 All ER 490; *Riordan v The War Office* [1959] 1 WLR 1046 at 1053-1054 per Diplock J; *R v Civil Service Appeal Board, ex parte Bruce* [1988] IRLR 338 at 340 per Dillon LJ). Certainly the rule may not be excluded simply by providing for a fixed term of service or a fixed notice period: it has been applied in several cases in the face of contractual terms of this kind (*Dunn v The Queen*, above; *Riordan v The Home Office*, above; *Denning v Secretary of State for India* (1920) 37 TLR 138; and see *Hales v The King* (1918) 34 TLR 589). However, there are some dicta stating that the rule is capable of exclusion by contract if it is made very clear that this is intended (*Shenton v Smith*, above; *Robertson v Minister of Pensions* [1949] 1 KB 227 at 231 per Lord Denning). This might arguably be achieved, for example, by including a fixed term or notice period and a provision stating either that there may be dismissal only for cause, or that the right to dismiss at will is excluded. This, it seems, is what is required in a statute for the right to dismiss at will to be regarded as excluded by the statute : mere provision for a fixed term or notice is insufficient (*Reilly v The King* [1934] AC 176; *Gould v Stuart*, above, where it was held that the dismissal at will rule had in fact been excluded).

In practice the question of whether the rule may be excluded by contract is not important, since the Civil Service Code, and the model letter of appointment issued to Crown servants, expressly reserve the Crown's right to dismiss at pleasure (see Fredman and Morris, above, at p.68).

The common law principle allowing dismissal at will has rightly been criticised (see, for example, Wade, at pp. 68-69; Craig, at p.511; Hogg, at p.175; Fredman and Morris, *The State as Employer: Labour Law in the Public Service*, at p.69). The rationale for the principle was that the State may need to rid itself of servants who might act in a manner detrimental to important national interests; but this has no application to the vast majority of civil servants, who carry out routine work. Even with more important posts, this explanation can only justify refusing specific relief, and not the denial of a remedy in damages.

Although the law of contract does not protect a Crown servant from dismissal without cause and without notice important protection is, however, provided by statute. In particular, the provisions on unfair dismissal contained in the Employment Protection (Consolidation) Act 1978 apply to Crown servants (s.138). Most Crown servants will fall within the Act, and thus the gap in the common law becomes largely irrelevant. However, some servants are not covered - for example, the Act excludes certain part-time workers and those employed less than two years. There is also a power given to the Secretary of State to certify that certain groups of civil servants as specified by him should be excluded from the Act on the grounds of national security (s.138(4)).

In addition, Crown servants may sometimes be protected against dismissal by the operation of the public law principles of judicial review. These are considered at 4.4 below.

4.3.   Office Holders

It was seen at 4.2.2 that Crown servants arguably have no contract. In addition some other groups working in the public sector are not engaged under contract. An important example is the police. The terms and conditions of their engagement are not contractual, but are set out in detail in the Police Regulations 1987. They are also not considered "employees" under the common law - for example, there was no question of vicarious liability for the actions of a police officer until this was imposed by statute on the Chief Constable, (Police Act 1964, s.48). Likewise, those on the staff on Parliament are not employed under contracts, and the terms of their engagement are also largely contained in legislation (see Fredman and Morris, *The State as Employer: Labour Law in the Public Services* (1989), at pp. 73-74).

It was once considered that all servants classed as "office holders" served without contract. "Office holders" are a special legal category whose office was once seen as a form of property, and who were for this reason given special privileges, such as rights in public law. However, the common law had never defined "office holder" with precision. Relevant factors include whether the position is established by statute and whether it continues to exist though there is no current holder of the post (see further Fredman and Morris, above, at pp.74-76). On the whole, however, a "rather impressionistic", and often arbitrary approach, which certainly does not depend on the importance of the position held, has been adopted to classification (Rideout, *Principles of Labour Law* (5th ed. 1989) at pp.17-18). It has now been held that office holders may sometimes have a contract of employment (*Barthorpe v Exeter Diocesan Board of Finance* [1979] ICR 900), reducing the significance of the concept in the context of contract. The courts have also recently indicated that where an office holder enjoys legal rights which are not derived from contract but from his status as an office holder, they will generally be construed to be as close as possible to those which would arise in a contractual situation. Thus in *Miles v Wakefield MDC* ([1987] AC 539) the House of Lords held that the position of a person seeking to recover pay when only part of his duties have been performed is *prima facie* the same whether or not there is a contract of employment.

4.4.   Employment and Judicial Review

4.4.1   Introduction

A person engaged in the public service may sometimes be able to claim the protection of the public law principles of judicial review, such as natural justice and unreasonableness. Not every decision adversely affecting a public servant, however, is subject to judicial review. The courts have said that decisions affecting a public engagement may be classified into decisions in public law and decisions which belong purely to private law, and it is only the former which are subject to review. This division into "public" and "private" law employment decisions became embedded in the law following the decision of the Court of Appeal in *R v East Berkshire Health Authority, ex parte Walsh* ([1985] QB 152), discussed at 4.4.2 below.

This public-private distinction is important, first, in determining the scope of the substantive principles of review. This is not as important as it might once have been since in relation to dismissal, which is the cause of most complaints, employees generally now have protection which overlaps to some extent with that given by administrative law principles. In particular, it seems that there is a right to a hearing under the common law for an employee, whether in the public or private sector, whenever the employer is under some sort of restriction on the grounds for dismissal (see *Stevenson v United Road Transport Union* [1977] 2 All ER 941 at 948-949, per Buckley LJ; *R v British Broadcasting Corporation, ex parte Lavelle* [1983] 1 WLR 23). Such restrictions apply to the dismissal of many employees, if not under their contract of employment then under the Employment Protection (Consolidation) Act 1978. In addition, whether an employee has been given an opportunity to present his case before dismissal is one important factor in deciding whether a dismissal has been "unfair" for the purposes of protection against unfair dismissal, which is given by the 1978 Act (see *Polkey v Dayton Services Ltd* [1988] AC 344; Bowers and Honeyball, *Textbook on Labour Law* (1990), at pp.166-168). This provides a further safeguard for those within the scope of these provisions. Finally, a right to a hearing is frequently provided for in any case under an employee's terms and conditions of employment, or at least is given as a matter of practice (on existing procedures in the public sector see Fredman and Morris, *The State as Employer: Labour Law in the Public Services* (1989), at pp.275-278). Hence, it will not be often in practice that a public employee will need to turn to public law to obtain a hearing. However, other public law principles often do not have any clear parallel in private law - for example, the principle of unreasonableness or the relevant considerations rule (invoked in *R v Hertfordshire County Council v NUPE* [1985] IRLR 258). Probably these will only apply where the decision is within the Walsh concept of a "public law" decision. This was accepted at first instance in *NUPE*, and also by Sir John Donaldson in the Court of Appeal (see p.259); but, strangely, the existence of a public law element in the particular case was not really dealt with in the appeal. Although there may be some overlap between the public law concepts of unreasonableness and proper purposes and restrictions under the contract of employment and the 1978 Act relating to dismissal, often the public law principles might apply in situations where there is no other redress.

Second, even where there has been infringement of a right under contract or the 1978 Act, a party may wish to invoke public law in order to use the Order 53 procedure, instead of either suing by writ or summons for breach of contract, or bringing a claim before an Industrial Tribunal. Thus, for example, he may have a right to a hearing under all three, but may choose to sue in public law because he prefers the procedure of Order 53. It is only where the right in respect of which he sues is one in "public law" that the Order 53 procedure is available (*Walsh*, above). It seems, however, that the court may now refuse use of Order 53 in its discretion, where a remedy is available before a Tribunal: this is considered further at 4.4.2 below. A party may, probably, on the other hand, be permitted to claim under Order 53 instead of in contract where he has both public law and contractual rights of a similar nature (see 1.3 above). Conversely, he may choose to sue by writ in contract if he prefers: he is not compelled to use Order 53 just because it is available.

Whether a claim is based on public or private law may also be relevant to the nature of relief available. In particular, it has generally been considered that where the complaint is one relating to dismissal, reinstatement is more readily available where the dismissal results from a breach of public law than from infringement of a right derived from private law. This question is examined at 4.4.3 below. It will be suggested, however, that there is no difference between the two cases in the nature of relief available.

4.4.2.   *The scope of public law*

The starting point in discussing the public-private divide in this context has been that a decision relating to employment is *prima facie* a decision in private law, and some special feature will have to be shown for the case to be brought within the realm of public law. This approach is exemplified in the leading decisions of *Ridge v Baldwin* ([1964] AC 40) and *R v East Berkshire Health Authority, ex parte Walsh* ([1985] 1 QB 152). However, in recent cases the courts have so expanded the category of special "features" which will put a decision into the realm of public law, that in practice public law decisions may almost be considered to have become the norm, rather than the exception. The law in this area is currently in a state of great flux, and hence uncertainty. It was recently emphasised by the Court of Appeal in *R v Derbyshire CC, ex parte Noble* ([1990] IRLR 332) that there is no "universal test" of what constitutes a public law case, and new categories may be created in the future. (For further discussion of recent developments see Walsh, [1989] PL 131; Fredman and Morris, *The State as Employer: Labour Law in the Public Services* (1989), ch.7 and (1991) 107 LQR 298; Freedland, (1990) 19 ILJ 199; Carty, (1991) 54 MLR 129).

Several categories of "public law" are recognised by the courts. First, it was said in *Walsh*, above, that a dismissal will be a decision in public law where there is some "statutory underpinning" or "statutory element" present.

This has been interpreted by the Court of Appeal in *R v Derbyshire CC, ex parte Noble* ([1990] IRLR 332) as meaning that there must be a statutory element "which has a bearing upon the procedure for dismissal" itself. It is insufficient that, for example, the power to *appoint* persons to the particular type of post is given by statute. In *Noble* a deputy police surgeon sought review of a decision not to employ him further, alleging a breach of natural justice. It was held that any claim to a hearing could only be a claim in private law, and could not be pursued in an action for judicial review. Though the power to appoint police surgeons was given by statute there was nothing in the statute on dismissal. In order for this requirement to be satisfied it also seems that the provisions on dismissal must derive their force directly from statute. In *Walsh,* which concerned an application for judicial review by a senior NHS nursing officer who had been dismissed, it was argued that there was a sufficient statutory element, in that the terms of such employees' engagement were required by statute to be included in their contracts by the employing Health Authority, once they had been approved by the Secretary of State. However, this was considered insufficient. Although there could have been an action for judicial review to ensure the terms (including those on dismissal) were included, they derived their actual effect only from the contract, and not directly from the statute.

A case where judicial review was held to be available, on the other hand, is *R v Secretary of State for the Home Department, ex parte Benwell* ([1985] 1 QB 554), where it was held that a dismissed prison officer could proceed by way of judicial review, where the procedures relating to dismissal were embodied in a legislative code. Uncertainty in this area is exacerbated by the fact that it may not be in every case where statutory procedures have a bearing on the decision that "public law" will apply: it was stated in *Noble* by Woolf LJ (at 374) that this is merely a "significant indication" that the decision is one in public law.

Finally, on this category, although the cases have concerned dismissals the same test - the need for a statutory element which relates to the actual decision challenged - will no doubt also apply to matters such as suspension and demotion.

Two further categories of "public law" case were recently outlined in *obiter dicta* by Woolf LJ in *R v Secretary of State for the Home Office, ex parte McLaren* ([1991] IRLR 338), in which he sought to rationalise some of the previous decisions. First, he said that judicial review is available "where there exists some disciplinary or other body established under statute to which the employer or the employee is entitled to or required to refer disputes affecting their relationship", provided that it is not a purely domestic or "wholly informal" tribunal (at 342). On this basis decisions relating to civil servants would generally be reviewable, since such decisions are generally within the ambit of the Civil Service Appeal Board. Such decisions were held renewable in *R v Civil Service Appeal Board, ex parte Bruce* ([1988] 3 All ER 686), which Woolf explained in McLaren as based on the "tribunal" ground, though the reasoning of the court was rather different (see further below), and also *R v Civil Service Appeal Board, ex parte Cunningham* ([1991] 4 All ER 310). It has been held that the internal disciplinary proceedings of a government department, on the other hand, are a "domestic" procedure for the purpose of this rule, and not amenable to review (*R v Lord Chancellor's Department, ex parte Nangle* [1991] IRLR 343).

Second, Woolf LJ considered that review would be available where the employee is "adversely affected by a decision of general application" (at 342), as opposed to a decision taken about him particularly. On this basis he explained the decision in *Council of the Civil Service Unions v Minister for the Civil Service* ([1985] AC 374), in which the House of Lords held that a decision to ban union membership amongst staff at the government's communications headquarters was in principle subject to review (although the unions' claim to a hearing was denied on the facts for national security reasons). The question of the presence of a sufficient "public law" element for review had not been raised in the *Civil Service* case itself. The availability of review in this type of case seems to be accepted by Nolan J in *R v London Borough of Hammersmith and Fulham, ex parte NALGO* ([1991] 1 IRLR 249), although there was held to be no unlawful conduct on the facts.

In addition it may be that all those who work for public bodies who do not have a contract of service may obtain the benefit of judicial review. This was the approach in *Bruce*, above. It was held by the Divisional Court that the fact that the servant did not serve under a contract was conclusive of the fact that a sufficient element of public law existed for review of decisions relating to the engagement. This suggests that it is only where there is a contract of employment that there is a need to look for some "special" element of public law, such as the "statutory underpinning", the tribunal, or the "general" decision: it is the fact of the existence of the private law contractual relationship which puts employment decisions, *prima facie*, into the "private law" category. It was explained at 2.9 above that the courts have generally been reluctant to review contractual decisions and have traditionally required some special public law element before they will do so, and *Bruce* appears to rationalise the exemption from review of employment decisions as turning on this general rule. However, it was also explained at 2.9, that the courts now appear, quite rightly, to be abandoning this restrictive approach to contract in other contexts, and *Bruce* is an unfortunate decision insofar as it tends to reinforce the old approach. More recently Woolf LJ in *McLaren*, as just explained, suggested that *Bruce* turned on the fact that the decision challenged was one by a formal disciplinary tribunal; and in *Nangle*, above, the court also rejected the suggestion in *Bruce* that all non-contractual powers are reviewable.

Finally, there is some suggestion that "office holders" may have an automatic right to judicial review. This was the reason for affording a right to a hearing under public law for a Chief Constable who was dismissed in the famous case of *Ridge v Baldwin*, above. As was explained at 4.3 above, the scope of the category of office holders is unclear. In most cases, a decision affecting an office holder will be a public law decision under one of the other categories outlined above. For example, public law will generally apply to the police both because police officers have no contract and because the terms of their engagement are laid out in regulations (see 4.3 above). Probably, however, it is also recognised as a separate category. This was accepted at first instance by *R v Hertfordshire CC, ex parte NUPE;* though it was doubted by Sir John Donaldson an appeal (see [1985] IRLR 258).

It is clear that the courts have recently been prepared to widen the definition of "public law" in the employment context. Thus more cases are potentially within the scope of public law rules, remedies and procedures. However, the importance of this in practice appears to have been reduced by the recent decision of the Divisional Court in *R v Civil Service Appeal Board, ex parte Bruce*, above. Although it was held that the case did fall within public law, the court refused, in the exercise of its discretion, to grant a remedy, since the applicant was pursuing his case before the industrial tribunal, and this was regarded by the court as a more convenient and expeditious forum. The Court of Appeal refused to interfere, on the basis that the exercise of discretion was not manifestly wrong (see [1989] 2 All ER 907). As was explained at 4.4.1 above, an employee with public law rights relating to dismissal may frequently have an alternative remedy before a tribunal. It was, in fact, probably this desire to compel public servants to use tribunals, where available, which led the Court of Appeal in *Walsh* to take a restrictive approach to the definition of public law. If this policy of pushing individuals towards tribunals is accepted, the exercise of discretion to refuse a remedy is a better way of implementing it than by adopting a restrictive definition of public law, since the latter approach will exclude many cases where there is no other remedy, as well as those where there is. Thus recent developments towards widening the class of cases within public law and recognising a discretion to refuse a remedy are to be welcomed. Many of those whose employment is outside the scope of tribunals - for example, certain part-time employees, or those employed for less than two years - thus now have some protection, through public law; and those who are excluded generally from statutory protection on grounds of national security (see 4.1 above) may also often be within the scope of public law, though in practice a claim may be refused where national security considerations arise, as in the *Civil Service* case. General decisions which do not relate to particular individuals will also, of course, generally be resolved in the public law forum, since tribunal proceedings are not appropriate in this type of case. Those who do have a remedy before a tribunal, on the other hand, must use it.

However, although the specialist tribunal system may indeed provide a better forum for dealing with all employment questions, there are difficulties with the exercise of the courts' discretion in this area. In many cases, a remedy before a tribunal may not be as favourable as one in public law: the substantive protection given may not be so generous and, perhaps more important, reinstatement is not normally available before a tribunal, but is considered to be generally available in a public law action (though see further 4.4.3 below). It seems unfair for the court to exercise its discretion to deprive the applicant of a public law remedy in such a case. This means that public employees deliberately excluded from the employment protection legislation may, ironically, often be in a better position than those within it, since they *will* be able to rely on public law. It is not entirely clear how "equivalent" tribunal protection must be in order for the applicant to be deprived of a public law remedy, but it seems from *Bruce* that he will normally be required to go to a tribunal even if his remedies there are less satisfactory: May LJ said (at 664) that judicial review will be allowed only in a "very exceptional case".

The current position may be criticised. First, the definition of "public law" is difficult to defend. Why, for example, should an employee have public law rights when the decision affects a whole group, but not where it affects him alone? Similarly, the question of whether there is a "statutory underpinning" to an employment relationship is largely a product of historical accident, and does not provide any sensible basis for determining which decisions should be subject to judicial review. It is, in fact, difficult to see why a distinction should be made between different types of public employment at all, and arguably all should be reviewable in the same way. Similarly, it has been argued that *all* contractual activities should *prima facie* be subject to review (see 2.9 above).

Second, some difficulties arise from the fact that there is more than one forum for dealing with public employment disputes: remedies may be available under Order 53, in tribunals, or, with an action for breach of contract, in the High or County Court. Many recent cases have been concerned with issues relating to the correct forum for procedure, a wasteful state of affairs. The availability of different forums also makes it more difficult to develop coherent and consistent principles: it seems odd that the scope and nature of the hearing required before dismissal, for example, may differ under public law, the "private" common law and the Employment Protection (Consolidation) Act 1978. It is also strange that the availability of remedies governing reinstatement appears, theoretically, to be based on totally different principles according to whether the action is one for breach of contract, breach of public law, or breach of the 1978 Act (see further 4.4.3 below). Fredman and Morris have argued that questions relating to public employment should all be dealt with in a single forum (see (1991) 107 LQR 298; *The State as Employer: Labour Law in the Public Services* (1989) at pp.270-271), and it is difficult to disagree with this conclusion.

4.4.3.   *Consequences of a breach of public law*

As was explained at 2.10, the consequence of a breach of public law in the purported termination of an employment relationship, whether contractual or non-contractual, is that the action will not be effective to bring the relationship to an end (*Ridge v Baldwin* [1964] AC 40; *Malloch v Aberdeen Corporation* ([1971] 1 WLR 1578). It was suggested that the exercise of other private law rights is likewise ineffective when done in breach of public law.

   Some problem arises over the effect of the remedies available in such a case. It has generally been assumed that where there is a dismissal in breach of public law a remedy will be given to reinstate the applicant, even though a specific remedy would not be granted under the ordinary principles of private law (*Ridge v Baldwin*, above; *Malloch v Aberdeen Corporation*, above, per Lord Reid and Lord Wilberforce; *R v Derbyshire CC, ex parte Noble* ([1990] IRLR 332 at 337 per *McCowan* LJ; and see the views of Collins, (1984) 13 ILJ 174 at p.174). Originally this was because only those regarded as "office holders" were entitled to the benefit of public law, and reinstatement was seen as justified in order to restore the "property" in the office to the applicant. However, public law has now extended far beyond this class (see 4.4.2), and the availability of specific relief has been assumed to be extended with it. However, as was argued at 2.10 above, it is illogical that the principles governing specific relief should be different according to whether or not the dispute between the parties arises from a breach of public law.

   Recent cases have expanded the availability of specific remedies in private law, and it is suggested that the cases where such relief has been given in public law can now be reconciled with the private law rules. It seems that, provided it can be shown that damages are an inadequate remedy, specific relief will generally be given under the private law where such relief would be "workable" : this was the formulation of the test in the recent High Court decision in *Robb v London Borough of Hammersmith and Fulham* ([1991] IRLR 72). This will normally apply where there is still "trust and confidence" between the parties, which seems to apply where the employer has confidence in the ability of the employees to do the job, and the employee has a satisfactory relationship with those with whom he will be working (these principles can be extracted from *Hill v Parsons* [1972] Ch 305 and *Powell v London Borough of Brent* [1988] ICR 176). The court may also give specific relief to the extent that the applicant does not seek to be reinstated to his post, but simply wishes to hold the contract on foot for some other purpose. Thus in *Robb*, above, an injunction was granted to prevent the authority from dismissing the applicant without carrying out the contractual hearing procedures which were required before a dismissal, where the plaintiff did not seek reinstatement but simply to justify himself at a hearing. In such a case there is no difficulty with the workability of a limited order which does not require actual reinstatement.

The leading public law cases where specific relief has effectively been given seem to be explicable in accordance with these criteria. The foremost decision of this type is *Ridge v Baldwin*, above; but in this case the dismissed party, a Chief Constable, did not wish to return to work, but merely to establish that this dismissal had been ineffective, so that he could claim pension rights. In *Malloch v Aberdeen Corporation*, above, the House of Lords considered that reinstatement of a dismissed schoolteacher would follow from the reduction of an invalid decision to dismiss; but this was a case where there appeared to be no problems of "workability" in the relationship. The teacher was dismissed because the authority considered itself bound in law to dismiss a teacher who was not on the appropriate register.

In other cases relief has been denied, and these can be cited to support an argument that the fact of a breach of public law should make no difference to the principles which apply in granting relief. In *Chief Constable of the North Wales Police, ex parte Evans* ([1982] 1 WLR 1155) the House of Lords considered a case where a Chief Constable of Police had resigned after being offered a choice between resignation and dismissal. He sought reinstatement, on the grounds that the decision to dismiss him, and thus the demand for his resignation, was invalid for breach of natural justice. The House refused to grant an order for mandamus to compel the authority to accept the applicant's services in this case, but instead gave a declaration that the applicant was to be treated as if he had not resigned, *except* for the question of reinstatement. The House did not make express references to private law principles, and indeed seemed to accept a presumption in favour of reinstatement. Clearly, however, it was primarily influenced in refusing relief by the fact that a continued relationship was not "workable", and the case is now best explained as an example of the ordinary private law rules. A case which supports the private law approach more explicitly is *Francis v Municipal Councillors of Kuala Lumpur* ([1962] 1 WLR 1411), in which a municipal employee was dismissed in a manner alleged to be *ultra vires* since it was not carried out by the party to whom the function of dismissal was entrusted by statute. The Privy Council advised that if *ultra vires* were proved a declaration should not be made that the contract was still in effect, because of the principle that there cannot normally be specific performance of a contract of service (see pp.1417-1418; and see also the views of Lord Guest in *Malloch v Aberdeen Corporation*, above, at 1594). It is submitted that the courts should in all cases grant specific relief according to the principles which generally apply in private law; and that those cases which appear to espouse a more generous approach where a remedy is sought in public law must now be explained as turning on the operation of the ordinary rules. This ought to apply whether or not the employment is in the nature of an office.

5

Tort: General Principles

5.1. Application of the Private Law of Tort

With tort, as with other areas of civil liability, the basic principle is that the ordinary private law, administered by the ordinary courts, applies to public authorities. There are, however, many qualifications and modifications to the private law model, as well as rules to deal with problems which are special to government - for example, the question of liability for *ultra vires* action. All these matters may be considered as part of the law of government torts.

Two related aspects of the private law model need to be emphasised.

The first is that the substantive torts of private law apply to government: it is subject in principle to the ordinary rules of negligence, nuisance, trespass and so on. Conversely there is no general regime of public law torts which applies to the State but not to others, though there is one tort, misfeasance in public office, which can be said to be a special public law tort, and also a number of special principles of liability imposed by statute. These matters, along with the question of *ex gratia* compensation, which is an important feature of public "law" in this area, are examined in chapter 9.

The second - related - feature of the private law approach is that where loss results from government activity both the public authority concerned and the individuals who were engaged in carrying out that activity on its behalf are treated in the same way as if the State were a private person. This gives rise to three main types of liability : the personal liability of those who act for the State; the vicarious liability of the State for the torts of those who act on its behalf; and the direct liability of public authorities themselves.

As to the first of these, the "private law" approach means that individuals doing work for the government are personally liable under the general law for losses which they cause whilst engaged in government business, in the same way as an individual is personally liable for the torts which he commits during the course of his work for a private employer. A driver who carelessly injures a pedestrian, for example, is liable personally in tort, whether driving for pleasure, or driving for his employer on business; and this applies equally where the employer is a public authority. It may be noted here that a person is liable himself where he directs or authorises another to commit a tort, and this principle has sometimes been used to hold senior government officials liable for torts committed by their subordinates. A famous illustration is found in the Supreme Court of Canada decision in *Roncarelli v Duplessis* ([1959] 16 DLR 2d 689) where the Prime Minister of Quebec was held personally liable for misfeasance in public office for ordering a government servant to cancel a liquor licence for reasons known to be improper - namely, the fact that the licensee was a Jehovah's Witness. It was this feature of our law, the personal liability of government servants under the ordinary law, which was emphasised by Dicey in his eulogy of our system of governmental liability (see *Introduction to the Law of the Constitution* (10th ed., 1959) and the discussion at 1.1 above).

As will be seen in the following chapters, although the private law applies in principle, there are modifications to take account of the fact that an individual is acting in the conduct of government business. Thus, for example, the defences of statutory authority (see 5.2.4) and judicial immunity (see 5.2.2) operate to protect individuals from personal liability; and likewise those acting for public authorities are screened from any personal liability by the general immunity from liability in negligence given in respect of certain government policy decisions (see 6.2 below).

It has sometimes been suggested that any personal liability on the part of state servants should be abolished entirely, leaving a victim of what would otherwise be tort by the servant solely to a remedy against the State. Where a public servant commits a tort in the course of his employment the State will normally be vicariously liable, and it would clearly be possible to impose some liability on the part of the State, whilst abolishing the personal liability of the servant himself. (The State's liability would probably not then be designated vicarious since vicarious liability depends on showing a tortious act by another, as explained below). The arguments for personal immunity are that no remedy is needed since the State will provide a solvent defendant; that potential personal liability in damages is an unduly harsh potential penalty and may lead to undue caution by public officials in the execution of their duties; and that misconduct can be dealt with adequately by internal disciplinary procedures. Hogg, however, has opposed such a suggestion, arguing persuasively that there is no evidence to support the "undue caution" theory, and that, on the other hand, "an immunity for Crown servants detracts from the powerful symbolism of equal treatment of public and private employees" (at p.145).

A person is vicariously liable for the torts of his servants committed in the course of their employment, and sometimes for the torts of other persons; and these principles apply equally to public authorities. For liability, there must normally have been a tort committed by the person for whom the authority is responsible. Thus if a servant has immunity - for example, because he is acting within jurisdiction in the exercise of a judicial

function (see 5.2.2) - the authority will not be liable. A possible exception
to this principle may have been created in cases holding that an employer
could be liable for a husband who in the course of employment negligently
injured his own wife, though at the time a wife could not sue her husband in
tort (*Smith v Moss* ([1940] 1 KB 424; *Broom v Morgan* [1953] 1 QB 597 -
where the decision was explained on the basis that there was a tort, but no
action could be brought). These are considered "anomalous cases decided on
pragmatic grounds" (McKendrick, (1990) 53 MLR 770 at 780) and others
are unlikely to arise.

Although the principles of vicarious liability have long been applied to
public bodies other than the Crown, until 1947 the Crown itself could not
be held vicariously liable (see further 5.4.1 below). This represented an
important gap in the system of public liability in the United Kingdom, and
Dicey has frequently been criticised for his failure to give it due attention.
Another exception to the principle of vicarious liability was that there could
be no liability for persons exercising an "independent discretion" in carrying
out government functions; but this exception has also now been abolished
(Crown Proceedings Act 1947 s.2(3)).

Finally, a public authority is directly liable for torts attributable to the
authority itself. Thus, for example, an authority which occupies land is
subject to the usual civil duties of an occupier; and as an employer it is
under the duties owed generally by employers to their employees.

Until 1947 the Crown was largely immune from direct as well as
vicarious liability (see 5.4.1). The 1947 Crown Proceedings Act has
substantially, although it seems not entirely, abrogated this general
immunity (see 5.4.4 below).

5.2. Immunities from Suit

Although the private law applies in principle the government enjoys certain
immunities from suit. Some can best be examined in relation to the
operation of individual torts, but others can be considered here in general
terms.

5.2.1. Acts of State

The defence of act of state may apply in circumstances to negate liability in
tort. (For further discussion see Hogg, at pp.143-144; Wade and Bradley,
Constitutional and Administrative Law (10th ed. 1985) at pp.316-320; Hood
Phillips and Jackson (7th ed. 1987), at pp.278-284). Where it applies it will
shield both the individual and the Crown from any liability.

The defence applies in certain cases where an act is committed on the
orders of the Crown. There is little authority on the question of whose act

may be considered to be the act of the Crown for this purpose, but it seems that the defence should only apply in relation to the act of the Cabinet, or possibly, an individual Minister (see Hogg, at pp.143-144; and for discussion *AG v Nissan,* [1990] AC 179 (Lord Reid). It is generally considered now that this defence is not available at all against a British subject (see *AG v Nissan,* above). It may, however, still apply in certain cases to actions brought by aliens. It seems that it is available against any alien with respect to acts done outside the jurisdiction (*Buron v Denman* (1848) 154 ER 450). With respect to an act done inside the jurisdiction it appears not to be available against aliens generally (*Johnstone v Pedlar* [1921] 2 AC 262); but it may be available against those who are enemy aliens.

5.2.2. Judicial immunity

5.2.2.1. Introduction
Judicial officers acting in a judicial capacity have a wide immunity from suit in tort (see further Brazier [1976] PL 397; Thompson (1958) 21 MLR 517). Hogg (at p.146) suggests that this may be regarded as an example of the general immunity enjoyed by public officials acting within the scope of their statutory or prerogative authority (see 5.2.4 below). In applying this general defence, the question of what acts have been authorised is a matter of construction of the power - conferring provisions in each case. In the case of judicial officers a particularly wide immunity from tort liability is conferred, as is outlined below. On Hogg's theory, this wide judicial immunity is explained on the basis of a presumption that Parliament generally intends to give such officers a particularly wide jurisdiction. An alternative explanation, however, is that it is an immunity given by the common law of tort. In relation to negligence this might be framed by saying that judicial officers do not owe a duty of care; with other torts it may simply be said that judicial officers have exemption in certain circumstances. This latter approach has been adopted in developing an immunity from negligence for some other public officers for policy reasons (see 6.2 below). It seems preferable to an approach which requires the law to say that Parliament has "authorised" the commission of acts which would otherwise be tortious. The immunity is not based on the fact that such acts are justifiable or acceptable - which is suggested by the idea of statutory authorisation - but on broader policy grounds.

The main argument in favour of immunity is that judges should be able to act with freedom and independence of thought, and should not be inhibited by a fear of legal actions, which might, moreover, be vexatious: "It is better to take the chance of judicial incompetence, irritability, or irrelevance, than to run the risk of getting a bench warped by apprehension of the consequences of judgements which ought to be given without fear or favour" (Winfield and Jolowicz, at p.664). It has been suggested, however, with some force, that the concerns behind the immunity doctrine do not justify the absolute immunity which is generally given at present, but only a rule of qualified immunity, which would not preclude liability where a judge acts "maliciously" or "recklessly" (see Olowofoyeku, (1990) 10 LS 271).

The tort system which currently governs the question of compensation for judicial errors is arguably ill suited for the task. There is a widespread feeling that the burden of judicial errors should be borne by public funds and not by innocent persons who are prejudiced by them, particularly where this prejudice is serious - for example, where a person serves a term of imprisonment when he is in fact innocent of any crime. The present system is predicated on the need to affix responsibility for a wrong on a particular individual, and consequently to balance the need to protect that individual from liability against the interests of the victim. This has led to the immunity rules, and means that many victims may go uncompensated, as explained below. A better system would probably be one which provides automatic compensation from State funds for certain types of losses resulting from judicial errors, which does not depend on any notion of "wrongful" conduct by a judicial officer. This view is reflected to a certain extent in cases of unjustified imprisonment in section 133 Criminal Justice Act 1988, which now provides a right to compensation for those wrongfully convicted, in limited circumstances, and in the government's practice of making *ex gratia* payments to victims in some cases. These developments are discussed further at 9.3 below. What follows is an outline of the position under the law of tort.

5.2.2.2. The immunity of superior court judges

The immunity from suit of superior court judges is wide. There has, in fact, been no reported case in which a superior court judge has been held liable in tort for an act done in his judicial capacity. However, some liability may exist: in the House of Lords in *Re McC* ([1985] AC 528) Lord Bridge stated (at p.540) that a superior court judge could be liable if he does an act which he *knows* that he has no right to do. Thus the Lord Chief Justice, he said, would be liable if he were to order the imprisonment of a defendant acquitted of a criminal offence by a jury, because the Chief Justice believed the jury verdict to be perverse. It seems clear, on the other hand, that there can be no liability on the part of a superior court judge who believes himself to be acting within his powers, even though he is actuated by malice (Anderson v Gorrie [1895] 1 QB 668; *Sirros v Moore,* [1975] QB 188 at 132-133; *Re McC,* above, at 540-541 per Lord Bridge).

5.2.2.3. Immunity of other judicial officers

Acts within jurisdiction
A judge of an inferior court will, under the common law, be immune from
liability provided he acts within jurisdiction. As with superior court judges
the immunity will apply even though he is actuated by malice (*Anderson v
Gorrie* [1895] 1 QB 668; *Sirros v Moore* [1975] QB 118; *Re McC* [1985]
AC 528 at 540-1 per Lord Bridge and 559 per Lord Templeman).

There was at one time some debate as to whether this general common
law immunity extended to justices of the peace. One view was that they
could be liable for acts within jurisdiction where they acted maliciously and
without reasonable and probable cause (for discussion and authority see
Thompson (1958) 21 MLR 517). On the other hand, in the House of Lords
in *Re McC* ([1985] AC 528), Lord Bridge, with whom Lord Elwyn Jones
agreed, and Lord Templeman, opined that no such liability exists. The
question had not, however, been argued before the House and for this reason
Lords Keith and Brandon expressly declined to consider it, so that the
common law position might still be considered to be open. Section 44 of
the Justices of the Peace Act 1979, as amended by the Courts and Legal
Services Act 1990, section 108, now provides that no action shall lie
against a justice of the peace or a justices clerk where he acts in the
execution of his duty with respect to any matter within his jurisdiction.

Acts outside or in excess of jurisdiction
A judge who acts outside his jurisdiction does not enjoy any immunity from
tort. A famous illustration is *The Marshalsea Case* ((1612) 77 ER 1027).
The court had jurisdiction only over members of the King's household, but
purported to order the imprisonment of a person who was not a member.
The judge was held liable in damages for false imprisonment. Liability at
common law will exist even though the judge believes in good faith that his
act is within jurisdiction (Re McC [1985] AC 528).

A judge will not be required to compensate for any act outside his
jurisdiction which causes damage, but only where his act constitutes a tort
under the general private law. This is an aspect of the general principle that
there is no automatic liability for damage caused by unlawful administrative
action (see 9.2.1 below).

The meaning of the concept of jurisdiction for the purpose of the
general law of judicial immunity was discussed in *Re McC,* above, by Lord
Bridge (at 544-552; and see also Lord Templeman at 558). Lord Bridge
considered that a judicial officer would be acting outside jurisdiction if he
had no competence to entertain proceedings at all, for example, because there
was no jurisdiction over the person (*The Marshalsea Case,* above), the place
(*Houlden v Smith* (1850) 14 QB 841) or "the subject matter" (*Polley v*

Fordham (No.2) [1904] 2 KB 345, where the court purported to try an action which was out of time; and see also *R. v Manchester City Justices ex parte Davies* [1989] QB 631 per Neill LJ). His Lordship also considered (at 546) that magistrates would be acting outside jurisdiction where they failed to inform the defendant of his right to jury trial. On the other hand, where justices have "duly entered" on the trial, he considered that "only something quite exceptional occurring in the course of their proceeding to a determination can oust their jurisdiction so as to deprive them from protection from civil liability for a subsequent trespass". His Lordship made it clear that a judicial officer would not be treated as acting outside jurisdiction for immunity purposes in every case where his jurisdiction could be quashed for "excess of jurisdiction" under the principle of *Anisminic v Foreign Compensation Commission* ([1969] 2 AC 147, as to which see Craig ch.9; Wade ch.9). In *Re McC,* however, it was held that there *was* an excess of jurisdiction in sentencing a juvenile to detention without first informing him, as required by statute, of his right to apply for legal aid. Lord Bridge stated that there might also be excess of jurisdiction for the purpose of judicial immunity where there was other "gross and obvious irregularity of procedure" or breaches of natural justice, giving examples of where a judge absented himself from part of the hearing, or the court refused to hear the defendant's evidence.

An excess of jurisdiction arising from the conduct of an inquiry which has been "duly entered" was also found by the majority of the Court of Appeal in *R v Manchester City Justices, ex parte Davies*, above. A trader had been sentenced to imprisonment for failing to pay rates. This sanction was available to the court only where the failure to pay resulted from culpable neglect, but the justices had failed to make inquiry into the question of culpability, and their order was quashed. It was held that the failure to make the inquiry took the justices outside their jurisdiction. Under the old law by which this case was decided an action for false imprisonment was thus available though this would no longer be the case in the absence of bad faith (see the discussion of the Justices of Peace Act 1979 below). Ormrod LJ dissented on the jurisdiction point, on the basis that such a narrow view of jurisdiction would substantially reduce the protection available to judicial officers under the common law.

Despite the statement of Lord Bridge in Re McC that only rarely will an error in the course of an inquiry "duly entered" take an officer outside jurisdiction, the decisions in Davies and in Re McC itself do seem to suggest that the courts have not been reluctant to find an excess of jurisdiction when actually faced with an innocent victim of a judicial error. The individual officer responsible will often be indemnified from public funds and these cases have shown sympathy for the view that the cost of any error should be borne by public funds rather than the innocent victim himself. As has been indicated (see 5.2.2.1), a policy of allocating the cost of judicial errors to the State is now reflected in a statutory provision giving compensation in certain cases of wrongful conviction, and in the practice of making *ex gratia* payments to some of those affected by such errors.

With respect to justices of the peace and their clerks who act outside jurisdiction liability is, however, governed expressly by statutory provisions, which contrary to the policy of *Re McC,* provide for only very limited liability. Under the old section 45 of the Justices of the Peace Act 1979, it had been expressly provided that there could be liability for acts done outside jurisdiction though there was no malice or absence of reasonable and probable cause. Under a new section 45, however, which was substituted by s.108 of the Courts and Legal Services Act 1990, it is provided that with respect to an act or omission by a justice or his clerk in the proposed execution of his duty with respect to a matter not within his jurisdiction, there is liability only if it is proved that he acted in bad faith. The decisions in *Davies* and *Re McC* were based on the old rule of general tortious liability, and there would be no liability on the facts of either case under the new provision. This is unfortunate.

5.2.2.4. *Immunity under the law of defamation*

The above principles apply to tort generally. With regard to the tort of defamation there is a special rule which gives an absolute immunity from suit to all those involved in judicial proceedings. This includes, of course, those involved as judicial officers (*Glick v Hinchcliffe* (1967) 111 SJ 927. On what constitutes "judicial proceedings for this purpose see Winfield and Jolowicz, at pp.333-334).

5.2.3. *Immunity of the Post Office*

A specific statutory immunity from tort liability in respect of any act or omission in relation to postal packets is given to the Post Office and its servants and agents by section 29 Post Office Act 1969. This applies also to any claim framed in bailment (*American Express Co. v British Airways Board* [1983] 1 WLR 701). It was explained at 2.2.2 above that there is normally no action in contract in such a case either. However, if a person does not wish to take the risk of loss or damage himself it is open to him, in the case of inland mail, to pay to send the package by registered mail. In this case there is a statutory cause of action which allows recovery where damage is caused by the wrongful act, neglect or default of an agent or servant of the Post Office (s.30(1) Post Office Act 1969), such default etc being presumed unless it is shown otherwise (s.30(2)). Damages are assessed on a tortious basis (*Building and Engineering Scheme Holidays*

Management v Post Office [1966] 1 QB 247) subject to limitations in
section 30(3) of the Act, which provides for a maximum liability of the
market value of the package, or of the amount set out in a scheme made in
regulations under the Act, whichever is the less.

5.2.4. The defence of prerogative or statutory authority

The law of tort is seen as imposing liability for acts which are wrongful.
Where an act is authorised by law, either by statute or under the prerogative,
it cannot be wrongful, and it cannot therefore give rise to liability in tort,
though there would be liability in the absence of specific authorisation.
Thus, for example, where statute authorises the construction and operation
of public works which inevitably interfere with the interests of
neighbouring landowners, these landowners cannot maintain an action in
nuisance, though there would be a nuisance in the absence of any
authorising statute (see further 8.1.2 below). Similarly, where a person is
arrested within the lawful authority to arrest given to the police, and
subsequently released because his innocence is established - a mistake was
made - he cannot claim damages, though the act of detention would
constitute the tort of false imprisonment in the absence of any authority for
the arrest. It need not, of course, follow that because the act is lawful
compensation should not be payable, but the courts have generally held that
no compensation is due in the absence of a tort : see further 9.3 below.
   The scope of the authorisation is determined by the construction of the
statute in each case - or by the principles of the common law where the
authority relied on derives from the prerogative. How far a general authority
conferred on a public body is intended to confer the power to do an act which
would otherwise be a tort is often a difficult question, and in some contexts
the courts have worked out detailed principles of statutory interpretation to
deal with the issue. The most important are examined later in considering
liability under specific heads of tort (see chapter 6 (negligence); chapter 8
(nuisance and liability under *Rylands v Fletcher*); and in relation to false
imprisonment see *Hague v Deputy Governor of Parkhurst Prison* [1991] 3
All ER 733).
   It has generally been assumed that where legislative authority is given
to a party to do an act which would normally be tortious, that act may be
done not only by the named party and his servants but also by his
independent contractors (see, for example, *Darling v Attorney General*
[1950] 2 All ER 793).

5.3. Liability for Ultra Vires Action

There has never been serious doubt that where a tort occurs in the course of *intra vires* activity the government may be liable, either directly or vicariously. It might be said that any tortious act by the authority itself, at least by a statutory authority of limited capacity, is by definition *ultra vires*: Parliament cannot be said to have authorised the commission of wrongful acts. This does not affect liability, however : the argument that a local authority can not be directly liable for an act of nuisance because such an act cannot itself be said to be authorised was expressly considered and rejected in *Campbell v Paddington Corporation* ([1911] 1 KB 869).

It has also been held that liability in tort may result from an act which is not only *prima facie* wrongful under the private law but also *ultra vires* under public law principles. Indeed with the tort of misfeasance in public office, for which liability may be either direct or vicarious, the existence of an *ultra vires* act is a precondition of liability in many cases (see 9.1.2). The range of situations in which liability for an *ultra vires* act may arise is outlined at 9.2.1 below. The argument that there can be no vicarious liability in such a case was expressly rejected by the High Court of Australia in *James v Commonwealth* ((1939) 62 CLR 339) in which the Commonwealth was held liable for the seizure by a government officer of the plaintiff's property. This was done under the purported authority of statute, but the statute in question was invalid as unconstitutional, so that the seizure was unlawful. It was argued that since the officer was acting unlawfully he could not be acting in the course of employment. The Court rejected the argument, holding that a State servant acts in the course of employment where he has *de facto* authority to act, and not only where there is legal authority. A similar approach, of looking to the de facto position, can be used to attribute the *ultra vires* acts of servants to the authority, for the purpose of establishing the latter's direct liability, should the issue of direct liability ever be contested. In this case there is clearly no policy objection to liability. Indeed, quite the contrary : the effect of liability here is to compensate the very persons for whose benefit the *ultra vires* rule operates.

There may be more debate, however, over the issue of liability in tort for acts done in the course of an activity which is itself *ultra vires*, where the purpose of prohibiting the activity is to prevent public funds being spent or put at risk in that way. For example, if a public body carries on a passenger transport service when it is not authorised to do so, should it be liable for any public nuisance caused by the operation of its vehicle depots, or be vicariously liable for negligent acts of its vehicle drivers which cause injury? There is no reason of logic why liability should be precluded simply because the act which gives rise to liability is *ultra vires*, as explained at 1.4.1. Indeed this is amply illustrated by the many cases holding public bodies liable for *ultra vires* acts - for example, under the tort of misfeasance. It might be contended, though, that no liability should arise where this would be contrary to the protective policy of the rule. However, it is submitted that policy clearly favours the imposition of liability: the public interest here is far outweighed by the private interests protected by the tort system. That liability should exist is the view taken by most writers (for example, Winfield and Jolowicz, at p.676; Warren (1926) 2 CLJ 180; though for a contrary view see Goodhart (1926) 2 CLJ 350). Such authority as exists also favours the imposition of liability: in *Ormiston v Great Western Railway* ([1917] 1 KB 598 at 602), Rowlatt J expressed the view that vicarious liability could probably arise for the acts of servants in respect of *ultra vires* activities, though it was unnecessary to decide the point. It is argued elsewhere in this book that the fact of *ultra vires* should not preclude claims in contract (see 2.3.3) and restitution (see 11.4.2), and the case for liability in tort is even stronger.

Whatever the position with public bodies generally, the Crown, in relation to torts within the Crown Proceedings Act 1947, is made liable as if a person of full age and capacity (see 5.4.2 below). This would seem definitely to preclude any plea of *ultra vires* as a defence to liability in tort.

5.4. The Crown and its Servants and Agents

5.4.1. Introduction

At one time the Crown enjoyed a general immunity from suit in the courts (see 1.2.1.3). In the nineteenth century the petition of right procedure developed to allow Crown liability, including most questions of contract and restitution, to be determined by the courts according to the ordinary law (see 1.2.1.3). However, it could not be used to hold the Crown liable in tort, either directly, or vicariously for the torts of others (*Viscount Canterbury v The Queen* (1843) 12 LJ Ch.281; *Tobin v The Queen* (1864) 143 ER 1148; *Feather v The Queen* (1865) 122 ER 1191). An exception was certain actions concerned with the taking of property: actions for the recovery of property could be brought using the petition of right procedure, and were not regarded as precluded by the general tort immunity, probably because such claims were not considered to be based on tort. There was some dispute as to whether claims for compensation for property taken, as opposed to claims for the recovery of property itself, were also within the procedure (see Robertson, *Civil Proceedings by and against the Crown* (1908) at pp.335-336). It may be noted that the Crown's general immunity from suit in tort was held in *Tobin v The Queen*, above, not to be affected by the Petitions of Right Act 1860, an Act for simplifying the procedure for bringing a petition, though similarly worded provisions, modelled on this British Act, were later held in some other jurisdictions to remove the Crown's substantive immunity in tort, as well as simplifying procedure (*Farnell v Bowman* (1887) 12 App Cas 643 (P.C.), on New South Wales, and followed in other Australian jurisdictions; *R v Cliche* [1935] SCR 561 (Quebec). The British view was adopted elsewhere in Canada: see Hogg, at pp.80-81).

The conclusion that the petition of right could not be used to bring claims in tort was based on the ancient maxim that "The King can do no wrong". This was interpreted to mean that it was not possible to hold the King liable for action which would amount to a legal "wrong" if carried out by another person, although it seems that the original meaning of the maxim was quite the opposite: that the King was not permitted to do wrongful acts (see Ehrlich, in Vinogradoff ed. 6 *Oxford Studies in Social and Legal History* (1921) 54). The Crown could be held neither directly nor vicariously liable for a tort. It might be thought that the maxim would have had no application to vicarious liability which is not now considered to be based on a wrong by the defendant himself, but the nineteenth century view was that such liability was based on either the defendant's "fault" in choosing incompetent agents or on the fiction that he had impliedly authorised the act.

There was no other way under the common law to pursue a remedy in tort against the Crown itself. However, under statute the Minister of Transport was himself early on made liable for the torts of his subordinates in respect of inland transport (Glanville Williams at p.20). It was also probably possible, as now, to sue an incorporated Crown agent directly for torts committed by the entity (see 5.4.7) - though such an entity would not be liable for the torts of individuals involved in its activities since their employer was, and is, the Crown (see 5.4.3.2). Subject to these very limited exceptions, however, the only recourse in law for a party harmed by the Crown's activities was to sue any individual servant responsible for the loss. These individuals remained personally liable in accordance with the ordinary law: they did not share the immunity from tort liability enjoyed by the Crown.

Where a tort was committed by a Crown servant, it was unsatisfactory that the only remedy was against that individual, who might be unable to meet a judgement. However, it became the practice of the Crown to negotiate any settlement on behalf of its servants and to pay any sum agreed by way of damages; and if the matter could not be settled the Crown would conduct the litigation and pay any damages and costs awarded against the servant. This practice, as Hogg points out (at p.82) "was probably the reason why the scandalous gap in the law was not filled much earlier". Although the practice did largely plug the "scandalous gap" the position was not entirely satisfactory. If the Crown disputed the issue of vicarious liability - for example, arguing that the alleged tortfeasor was not a servant or the tort had not occurred in the course of employment - there was no method to resolve the question in the courts. It became the practice to submit such matters to arbitration (Glanville Williams, at p.17), but this meant the possibility of proceedings in two separate forums. Difficulties would also occur when it was known that a Crown servant was responsible, but it was impossible to identify the servant. Finally it was also unsatisfactory in principle that compensation should be a matter of grace.

Where damage occurred for which the Crown, but for Crown immunity, would have been *directly* liable, the courts were often able to consider the case by virtue of a practice of the Crown's nominating a particular servant as a defendant - for example, as the "occupier" of premises. The court would give judgement on liability as if this person were the occupier, and the Crown would meet any judgement and costs against him. However, in 1946 this practice was condemned by the House of Lords in *Adams v Naylor* (1946 AC 543) where it was stated, *obiter*, that the court would only find liability if it could be proved that the named defendant had committed the tort. This seemed contrary to the usual principle that the court only dismisses an action on the grounds argued by the parties. However, their Lordships' views were followed by the Court of Appeal the next year in *Royster v Cavey* ([1947] 1 KB 204) in which an action for negligence and breach of statutory duty, arising from an accident in a factory run by the Crown, was dismissed on the basis that it was not the named defendant but the Crown who owed the relevant duties.

These developments prompted the long overdue reform of the law of Crown liability, by the Crown Proceedings Act 1947. This Act aimed to put the Crown in a similar position to any other person with respect to liability claims, including by putting an end to the anomalous immunity from the substantive law of tort which the Crown previously enjoyed.

5.4.2. The general approach to reform

The 1947 Crown Proceedings Act aimed substantially to place the Crown in the same position as any other litigant with respect to the substantive law of civil liability. By 1947 actions in contract and restitution could already, as indicated, be determined by the courts in accordance with the ordinary law by using the petition of right procedure (see 1.2.1.3), so that all that was needed was to provide for enforcement without the fiat of the Crown. With tort, however, it was necessary to provide for substantive liability. This might have been done by stating a general principle that the Crown should be liable to the same extent as any private person, an approach adopted in some Commonwealth jurisdictions (see Hogg, at p.86). However, instead of making the Crown liable under the ordinary law in general terms the United Kingdom Act imposed liability under certain specified heads of private law. With vicarious liability the Act makes the Crown liable for the torts of its "servants and agents" (s.2(1)). In relation to direct liability the Crown is made liable for breach of duties owed as employer (s.2(1)); breach of duties attached to property (s.2.(1)); and breach of statutory duty (s.2.(2)). Although it seems the Act was intended to render the Crown liable under all recognised heads of tort, probably it has failed to do so: there appear to be some categories of liability which are not within these specified heads (see in particular 5.4.4.4 below). The approach adopted is thus open to criticism : probably it would have been better to adopt some more general formula of liability.

5.4.3. *Vicarious liability*

5.4.3.1. *General principle*

Section 2(1) of the Crown Proceedings Act provides:

"Subject to the provisions of this Act, the Crown shall be subject to all those liabilities in tort to which, if it were a private person of full age and capacity it would be subject: a) in respect of torts committed by its servants or agents ..."

5.4.3.2. *Liability for servants*

The Crown is stated by the above provision to be liable where a tort is committed either by its servant or its agent.

In deciding which individuals are servants of the Crown the same test applies as in deciding whether any other person is a servant of the alleged employer, the main criterion being the extent of control exercised over the alleged employee (Jones, at pp.254-259; Winfield and Jolowicz, at pp.562-577). One special problem is deciding whether a person is the servant of the Crown itself or of the particular public authority - for example, a Minister or departmental corporation - under whose auspices he acts. The general principle is that, in the absence of express statutory provision to the contrary, where the public authority is classified as a "Crown agent" those working in its activities are regarded as servants of the Crown rather than as servants of the specific authority (*Bainbridge v Postmaster General* [1906] 1 KB 178 (CA). Thus the Crown is vicariously liable for their torts, and the specific authority is not (*Bainbridge,* above).

A limitation on the Crown's liability for its servants is contained in section 2(6) of the Crown Proceedings Act. This states that there is no liability for any officer of the Crown - which includes any Crown servant and not just office holders *strictu sensu* (s.38(2)) - unless 1) that officer was directly or indirectly appointed by the Crown and 2) he is paid out of the Consolidated Fund, moneys provided by Parliament or some other fund certified by the Treasury for the purposes of the section, or would normally be paid from such a fund or moneys. One effect of the provision is probably to exclude vicarious liability for torts of the police. (Vicarious liability for these torts is now imposed by section 48 of the Police Act 1964 on the relevant Chief Constable, and damages and costs in respect of this liability are payable from police funds). Section 2(6) also has the effect of excluding vicarious liability on the part of the Crown for those working for Crown agents who, although servants of the Crown, are paid from funds belonging to the agent itself.

A master is generally only liable for torts committed by his servants in the course of their employment, and the same applies to the liability of the Crown for its servants: as explained, section 2(1) only subjects the Crown to that liability to which it would be subject if it were a private person.

A person who is a servant of the Crown sometimes has public functions conferred on him directly, either by statute or under the common law. In such a case he may be considered, for some purposes at least, to exercise these functions in an independent capacity, rather than on behalf of the Crown: thus, the prerogative orders may be granted to compel proper performance of the function, though such orders cannot be granted against the Crown (see 1.2.1.2 above). At common law it was held that in such a case the Crown was not liable for torts committed in the exercise of these functions, since the functions were not carried out in the course of employment with the Crown (see Hogg, at pp.94-96). The effect of this rule is now altered by section 2(3) Crown Proceedings Act, which makes the Crown liable. It provides that where functions are imposed on an officer of the Crown as such by statute or common law, and the officer commits a tort whilst performing or purporting to perform those functions, the Crown shall be liable as if those functions had been conferred or imposed on him by the Crown.

Whether public authorities which are Crown agents may be treated as "servants" of the Crown for the purpose of vicarious liability is considered at 5.4.3.4 below.

5.4.3.3. Liability for agents

As well as being liable for the torts of its servants, the Crown is also stated to be liable for the torts of its agents. In private law there is no general liability for the torts of persons who are designated as "agents" for other legal purposes: liability for those agents who are not servants exists only in very limited and well defined circumstances (see Winfield and Jolowicz, at pp.579-581). It is clear that the Crown's liability is also confined to those limited circumstances since section 2(1) imposing liability for the torts of others subjects the Crown only to those liabilities to which a private person would be subject. With respect to independent contractors this point is also expressly made in section 40(2)(d), which states that, unless expressly provided otherwise, the Act does not subject the Crown to greater liabilities for its independent contractors than those to which it would be subject if it were a private person.

As to who falls within the definition of agent, section 38(2) states expressly that agent includes an independent contractor, and the Crown will thus be vicariously liable for the torts of its independent contractors where such liability exists under the general law. The general rule is that a person is not liable for torts committed by his independent contractors. However, liability exists in some exceptional cases - for example, where the contractor is engaged in some particularly hazardous activity; in some circumstances, where a nuisance is created by an independent contractor; where goods under a bailment are damaged by one's contractor; or in certain cases where a contractor causes damage when employed to do work under a statutory power (see Jones, at pp.268-273; Winfield and Jolowicz, at pp.581-586; McKendrick, (1990) 53 MLR 770; and 6.11 below). It is possible, however, that in all these cases the liability is direct, arising by virtue of breach of a non-delegable duty by the party employing the contractor, and not vicarious (Jones, at p.268; Winfield and Jolowicz, at p.582). Probably section 2(1)(a), imposing liability for the torts of servants and agents, itself does not impose any direct liability; thus other provisions of the Act, which are concerned with direct liability, will have to be relied on to hold the Crown liable for its independent contractors in the circumstances listed above (on these see 5.4.4.4). If, indeed, liability for independent contractors is direct and not vicarious, section 2(1)(a) will then have no relevance as regards liability of the Crown for such contractors, though they are specifically included in the definition of "agent".

Whatever the position with independent contractors, there are some other circumstances in which there may be vicarious liability for the acts of another who is not a servant (see generally Winfield and Jolowicz, at pp.579-581). For example, a person is liable for the torts of another who drives his car at his request, where the owner has an interest in the journey (*Ormrod v Crossville Motor Service* [1953] 1 WLR 1120; *Morgans v Launchbury* [1973] AC 127). In such a case the driver is said to be the owner's "agent" (*Morgans v Launchbury,* above), so this principle would seem to apply to the Crown.

Whether a public body such as a Crown corporation, which acts on behalf of the Crown generally may in carrying out its functions be considered an "agent" for the purpose of vicarious liability is considered immediately below.

5.4.3.4. *Public bodies which are "Crown agents"*

An unresolved question, alluded to above, is the extent to which the Crown is vicariously liable for the torts of public authorities which are classified as Crown agents for the purpose of taking advantage of certain Crown privileges and immunities (see 1.2.1.7 above). The extent to which such bodies may be directly liable in tort is considered at 5.4.7.2 below. It will be explained that such liability will in fact rarely arise, but where it does, it may be necessary to know whether there is also any liability on the part of the Crown. Hogg has suggested that for the purpose of vicarious liability, such an authority "is equivalent in law to an individual Crown servant" (at p.259; and see also p.90), and that the Crown is thus vicariously liable for its torts because it is a servant. The same view is adopted by Glanville Williams (at pp.31-37). If this were so the Crown would *prima facie* be liable for all the torts committed by such bodies in the course of carrying out Crown activities. However, if such liability arises on the basis that the body is a servant, it may be argued that in practice it would be precluded in most cases because of the operation of section 2(6), which as explained above (see 5.4.3.2) provides that the Crown is liable only for servants who are paid from the funds of Parliament etc and appointed by the Crown. Crown agents are not paid at all, and are appointed by Parliament not the Crown (Glanville Williams, at p.34; Treitel [1957] PL 321 at 322). Thus liability would seem often to be excluded by this limitation, if, indeed, any liability which arises does so on the basis that these bodies are servants of the Crown.

An alternative view is that such bodies are not "servants", since they are not paid and employed in the normal manner of the service relationship (see Treitel above, at p.327, and Atiyah, *Vicarious Liability in the Law of Torts* (1967), at p.397; and see also *British Medical Association v Greater Glasgow Health Board* ([1989] AC 1211, in which the House of Lords took the view that the Board was not a Crown servant for the purpose of immunity from the grant of an injunction: see further 5.4.7.2 below). If they are not servants what is the extent of the Crown's liability? The basic principle is that the Crown is liable for its agents who are not servants when a private party would be liable. The problem is that there is no clearly analogous situation in private law, the nature of the relationship between the Crown and this type of agent being unique in practice. This illustrates the difficulties of relying too closely on a private law model to determine principles of liability in public law.

One possibility if they are not servants is to regard them as independent contractors : if this is correct liability for their acts would be rare and, as explained, would probably be direct, not vicarious. However, it is submitted, as Treitel also argues ([1957] PL 321, at 328), that they are not within this category, one reason being that most Crown agents are subject to a close degree of control by the Crown - indeed, control by the Crown is the most important element in the test to decide which authorities are Crown agents (see above at 1.2.1.7).

Another possibility is that the Crown will generally be liable for the torts of these bodies even though they are not strictly "servants". This is the view of Treitel (at pp.330-331 above) though he does not attempt to explain the basis of such liability. The best explanation would be that this is simply a distinct category of vicarious liability based on "agency", arising from the special relationship between the parties, to be classified with the other "miscellaneous" categories of vicarious liability, such as that of a motor vehicle owner for torts of a driver. There is no need, it is submitted, to find a close private law analogy. Atiyah has argued that this view cannot be correct since it would entail the unacceptable proposition that private corporations would be liable for the torts of their subsidiaries (above, p.394, note 12). However, this need not be the case. The relationship between a Crown and its agents is a very special one, as indicated by the fact that for certain other purposes, such as the enjoyment of the Crown's immunities, they can be equated with the Crown : no doubt a subsidiary of a private company would not be permitted to participate in any similar privileges given by statute to its parent (on equating a subsidiary with a parent for legal purposes, see Pennington, *Company Law,* (6th ed. 1990) ch.2, at pp.37-38). Such liability would not seem generally to be excluded by section 2(6), which applies only to Crown "officers" (defined to include servants) : if not servants, it is difficult to see that Crown corporations would be within the definition of "officer".

To allow recourse against the Crown is desirable in view of the fact that these public authorities bodies may sometimes not hold their own funds, and it is submitted that the position put forward in the previous paragraph is the one which the courts ought to adopt. The extent and basis of the Crown's vicarious liability, if any, for these entities, however, currently remains uncertain. Probably, as explained, it is of very little importance.

In practice most torts committed in the course of the activities of a Crown agent will be committed by individuals and not the agent itself. It has already been seen that the Crown is generally vicariously liable for the torts of these individuals since the Crown, and not the agent, is the employer.

5.4.3.5. *Is any vicarious liability inapplicable to the Crown?*

The Act does not impose any vicarious liability on the Crown except for the acts of servants or agents. If the law were to impose liability under the general law for the acts of other categories of persons, then this liability would not apply to the Crown. However, no such liability currently exists. This is because in those cases where liability has been imposed outside the traditional and master and servant category, as in the case of a person driving a car at the owner's request, the courts have explained this as depending on the existence of an agency relationship between the parties. The concept of agency in these cases seems to mean no more than that this is within the category of relationships capable of giving rise to vicarious liability, since it is doubtful if the designation of the relationship in this way has any other legal significance. In other words, the term "agent" is a conclusory label, used to express the view that vicarious liability should be imposed. So long as the courts continue to adopt this approach of attaching the label of agent wherever such vicarious liability is recognised, liability in such cases will always attach also to the Crown, as liability for an agent. Should the courts ever recognise liability in a situation which is not designated as one of agency, however, the Crown could not be vicariously liable, and there would be a gap in the law.

Since section 2 only imposes liability for the torts of servants and agents, there is also a potential gap in the law if there may ever be liability for an act of another which is not a tort. Glanville Williams (at pp.43-45) has criticised the provision for this reason. As explained at 5.1 above, however, the only case where this has been held to apply, that is in relation to liability for injury caused by husband to wife, can no longer arise since a wife may now sue a husband in tort. Were the courts by analogy to recognise the possibility in other cases, however, clearly a gap would exist.

5.4.2.6. *Requirement for a tort*

It is expressly stated in a proviso to section 2 of the Crown Proceedings Act 1947 that no proceedings lie against the Crown for the act or omission of its servants or agents unless the relevant act or omission would apart from the provisions of this Act have given rise to a cause of action in tort against that servant or agent or his estate. This provision seems to have been inserted to make it clear that where the defence of act of state is available to a servant in respect of an act which would otherwise be tortious, the Crown is not to be liable either. It is unnecessary, since liability for servants and agents under 2(1)(a) generally arises anyway only with respect to the *torts* of those servants and agents (see 5.1 above).

5.4.3.7. Judicial functions

Section 2(5) of the Crown Proceedings Act 1947 states that no proceedings lie against the Crown for the torts committed by its servants or agents while "discharging or purporting to discharge any responsibilities of a judicial nature" vested in them, or any responsibilities which they have "in connection with the execution of the judicial process". As explained above (5.2.2.2), there is a substantial immunity from tort liability for persons acting as judges. In these cases there is no personal liability and so there probably can be no vicarious liability on the Crown. However, the judge of an inferior court acting outside jurisdiction is liable in some cases, though acting in the exercise of judicial functions, as is a superior court judge knowingly acting outside jurisdiction (see 5.2.2); and other authorities exercising judicial functions may attract liability. The effect of the section is to preclude vicarious liability on the Crown in these cases. Wade justifies this on the basis that the Crown as the Executive has no control over the manner in which the judicial function is exercised and often very restricted control over dismissal (Wade, at pp.817-818). However, it is questionable whether it is desirable that an individual victim should be left with only a personal remedy.

5.4.4. Direct liability

5.4.4.1. Employers' duties

The Crown Proceedings Act imposes direct liability on the Crown in three categories. First, section 2(1) states that the Crown is subject to those liabilities in tort to which, if it were a private person of full age and capacity, it would be subject "(b) in respect of any breach of those duties which a person owes to his servants or agents at common law by reason of being their employer". An employer has, for example, common law duties to his employees to provide a safe system of work, competent servants and safe plant (see Jones, ch.5; Winfield and Jolowicz, ch.8), and the Crown is made subject to such duties by this provision.

5.4.4.2. Duties attaching to property

Section 2(1) also makes the Crown liable as if it were a private person of full age and capacity "(c) in respect of any breach of the duties attaching at common law to the ownership, occupation, possession or control of property". Thus the Crown is made liable, *inter alia,* in nuisance and under the rule in *Rylands v Fletcher* (see ch.8). Many duties attaching to property - such as the duty of care owed by occupiers - are now contained in statute and the Crown's liability under these will be governed by the provisions on liability for breach of duties imposed by statute (see 5.4.4.3 below). Section 40(4) of the Act limits liability for property "involuntarily" acquired by the Crown, as may occur, for example, when property vests in the Crown as *bona vacantia*. It provides that where any property vests in the Crown by virtue of any rule of law which operates independently of the acts or intentions of the Crown "the Crown is not to be liable under the Act by reason of the property being so vested". It is provided, however, that liability will arise once the Crown has taken possession or control, or entered into occupation of, the property.

5.4.4.3. Statutory duties

Under section 2(2), where the Crown is bound by a statutory duty and fails to comply with that duty, it is subject to any liabilities in tort as if it were a private person of full age and capacity.

Under the general law civil liability does not arise for every breach of a statutory duty (for the general principles see Jones ch.9; Winfield and Jolowicz, ch.7; and on public duties see ch.7 below). Obviously the section makes the Crown liable in the same circumstances in which any other party would be liable. In addition it should be emphasised that the Crown is only normally bound by statute by express provision or necessary implication (see 1.2.1.6). Section 2 of the Crown Proceedings Act expressly states that liability for breach of statutory duties can arise only where "the Crown is bound by a statutory duty", and thus makes it clear that the possibility of civil liability will only arise where the statute is one which otherwise binds the Crown.

It is also stated in section 2(2) that liability only arises under this section if the duty is one which also binds persons other than the Crown. It seems that it is sufficient that the duty also binds other public authorities - there is no rule that the duty must be one which also binds some *private party*. The purpose of this qualification may have been to ensure that no liability for damages is imposed for breach of duties of a political nature which it is not appropriate to enforce through actions by private individuals. It is true that many duties owed by the Crown are of this kind but so are many duties owed by other public authorities, and in such cases the courts have held that as a matter of construction of the statute an individual has no right to enforce the duty (see 7.2 below). Since some duties owed by the Crown will, on the other hand, be suitable for individual enforcement, it would have been better to impose liability for duties owed solely by the Crown, and to leave the courts to decide when a remedy should be available, in accordance with the general principles outlined in chapter 7.

As was explained in chapter 1 (see 1.2.1.1), it is the practice for duties
on the central executive to be placed on named Ministers, rather than the
Crown itself. It was held by Popplewell J in *R v HM Treasury, ex parte
Petch* (Feb. 28 1989; Lexis) that in such a case any action in tort for breach
of the statutory duty must be brought against the Minister himself, and not
against the Crown, with the Crown's being vicariously liable for the tort of
the Minister. On this basis it was held that the restriction of the Crown's
liability to a case where the duty is shared by others as well as the Crown,
contained in section 2(2), had no application: the duty was not a duty on
"the Crown". This is consistent with the courts' view that mandamus
(which is not available against the Crown) can be granted to enforce duties
placed on a Minister in his own name; but it is hard to reconcile with the
line of authority stating that injunctions are not available to enforce such
duties, which takes the view that they are duties owed by the Crown (on the
question of the independent capacity of Ministers generally see 1.2.1.2
above).

It might be argued that the provision for liability on the part of the
Crown for breach of statutory duty is unnecessary, since such liability
derives from the specific statute enacting the duty and overrides any
common law immunity from tort actions. If so restrictions - such as the
requirement that the duty apply also to some person other than the Crown -
might effectively be disregarded. However, even if each duty can be said to
derive from the specific statute, section 2(2) might be construed,
alternatively, as imposing restrictive conditions on recovery under such
statutes. It was assumed in *Petch*, above, that section 2(2) does apply to
restrict the liability of the Crown in cases where the duty is owed by the
Crown.

5.4.4.4. Other heads of direct liability

The Crown Proceedings Act 1947 imposes liability on the Crown only in
the three areas just outlined. Under the general law, however, artificial legal
entities, including public authorities, have been held directly liable in tort in
circumstances which do not fall within any of these categories. For
example, an education authority has been held directly liable for an accident
caused by a young child who was not subject to proper supervision
(*Carmarthenshire County Council v Lewis* [1955] AC 549) and a hospital
for failing to establish a proper system for the administration of drugs
(*Collins v Hertfordshire CC* [1947] KB 598). It also seems that liability for
the acts of an independent contractor - for example, for a contractor engaged
in extra hazardous activities - is direct and not vicarious liability, and this
may arise in circumstances which are not within one of three categories (see
5.4.3.3). It seems that the Crown will not be liable in such cases, or in

others which might arise in the future (on this, and for examples which have arisen in other jurisdictions see Hogg, at pp.102-104). This is an unfortunate gap in the law.

Can section 2(1)(a) which imposes liability for the torts of servants and agents (see 5.4.4 above) be used to impose *direct liability*, as well as vicarious liability? If so, this would narrow the unfortunate gap referred to above. The provision does not expressly state that it is concerned only with vicarious liability. It does, however, refer to liability for torts of servants or agents. Thus it could only be used, if at all, where there is a tort by the servant or agent. In *Carmarthenshire County Council v Lewis* there was no tort by the individual with care of the child. However, in some cases there may be a tort. For example, when a contractor engaged in an extra hazardous activity causes damage the contractor himself will be liable if he has been careless; and there was actionable negligence in *Collins*. It is probable, however, that even here the provision does not apply, since the existence of a tort by the servant or agent is coincidental, and the liability of the Crown is not *in respect of* that tort.

5.4.5. The armed forces

Previously section 10 of the Crown Proceedings Act 1947 denied recovery in tort for personal injury to a member of the armed forces who was on duty, or was on land or premises, or a vehicle, ship or aircraft, being used for services purposes, where the injury was caused by another member of the forces on duty. This applied only where the injury was one attributable to the service for pension purposes. The main objective seems to have been to prevent double compensation, by way of both pension and damages. Where the section applied neither the tortfeasor nor the Crown could be sued. (For further detail on the objectives, history and interpretation of the section see Boyd [1989] PL 237).

It became apparent that the provision worked injustice where the pension was less than damages which would be obtained by suing in tort (as in *Adams v War* Office [1955] 1 WLR 1116). The absence of a legal right of action also deprived victims and their relatives of a method of establishing responsibility for any injury. These considerations led to the suspension of section 10 by Section 1 of the Crown Proceedings (Armed Forces) Act 1987. The effect of this reform is to make possible claims against both the Crown and the individual wrongdoer. Pension entitlements are not affected, though the Secretary of State does have a power to reduce a pension, which power may be used to take account of any damages awarded (Article 55, Naval Military etc (Disablement and Death) Service Pension Order 1983, S.I. 1983 883). The provision applies only to acts or omissions occurring after its enactment, a feature of the legislation which has been criticised (though for a defence see Boyd, above, at pp.246-247).

As indicated, section 1 of the 1987 Act merely suspends section 10 of the 1947 Act, and does not repeal it. Section 2 of the 1987 Act provides for the revival of the no-liability provision by the Secretary of State whenever this appears to him to be necessary or expedient by reason of "imminent national danger" or "any great emergency" or "for the purposes of any warlike operations" outside the United Kingdom. It has been suggested that the reason for this revival provision is not the potential cost of claims in the situation which it covers, but a belief that it is inappropriate to allow judicial scrutiny of the activities of the forces when on active service (Boyd, above, at pp.247-248).

5.4.6. Crown immunities

A number of the general Crown immunities discussed in chapter 1 (see 1.2.1.4-6) may be relevant to an action in tort. Thus, for example, an injunction is not available to prevent the Crown from acting in a tortious manner, nor is execution available to enforce a judgement in tort.

One important general immunity is the immunity from the burden of statutes (see 1.2.1.6 above). Many important statutes on tort expressly state that they are to bind the Crown (see for example, Occupiers' Liability Act 1957 s.6; Occupiers Liability Act 1985 s.6; Defective Premises Act 1972 s.5). Statutes passed before the Crown Proceedings Act 1947 on indemnity and contribution apply by virtue of section 4 of the Act, which subjects the Crown to the general law on these questions, and the section also expressly applies the Law Reform (Contributory Negligence) Act 1945 to the Crown (for discussion see Treitel [1957] PL 321 at 322-4).

An argument may be made that statutory provisions imposing tort liability automatically bind the Crown since, with respect to the matters for which liability is imposed by the Act, it is provided that the Crown shall be liable as a private person of full age and capacity. Thus, it might be argued, statutory provisions on these matters which apply to a person of full age and capacity should also apply to the Crown. This would make the provisions in the Act on specific statutes dealing with tort liability unnecessary, and they may be regarded as inserted *ex abunante cautela*. The strongest argument against this view is that it is expressly provided by section 40(2)(f) that nothing in the Act shall "affect any rules of evidence or any presumption relating to the extent to which the Crown is bound by any Act of Parliament." The matter is discussed in detail by Treitel ([1957] PL 321), where he demonstrates that different statutes passed between 1947 and 1957 are based on different views on this question.

5.4.7. *Crown servants and agents*

5.4.7.1. *Servants*

Crown servants, like other public servants, are personally liable for torts which they commit in the course of their public employment. This was so before 1947: Crown servants never shared the immunity from tort liability enjoyed by the Crown itself. Certain immunities still existing also attach only to the Crown and are not shared by its servants, even in relation to torts occurring in the course of employment - for example, immunity from execution. Others, such as the presumption of immunity from statute, protect servants personally (*Cooper v Hawkins* (1904) 2 KB 164). Crown servants may, of course, like other public employees, benefit from general public law rules such as the immunity from suit in negligence for certain policy decisions, or judicial immunity.

With regard to injunctions against Crown servants section 21 of the Crown Proceedings Act 1947, which prohibits injunctions against the Crown states also (s.21(2)) that there may be no injunction against an officer or servant of the Crown if the effect would be "to give any relief against the Crown which could not have been obtained in proceedings against the Crown" (see 1.2.1.5 above). The effect of section 21(2) is probably to preclude an injunction against a servant in his personal capacity, where he is acting within the scope of his duties in committing a tort. It is suggested by Evans in *de Smith's Judicial Review of Administrative Action* (4th ed. 1980) (at p.446) that an injunction would not issue "unless his act was so far removed from the proper sphere of his official duties that the award of an injunction could not be regarded as an indirect form of relief against the Crown".

As explained above (at 5.4.3), the Crown is vicariously liable for the torts of its servants.

5.4.7.2. *Agents*

Special consideration is required of the position of Crown agents who are non-natural persons, such as Crown corporations (see above at 1.2.1.7). The predominant view of writers is that "A public corporation that is an agent (or servant) of the Crown, is generally in the same situation as an individual Crown servant" (Hogg, at p.142), and thus, like any servant, may be directly liable in tort (and see Atiyah, *Vicarious Liability* (1967), at pp.393-4; Treitel [1957] PL 321, at 331). If direct liability exists at all it will not arise often, since under most possible heads of direct liability, this will lie on the Crown itself: for example, any employers' liability will often attach to the Crown not the corporation since the general principle is that the Crown is the employer (see 5.4.3 above). The corporation could be directly liable though, for example, if it were expressly to authorise a tort by a Crown servant (as is any person who directs another to commit a tort). If a corporation is directly liable, it seems the Crown would be vicariously liable, though the precise basis of liability is unclear (see 5.4.3.3).

An alternative view is that a Crown agent cannot be sued in tort but that its acts should all be attributed to the Crown for the purpose of tortious liability (Glanville Williams at p.21). This seems a better approach, since these bodies often have no independent assets. (The same point was made in arguing that these bodies should not be recognised as having an independent capacity to make contracts : see 2.3.1.2 above). The authority is inconclusive on the point. In *Roper v Commissioners of Works* ([1915] 1 KB 45) it was held that such a body could not be liable, and that the position was unaffected by the fact of incorporation; but this was doubted by Atkin LJ in the Court of Appeal in *Mackenzie Kennedy v Air Council* ([1927] 2 KB 517 at 532-533).

If it is the case that the authority may be sued directly, may an injunction be granted against it? Section 21 of the Crown Proceedings Act 1947 provides, first, that no injunction shall be granted in "proceedings against the Crown". It seems that proceedings against a Crown agent where the agent is directly liable in tort would not constitute "proceedings against the Crown" for the purpose of this provision, even though the agent carries on all its functions on behalf of the Crown and is entitled to share general Crown immunities such as immunity from taxation (see 1.2.1.7 above). This conclusion is suggested by the House of Lords decision in *British Medical Association v Greater Glasgow Health Board* ([1989] AC 1211), in which it was stated that "proceedings against the Crown" for the purpose of section 21 refers only to proceedings brought against an authority which is being sued as nominal defendant for the Crown under section 17(3) of the Act - that is with respect to an obligation incurred by the Crown (see 1.2.1.3) - and not where a Crown agent is sued with respect to liability which the agent has incurred itself. In some statutes Crown agents are stated to be liable to suit in their own name as principals in respect of torts committed by the Crown itself, and not merely as nominal defendants for the Crown. In this case also it seems from the *Glasgow* case that these proceedings are not "proceedings against the Crown" for the purpose of section 21. It is clear that the courts have desired to give a narrow construction to section 21 in order to avoid applying the Crown immunity rule.

As explained (see 1.2.1.5) section 21(2) precludes the grant of an injunction against an officer of the Crown where the effect would be to give relief against the Crown. The court in the *Greater Glasgow Health Board* case took the view that the Board was not an "officer" of the Crown for this purpose. Thus it would seem an injunction could be granted for a tort committed by such a body where the effect would be to give relief against the Crown, though an injunction could not have been obtained in proceedings against officers of the Crown or the Crown itself. Thus this type of agent is in a different position from individual Crown servants in this respect.

Since it is normally the Crown, not the agent, which is the employer of those engaged in the agent's activities, it will normally be the Crown, and not the agent, which is vicariously liable for the torts of those persons.

5.5.   Exemplary Damages

5.5.1. General

The main object of an award of damages in a tort action is to compensate the plaintiff for loss suffered. The manner in which the tort was committed may affect the amount of compensation since this may aggravate the injury: a tort committed in a malicious or insulting manner, for example, may affect the plaintiff's pride or dignity, and the compensation awarded will reflect this (see *Cassell v Broome* [1972] AC 1027 at 1085 per Lord Reid). Additional damages awarded because of the manner of commission are termed "aggravated" damages; but their function is compensatory, and not punitive.

In the vast majority of cases only damages by way of compensation, which may include aggravated damages, will be awarded. In limited circumstances, however, the court may also award "exemplary" (or "punitive") damages: that is, damages which are not limited to an amount to compensate the plaintiff for his loss, but are designed to punish the defendant for the way in which he has acted in committing a tort. The earliest cases in which exemplary damages were given concerned torts committed by public officials in attempting to suppress the publication of the *North Briton* back in the eighteenth century (*Huckle v Money* (1763) 95 ER 768; Wilkes v Wood (1763) 98 ER 489). It was once considered that the court could award exemplary damages in any case where it considered this appropriate because of the nature of the defendant's conduct. However, it was held by the House of Lords in *Rookes v Barnard* ([1967] AC 1129), and affirmed by the same court in *Broome v Cassell*, above, that such damages can be awarded only in three types of case: where there is express authorisation by statute; where there is "oppressive, arbitrary or unconstitutional" action by servants of the government ([1967] AC 1129 at 1226 per Lord Devlin); and where the defendant's conduct has been calculated to make a profit which may exceed any compensation payable. Even within these categories Lord Devlin emphasised that exemplary damages should be considered an exceptional weapon, to be used with restraint. This section will examine the scope of the second category, relating to tortious conduct by public officials. (For an account of the others and the general principles relating to exemplary damages see *McGregor on Damages* (15th ed. 1988) Ch.11; Ghandi, (1990) 10 LS 182).

Strong criticism has been made of the very existence of exemplary damages. It is argued that to allow punishment through the civil law avoids many safeguards for the protection of alleged offenders which are provided in criminal proceedings (see, for example, *Cassell v Broome*, above, at 1087 per Lord Reid), and that it is anomalous that the amount of the "fine" imposed through the means of exemplary damages should go as a windfall to the plaintiff rather than going to the State. The current operation of the principle can also be criticised in that the circumstances in which "punishment" may be given are not clearly defined. Many cases where this question may arise are determined by a jury and it will be the jury which decides whether to award such damages and how much, exacerbating the uncertainty though section 8 of Courts and Legal Services Act now provides for rules to be made giving the Court of Appeal power to substitute its own damages figure for that of a jury.

It is clear that the House of Lords in *Broome* (with the possible exception of Lord Wilberforce) did not favour the recognition of exemplary damages but felt compelled to do so because of a long line of prior authority in which such damages had been awarded: Lord Reid (at 1087) considered that such damages were so firmly embedded in English law that only Parliament could remove them. It is this attitude which underlies the restrictive approach adopted by the House: the House confined the award of exemplary damages to those situations where such an award has been recognised unequivocally in the earlier case law or by Parliament, and called generally for restraint in the award of such damages. In this light, the logic of the special category for actions by government servants can be called into question. Lord Devlin in *Rookes v Barnard* (at 1226) justified this category on the basis that servants of the government are also servants of the people and the use of their power subordinate to their duty of service. However, as suggested by McGregor (above, at p.415): "It may be a matter for speculation how far the House, in selecting this category, was really impressed by the difference in the context of damages between the public and private sectors and how far it was motivated by the need to retain some scope for exemplary damages in order not to appear to be acting too cavalierly with the doctrine of precedent; in such a search, what better authorities to leave standing than those in which exemplary damages had originated?" This needs to be borne in mind in considering the proper scope of the second category. A similar view was expressed by Neill LJ in *Arora v*

Bradford CC ([1991] IRLR 165, at 169), suggesting that it was anomalous to allow exemplary damages against a small local authority but not against a powerful private enterprise.

5.5.2. Exemplary damages against government servants

5.5.2.1. General
Until relatively recently there had been few reported successful claims under this head; but a number of awards have been made in recent years, mainly in relation to unlawful conduct by police officers (see Ghandi, (1990) 134 Sol J 357). The torts most commonly involved are false imprisonment, assault, battery, trespass to goods and malicious prosecution. Although their Lordships in *Cassell v Broome,* with the exception of Lord Wilberforce, seemed to think that exemplary damages could only be awarded for torts for which awards had been given in previous cases, awards have recently been made for torts for which there was no precedent (see Ghandi, (1990) 10 LS 182, at 194-196); and it is arguable that they may now be given for any tort. Thus such damages could probably be awarded in a case of misfeasance in public office despite the absence of an English precedent (though they were awarded in *Farrington v Thomson* ([1959] VR 286).

5.5.2.2. "Governmental acts"

To which persons and activities does the second, "public law", category of exemplary damages extend? It was made clear in *Cassell v Broome* by Lords Hailsham, Diplock and Kilbrandon that it applied not only to servants of the Crown but also to other "government" servants, including those of local government. The category has been held applicable to a prison doctor (*Barbara v Home Office* (1984) 134 NLJ 888); to the army as well as to civil Crown servants (*Lavery v Minister of Defence* [1985] 3 CL 249); and even to a solicitor acting as an officer of the court (*Columbia Pictures Industries v Robinson* ([1987] Ch 38 at 87). It is not clear whether it would be applied to publicly funded corporations exercising commercial type functions - whether Crown corporations or not - such as those established to carry on particular development projects, or the newly privatised utilities.

In addition to the requirement of action by a government servant, it was stated by the Employment Appeal Tribunal in *Bradford CC v Arora* ([1989] IRLR 442) that the second category applies only to acts which "fall within the execution of public powers as opposed to powers which are shared with private individuals" (at 69, per Wood J giving the judgement of the tribunal). In support of this view the tribunal cited statements of Lord Reid in *Rookes v Barnard* (at 1087) referring to "governmental functions" and "functions of a governmental character". He cited also the statement of

Lord Diplock in *Broome v Cassell* (at 1129) that the category applies to powers conferred by virtue of an "official status or employment" (though this could equally well support the view that all acts of government servants are within the principle). The tribunal concluded that exemplary damages could not be awarded in this case, which concerned the act of selecting an individual for employment, since the authority was not "exercising a power within the public domain".

The Tribunal's decision was overturned by the Court of Appeal ([1991] IRLR 165), which held that an exemplary award could be made. It was held irrelevant that judicial review would not apply to this type of function. However, the court did emphasise the seniority of the appointment in question (of Head of Teaching Studies at an Education College), the seniority of the appointing officials, and the fact that express responsibility was given by statute to the council itself with respect to the post; and it was suggested that certain acts of junior officials of the council might not constitute the exercise of a "public function" for the purpose of exemplary damages. This suggests that the court might not have accepted the appellant's submission that all functions of the authority were "public functions" for this purpose. The court's approach is likely to create a great deal of uncertainty : it would be better to recognise that all torts by public officials may attract exemplary damages. Exemplary damages have been awarded for the wrongful injection of a remand prisoner with a tranquiliser by a prison doctor ((*Barbara v Home Office* (1984) 134 NLJ 888), a decision which is difficult to reconcile with the restrictions suggested in Arora.

5.5.2.3. *"Oppressive, arbitrary or unconstitutional action"*

Exemplary damages may be awarded when the action complained of is "oppressive, arbitrary or unconstitutional". There is no requirement, however, that they be awarded in every case falling within this category (*Holden v Chief Constable of Lancashire* [1987] QB 380).

What is "oppressive, arbitrary or unconstitutional" action has not been clearly defined. The only significant decision on this point is that of the Court of Appeal in *Holden* above. Here it was held that the terms denote three separate categories of behaviour capable of giving rise to an exemplary award, a conclusion said to be based on the need to give effect to the word "or" used by Lord Devlin. It is doubtful, however, that Lord Devlin was intending to lay down a precise test, and it is difficult to develop any coherent principles by trying to give separate meaning to these three terms. In the case before it the court held the conduct in question, an unlawful arrest of a police officer, to be "unconstitutional", and hence capable of giving rise to an exemplary award though there was no element of arbitrariness or oppression. Purchas LJ, giving the leading judgement, said that he found "surprising" the proposition that every unlawful act of a police officer is "unconstitutional" (at 387). This suggests that not every *ultra vires* act of government is an "unconstitutional" one. However, no guidelines were given as to the meaning of unconstitutional in this context. In fact there seems no reason to distinguish between different categories of unlawful act.

Where an act is not "unconstitutional" (whatever this means), oppression or arbitrary conduct is required before an exemplary award can be made. Arguably, this might suggest the need for a significant detrimental effect on the plaintiff, whereas this is not required where the conduct is unconstitutional.

The question of what mental element, if any, is required is not entirely clear. It is submitted that an exemplary award should only be allowed where the defendant acts with malice, or where he knows his conduct is unlawful, or is reckless as to this; it is only conduct of this type which should be punishable (though for a contrary view see Gandhi, [1990] 10 LS 182 at p.187). The fact that the conduct has a serious effect on the plaintiff should not be sufficient: this is taken account of in awarding compensatory damages. This proposition is consistent with the views expressed in the case law. In *Moore v Lambeth County Court Registrar* ([1970] 1 QB 560 (CA)) both Sachs LJ and Russell LJ seemed to contemplate that malice would normally be necessary for such an award, and that exemplary damages could not be awarded where the act in question was done in good faith as a result of a mistake. Similarly in *Barbara v Home Office* ((1984) 134 NLJ 888) Leggatt J stated that he was "not attracted" by the idea of imposing liability for "mere negligence", even though the conduct was "oppressive" from the plaintiff's point of view, expressly making the point that this was a matter for compensatory damages. He stated, rather obscurely, that "malice" was not the only state of mind which might warrant an award of exemplary damages; but this could refer to the fact that such damages may be available where the tortfeasor knows that he acts unlawfully, though he does not act out of spite towards the plaintiff. It may also be noted that in *Holden* it was suggested by Purchas J that exemplary damages might only be awarded for unconstitutional action which is "improper", which could be interpreted as referring to the need for a mental element.

6

Negligence

6.1. Introduction

It is well established that a public authority may be liable in negligence. Its employees are liable personally for damage which they cause - for example, for negligent driving on government business; and the authority is vicariously liable for such negligence. The authority may like any other non-natural person also be fixed with direct liability. Thus, for example, a school authority was held liable where a young child escaped from a school as a result of the authority's careless fa...:ure to establish a proper system of supervision, and caused an accident (*Carmarthenshire CC v Lewis* [1955] AC 549). The Crown is only directly liable for carelessness in respect of the categories specifically set out on section 2 of the Crown Proceedings Act 1947 - that is, for breach of duties owed as an employer, or as an owner or occupier of land, or duties imposed by statute: see 5.4.4 above.

In some early cases it was argued that when an activity was being carried out under the authority of statute the loss-causing action must be regarded as authorised by Parliament, and thus could not be considered tortious. This argument was rejected: "an action does lie for doing what the legislature has authorised if it be done negligently" (*Geddis v Proprietors of Bann Reservoir* (1878) 3 AC 430 at 455-6 per Lord Blackburn; and see *Gibbs v Mersey Docks and Harbour Board* (1866) 11 HLC 686). To put it another way, it can be said that the authority given generally extends only to the carrying out of activities in a non-negligent manner: the legislature is presumed not to have authorised any negligent activity.

A few writers have criticised the application to public bodies of ordinary negligence principles. It has been suggested that in times of financial stringency local authorities may have insufficient resources to perform all their statutory duties, or at least to provide the level of services which has become reasonably expected of them. In this climate the function of the law of negligence in minimising the total cost of accidents and accident prevention cannot be achieved, since there are simply insufficient resources available to spend on prevention. A public body, unlike a private individual, cannot divest itself of responsibilities and functions because it cannot meet the legal obligations which arise out of them. An employer who cannot meet his obligations, for example, can always cease business or curtail his

168

activities, but the former option is not open to a public authority, and the latter impossible to the extent that statutory duties are placed on the authority. In such a situation, it has been suggested, it may be better to use the limited resources available to prevent accidents in the future than to compensate those who have suffered damage in the past (see Weir, [1989] PL 40). It has also been argued that the law of negligence has minimal deterrent effect on public bodies (see Cohen and Smith, (1986) 64 Can Bar Rev 1; Cohen, (1990) 40 U of TLJ 213). Such arguments have not, however, prevented the courts holding authorities liable under ordinary negligence principles, although the inadequacy of resources argument may have contributed to their reluctance to impose liability for careless failure to confer benefits (see 6.4 below).

It is, then, in principle, the ordinary private law of negligence which is applied to determine liability. A number of matters of particular relevance to public authorities require consideration however, and it is these which will be examined in this chapter.

6.2. Immunity for Discretionary Decisions

6.2.1. The principle of immunity

Although public bodies are liable in negligence in principle, there is some government decision making for which the possibility of negligence liability is excluded. This is because it is considered inappropriate that the courts should assess the "reasonableness" of that conduct. Public authorities making discretionary decisions must balance the different interests affected as they think fit, and it is accepted that the courts should not always "review" this process by imposing liability in negligence.

The case of *Home Office v Dorset Yacht* ([1970] AC 1004) illustrates the general principle. The government has a discretionary power to decide how to dispose of and treat young offenders who have been given a custodial sentence. In deciding how to exercise this power the government must weigh and balance a range of concerns. For example, in deciding whether these offenders should be permitted to spend time working in the community, or to engage in activities outside their institution of confinement, a number of factors must be considered. On the one hand are the possible rehabilitative effects of outside activities, and the ultimate benefit to the community from rehabilitation. On the other, are the costs of a more "open" corrective regime, including administration and supervision costs, and the costs in terms of damage which might be caused by the youngsters. If it is decided to implement an "open" training policy under which access to the community is provided, and damage is caused by the youngsters to persons or property, should those who suffer damage be able to sue in negligence, on the basis that it is unreasonable for the government to adopt such a policy? Negligence liability exists where a person has not acted as a "reasonable" man (or government). In deciding unreasonableness one must weigh all the pros and cons of the action. In the example given, this would require the court to weigh the benefits of the "open" training policy against the costs. If the courts did not agree that the decision reached was justified, because the costs outweighed the benefits, it would categorise the decision as tortious - as a "wrong" - and the authority would be required to pay damages for any loss caused. It is in fact considered inappropriate for the court to determine whether the decision made was reasonable in this sense: the question of what action should be taken is for the authority to decide. In *Dorset Yacht*, which concerned damage allegedly caused to the plaintiff's yacht by escaping borstal trainees who had been working in a harbour as part of a rehabilitation programme, it was held that there could be no liability for the government's policy decision to adopt an "open" regime. This conclusion was expressed by saying that no duty of care was owed in making the decision. Such an immunity, expressed at the duty level, covers many decisions involving the allocation of resources, or the allocation of risks or benefits to one sector or activity, at the expense of another.

It must be stressed, however, that the immunity is limited to the making of discretionary decisions which it is considered inappropriate for the courts to "review" : the general principle is that public authorities *are* liable in negligence in *carrying out* their activities. Thus in *Dorset Yacht* it was said that, though there could be no liability for the policy decision which increased the risk of damage occurring, the government would be liable if the escape had resulted from a careless failure to supervise the youngsters in accordance with Home Office instructions.

The distinction between reviewable and unreviewable decisions is often expressed by reference to a distinction between the "policy" and "operational" levels of government activity: it is said that the government will generally be liable for carelessness   at   the "operational" level but not for a decision made at the "policy" level. This approach originates from the United States (though the courts there tend to use the term "planning" rather than "policy"). It became established in English law following its adoption by Lord Wilberforce in *Anns v Merton LBC* ([1978] AC 728). However, although it is sometimes said that to categorise an act as occurring at the policy or operational level is dispositive of the existence of a duty of care, the terms were not used by Lord Wilberforce in this dispositive sense. He stated as follows (at 754):

"Most, indeed probably all, statutes relating to public authorities or public bodies, contain in them a large area of policy. The courts call this 'discretion' meaning that the decision is one for the authority or body to make, and not for the courts. Many statutes also prescribe, or at least presuppose, the practical execution of policy decisions: a convenient description of this is to say that in addition to the area of policy or discretion, there is an operational area. Although this distinction between the policy area and operational area is convenient, and illuminating, it is probably a distinction of degree; many `operational' powers or duties have in them some element of `discretion'. It can safely be said that the more 'operational' a power or duty may be, the easier it is to superimpose upon it a common law duty of care."

Clearly it was not intended to say that activities at the operational level will *always* give rise to a duty of care: the terms "policy" and "operational" are used merely as a sort of "layman's" shorthand to refer to the kind of activity which is likely, or not likely, to be subject to review.

Whether there is immunity has sometimes been expressed as a question of whether the authority has acted within the limits of a discretion conferred by Parliament (see, for example, *Fellowes v Rother DC* [1983] All ER 513 at per Goff J). In other words, it is said that with statutory powers the immunity principle is an aspect of the defence of statutory authority: the immunity arises because statute has provided that within a certain area the authority is authorised to act as it chooses. This is indeed a formal reason for immunity. It tells us little, however, about the factual circumstances in which an authority is immune, since the precise circumstances in which the court should refrain from imposing liability will be far from clear from the terms of any given statute. It is general constitutional principles concerning the relationship between the courts, Executive and Legislature which determine the appropriate method of "construction" of the statute to establish the limits of the authority's powers. Other principles of administrative law, such as natural justice have similarly been framed as principles of statutory construction: they apply because Parliament "intended" that the powers of public authorities be defined by these limits (*Fairmount Investments Ltd v Secretary of State for the Environment* [1976] 1 WLR 1255 at 1263 per Lord Russell). But it is constitutional principle and policy, as determined by the courts, which sets the precise limits on the powers.

However, like other administrative law principles, negligence immunity cannot, anyway, be explained entirely in terms of the scope of statutory discretion. First, like other public law principles, it should apply equally to common law powers. Second, there may probably also be immunity where the authority is operating at a policy level, though it acts *ultra vires* (see 6.3 below). The key to the principle is that where public authorities have been set up in relation to a certain area of activity, policy choices in that sphere ought to be left to the authority as a more appropriate body than the courts for making such choices. This is not to say that the courts are incapable of adjudicating on the matter; simply that it is sometimes more appropriate that another established institution should do so instead.

6.2.2.   Operation of the immunity

In what cases it is inappropriate to review public authority actions through the law of negligence? Some decisions are quite obviously not reviewable. Thus, the courts are hardly likely to entertain a claim for damages by an unemployed person who considers that he has suffered loss from the negligent handling of the economy! (Bowman and Bailey (1986) CLJ 430). The view of the House of Lords that the implementation of an open training regime for borstal boys is immune from review, has already been mentioned (see 6.2.1 above); and in a similar vein the Court of Appeal has stated that determining the care to be given to potentially dangerous juveniles is for the responsible authority (*Vicar of Writtle v Essex CC* (1979) LGR 656 at 672).

Another leading case is *Anns v Merton LBC* ([1978] AC 728). This concerned the powers of a local authority to inspect new buildings for compliance with certain legislation which was designed to ensure sound construction. It was held that the decision on what resources to devote to inspection - how many houses to inspect, for example - was for the local authority: it was for that body to weigh the benefits of inspection in terms of securing proper construction against the financial costs of an inspection policy. However, it was stated that liability would exist where a choice was made to inspect in a particular way, and the inspection was carried out in a careless manner. It should be noted that there are now some doubts whether a duty of care is owed in the exercise of this power at all, because of the restrictions on liability where no extra damage is caused, discussed at 6.4 below. (Certainly, there is no duty in relation to economic loss: see 6.7 below). If there can be no liability for a careless inspection for the reasons discussed in 6.4, the dividing line between the policy and operational levels here becomes irrelevant in English law, though still relevant in some other Commonwealth jurisdictions (see 6.4).

Other examples of decisions held immune from scrutiny include *Rigby v Chief Constable of Northamptonshire* ([1985] 1 WLR 1242), holding that a decision to end a seige by using an inflammable form of CS gas as opposed to one less inflammable, but with other potential dangers, was properly within the discretion left to the Chief Constable; *Alison v Corby DC* ([1980] RTR 111) where a cyclist injured by roaming dogs could not claim in negligence for the Council's failure to devote more resources to the problem of capturing strays; and *Department of Health and Social Security v Kinnear* ([1984] 134 NLJ 886; and Lexis), holding that the formulation of a vaccination policy was within the authority's discretion so that those suffering serious side effects could not sue the Department in negligence.

A wide view of the scope of immunity is that an authority's actions should not be reviewable wherever they result from a conscious decision to allocate resources in a particular way, or to inflict or permit damage in order to achieve a benefit for other parties. The decided cases suggest, however, there will not be immunity in every such case. This is illustrated by the decision of the Court of Appeal in *Bird v Pearce* ([1979] 77 LGR 753). The authority had established a system of priority at a junction as between the users of certain roads. This was normally indicated by white lines on the road. However, during resurfacing work the lines became obliterated and before they could be replaced an accident occurred. It was held that the Council had been negligent in failing to provide temporary warning signs, even though the decision not to do so had been one deliberately taken by the Council on the basis that the risk to be averted was too small to justify the cost. Another such case is *Rigby,* above, where, though the authority's choice of which gas to use was not reviewable, it was held to be negligent to have used the more inflammable gas without firefighters present (an absence known to the person responsible for its use); whilst in *Reffell v Surrey CC* ([1964] 1 WLR 358) it was held that the authority was negligent in failing to replace dangerous glass panels in its schools, although it had deliberately adopted a policy of "phased" replacement over a period of time. Once it is accepted that some choices are reviewable, however, it may be difficult to decide where to draw the line between those which are and those which are not.

One factor which is clearly important is whether the situation is one in which a private person would owe a duty of care. It has been argued that the matter is always justiciable in such a case: according to Oliver "it would be unthinkable that a public authority which is under a duty of care either at common law, or under a statute (such as the Occupiers Liability Act), might be able to plead in its defence that, for example, the public interest or the rival claims of efficiency and thrift, as evaluated by the authority, entitled it to neglect its duty" ([1980] CLP 269; and see Bowman and Bailey, above). It seems clear that the courts are likely to hold an authority to the ordinary standards of liability under the Occupier's Liability Acts as indicated by *Reffell v Surrey CC,* above. It was also held in *Page Motors v Epsom and Ewell BC* ((1982) 80 LGR 337) that the "policy" immunity has no relevance to a local authority acting as a landowner: it is for the court, not the authority, to weigh the competing policies and interests (on this see further 8.1.5 below). It seems also to be accepted that a driver in a police chase owes a duty of care under ordinary principles (*Marshall v Osmond* [1983] QB 1034); the court will thus be prepared to review an officer's decision to take risks in the public interest. Similarly, in *Knight v The*

Home Office [1990] 3 All ER 237, PiILJ held that the question of what constituted "reasonable" supervision of an inmate of a prison hospital, known to be a suicide risk, was for the courts, as it would also be in relation to an inmate in any psychiatric hospital. The judge rejected the argument that it was for the prison authorities to decide how much of their limited resources should be devoted to this. (The judge did, though, accept that the standard of care required would be lower than in in ordinary psychiatric hospital since the legislature had not intended to provide the resources for care to be given in prisons at the same level as in specialist hospitals). It was also stated in *Knight* (at 743) that the court would impose liability on ordinary negligence principles if the authority decided not to give attention to maintaining its vehicles in order to spend its resources on other things, and an accident thereby resulted.

Although the test of whether there would be a duty under the general law is a useful guideline, however, it should not be conclusive. *Rigby* can be cited to support this view - a private individual attempting a rescue with dangerous equipment would be required to act reasonably, though a generous view of what is reasonable would no doubt be taken. (Proponents of the "private duty" test might argue that *Rigby* is wrong on the duty of care point, and best explained as a case where the conduct was reasonable (see Bowman and Bailey, above) - a ground which the judge did mention as an alternative basis for the the decision). Similarly, a doctor implementing a vaccination policy on his own initiative might be liable in negligence, though it was held in *Kinnear* that the Department of Health was not. In other cases, it is unrealistic to ask whether there would be a duty of care in private law since the situation is not one which has a close private law parallel - for example, where an authority has care of offenders, or suspected offenders (as in *Writtle and Dorset Yacht*). This cannot be compared with a parent's control of a child, given the authority's public law obligation to take action to punish and/or rehabilitate. In such a case it is submitted that it is generally appropriate for the policy choices to be made by the authority.

It must be recognised that certainty is not possible in this area, and that inevitably there will be differences of opinion on the width of the discretion to be given to public bodies. This is true also of the rules relating to judicial review of administrative action, but the uncertainties in both areas of the law must be tolerated to allow public authorities a reasonable freedom of action whilst maintaining some degree of judicial control.

Where damage is caused by inadvertence or failure to adhere to a policy set by the authority itself, as opposed to a deliberate policy choice by that authority, there is no problem in the courts' reviewing that conduct according to a reasonableness standard. Thus in *Dorset Yacht*, for example, it was said that there would be liability if, as alleged, the boys causing the damage had escaped because the officers in question had disregarded Home Office instructions as to the manner in which they were to be looked after.

6.2.3. *Need for a special public law rule*

Several writers have argued that the latitude given to public authorities in the exercise of their discretion can adequately be dealt with through the ordinary concepts of private law, and that there is no need to talk in terms of an "immunity" for public bodies (see for example, Bowman and Bailey [1986] CLJ 430; *Harlow Compensation and Government Torts* (1982) at pp.56-57). Bowman and Bailey have pointed out that the courts show some reticence in reviewing the discretion of professionals such as doctors, which is done by giving deference to the judgement of those professionals in determining what is required by the standard of care, and these writers argue that the same techniques should be adopted in reviewing the activities of public authorities.

However, there is an important difference in review of the two groups. With professionals the court defers to their view as *evidence* of reasonable practice. However, in principle the court retains control as the arbiter of values to be given to competing interests, and indeed as the finder of fact, and should retain the right to substitute its own judgement if appropriate (see *Sidaway v Bethleman Royal Hospital* [1985] AC 871 at 900 per Lord Reid). With public authorities the court does not retain this control even in theory: the authority's decision is not just evidence of what is reasonable, but the responsibility of deciding what should be done is with the authority itself. The concept of an "immunity" is appropriate to express this important difference of principle.

It is true, however, as Harlow has pointed out (at pp.56-57) that the use of the policy/operational dichotomy involves "an incredibly complex reasoning process". It would be more satisfactory to drop this and to focus directly on whether the particular decision is of a kind which is which is better left to the public body.

Critics have also suggested that the "immunity" approach might lead the courts to err on the side of giving too much discretion to public authorities. From this perspective, views as to whether the "immunity" approach is the best one will differ according to one's views on the degree of freedom which ought rightly to be given to public bodies. It is the author's view that the biggest danger is that any other approach will result in undue interference with public authority decision making.

6.2.4.   Ultra vires and the public law immunity

The decided cases where immunity has been given for policy decisions are
cases where a public authority has acted *intra vires*. What would the position
be if its action were *ultra vires*? Consider, for example, a person refused a
licence to trade because an authority considers there are already too many
licence holders. This turns out to be a consideration which is irrelevant to
the grant of licences: the only relevant consideration is the fitness of
applicants. Pending a determination of the legality of the authority's action,
the applicant suffers loss of profits through being unable to trade. In
weighing the factors relevant to a grant of a licence the authority, when
acting *intra vires*, will be immune from liability. Is the position affected by
the fact that the authority took into account an irrelevant factor and hence is
acting outside jurisdiction? In other words, may the applicant for the licence
claim damages in negligence if he considers the authority's judgement was
wrong?
   In deciding this the court would have to balance the various factors for
and against the grant of the licence: that is, to engage in the kind of
assessment which is considered inappropriate where the authority act *intra
vires*. Craig (at pp.455-457) has argued that it is no more appropriate for the
court to make such an assessment where the authority has acted *intra vires*.
This is surely correct. Lord Diplock in *Dorset Yacht Co. v The Home
Office* ([1970] AC 1004, at 1183-84) suggested that *ultra vires* had
"replaced" negligence as the test of liability in public law; but this should
only be taken to mean that the authority will *not* be liable where it acts in
the exercise of a valid discretion, and not that negligence liability may be
imposed for a "policy" decision which is *ultra vires*. The view that public
law immunity does not turn on whether or not the authority is acting in the
exercise of valid discretion, but rather on whether the question in issue is
suitable for judicial resolution, finds support in the speech of Lord Keith in
Rowling v Takaro Properties Ltd [1988] AC 473.

6.3.   Exceeding or Failing to Exercise Powers

One important issue yet to be fully resolved is whether a public authority
should be liable for any careless failure to keep within its powers, or for a
careless failure to exercise its discretion at all. In the case of a refusal of a
licence on the basis of an improper consideration, for example, could the
applicant sue for damages in negligence if the authority ought to realise that
the factor on which it based its decision was irrelevant? Ensuring that a
public body has legal authority for its actions - by checking the statute and

seeking legal advice - and taking reasonable care to comply with this authority could be regarded as a function at the operational level and therefore reviewable by the courts.

6.3.1. Liability for ultra vires action

The existence of a duty to take care not to make an invalid decision has been raised in two cases before the Privy Council. In the first, *Dunlop v Woollahra Municipal Council* ([1982] AC 158) it arose in relation to a decision by the council to limit the number of storeys which the plaintiff's building could contain. It had no power to do so and it was argued, *inter alia*, that the council had been negligent in not realising this. The Privy Council expressed doubts whether there was a duty of care on the authority to act within its powers, but found it unnecessary to decide. The matter came up again in *Rowling v Takaro Properties* ([1988] AC 473), where it was argued that the Minister had been negligent in taking account of an irrelevant consideration in refusing consent for the sale of the plaintiff's shares to an overseas company. It was again held unnecessary to determine the duty of care point but Lord Keith expressed serious doubts as to whether a duty existed. The main reason given was a fear that imposing a duty might induce undue caution by public officials; he considered that actions of this kind would rarely succeed because of the difficulties - discussed below - of showing carelessness and of proving damage, so that there was little to be gained by allowing them, whilst, on the other hand, the adverse effect on bureaucratic behaviour might be significant. This is similar to the argument used to justify judicial immunity (see 5.2.2 above). It has also been used to give some immunity to barristers in connection with litigation (*Rondel v Worsley* [1969] 1 AC 191; see Winfield and Jolowicz, at pp.102-106), and it has sometimes been suggested that it should be extended to other professionals, such as doctors, who may be led to practise defensive medicine through a fear of legal liability. However, this sort of argument is generally unconvincing: such problems should (with perhaps the exception of judicial immunity) be met by setting the standard of care at an appropriate level, rather than by denying the existence of any duty.

The problem of the duty owed by public authorities was also considered by the Supreme Court of Canada in *Welbridge Holdings v Greater Winnipeg* ([1971] SCR 957) where it was held that the authority owed no duty to take reasonable care in ensuring that it adhered to the necessary procedural requirements in enacting a zoning law. The reasoning was that the exercise of "legislative powers" was not capable of giving rise to liability in negligence. This reasoning is also open to criticism: it is true that there can be no liability with respect to a decision on the *content* of bye-laws, but this is a quite separate matter from whether the authority has been negligent in failing to keep within its powers.

It is submitted that English law should recognise the possibility of a duty to take care to ensure that action is *intra vires*. This finds some support in English cases, discussed below, suggesting that there may be a duty to take reasonable care to *consider* the exercise of discretionary powers, and to make a prompt and valid decision where there is a duty to act - although it is true that the "undue caution" argument is not so relevant where there is a complaint of an unlawful failure to act, as opposed to invalid action.

Even if a duty may arise in principle, it must be emphasised that no duty will be owed where the other requisites of a duty of care are not satisfied. Thus it may be debated whether any duty of care could be owed on the facts of *Takaro*, for example, given that the loss caused was economic loss (on this see 6.7 below). There are also a number of other restrictive rules such as those governing liability for failure to confer a benefit (see 6.4), which means that successful actions will be rare in practice.

To establish liability it must also be proved that the authority did not take reasonable care. The interpretation of statutes conferring powers on public authorities is a matter of considerable difficulty and uncertainty, and frequently an authority would not be negligent in failing to appreciate the scope of its powers (as was recognised in *Takaro* itself). However, the authority may be said to have acted carelessly where the action is quite obviously outside the scope of its powers, as may often be the case with conduct which is "unreasonable" in the public law sense (though not invariably : for example, the decision on unreasonableness in *Wheeler v Leicester City Council* [1985] AC 1054 was probably unpredictable). There may also be negligence where the conduct proposed is controversial and no legal advice has been sought.

An action may also fail because of the difficulty of proving loss, as again was pointed out in *Takaro*. Thus, for example, where a licence is refused for some irrelevant reason, an applicant should only obtain damages where he can show that if the authority had acted lawfully its discretion would have been exercised in his favour (on this see 1.4.2 above).

6.3.2.   *Unlawful failure to determine*

A public authority has a general public law duty to give a proper consideration to whether to exercise its powers (*Anns v Merton LBC* [1978] AC 728). It may also have a duty to make certain specific determinations - for example, whether an applicant is entitled to a particular benefit or grant - and there is an implied obligation to make such public law decisions promptly (see Harding, *Public Duties and Public Law* (1988), pp.35-43; *R v HM Treasury ex parte Petch*, 24 Feb 1989 and *Petch v HM Treasury* (CA), 15 Jan 1990, Lexis).

It was stated by Lord Wilberforce in *Anns* that a public authority could be liable for failure to consider the exercise of its statutory powers. This would also suggest that there would be liability for a careless failure to make a determination which the authority is under a duty to make. This view is supported by Popplewel LJ in *Petch,* above, at first instance, who considered that there was a duty of care to make a required determination with reasonable promptness (and see also *Graves v Secretary of State for Social Security*, 17 Oct. 1988, Lexis, where Croom Johnson LJ, granting leave to appeal from a first instance decision to strike out the action as an abuse of process said that "perhaps" such a claim may be available; and *Lonrho v Tebbitt* [1991] 4 All ER 973). To establish a duty in any particular case, however, it will again be necessary to satisfy all the other requisites of a duty of care. It will also be necessary to show no reasonable care has been taken (see 6.3.1 above). On the latter issue it may be noted that Popplewell LJ in *Petch* considered that the question of what resources are to be devoted to the expeditious hearing of claims was a matter for the authority, and a conscious decision to allocate limited resources could not be reviewed through a negligence action. However, it is submitted that the question of what is a reasonable time for determination should normally be for the court.

To succeed it will again also be necessary to prove loss, which will require the applicant to show at any discretionary determination would have been made in his favour (see 1.4.2 above).

6.4. Omissions and Conduct not Creating "Fresh Damage"

6.4.1. Introduction

A person is not normally liable for a negligent omission: a man owes no duty to take positive action to help another (see Jones at pp.36-39; Winfield and Jolowicz at pp.91-96). Thus there is no liability for failing to save another from harm - to give the classic example, a man is not liable where he unreasonably stands by whilst a child drowns in a small pool of water. Similarly he is not generally liable for failing to confer a positive benefit - such as a gift or grant - on another, though a reasonable man would have done so. There is also no liability on someone who begins an act of rescue, or a task which would benefit another, but is unsuccessful because he is careless (Jones at pp.39-42; Winfield and Jolowicz, above; Bowman and Bailey [1984] PL 277): if he is not liable for refusing to act at all, he should not be held liable for attempting to act but failing. In such a case he will only generally be liable if the effect of his conduct is not merely to fail to improve the other's position, but to make it worse. For example, if a man carelessly fails in an attempt to rescue a drowning child, he will not come under any liability if without his intervention the child would have drowned anyway. However, if the effect of his intervention was to deter other rescuers who would have saved the child, then he may be liable. These rules can be summed up by saying that there is no liability for omissions or conduct which do not produce "extra damage". There are some exceptions (see Jones at pp.39-44; Bowman and Bailey, above); thus a number of relationships, for example, give rise to positive duties to assist - for example, that of employer and employee, and hotelier and patron; and a party may also have a duty to prevent certain persons within his control causing damage to others - for example, a parent with respect to his children.

An important question of public law is the extent to which a public authority owes a duty of care in relation to acts or omissions which do not involve the creation of extra damage. Public authorities are often given statutory powers to take action to prevent harm to the public - for example, through the regulation and inspection of trade, and   of safety standards. They are also given many   important discretionary powers which allow them to confer positive benefits, such as grants, welfare payments and scholarships. If an authority carelessly fails to exercise these powers at all, or exercises them in a careless manner, may an individual who might have benefitted from their proper exercise sue in negligence?

6.4.2.   The traditional approach

The present law is not entirely certain. The traditional view has been that public bodies are in the same position as private individuals with respect to acts which do not cause extra damage: liability is recognised only in very limited situations, which can be seen to have some analogy with situations where a positive duty to act is imposed in private law. In other words, the traditional view is that the public character of the entity does not affect liability. Thus there is a duty to take reasonable care to prevent damage being caused by youngsters under the care and control of a public body (*Dorset Yacht Co. Ltd. v Home Office* [1970] AC 1004; *Carmarthenshire County Council v Lewis* [1955] AC 549) and it has been held that the police are liable for negligently failing to prevent the suicide of a prisoner in their custody (*Kirkham v Anderton* [1990] 2 WLR 987; *Knight v The Home Office* [1990] 3 All ER 237), but these duties clearly have analogies with private law duties to control and to take care of persons for whom one has assumed responsibility. An authority has not, on the other hand, generally been considered liable for negligently refusing grants or welfare payments, or for a negligent exercise of (or failure to exercise) its regulatory powers. In *East Suffolk Catchment Board v Kent* ([1941] AC 74) the House of Lords declined to impose liability for the exercise of a power to assist the plaintiff in draining his flooded land, which it was alleged had been carried out in a careless manner. This case was regarded until recently (see 6.4.3) as authority for a general proposition that liability does not normally arise without extra damage.

It may be noted that some liability has always been imposed for the negligent performance, or non-performance of statutory duties (as opposed to the exercise of permissive powers). In particular, a highway authority has been held at common law to be liable for a negligent repair done in pursuance of its statutory duty to maintain and repair the highway (see generally Harding, *Public Duties and Public Law*, pp.239-245). Although the common law did not hold the authority liable for negligently failing to act at all, such liability has now been imposed by statute (Highways (Miscellaneous Provisions) Act 1961 s.1(1); Highways Act 1980 s.58). It may be noted that the burden of proving reasonable care is, under the statute, on the authority (s.1(2)), though the significance of this reduced by the fact that no breach of the duty to maintain and repair occurs unless there has been a *prima facie* reasonable time elapsing since the damage to make it reasonable for repair to have been effected (*Haydon v Kent CC* [1978] QB 343).

6.4.3. The decision in Anns v Merton LBC

A move towards wider liability under the common law for public authorities where no extra damage has resulted seemed at one time to have been heralded by the decision of the House of Lords in *Anns v Merton London Borough Council* ([1978] AC 728). Although it is now debatable whether *Anns* has any lasting significance at all in widening liability, the position is not entirely clear. It is argued below that this decision could and should be invoked to widen liability, provided that the courts proceed with some caution.

Anns concerned the question of whether an authority is under a duty to take care in the exercise of its powers of inspection. It was held by the House of Lords that, despite the fact that any "damage" caused by the absence of inspection or careless inspection would simply be a failure to prevent damage from occurring, a duty of care was in fact owed. The reason given by Lord Wilberforce was that a public authority is not, like a private individual, completely free to decide whether or not to exercise its powers, but is under a public law duty to give proper consideration to whether they should be exercised. This reasoning applies, of course, to all discretionary powers (and, of course, to duties) and is not confined to the type of power in issue in *Anns*. That Lord Wilberforce indeed envisaged that liability would be extended in future beyond the facts of the *Anns* case itself in seen in the fact that the decision of no liability in *East Suffolk* (above) was explained as based on the fact that the conduct complained of was a discretionary decision which was not justiciable (*Anns* at 756-757), rather than - as appeared from the judgements in *East Suffolk* itself - that there could be no duty of care where the authority had not added to the damage. The reasoning in Anns, then could be used to support an argument that a *prima facie* duty of care arises with respect to the exercise of discretionary powers, even in the absence of extra damage. More narrowly, it might at least be suggested that the court should be more willing to recognise new duties in this kind of case.

6.4.4.   The law since Anns

The approach in *Anns* has been subject to much criticism (see, for example, Smith and Burns, (1983) 46 MLR 147; Bailey and Bowman [1984] PL 277), and the decisions since then show a reluctance to impose liability without "extra damage". In many, liability has been precluded by a restrictive application of other rules, rather than any rule concerned with the need for extra damage *per se*. Thus liability is limited by the principle that there may be compensation only for interests the protection of which is within the object of the statute conferring the relevant power (see 6.6), and by restrictions on the recovery of economic loss (see 6.7). The decision in *Anns* itself, where economic loss was claimed, has now been overruled by the House in *Murphy v Brentwood DC* ([1990] 3 WLR 414) on the basis that the general test for the recovery of economic loss was not satisfied - though whether a duty may still be owed in relation to other types of loss was left open (see further below). In addition the possibility of liability has been excluded in many cases for specific "policy" reasons, notably that public authorities should not be rendered too cautious in their activities because of a fear of liability (see 6.8 below). These restrictions mean that even if a duty is not generally precluded by the absence of extra damage, it is likely in practice to be negatived for some other reason.

Further, other cases suggest that the absence of extra damage is still in itself an important indicator of the absence of a duty of care. This seemed to be the view of the House of Lords in *Hill v Chief Constable of West Yorkshire* ([1988] 2 All ER 238). In this case the mother of a young girl murdered by the notorious killer nicknamed "the Yorkshire Ripper" sued the Chief Constable on behalf of the estate, alleging the police had been careless in failing to catch the murderer earlier. It was held that the police generally owe no duty to individual members of the public in apprehending criminals. A number of grounds were given for this conclusion, one being, it seems, that a duty arises only where there is some special relationship between the parties: mere foresight of damage, even though it is physical damage, is insufficient for a duty to arise. *Dorset Yacht*, above, was distinguished on the basis that in *Dorset Yacht* there existed a special relationship between the Home Office and those living in the vicinity of the borstal "camp", arising by virtue of the fact that the Home Office had created a special risk of danger to those living in the area (and see *Alexandrou v Oxford* (The Times, Feb. 19 1990) holding the police owe no duty of care to prevent damage after being summoned to the scene of a crime by a burglar alarm; *Clough v Bussan* [1990] 1 All ER 431, holding the police owe no duty of care to motorists in failing to respond to information about non-functioning traffic lights).

A restrictive approach was also taken by the Privy Council in *Yuen Kun Yeu v Attorney General of Hong Kong* ([1988] AC 175). The Commissioner, who controlled the registration of those wishing to become deposit taking companies, was sued by investors who had lost money on the collapse of such a company. They argued that the Commissioner had been negligent in registering the company or in failing to remove its registration. It was held that no duty of care was owed, despite the fact that one of the functions of the statute was the protection of depositors. Again, a number of reasons were given. They were not, unfortunately, clearly distinguished in the judgement, but one seems to be that a duty of care to prevent damage is owed only in exceptional cases. It was expressly indicated that no duty is normally owed by regulatory authorities - including factory inspectors, who are concerned with physical safety, as well as bodies concerned with economic regulation (see further McLean, (1988) 8 OJLS 442).

The trend of the cases since *Anns* is clearly towards restricting liability and it is no doubt untenable to argue that there is a *prima facie* duty of care for the exercise of discretionary powers even in the absence of extra damage. It might be argued that the significance of *Anns* should now be limited to its particular context. Indeed, in *Murphy* four of their Lordships left open the question of whether any duty exists at all in the exercise of the powers in issue in *Anns* itself, even in relation to physical damage (see [1990] 3 WLR 414 at 419 (Lord MacKay), at 425 (Lord Keith, who considered there was no liability for properly damage), at 451 (Lord Jauncey), and 439 (Lord Bridge). As to the scope of such a duty if it does exist see *Dennis v Charnwood BC* [1983] QB 409; *Investors in Industry Commercial Properties Ltd v South Bedfordshire DC* [1986] QB 1034; *Richardson v West Lindsey DC* [1990] 1 All ER 296).

However, the existence of a public law duty to consider the exercise of discretionary powers, which was mentioned by Lord Wilberforce in *Anns,* does provide a good reason for the courts to be more willing to impose liability without extra damage than they are with private individuals: one of the main policy reasons for the reluctance to develop duties in private law is that it would impose an unfair burden, and constitute an excessive interference with private autonomy, to require positive action. This argument has no application where there is a public duty to consider whether and how to exercise a particular power. The existence of these duties are thus capable of justifying a fundamental difference in approach where public authorities are concerned.

The proper approach, it is submitted, is for the courts to consider each public law case where there is no creation of extra damage on its merits, without adopting a presumption for or against liability. They should be prepared to develop duties on an incremental basis, after careful consideration of the policy issues in each case. The refusal to recognise any duty in both *Hill* and *Yuen Kun-yeu* can be justified. *Hill* involved responsibility for the acts of a third party, for which the courts are reluctant to hold the defendant liable even where he has positively contributed to the damage, let alone failed to prevent it; and with respect to *Yuen Kun-yeu* it can be argued as a matter of policy that individuals have no right to protection from investment decisions, which are inherently risky. It is more arguable whether there should be liability for a negligent factory inspection, or whether a duty should be owed in the *Anns* situation itself.

One class of cases where a duty ought to be recognised is in relation to failure to confer welfare benefits and, perhaps certain types of scholarships and grants. In addition a claim should perhaps be recognised where the "benefit" conferred amounts to permission to exercise rights which existed under the common law, as for, example, with refusal of a licence to exercise a restricted trade or profession. The possibility of liability in respect of welfare payments was doubted by Slade J in *Jones v Department of Employment* ([1989] 1 QB 1), but the decision actually turned on the availability of an appeal (see 6.9 below). Subsequent decisions are more favourable. Clear support for liability is found in *R v H.M. Treasury ex parte Petch* (Feb 24 1989; Lexis), in which Mr. Petch claimed damages for mental distress allegedly caused by the Treasury's failure to consider promptly his claim for certain injury and pension benefits. Popplewell LJ held at first instance that a duty of care was owed, though the claim failed since on the facts there had been no unreasonable delay. The judge also indicated that an action should be available in respect of the refusal of licences, planning permission or legal aid (though on planning permission cf. *Strable v Dartford* [1984] JPL 329). *Petch* was upheld by the Court of Appeal (Jan 15 1991; Lexis) on the grounds that there was no undue delay, and the Court thus found it unnecessary to consider the duty of care point, although Parker L.J. did comment that the court's silence was not to be taken as endorsement of the judge's view of the law. The same issue also arose in *Graves v Secretary of State for Social Security* (Oct 17 1988;

Lexis), in which the plaintiff sought damages for an alleged failure to determine promptly his eligibility for welfare payments. Croom Johnson LJ, granting leave to appeal from the judge's decision to strike out the action as an abuse of process, indicated that "perhaps" such an action would be available. Of course, many of these cases concern economic losses, and to recover it will be necessary to show that the requirements of "proximity" are satisfied; but the courts ought to be willing to develop new duties of care to avoid causing economic loss in this sort of case (see 6.7 below).

The difficulties which the question of liability for failure to prevent damage or to confer benefits has caused can be seen by the different reaction to *Anns* in other jurisdictions. It has been applied to similar facts by the Canadian Supreme Court (see *Kamloops v Nielsen* [1984] 2 SCR 2); and in a recent decision the Court also held that an authority exercising a discretionary power to provide a fire fighting service owed a duty of care with respect to the operation of that service, and could be liable for failing to save the plaintiff's property (*Laurentide Motels v Beauport* [1989] 1 SCR 705. The decision can be criticised, however, on the basis that plaintiffs suffering fire damage are usually insured, and it is preferable to leave the loss with the insurance company). *Anns* has also been followed in New Zealand (see *Steiller v Porirua C.C.* [1986] 1 NZLR 84; *Craig v East Coast Bays C.C.* [1986] 1 NZLR 99). However, in the High Court of Australia in *Sutherland Shire Council v Heyman* ((1985) 60 ALR 1) Brennan J took the view that no duty of case existed with respect to a power to carry out building inspections, a power similar to that in *Anns*. Mason took the view that there could be liability for failing to prevent harm in certain cases where there is a "general reliance" by the public on the authority's performing the task properly, without the need for specific reliance by the plaintiff, in the sense that he would have taken other steps to avoid the damage, but for the authority's powers. He did not, however, consider whether the "general reliance" doctrine applied to the present power, since the case had not been argued on this basis. Deane J thought there was no liability but based his view on the absence of a legislative intention to protect against economic losses; whilst Gibbs J and Wilson J based their conclusion to the same effect on the absence of any breach of duty.

In retrospect *Anns* certainly appears as a high watermark of liability; but its precise boundaries are still not fixed. Whilst in many cases it may be undesirable to impose liability for failing to prevent damage, it is to be hoped that the courts will be willing to recognise the important interests which people have in receiving public benefits and services, and will impose liability in appropriate cases.

6.5.   Negligence and Public Duties

Sometimes a duty to take or refrain from specific action is imposed by statute. The precise nature of the obligation will depend on the construction of the particular statute : the duty may, for example, be strict or it may simply require the authority to take reasonable care (see further 7.2). An individual prejudiced by the non-performance, or improper performance, of a statutory duty may wish to obtain compensation. Not every breach of duty automatically gives a right to compensation, but this depends on whether the legislature intended to provide compensation as a remedy for breach. An action brought on this basis is called an action for "breach of statutory duty", and is discussed in chapter 7. Where such an action is available, it will be unnecessary to establish negligence. Where, however, there no action for breach of statutory duty lies and it is alleged that the authority has been careless in performing the duty, or has carelessly failed to perform it, the tort of negligence might be invoked.

In principle, negligence should apply in the same way to the performance of a duty as to the exercise of a power: a duty is simply a power which the authority is obliged to exercise. Thus if the authority is careless there should be liability, subject, of course, to the restrictions and qualifications outlined elsewhere in this chapter, such as the restrictions on the recovery of economic loss (see 6.7), or for conduct which does not cause extra damage (see 6.4). It was suggested by Lord Denning in *Haydon v Kent County Council* ([1978] QB 343) that the *Anns* principle on liability without extra damage has no application to statutory duties, but this is clearly illogical: the effect would be that where there is a duty to provide a benefit - for example, to inspect houses, or operate a fire brigade - there can be no liability for its careless performance, whilst liability could arise where the authority has a choice as to whether to provide the same benefit or service. It is thus generally assumed that the same principle applies to duties (see for example, *Murphy v Brentwood D.C.* [1990] 3 WLR 414).

In practice negligence is most likely to be relevant where there is a *strict* statutory duty, but no action for breach of statutory duty lies. It is unlikely, on the other hand, that negligence liability can be found where there is a statutory duty to take reasonable care, where there would not also be an action for breach of statutory duty. First, where there is an existing common law duty in respect of the matter covered by the statutory duty, the courts will generally construe the statute as imposing liability for breach, so that there is no need to rely on any duty at common law (see 7.4.1 above). Where, on the other hand, there is no duty of care at common law under ordinary private law principles, liability in negligence must arise from the imposition of the statutory power/duty, under the *Anns* principle (see 6.4

above). Whether the statute has, in fact, the effect of creating a duty to pay compensation for careless conduct should be determined in the same way whether the question is considered from the angle of breach of statutory duty or of negligence. In other words, liability both in negligence and for breach of statutory duty depends on whether there is a legislative intention to create an action in damages, and this question has only one answer. These matters are discussed further in Chapter 7.

If the standard set out for the authority's performance is *lower* than a negligence standard, any liability for negligence should be considered to be excluded by implication, at least in so far as liability in negligence depends on the existence of the statutory power/duty in question under *Anns*. This view was stated by Goff J in *Haydon*, above (at 108). In such a case any action for damages can be based only on the tort of breach of statutory duty. Whether an express duty of this kind would exclude by implication an existing duty under the common law, which does not depend on the *Anns* principle, is perhaps more debatable.

6.6. Purpose of the Statutory Power

In some cases, at least, there will only be liability for the negligent exercise of a power if it can be shown that the power was conferred for the purpose of protecting the plaintiff's interests. Thus in *Peabody Trust v Sir Lindsay Parkinson* ([1985] AC 210) the House of Lords held that the principle put forward in *Anns v Merton LBC* ([1978] AC 728), that there should be liability for the careless exercise by a local authority of powers of building inspection, did not allow a developer to recover for the cost of repairing premises, which costs it was alleged would have been avoided had the authority not been careless in carrying out its supervisory duties. The reason given was that the purpose of these duties is to protect occupiers, and not the financial interests of property developers. This case could today be decided on the basis that it concerned economic loss of a type which is irrecoverable (see 6.7), but it is still authority for the separate principle that the interests affected must be the type the statute was concerned to protect (and see also *Murphy v Brentwood DC* [1990] 3 WLR 414 at per Lord Keith; and *Investors in Industry Commercial Properties Ltd. v South Bedfordshire D.C.* [1986] QB 1034).

It is logical that there can be no recovery for interests outside the protection of the statute in cases like *Anns* and *Peabody* where the duty arises from the statute itself: as explained at 6.4, any duty in these cases arises from the public law duty to give consideration to the powers conferred by statute. This requirement should not be determinative, on the other hand, where a duty of care exists under ordinary common law principles. It may, however, be a relevant factor, as illustrated by the House of Lords decision in *Curran v Northern Ireland Co-ownership Housing Association* ([1987] AC 718 (and see also *Strable v Dartford BC* [1984] JPL 329). In *Curran* the Association had a discretion to award grants for housing improvements and conversions, in order to encourage improvements to the housing stock. It had a duty to withhold a grant where certain standards of work were not met. It was held that there could be no action against the authority which had handed over a grant for a careless failure to spot any defect, because the purpose of the statute was not to protect the interests of owners and occupiers, but to protect the public revenue, which should not be expended on unsatisfactory projects. The case was argued on the basis of "extra damage" - it was alleged that the plaintiff would not have bought the property had it not been able to assume that the extension was sound because of the fact a grant had been made (something which would no doubt be difficult to show in practice). This case can be regarded as an illustration of the more general principle, not confined to the public sphere, that the purpose for which a statement is made is a relevant factor in deciding whether there may be recovery for economic loss suffered in reliance on that statement (*McNaughton (James) Papers Group Ltd v Hicks Anderson & Co* [1991] 1 All ER 134 (C.A. at 114 per Neil LJ.)). It is not clear how far this factor is relevant in physical damage cases. Alternatively, in this sort of situation it may often be said that any reliance was not reasonable, on the basis that it is not normally reasonable to rely on a statement made in the exercise of a statutory power unless that power is granted for your own protection. However, the possibility of recovery in exceptional cases cannot be ruled out. It has been held that a purchaser of domestic property may recover for loss suffered in reliance on a building society survey concerning the property, though he is expressly informed that it is not for his benefit (*Smith v Bush* [1989] 2 WLR 790), and there might be cases in public law where there can be recovery because of reliance on a power not conferred for one's own protection.

6.7. Economic Loss

Restrictions on the recovery of economic loss play a significant role in limiting the negligence liability of public authorities. A duty to avoid such loss arises only where there is a special "proximate" relationship between the parties. The recognised number of "proximate" relationships is small, and although the courts can create new ones it is now difficult to persuade them to do so (see Jones at pp.57-93). This approach to the recovery of economic loss was confirmed by the House of Lords in *Murphy v Brentwood D.C.* ([1990] 3 WLR 414), and although Lord Oliver indicated a willingness to extend and develop the categories of proximate relationship, this was not shared by the other members of the House. In determining the scope of a duty owed by a public authority, the courts apply these restrictive principles on economic loss in the same way as they do to private individuals. This "private law" approach is illustrated, for example, by the Privy Council decision in *Yuen Kun - yeu v A-G for Hong Kong* ([1988] AC 175), discussed at 6.5 above, in which one of the reasons for refusing to recognise a duty of care was that the loss suffered was economic, and that the plaintiffs case did not fall within one of the recognised categories where a duty is owed. (Another, apparently distinct, reason was that the authority's role was merely to fail to prevent damage occurring : see 6.4.4). The fact that one purpose of the statute was to protect the investing public was insufficient to create a duty of care with respect to economic loss where such loss would not generally be recoverable on common law principles. Another illustration is *Murphy* itself, which concerned the scope of the duty of care of a public authority in carrying out its statutory duty to examine and approve building plans, to ensure that they are not defective and that they comply with building byelaws. In its previous decision in *Anns v Merton London Borough Council* ([1978] AC 728, discussed further at 6.2 and 6.4 above), which was concerned with the statutory power to inspect the construction work actually done, the House had held that where there was a breach of the duty of care owed by the authority in exercising its supervisory powers over building work, an occupier prejudiced by the breach could recover the costs of restoring any dangerous building to a safe condition. However, in *Murphy* the House took the rare step of overruling one of its own decisions, and held that no duty was owed in respect of this type of loss : the loss was pure economic loss and as such irrecoverable.

Recovery will, of course, be allowed where the loss falls within one of the recognised categories - for example, where the loss is consequent on physical injury to the plaintiff or damage to his property, or where the plaintiff has reasonably relied on the defendant's statement, under the principle in *Hedley Byrne v Heller* ([1964] AC 465). This principle might be invoked where loss results from reliance on negligent official advice. However, even in the case of advice given to the plaintiff individually and personally - rather than in a general brochure, for example - it is likely to be difficult to succeed in the light of the restrictive approach adopted in recent cases (*Caparo Industries v Dickman* [1990] 2 AC 605; *MacNaghton (James) Papers Groups Ltd v Hicks Anderson & Co* [1989] 1 All ER 134). It may be noted, however, that the area of misleading official advice is one in which the Parliamentary Commissioner for Administration has frequently been willing to recommend, and able to secure, compensation for citizens (see

Mowbray [1990] PL 68). There might also be recovery for economic loss where there has been reasonable reliance on an act, as well as on a statement (see Jones at pp.77-93). It might in some cases be argued that the plaintiff has relied on the exercise of a regulatory power - for example, where a person buys a building or other product which is subject to a regime of inspection, or invests in or trade with a body which has been given a particular licence or registration, when he would not have done so but for the existence of the regulatory power. Even if this can be shown, however, it must also be demonstrated that the reliance was reasonable, a flexible device to preclude recovery in appropriate cases. In *Yuen Kun-yeu*, where an argument of this kind was made, it was held that the supervision exercised by the Commissioner was not sufficiently close to prevent fraudulent practices in particular instances, and any alleged reliance by the depositors was therefore not reasonable.

A case of public authority liability which does fit the clearly recognised categories is *Ministry of Housing v Sharp* ([1970] 2 QB 223). A clerk had carelessly issued a certificate on a local land charges search which omitted to mention a charge held by the Minister. The purchaser thus took free of the charge, and it was held that the clerk was liable to the Ministry for its economic loss. The principle on which the case is based is not clear, and it is not beyond doubt whether it would now be recognised by the House of Lords, though Lord Oliver in *Murphy* clearly regarded it as valid authority. It might be considered authority for a general proposition that there may be recovery for economic loss resulting from reliance by a third party on the defendant's statement: Lord Oliver in *Murphy* suggested that the case might be explicable as one of "reliance". If it is indeed regarded as extending *Hedley Byrne* in this way, it is important in showing that there may be liability for a negligent misstatement made pursuant to a duty, as well as one made voluntarily.

The courts' approach in the area of economic loss can be criticised in that the existing categories of recovery - as well as the unwillingness to acknowledge new ones - are arbitrary: they are not sufficiently directed to the policy concerns which demand a restrictive approach, such as the availability of more efficient or "reasonable" protection (through first party insurance or the negotiation of contractual protection with the defendant); or the undesirability of redistributing large numbers of small losses. (For detailed criticism see Stapleton, [1991] 107 LQR). Many of the individual decisions can be justified on policy grounds: it can be argued that purchasers cannot expect protection in relation to financial investment - an inherently risky activity - or in relation to unlucky purchases of real property (see Stapleton, above). However, the reasoning in these decisions is unfortunate in suggesting that the courts will not be prepared to find that a duty is owed by a public authority - or anyone else - in novel situations, even where policy might suggest recovery should be allowed. Arguably duties should be recognised in relation, for example, to the payment of welfare benefits, grants, and scholarships, or the grant or withdrawal of licences: these are important interests which deserve protection. It was argued above (see 6.4) that a duty of care may exist in principle even though these cases involve merely a failure to confer a benefit; and this should be extended to allow recovery for economic losses which result from failure to pay. There also seems no objection to recognising the duty imposed by the Court of Appeal in *Sharp*. A general category of proximate relationships created by statute could be recognised to cover these situations. An argument for proximity based on a relationship created by a regulatory statute was in fact made in *Yuen Kun-yeu*; and though the Judicial Committee (rightly) rejected its existence on the facts, they did not specifically reject the very concept. Although recognition of such a category would be a desirable development, it seems unlikely, however, in the current climate.

6.8. Limitations of "Policy"

As well as limitations based on the need for a proximate relationship between plaintiff and defendant, a duty of care may be limited by miscellaneous considerations of "policy". The limited immunity which public authorities enjoy in making discretionary decisions, discussed at 6.2, is often placed in this category.

Another "policy" which has made a frequent appearance in recent cases involving public authorities is that of preventing "undue caution" : negligence liability should not be imposed for the exercise of certain functions, lest fear of litigation should make public officials too cautious. This argument was firmly rejected in *Dorset Yacht Co. v Home Office* ([1970] AC 1004), in which the House of Lords held there could be liability for the negligent supervision of young offenders. However in more recent cases the courts have used it very readily to deny a duty of care. Thus in *Rowling v Takaro Properties* ([1988] AC 473) the Privy Council suggested that for this reason there may be no duty on an authority to take care to keep within its powers (see 6.3 above, where it is argued such a duty should in fact be recognised). A similar argument has been used to preclude liability with respect to certain sectors of government activity. Thus the argument was accepted in *Hill v Chief Constable of West Yorkshire* ([1988] 2 All ER 238, discussed at 6.4 above) and *Clough v Bussan* ([1990] 1 All ER 431) as grounds for holding that the police owe no duty to the public in apprehending criminals and maintaining law and order; in *Yuen Kun Yeu v Attorney General for Hong Kong* ([1988] AC 175

(P.C.)) as precluding a duty to investors by the registrar of registered deposit taking companies; in *Calveley v Chief Constable of Merseyside* ([1989] AC 1228), another Lords decision, as precluding liability for conduct of disciplinary proceedings against police officers; and most recently in *Hughes v NUM* (1991) 4 All ER 278),where May J held that no duty is owed by senior to junior police officers in respect of on-the-spot decisions on the deployment of forces in a situation of public disorder.

It was suggested at 6.3 that this argument is not convincing, and that only rarely can it justify a blanket immunity. In all the cases just referred to there were also other possible grounds for the decision; and it is unfortunate that it was thought necessary to invoke also this very wide ground of immunity.

6.9.   The Effect of Remedies by Way of Appeal and Review

The relationship between actions in negligence and other remedies was considered by the Court of Appeal in *Jones v Department of Employment* [1989] 1 QB 1). It was held in that case that there could be no action with respect to an alleged negligent refusal of a welfare benefit, since decisions on the grant of benefits were subject to appeal. The existence of the statutory appeal framework, said the court, meant that there was already an "adequate" remedy, and that therefore no duty of care should be imposed.

The principle that there can be no negligence action where the sum claimed can be obtained through an appeal is unobjectionable, since appeal provides a more appropriate remedy than a challenge in the High Court or county court. The principle can be compared to the rule that a right of appeal must normally be exercised before a decision can be challenged by way of judicial review (see Craig at pp.430-431). However, it is arguable that the court stated the principle too widely in holding that no duty of care is owed, since appeal may not be an adequate remedy. In *Jones* itself the plaintiff did not claim the amount of the benefit denied: the right of appeal had already been successfully exercised, and the benefit awarded. In the negligence action the plaintiff claimed damages, for the legal expenses and the anxiety of the appeal. It was held that these could not be recovered, since no duty was owed at all. The court was no doubt influenced by the apparently trivial nature of the consequential losses claimed in this case, but sometimes serious losses might occur, and they ought to be recoverable in principle. It would be better to adopt a narrower principle, which requires the statutory appeal right to be used only to the extent that it in reality adequate. Another ground for the decision was that a specific clause in the statute precluded challenging a decision by any method other than statutory appeal (see 6.10 below). The decision in *Jones* is best regarded as turning on this basis.

Glidewell LJ also seemed to suggest that no negligence action should be available where the decision can be challenged by judicial review. However, this was rejected by Popplewell LJ in *R v HM Treasury ex parte Petch* (Feb. 28 1989; Lexis; and discussed at 6.4.4 above). Here it was held that a duty of care was owed in relation to a public law duty to make a prompt determination of a welfare claim, though the failure to do so could have been challenged by judicial review. Glidewell's view in *Jones* is also inconsistent with the view of Lord Wilberforce in *Anns v Merton L.B.C.* (1978) AC 728) that there may be liability for negligent failure to exercise a discretionary power (see 6.3.2 above), and is difficult to reconcile with the fact that damages may be available for breach of statutory duty even though there is a right to judicial review (see 7.2 below). It is submitted that the availability of judicial review should not affect the right to bring an action in negligence.

6.10. The Effect of Ouster Clauses

Parliament has sometimes enacted clauses stating that certain decisions are to be "final", or are not to be subject to legal challenge. The courts have generally adopted a narrow and often artificial construction of the clauses to avoid this result (see Wade at pp.719-733; Craig, ch.14). Thus it has been held that a clause stating that a "determination" is final does not preclude review where the decision is invalid, on the basis that an *ultra vires* determination is not a "determination" for the purpose of the statute (*Anisminic v Foreign Compensation Commission* [1969] 2 AC 147). It has also been held that a similar clause does not preclude review for error on the face of the record, since express words are required to take away the usual right to the remedy of certiorari which exists in such a case (*R. v Medical Appeal Tribunal, ex parte Gilmore* ([1957] 1 QB 174).

In *Jones v Department of Employment* ([1989] QB 100), discussed at 6.9 above, the Court of Appeal declined to adopt such a restrictive approach in relation to the right to sue in negligence. It was held here that a negligence action was barred by a clause stating that the "decision" was to be "final". It appears in this case that the error complained of did not render the decision invalid but was merely an error within jurisdiction. The court declined to apply the presumption against the ouster of certiorari, recognised in *Re Gilmore*, to the ouster of damages claims.

It can be argued, however, that where the decision is invalid the ouster clause will not apply, since following the reasoning in *Anisminic*, it is not a "decision" for the purpose of the statute. Hence an action could still, arguably, be maintained if the authority negligently exceeded its powers. As a matter of policy, however, it is difficult to see any distinction between negligent decisions which are valid and those which are invalid, so far as an action for damages is concerned.

6.11. Liability for Independent Contractors

6.11.1. General principle

A person is not generally liable for the negligence of an independent contractor. There are, however, some exceptions : there may be liability, for example, for a contractor engaged to carry out an extra-hazardous activity, or engaged in work affecting the highway; for some public nuisances created by a contractor; or where goods held under a bailment are damaged by a contractor (see Jones at pp.286-273;Winfield and Jolowicz at pp.581-586; McKendrick, (1990) 53 MLR 770). These exceptions have been explained as based on a non-delegable duty on the defendant to ensure that reasonable care is taken, which arises in these limited cases. They apply, of course, equally to public authorities as to private individuals. There are also some further exceptions which are of particular concern to public authorities, and these are considered below.

6.11.2. Special statutory authority

The first applies where a person is given authority by statute to do an act - such as enter onto private land - which would be wrongful but for the existence of the statutory authority. In such a case the authority given by statute is generally assumed to allow the authorised party to carry out the work through an independent contractor. It seems that in some such circumstances the person to whom the statutory authority is given will be liable for any negligence of the contractor occurring in the course of the authorised works. The leading authority is *Darling v Attorney General* ([1950] 2 All ER 793). The defendant had statutory authority to enter the plaintiff's land to explore for coal seams, and employed an independent contractor to do the work. The contractor left a pile of timber in the plaintiff's field and this caused injury to the plaintiff's horse. The House of Lords held that the contractor had been negligent and that the defendant was liable for the damage, by virtue of a duty placed on the defendant not to cause danger, which could not be avoided by employing an independent contractor.

The scope of the duty is uncertain. *Darling* seems to indicate that it is a general duty, applying wherever an undertaker relies on statutory authority for the power to do an act which would otherwise be tortious, and *dicta* in support of such a principle can be found in the earlier cases of *Hole v Sittingbourne and Sheerness Railway* ((1861) 158 ER 201) and *Hardaker v Idle District Council* ([1896] 1 QB 335 at 531 per Rigby L.J.). However, in *River v Cutting* ([1982] 1 WLR 1146) the Court of Appeal found there to be no liability in a case of this kind. The police had regulations to tow away private vehicles, and employed a garage to undertake this work. It was held that the police were not liable for damage to a vehicle negligently caused by the garage. The exact grounds of the decision are unclear. The only substantial judgement was delivered by Fox L.J. who put considerable emphasis on the fact that the provisions relied on conferred a distinct power to employ a contractor to do the work, as well as giving authority to the police itself. On this basis, the decision could be seen as a narrow exception to a general principle of liability, which is based on the interpretation of the particular statute. On the other hand, there are statements which suggest that the general rule is one of no-liability: "I see no reason why there should not be available to the police .... whatever defences would be available to a private person employing an independent contractor performing that task" (at 1149-1150). However, such a general rule is inconsistent with *Darling* which, though cited, was not mentioned in the judgement in *River v Cutting*. If it were desired to adopt a narrow liability rule it could be confined to the case which arose in *Darling* itself, where there is an exercise of a power to enter on another's land. *Hole and Hardaker*, above, can both be explained on the basis of the separate principle which exists regarding liability for negligence in carrying out work which affects the highway (see 6.11.1 above).

There is no clear principle discernible behind the cases where a person is held liable for an independent contractor so that the matter cannot easily be resolved by reference to principle (see McKendrick, (1990) 53 MLR 770). The argument for liability, as with other non-delegable duties, is to provide a solvent defendant in circumstances where the party who actually causes the damage might be unable to meet the judgement; but this is only justifiable where there is some special reason for holding the defendant responsible, arising from the nature of his relationship with a particular contractor, and most existing non-delegable duties appear anomalous. It is submitted that liability should be confined as far as possible, and a narrow interpretation of the *Darling* decision should be accepted (though cf. Atiyah, *Vicarious Liability in the Law of Torts* (1967) at pp.359-360, who supports the wider view).

6.11.3. Negligence which does not cause extra damage

It was held by the Court of Appeal in *Murphy v Brentwood District Council*
([1990] 2 WLR 944) that a local authority carrying out a statutory duty to
examine building plans, to ensure that they are not defective and that they
comply with building byelaws, is under a non-delegable duty of care. Thus
the authority was held liable when it engaged an independent contractor to
examine the plans, and the contractor was negligent: the authority had not
discharged its duty of care simply by appointing a competent independent
contractor. (The decision was overturned by the House of Lords on other
grounds, and this issue was not addressed : see 6.7). The court, however, did
not make it clear on what principle this decision was based, or how far such
a non-delegable duty extends. Some emphasis was given to the fact that the
council was under statutory duty to make the decision on whether to pass
the plans; but it is clear that it is not in every case that a public body is
liable for the negligence of a contractor whom it employs in carrying out a
duty (see for example, *S v Walsall M.B.C.* [1985] 1 WLR 1150, where it
was held that the council could not be held liable for injury to a child in its
care caused by the negligence of the foster parents with whom the child had
been placed).

   It is submitted that *Murphy* is based on the fact that the duty of care
owed by the authority arises only from its public   law obligations. In these
circumstances, the independent   contractor himself probably owes no duty
to the occupier, since there is generally no liability for failure to prevent
damage to another, but the public authority owes a duty because of its
obligations in public law (see 6.4 above). To allow the authority to fulfil
its private law duty of care by entrusting the task to a contractor would leave
the occupier without any remedy if the job is performed carelessly. If the
authority is under a non-delegable duty on the other hand, then the occupier
may sue the authority, which may in turn obtain an indemnity or
contribution from the negligent contractor. This seems to be the desirable
solution. The same principle should apply where a contractor is employed to
do work in connection with a statutory power, as well as a statutory duty. A
non-delegable duty should arise, of course, only when the authority would
have been liable had it chosen to carry out the activity itself.

7

Breach of Statutory Duty

7.1. INTRODUCTION

Where a duty is imposed by statute or under regulations, and there is a
breach of that duty, a person who suffers loss from the breach may
sometimes have an action in damages under the tort of breach of statutory
duty (see Jones, ch.9; Winfield, ch.7; Stanton, *Breach of Statutory Duty in
Tort* (1986)). It is not every breach of duty which gives rise to a cause of
action in damages, however: this depends on whether the courts consider that
the legislature intended that compensation should be an available remedy in
the particular case. This question is determined by considering matters such
as the existence of alternative remedies, and whether the duty was enacted for
the benefit of the plaintiff.

This tort applies to public bodies generally, and it applies to the Crown
by section 2 of the Crown Proceedings Act 1947 - though it cannot apply
where the Crown enjoys immunity from the particular statute, and probably
will not apply where the duty is one binding only on the Crown (see
5.4.4.3). Public authorities will thus be required to pay damages for a breach
of any general legislation for which liability is imposed under this tort - for
example, on health and safety in the workplace. The question of damages
may also arise in relation to specifically *public* duties - for example, duties
to provide welfare benefits or public services. It is this area of liability
which will be examined in this section. (For   other discussion see Stanton,
above, pp. 73-86, 113-115 and 148-152; Harding, *Public Duties and Public
Law,* at pp.230-253; Buckley, (1984) 100 LQR 204; Craig at pp.458-460,
at pp.772-776).

The tort may be used to claim damages both for breach of a duty
imposed by domestic law and for breach of a duty imposed by European
Community law. Problems arising in the latter context are dealt with in
chapter 10 on Community law.

7.2. The Nature of Public Duties

Before considering whether damages are available, it is first necessary to
determine whether any duty has been breached. Some provisions impose an
absolute requirement to achieve a particular result; in others the duty is only
one to take reasonable care. In some cases where a statute appears on its face
to create an absolute duty, the courts have construed the provision as merely
importing an obligation of reasonable care. Thus in *Read v Croydon
Corporation* ([1938] 4 All ER 631) a statutory duty to provide "pure and
wholesome water" was held only to require the authority to take reasonable
care to ensure that the supply was pure and wholesome, whilst in *Hammond
v The Vestry of St. Pancras* ((1874) LR 9 CP 316) a duty to clear sewers
was held to require only that the authority exercise reasonable care to do so.
More recently the argument that a public duty was absolute was rejected by
the Court of Appeal in *Ministry of Housing v Sharp* ([1970] 2 QB 223).
The case concerned a duty placed on the Land Registrar under section 17(2)
Land Charges Act, to make a search for land charges, and to produce a
certificate setting out the results. It was held that the provision did not
impose an absolute duty to produce an accurate certificate, but merely
required the Registrar to perform this function with diligence.

The courts have sometimes justified their refusal to recognise an
absolute duty on the basis that to do so might result in the imposition of
unreasonable and heavy liability on public authorities (see for example, the
statement by Brett J in *Hammond*, above, at 2.2.2). However, this concern
should not influence any decision on the nature of the obligation imposed,
but only the extent of any damages liability. It may in some cases perhaps
be appropriate to recognise that a duty is absolute - so that, for example,
mandamus can be obtained whenever the result specified is not achieved -
but to allow damages only where there is a failure to take reasonable care in
its performance. In such a case, the best approach is to classify the duty as
an absolute duty, but to deny a damages action for breach of duty *per se,*
imposing liability instead by recognition of a duty of care under the
common law of negligence. To take account of problems of liability in
determining the standard of conduct required may lead the courts to limit the
duty to one of reasonable care when such a limitation is not desirable from
the point of view of making other remedies available. In *Read* and
Hammond it was probably appropriate to construe the provisions as
imposing only a duty to take reasonable care; but arguably this is not so in
the case of the duty in issue in *Sharp.*

Difficulties sometimes arise where a public authority is given a degree
of discretion in performing function which is expressed as a duty (see
generally Harding, *Public Duties and Public Law* (1988), ch.7). Such a

provision was considered, for example, by the Court of Appeal in *Meade v Haringey L.B.C.* ([1979] 1 WLR 637), which concerned the obligation under section 8 of the Education Act 1944 to provide education. It is clear that the authority has a wide measure of discretion in deciding precisely how such an obligation is to be performed. In *Meade* school caretakers had gone on strike and the authority decided to close schools in order not to antagonise the trades unions. The plaintiff sought an injunction to prevent closure, claiming that this constituted a breach of section 8. It was accepted by all three members of the Court of Appeal that the authority had a discretion in carrying out the duty. Eveleigh L.J. and Sir Stanley Rees felt this discretion could extend to permitting the authority to close schools, provided that it based its decision on educational concerns - such as the need to maintain relations with the unions for the smooth running of schools in the future. Probably the statutory provision which was at issue in this case - and other apparent duties involving a wide measure of discretion - is one which is best analysed as involving a duty (here to provide a certain minimum amount of education), coupled with a discretionary power to make educational provision as the authority thinks fit (see Cane, [1981] PL 11). The duty   which arises in a case of this kind may sometimes   be unenforceable in the courts because of the difficulty of determining precisely what is required (as, for example, in deciding what is the minimum level of education envisaged by the statute), a matter discussed further below. Where the duty is potentially enforceable, however, damages should in principle be an available remedy.

In other cases, a public authority's obligation to take action - for example, to provide an individual with a particular service or benefit - may arise only following the exercise of a discretion by the authority: for example, to determine whether the individual concerned is a member of the class entitled to the benefit. Thus, the satisfaction of obligations to provide accommodation to homeless persons requires, first, that the authority determine whether an applicant for housing satisfies the statutory conditions precedent for assistance (*Thornton v Kirklees M.B.C.* [1979] QB 626; *Cocks v Thanet D.C.* [1983] 2 AC 286). Until a determination has been made that these conditions are satisfied, the authority cannot be compelled to provide assistance, though obviously there can be an action to require the authority to make a valid determination. It was held in *Cocks v Thanet D.C.*, above, that a private law writ action for breach of the duty may not, in such a case, be brought unless the discretionary decision on the applicant's eligibility (or the authority's failure to make any decision) has first been challenged in an action for judicial review (see 1.3.3 above).

An issue with duties of this type is whether damages can be recovered for the loss suffered in the period prior to the authority's making a determination of the applicant's eligibility. It was stated in *Cocks* that no duty to provide housing actually arises until the authority has made a determination in the applicant's favour. This suggests that no damages could be claimed for loss suffered from the temporary failure (pending the judicial review action) to give valid consideration to the claim, since there is no breach of the duty to house at that point. Insofar as the decision in *Cocks* was motivated by the desire to require challenges to these sort of decisions to be brought under Order 53, with its restrictions and safeguards, this does not, however, provide a reason to restrict the   damages recoverable in this way. Another reason for the decision in *Cocks* was also, however, suggested by Lord Diplock (at 294), which was that to award damages prior to a decision on eligibility by the authority would mean the court substituting its own view on the issue of eligibility. This is because in order to award damages it must be proved that loss has been suffered; to do this it must be shown that the applicant was eligible for housing (or the benefit in issue); and the question of eligibility is for the authority, not the court. Where the question of eligibility has actually been remitted to the authority this problem does not arise: either the applicant will be determined ineligible and hence unable to recover damages at all (since he has clearly lost nothing), or the authority will find that he is eligible, so determining the matter for the court if any damages action is subsequently brought. However, the question may arise where the applicant does not wish to have his case considered by the authority because, for example, he has in the meantime found his own housing, but simply wishes to obtain damages in respect of the period during which he was wrongfully refused housing. Should it be held, to avoid this last possibility, that damages can never arise until a favourable determination has been made? It may be noted that the desire to avoid interfering with any discretion given to the authority sometimes seems to have influenced the courts in reaching the conclusion that no damages remedy should be given at all (see, for example, *Wyatt v Hillingdon L.B.C.* (1978) 76 LGR 727).

It is surely wrong that the applicant should be deprived of damages for that period. There are many other instances where the courts are required to "guess" the result of the exercise of administrative discretion. This issue was discussed above at 1.4.2 where it was suggested that the courts ought to be willing to make this determination. This was the view taken by Megaw L.J. in *Thornton*, above, and it was not specifically disapproved in *Cocks*. Where the applicant does not wish the matter to be remitted to the public body (that is where the exercise of the discretion is no longer a "live" issue), the court should attempt to assess whether there would have been eligibility. Where the matter is remitted, the award of damages can be delayed unless it is clear that the authority would be bound to decide in his favour - for example, where their prior decision is held by the court to be unreasonable. Such an approach does seem to be contemplated in *Cocks* by Lord Diplock:

see p.294 (and see further 1.4.2 above). However, if a right to damages does arise before the authority exercises its discretion it is difficult to see how *Cocks* can be reconciled with other cases concerning the use of Order 53 (see 1.3 above). Thus it must probably be treated as authority for the view that no damages can be obtained at this point.

Finally, it may be noted that with some public duties the courts may not adjudicate on the question of breach at all, because they are of such a nature that it is not appropriate for the courts to determine their precise content. It is particularly likely to be held that no enforcement action is available to a private individual where a Minister is given a power by statute to compel action by the body on whom the duty is laid: this is taken to indicate that a political, and not a judicial, remedy is appropriate. A detailed discussion of this question of "non-justiciable" duties is outside the scope of this book on liability, but it should be noted that the fact of non-justiciability will by definition preclude any damages remedy as well as an action for damages or injunction. (For the case law see Harding, *Public Duties and Public law* (1988), at pp.104-114; and, for some of the decisions, the discussion below at 7.4.2).

7.3. Damages: General Principles

Once it has been shown that there is a breach of duty which is justiciable in the courts, it must be considered whether damages are intended to be provided as a remedy for the breach. Some early cases appeared to take the approach that *prima facie* damages could be recovered by anyone suffering loss from a breach of statutory duty (see Stanton, *Breach of Statutory Duty in Tort* (1986), at pp.2-4; and for public law cases taking this approach Craig, at p.455). However, it was later established that the tort was more limited in scope, and applied only where a legislative intention to give a damages remedy could be shown. In some statutes it is expressly stated that a right to damages is given for a breach of duty (for example, Highways (Miscellaneous Provisions) Act 1961, s.1(1), giving a right to damages for breach of obligations to maintain and repair the highway; Local Government Act 1988 s.19(7), providing damages for a breach of the duty on local authorities not to have regard to certain "non commercial" considerations in awarding commercial contracts, discussed above at 3.1.4). However, in most cases no express provision is made and it is necessary for the courts to determine the legislative "intention" from all the circumstances.

With many statutory duties a penalty for non-compliance is provided. In such a case there has been said to be a presumption that this is the only remedy available (*Doe dem Murray, Lord Bishop of Rochester v Bridges*

(1831) 109 ER 1001; *Atkinson v Newcastle and Gateshead Waterworks* (1877) 2 Ex D 441; *Lonrho v Shell Petroleum Co.* (No.2) [1982] AC 173). However, this presumption can be overridden; it is possible to show a legislative intention to confer a right to damages even where another method of enforcement is provided, and it is not difficult to do so, as will be seen from the decisions discussed at 7.4 below.

For a plaintiff to override the alleged "presumption", and to claim damages, it is necessary, first, to show that the duty was enacted for the plaintiff's protection, or for the protection of a class of which he is a member (see, for example, *Read v Croydon Corporation* [1938] 4 All ER 631, discussed below). It is also necessary that the damage suffered is of the kind which the statute was intended to prevent (*Gorris v Scott* (1874) LR 9 Ex 125).

This is not, however, sufficient: it is necessary to show not only that the measure was enacted to protect the relevant interest, but also that the legislature intended to confer a right to damages for infringement of that interest. This was spelt out by the House of Lords in the recent case of *Hague v Deputy Governor of Parkhurst Prison* ([1991] 3 All ER 733) in which it was held that there was no right to damages for a prisoner affected by a breach of the Prison Rules relating to segregation, even if one of the purposes of those rules was to protect the interests of prisoners. Clearly their Lordships thought that a right to damages for breach cannot have been intended, on the basis that a fear of damages liability would have an adverse effect on the efficient administration of prisons. An earlier case in which policy factors also precluded the court from finding a right to damages had been conferred on a protected class was *Clegg Parkinson & Co v Earby Gas* ([1986] 1 QB 592). Here it was held that damages could not be claimed against a public utility for breach of a duty to supply gas of a particular amount and quality, since this might lead to indeterminate liability to a wide class (a factor which has also influenced the courts' approach in negligence cases).

It has sometimes been said that there is no intention to confer a right to damages on affected individuals where the statute is intended to protect the public as a whole (see, for example, *Atkinson v Newcastle and Gateshead Waterworks Co* above; *Cutler v Wandsworth Stadium* [1949] AC 398). However, it is difficult to draw any meaningful distinction between the concept of a class and the "public as a whole"; "the public" means no more than that class of individuals who are placed in the circumstances with which the particular duty is concerned. This "distinction" in reality is invoked where the court does not wish to impose liability for policy reasons, even though it is clear the plaintiff's interest was of the type the statute was designed to protect. Thus in *Atkinson,* where it was relied on in support of a decision that there could be no damages claim for breach of the company's duty to provide water to fire plugs, the decision reached was clearly based on policy considerations; it was said to be unsatisfactory that the company should act as an "insurer" against fire damage, no doubt because it is the practice for householders to take out insurance against fire damage themselves. It would be better to disregard this "benefit of the public" criterion altogether, and to acknowledge the relevance of policy concerns as a separate factor, which is to be taken into account in determining whether there is a legislative intention to confer a right to damages. In other words, to succeed it must be shown both that the statute is for the protection of persons in the plaintiff's class, and that there are no policy reasons for denying liability in accordance with the principles laid down by the House of Lords in *Hague*, and as was done in *Clegg*.

It may be noted that Lord Diplock has said in *Lonrho v Shell Petroleum (No.2)* [1982] AC 173, following some *dicta* in earlier cases, that a breach of a "public right" may give rise to an action in damages on the part of a party who suffers "particular damage", as well as on the part of a person in the "protected class". It is unclear, however, what is meant by the concept of "public right". If it simply means a right created for the benefit of the public in the sense in which that term is used in cases like *Atkinson*, then this *dictum* is in conflict with earlier cases, including *Atkinson* itself, where the plaintiff had in fact suffered particular damage but was unable to recover. The principle would lead to an unacceptably wide liability, and seems inconsistent with the restrictive approach to recovery adopted in negligence cases (see ch.6). There may be a good reason to give a party standing to enforce the duty in a judicial review action in such a case, either for the benefit of the public or to allow the applicant to protect his own rights. However the imposition of damages liability may involve policy concerns which do not arise in a review action, and it certainly does not follow from the fact that a party has standing for review purposes that he should be able to claim damages. Lord Diplock's statement, insofar as it concerns a right to damages, has generally been criticised by writers (see, for example, Jones at pp.257-258; Buckley, above, at pp.225-230) and it is to be hoped that such a principle will not be applied in future cases.

The above discussion has concerned situations where a penalty is provided in the statute in question. It appears now that the position is the same where there is no penalty provided, but there is a remedy by way of judicial review. It seems in some earlier public law cases to have been assumed that where there is no express statutory remedy, there is *prima facie* a right to damages, an assumption based on *dicta* in *Bridges*, above, *Reffell v Surrey C.C.* [1964] 1 WLR 358, *Meade v Haringey L.B.C.* [1979] 1 WLR 637, and *Thornton v Kirkless M.B.C.* [1979] QB 626, all of which are discussed below. However, such a view seems clearly to be rejected by the House of Lords in *Hague v Deputy Governor of Parkhurst Prison*, discussed above, in which it was held that no damages claim will lie for a breach of the Prison Rules. This seems correct: if the principle stated in *Bridges* has any validity, it can only be on the basis that damages should be given where there is no other method of enforcement, in order to ensure the duty is more than a "pious statement", and to provide for some mechanism for enforcement in the public interest. This is not necessary where judicial review is an available remedy.

The relevant principles may thus be summarised as follows: (1) Where some remedy is available, whether a statutory penalty or a remedy by way of judicial review, there is a presumption against a damages remedy. (2) This presumption is a weak one, and may be overridden. To override it it is necessary to show the plaintiff's interest is of the type intended to be protected by the statute, but this is not sufficient: it must also be considered whether the legislature intended damages to be an available remedy. Policy factors, such as the need to prevent indeterminate liability, to leave losses to be dealt with by insurance, and to restrict liability for failing to avert harm, are relevant to this consideration of legislative intent.

The tort called breach of statutory duty may be invoked in relation to secondary legislation as well as Acts of Parliament. In the former case it is necessary to consider not only whether the party enacting the measure intended to confer a right to damages, but also whether the enabling Act intended to confer on that party the power to create a damages remedy. This issue was raised in *Hague,* discussed above, in which the defendant Governor contended that the Secretary of State to whom was delegated the power to make rules on prison management, had no power to create a right to damages for prisoners affected by a breach of the rules which he made. Lord Jauncey considered that this power did exist; Lord Jauncey, on the other hand, took the view that any purported creation of a right of damages would have been *ultra vires.*

7.4.   Damages: Specific Cases

7.4.1.   Duties not to cause harm

Under the law of negligence the courts are more willing to find liability for creating fresh damage than for failing to provide a benefit, or to prevent harm (see 6.4) and the same is true where it is sought to impose liability for breach of statutory duty. Where a duty is one which already exists under the common law the courts will generally construe the statute as creating a right to damages. For example, in *Read v Croydon Corporation* ([1938] 4 All ER 631) it was held that breach of a water company's statutory duty to take reasonable care to provide pure and wholesome water could give rise to a damages action. However, the scope of the duty was narrower than the scope of common law duties to take reasonable care in relation to this activity: it was held that the statute was enacted only for the benefit of ratepayers, and that hence a ratepayer's daughter, who contracted typhoid from drinking the water, could not recover breach of statutory duty (although she succeeded in negligence). In one way, however, the authority's liability seems to have been wider than that at common law : the plaintiff's father, a ratepayer, was allowed to recover financial losses incurred in relation to his daughter's illness, though such damage might not have been recoverable in negligence because of the restrictions on the recovery of economic loss. It can be argued that where the courts are dealing with a duty which parallels one under the common law there should be a presumption (although perhaps not a strong one) that liability is no wider than that at common law: it is illogical that a different approach should be taken to limitation according to whether the duty is imposed by statute or common law, unless there is some evidence that a wider right of action was intended to be conferred by the statute. For example, where the recovery of economic losses is concerned, rather than using distinct devices such as finding that the statute was enacted for the "benefit of the public as a whole" to limit recovery for policy reasons (see 7.3 above), the court should address the question in precisely the same way as in deciding whether there is a duty to avoid economic loss in negligence. (This is not to say that the courts approach to negligence liability is ideal. Policy issues are not addressed sufficiently explicitly in negligence cases, as to which see 6.7; but the point is simply that the approach to negligence and breach of statutory duty should be as consistent as possible). Under these general negligence principles it is not sufficient that the statute was designed to protect the plaintiff's economic interests: some special relationship of proximity must be shown (see 6.7). Some explicit support for this kind of approach is found in *Merlin v British Nuclear Fuels PLC* ([1990] 3 WLR 383), in which an express statutory right of compensation for "property" damage, imposed for breach of an absolute duty under section 7 of the Nuclear Installations Act 1965, was held not to apply to economic loss, one reason given being that such loss would not have been recoverable in a common law negligence action.

Where there is a statutory duty to avoid causing harm which sets a stricter standard than one of reasonable care, there should normally be no liability where not expressly provided for, but the question of damages should be left to the general law of negligence. However, there are exceptions. Under the general law an important class of duty giving rise to a damages action is duties concerned with health and safety (which are often absolute), and analogous duties applying to public authorities have been construed as giving rise to a damages claim when breached. Thus in *Reffell v Surrey C.C.* ([1964] 1 WLR 359) it was held that a duty under Regulations to ensure that the safety of occupiers of school premises should be "reasonably assured" did not merely require reasonable care by the party subject to the duty but was a duty to ensure that reasonable care was taken, and that a pupil injured through a breach of the duty had a right to damages.

7.4.2. *Duties to prevent harm or to provide a benefit*

More cases have concerned public duties to provide benefits or prevent harm, than duties to avoid *creating* harm. The courts have been reluctant to impose liability in negligence in the former case, and likewise should exercise caution in finding liability for breach of statutory duty. Where the statutory duty is one to take reasonable care, the presumption should be, as with duties to avoid creating harm, that liability is no wider than that imposed by the common law. (On common law liability see 6.4 above). Such a proposition might find implied support in *Clegg Parkinson & Co. v Earby Gas Co.* (1886) 1 QB 592), discussed at 7.3 above.

A *fortiori* where the duty is an absolute one, or the standard is in some other way higher than one of reasonable care, there should normally be no liability for breach of statutory duty, unless the common law would impose liability for a breach which is negligent. On the other hand, just because liability would be imposed for a negligent breach of duty, it does not of course follow that there should be liability for a breach which occurs without any negligence, where the statutory standard is higher than one of reasonable care. A number of cases have considered liability for breach of an absolute duty. Unfortunately, much of the case law is unsatisfactory, and it is sometimes difficult to reconcile the decisions.

One area which has been considered is the provision of welfare benefits. A person entitled to a benefit may obtain the amount of any benefit by an action to recover the sum due, if appropriate (see ch. 12), and may also have a judicial review remedy or a remedy before an appropriate tribunal or other appeal body. He may also, however, wish to claim damages, in negligence or for breach of statutory duty, for loss suffered from non-performance in the period before the review action. Such duties are generally absolute, though their existence may depend on the exercise of a discretion by the authority itself (see 7.2 above). Earlier cases seemed unfavourable to a right to damages for breaches of duties of this type: in *Southwark L.B.C. v Williams* ([1971] Ch 7 134) it was held that breach of local authorities' duties to house the homeless did not give rise to an action in damages, and in *Wyatt v Hillingdon L.B.C.* ((1978) 76 LGR 727) it was held that breach of a statutory duty to provide assistance under section 8 of the Chronically Sick and Disabled Persons Act 1970 did not give rise to a cause of action in damages. It is true that in both cases default powers were contained in the statute, and in such cases the courts are less likely to provide a remedy to an individual (see 7.2 above). However, in the latter case Geoffrey Lane LJ stated (at 733): "It seems to me that a statute such as this which is dealing with the distribution of benefits - or, to put it perhaps more accurately, comforts to the sick and disabled - does not in its very nature give rise to an action by the disappointed sick person." This might suggest a very broad principle that breach of such provisions do not give rise to damages.

However, in the latter case of *Thornton v Kirklees M.B.C.* ([1979] QB 626), the Court of Appeal distinguished these cases as turning on the existence of the default powers: it was held that damages were available for breach of an authority's duty to provide accommodation under a statute later than the one considered in *Wyatt*, from which the default powers had been dropped. The decision has been criticised (Stanton, *Breach of Statutory Duty in Tort* (1986), at pp.80-81), but arguably the right to receive proper consideration for benefits of a social (as opposed to commercial) nature is an interest of such importance that it should be protected by allowing a damages claim. It has already been suggested that an action should generally be available for a negligent failure to provide the benefit (see 6.4 above). However, such an interest ought arguably also to be protected by a remedy for breach of statutory duty, unless there are particular reasons of policy why this should not be done. In addition to *Thornton* the availability of a damages remedy based on breach of duty is supported by *R v H.M. Treasury ex parte Petch* (Feb. 24 1989; Lexis), where it was held that a damages claim was available for breach of a duty to consider, within a reasonable time, the applicant's claim to a pension and sickness benefit, under the tort of breach of statutory duty (and see also *Graves v Secretary of State for Social Services*, Oct 17 1988; Lexis).

It may be argued that this line of authority should be extended also to cases where there is a discretion to award a particular benefit, as well as where there is an entitlement once certain statutory conditions are satisfied (as in *Thornton and Petch*), since it is illogical to distinguish cases according to whether the legislature or the public authority makes the "entitlement" decision (a point made by Cohen and Smith, (1986) 64 Can Bar Rev 1). In such a case there may be said to be a public law duty to consider the exercise of a discretion and a damages remedy if this is not done; but it is perhaps unlikely that the courts will be willing to take this step.

On the other hand, damages should probably not generally be available for a failure to confer commercial grants or benefits. One such case was *Booth & Co. (International) v National Enterprise Board* ([1978] 3 All ER 624) where a claim was made for alleged breach of the defendant's duties in administering an industrial grant scheme. The complaint was not that the plaintiff had received no grant but that sums had wrongly been awarded to competitors. Forbes J refused to strike out the claim as disclosing no reasonable cause of action, but he did express his own view (at 635-636) that no damages remedy was intended to be given. However, an action in damages may be available in a commercial context where there is a breach of a duty in connection with a dominant trading position buttressed by statutory powers. This was held to be the case in *Austin v Milk Marketing Board* (March 23 1988; Lexis) where a breach of a duty by the Board to purchase the plaintiff's milk was held to be actionable in damages. Breach of the general obligation not to abuse a dominant market position under Article 86 of the Treaty of Rome has also been held to be actionable in damages, though this is not a duty imposed on public authorities alone (see further 10.2.1 below).

Another area of authority concerns the provision of firefighting capability. In the first case, *Atkinson v Newcastle and Gateshead Waterworks Co.* ((1877) 2 Ex D 441), the authority was under a duty to maintain fireplugs and to keep water supplied to them at a certain pressure. It was held that there could be no action for breach of this duty by a party whose property was damaged by fire, when the firefighting operation was prejudiced by the authority's failure to meet its duty. However, in similar circumstances in *Dawson v Bingley U.D.C.* ([1911] 2 KB 149), the Council was held liable by the Court of Appeal for breach of a duty to mark the site of fire plugs. It is difficult to see any sensible reason why the result should have differed here from that in *Atkinson*. Vaughan Williams L.J. distinguished the earlier case on the basis that there had been a statutory penalty for breach of the duty, whereas here there was no such penalty, but this point ought not to have been of importance: there would have been an action for judicial review in *Dawson* so that the court should not have relied on any rule that damages are more generously given where no other remedy is available at all. Probably no remedy should be given here - whether in negligence (see 6.4 above) or for breach of statutory duty - since plaintiffs are normally insured.

A further area considered is education. The position here has been complicated by the difficulties of deciding whether duties to provide education are justiciable in the courts at all, as well as of deciding whether a justiciable breach should give rise to a damages claim. *Dicta* suggest that, where the breach is justiciable, a right to damages arises in at least some cases. Thus in *Guardians of the Poor of Gateshead Unions v Durham C.C.* ([1919] 1 Ch 146), where an injunction was granted to restrain the authority from charging fees when they were under a duty to provide free education, Scrutton L.J. suggested that damages would be available for the breach, though this was purely *obiter* since no damages were sought. The possibility of damages is also supported by *dicta* in *Watt v Kesteven C.C.* ([1955] 1 QB 408). This case concerned an action for an alleged breach of the general duty under section 8 of the Education Act 1944 to provide education, and of the specific duty under section 76 of the Act to have regard to parents' wishes. The authority had refused to finance the plaintiff's son to study at a Roman Catholic school of his choice but instead had offered a place at the local grammar school. The court held that in the particular case the only remedy was the statutory one of complaint to the Minister, but the court accepted, on the authority of *Gateshead*, that damages might be available for some breaches. Finally, in *Meade v Haringey L.B.C.* ([1979] 1 WLR 367), the facts of which were outlined at 7.2 above, the courts held that a decision to close particular schools in the exercise of their discretion in the performance of the section 8 duty, which was unlawful because based on irrelevant considerations, could be subject to an action for judicial review as a breach of the section 8 duty. *Watts* - which, as indicated, also concerned section 8, and had held the question of breach to be non-justiciable - was distinguished as involving a different kind of decision, with both Eveleigh and Sir Stanley Rees distinguishing it as involving a positive act, instead of simple non-performance (a plainly illogical distinction in this context). Having accepted the question of breach to be justiciable, both Lord Denning and Eveleigh L.J. seemed to consider that damages would be available for breach. Their reasoning on this point, however, can be criticised. They seemed to assume that once the duty was shown to be justiciable, both injunction and damages must be available remedies, but this is not necessarily so. Damages were not in fact claimed. There is thus no case where damages have actually been recovered for a breach of duty in relation to education, and authority for the view that they are available consists purely of *obiter dicta*. It may be that the courts would not wish to follow these *dicta* in future cases.

Finally, the courts have held that no action in damages is available for breach of the Prison Rules (*Williams v Home Office* (No.2) [1981] 1 All ER 1211; *Hague v Deputy Governor of Parkhurst Prison* [1991] 3 All ER 1751); and that a breach of a duty owed to a police officer to give him notice as soon as possible of a disciplinary hearing against him also does not give rise to damages (*Calveley v Chief Constable of the Merseyside Police* ([1989] AC 1228).

8

Nuisance and Rylands v Fletcher

8.1. Nuisance

8.1.1. Application to public authorities

Public authorities are liable in principle for public or private nuisance. A private nuisance exists where conduct constitutes an unreasonable interference with the use or enjoyment of land by another; a public nuisance where there is interference with the reasonable comfort or convenience of a class of citizens. (See generally Jones, ch.7; Winfield and Jolowicz ch.14).

In determining what is unreasonable for the purpose of nuisance, the question is whether the degree of interference exceeds that which is acceptable. In contrast with a negligence action the court is not always entitled to weigh the benefit of the defendant's activity: although this is one factor in deciding whether an interference is reasonable up to a point, once interference reaches a certain maximum level which is considered unacceptable, it is no defence that the benefit to the defendant or the public outweighs the detriment to the plaintiff (see Winfield and Jolowicz, at p.388 and Jones at pp.218). Similarly, the cost of precautions to abate the nuisance is a factor in deciding whether the user is reasonable; but user may be held to be unreasonable in some cases even though all reasonable precautions have been taken.

Public authorities have an immunity from negligence liability in making certain discretionary decisions, on the basis that they, rather than the courts, are the best institution to weigh the competing interests which will be affected by the decision. Determination of liability in nuisance also involves the court in weighing competing policies and interests, although here, as just explained, the criteria of what is "unreasonable" are slightly different to those applying in a negligence action.

In principle, it seems that immunity should be available in relation to actions in nuisance as well as in negligence: where the public authority has taken a policy decision of a type considered non-justiciable through the imposition of negligence liability (see 6.2) it should likewise be, immune from liability in nuisance. In practice, however, most actions treated as a nuisance under the private law arises from decisions which would be regarded as justiciable.

Though it is normally for the courts to judge the reasonableness of user, however, the public body may be given authority by statute to do a specified action or class of actions which would otherwise constitute a nuisance. In such a case it will not be liable: the defence of statutory authority will apply (see 8.1.2 and 8.1.3 below). In some cases the statute will specify precisely what is permitted. In others it will allow some degree of discretion to the authority (see further 8.1.3). The effect of statutory authority, where discretion is involved, is that it is for the public body and not the court to weigh the competing interests affected in deciding how its land will be used. In other words, it is similar to the immunity principle in negligence. However, there is an important difference, in that where immunity from suit in nuisance is based solely on statutory authority, rather than a more general concept of immunity based on justiciability, the authority should be liable where it acts *ultra vires*. It was argued that this is not the case with the general immunity in negligence (see 6.2.4 above). This question is discussed below at 8.1.6.

8.1.2. The defence of statutory authority

As indicated, public authorities are liable in principle for nuisance, but there is no liability where a work or activity which would normally constitute a nuisance has been authorised by statute. This is because a tort is by definition a wrongful act, and an act authorised by Parliament cannot be wrongful. The defence of statutory authority is available generally in tort (see 5.2.4 above) but has been of particular significance in nuisance actions (see generally Linden, (1966) OHLJ 196; Kodilnye, (1990) 19 Anglo Am L Rev 72). Its availability was established in a line of cases which arose from the operation of locomotive railways authorised by statute (see *R v Pease* (1832) 110 ER 366 (no liability for noise causing interference to animal traffic on the nearby highway) and *Vaughan v Taff Vale Railway Co.* (1860) 157 ER 1351 (no liability for fire caused by sparks from the locomotives)). It was confirmed by the House of Lords in *Hammersmith and City Railway Co. v Brand* ((1869) LR 4 HL 171), holding that the defendant would not be liable for depreciation to the value of the plaintiff's land caused by the defendant's railway, where operation of the railway had been authorised by statute.

The basic principle, then, is simple, but its operation is far from straightforward. Very frequently a statute conferring a power is silent on the question of liability for nuisance. If, within the apparent terms of the power which is conferred, an action is done which would be a nuisance at common law, should it be regarded as authorised, or is there a presumption that any power must be exercised in accordance with common law rights? The courts have developed general principles of statutory construction, which determine this question when it is not expressly addressed in the legislation, and on the whole these principles have been favourable to public authorities. They are examined at 8.1.3 below. In other cases, express clauses have been inserted into statutes. Even in these cases, though, problems of interpretation have often arisen, and a separate body of case law has developed to deal with the construction of these clauses. This is examined below at 8.3.

It must be stressed that statutory authority operates as a defence. Once it has been shown by the plaintiff that the act complained of would constitute a nuisance at common law, the defendant has the burden of showing that the act was within the authority given by statute (*Manchester Corporation v Farnworth* [1930] AC 171; *Allen v Gulf Oil* [1981] AC 1001 at 1013 per Lord Wilberforce; *Tate and Lyle Food Distribution v GLC* [1983] 2 AC 509).

The defence applies to all bodies with statutory powers, public or private, and applies whether the Act conferring the power was a public or a private Act. Although there is a general principle that a private Act is to be construed strictly against its promoter, the principle has not caused the courts to adopt a different approach to private Acts in the present context. In *Allen v Gulf Oil,* above, the fact that the defendant was a commercial corporation and took its powers under a private Act was held to make no difference, and the majority of the House clearly considered the general principles which were laid down (discussed at 8.1.3.1 below) to apply equally to private and public authorities.

8.1.3. Statutory authority: construction of the legislation

8.1.3.1. Specified works and activities

When Parliament has authorised a specific activity at a specified place, any damage which is the inevitable result of the activity must be considered to be authorised, even though it is such as to constitute a nuisance at common law. This applies though there is no clause in the statute which authorises the commission of a nuisance in express terms. To hold otherwise, it is said, would mean that the power conferred could not lawfully be exercised, and would be redundant, and this cannot have been the intention of Parliament. This important principle was firmly established as a result of the decision in *Hammersmith and City Railway Co. v Brand* ((1869) LR 4 HL 171), where the House of Lords rejected the argument that an interference with private rights should only be permitted if the statute *expressly* says that a nuisance is to be permitted. A more recent illustration is *Allen v Gulf Oil* ([1981] AC 1001), where the House of Lords held that there could be no liability for the operation of the defendant's oil refinery, since its operation had been authorised by statute, though again the statute did not expressly state that the authority could create a nuisance. The principle applies whether the power given is in the form of a duty - that is, where there is an obligation to carry out the activity in question - or in the form of a permissive power - that is, where the body has a choice whether or not to exercise the power given to it, as in *Allen*. There is no liability in the latter case even though it might be argued that the nuisance could be avoided by choosing not to exercise the power: it is presumed that when Parliament gives powers it intends them to be exercised. This seems logical and correct. Whether there is a duty or power may, however, be relevant where there is an express nuisance clause, as explained at 8.3 below.

It has been argued that a nuisance should not be permitted unless power to carry on the nuisance-creating activity has been expressly and precisely authorised, on the basis that statutes should be presumed as far as possible not to authorise an interference with private rights. It seems clear from *Allen v Gulf Oil*, however, that a nuisance may be authorised by implication, where to hold otherwise would stultify the use of other powers given by Parliament. In that case the relevant statute had expressly authorised the compulsory purchase of certain lands for use for an oil refinery and also the construction of the refinery, but did not expressly refer to its operation. It was held (Lord Keith dissenting) that the operation of the refinery was authorised by implication. As Lord Diplock pointed out (at 1014): "Parliament can hardly be supposed to have intended the refinery to be nothing more than a visual adornment to the landscape in an area of natural beauty". The House reached this conclusion though there was no provision for compensation for the plaintiff in the statute (and see *Goldberg v City of Liverpool* (1900) 82 LT 362, where interference with the plaintiff's access to the highway by erecting a pole and fusebox for an electric tramway was held to be authorised though no compensation was provided). It is submitted that the approach of the majority is correct: the courts should adopt a reasonable, not an artificial, approach to the construction of such legislation.

On the same basis, the courts should permit activities which are reasonably within the express terms of the authority given by Parliament. They should not restrict artificially the meaning of express terms, even though, in contrast with the *Allen* case, there would be no question of making any powers or provisions completely redundant. A restrictive approach, however, is found in old railway cases such as *Jones v Ffestiniog Railway* ((1868) 3 LRQB 733). In this case it was held that statutory authority to make and use a railway did not give legal authority to use locomotives, but only extended to allowing wagons to be pulled along the tracks by men and beasts: the use of locomotives would require more specific authority, seemingly because of the "highly dangerous" nature of this activity (at 738 per Lush J). It is unlikely that the same statute passed today would be so construed, but a restrictive approach for particularly unusual or hazardous activities might still be adopted. If so, this approach should certainly be limited to cases where there is no provision for compensation in the statute.

Where an activity is authorised on a particular site, the implication is that the size of the operation is permitted to be in accordance with the size of the site (*Manchester Corporation v Farnworth* [1930] AC 171).

Even where the activity is authorised, there will be liability if the authority has not acted "with all reasonable regard and care for the interests of other persons" (*Allen v Gulf Oil,* above, at 1011 per Lord Wilberforce). In deciding whether the authority has acted reasonably the court will weigh the cost of precautions to reduce or eliminate the nuisance against the benefits to be gained by its reduction (*Farnworth*, above). What is not clear is the extent to which the court may take into account the benefit of the activity by requiring a reduction in the extent of the operation if it considers this reasonable when weighed against the reduction in the nuisance which would result: for example, in *Farnworth*, could the courts have required a reduction in output in order to reduce the nuisance? If so, the court clearly may not reduce activity to a level below that reasonably   contemplated by the legislature in authorising   the particular work, even though it considers this degree of activity to be unreasonable in the sense that that word is used in the law of negligence.

As indicated, statutory authority is a defence; and the defendant must show not only that his activity is within the terms of the statute, but also, as a question of fact, that due diligence has been exercised. Thus in *Farnworth* the House of Lords held that the corporation committed a nuisance in emitting poisonous fumes from an electricity generating station, though the operation of the station was authorised, since the corporation had not discharged the burden of showing that they had taken reasonable steps to minimise the damage (and see *Tate and Lyle Food Distribution v Greater London Council* [1983] 2 AC 509).

8.1.3.2. General discretionary powers

More difficulty arises where an authority has a discretion in that a precise site, or the scope or number of the authorised works, is not indicated specifically by the legislation. For example, an authority may be given a general power to build power stations or oil refineries as it thinks appropriate. Where the power cannot be exercised at all without committing a nuisance, it seems clear, by analogy with *Allen*, above, that some nuisance is authorised, since otherwise the power would be redundant. As in the case of a specified work, this should apply regardless of whether any compensation is provided by the statute.

What, on the other hand, of a case where the power *could* be exercised to some degree without any nuisance, though other exercises of the power might result in a nuisance? It would be possible to interpret the power to be exercisable only in accordance with private rights, without its being thus rendered entirely redundant. The argument for this approach is that where meaning can be given to a provision without construing it to authorise interference with private rights, this is the meaning which should be adopted. On the other hand, it may be that the legislature has not specified a site or details of the work because the public body is considered a more appropriate institution to do so. Certainly this is generally the case where statute authorises a variety of works - such as road improvements or drainage - to be carried out from time to time as the authority thinks fit. However, it may also apply where a particular work is authorised, but the site left unspecified. Alternatively, a site may not be specified because of chance factors, as where no suitable site has been found at the time of legislation. In such cases it may be that the legislature would have been prepared to allow some interference with private rights had it addressed the question. However, once legislation has been enacted, control over the details of the project and the balance to be made between the different affected interests has been removed from the Parliamentary process into the administrative sphere. It is difficult to develop rules to ensure that the administrative authority is left with an appropriate degree of discretion, whilst ensuring that it does not interfere unduly with private interests. As with the question of immunity from negligence liability, or indeed the principles of judicial review, it is probably impossible to attain certainty : whether the discretion may be exercised in such a way as to interfere with private interests can only be answered by considering the degree of discretion which seems appropriate in the context of the particular statute.

It has sometimes been suggested that the applicable principle is one which *would* give reasonable certainty: where the discretion can be exercised without interfering with private rights, then no interference is permitted, at least where the statute does not provide compensation. The case of *Metropolitan Asylum District v Hill* ((1881) 6 App Cas 193) can be read to support such a proposition. In this case the House of Lords considered a statute giving a power to establish small pox hospitals, without specifying any site(s). It was held that a hospital could not be built where it would constitute a nuisance. Lords Blackburn and Watson stated that where a wide discretionary power is given it should be interpreted as being exercisable only in accordance with private rights. In other words, given a choice, the hospitals should have been established in places where no nuisance would have resulted. The absence of a statutory right of compensation for those affected was stated to be a factor in reaching this conclusion.

This is a useful starting point: where there is doubt on the question, and no compensation is provided for, the court should conclude that there may be no interference with private rights. However, interference should not be precluded simply because the discretion may be exercised to some degree without interfering with rights: in some cases the *Hill* test would leave authorities with only a very narrow area of choice, which is far more restrictive than the legislature could have intended. The test should be whether the apparent discretion would be *substantially* stultified if private rights could not be interfered with.

Such a proposition is supported by the House of Lords decision in London, *Brighton and South Coast Railway Co. v Truman* ((1886) 11 App Cas 45). Here a company was authorised to run a railway for the specified purpose, *inter alia,* of carrying cattle, and to purchase lands for use for purposes ancillary to the railway. It was held, despite the decision in *Hill*, that there could be no liability for nuisance for the noise made by cattle on lands acquired to hold the company's cattle traffic, since this was authorised by the provision. A narrow explanation of this case would be that the authorised activity could not have been carried on at all without a nuisance (one of the distinctions between this case and *Hill* which was suggested by Lord Selborne; and see Buckley, *The Law of Nuisance* (1981) at p.87). However, this seems debatable on the facts, and it is clear that most of their Lordships, and probably Lord Selborne himself, did not consider the case to rest on this basis, but rather on the different width of the power given in the two cases. In *Truman* to hold that there could be no nuisance would substantially have stultified the exercise of the power; in *Hill* it would not. This was clearly the view of Lord Blackburn who himself had participated in *Hill*. It might also possibly be argued that *Truman* rests on the fact that in the case of the railway statutes Parliament has specifically provided compensation for some persons affected, so that it could be presumed that others were intended to be left without remedy: this possible distinction was also proffered by Lord Selborne. However, this should not be a significant factor. It was not mentioned in the later case of *Edgington v Swindon Corp.* ([1939] 1 KB 86). Here, it was held that the authority was permitted to erect bus shelters which interfered with individuals' access to the highway, even though it might theoretically be possible to construct some shelters without causing a nuisance, and though no provision was made for compensation. (And see *East Freemantle Corporation v Annois* ([1902] AC 213; and *Marriage v East Norfolk Rivers Catchment Board* [1950] 1 KB 284, holding that there was no liability for nuisance caused in the exercise of general power to carry on dredging works, since nuisance would generally result from the exercise of such a power, and must have been comtemplated. There was a compensation clause here, but the same conclusion should have been reached even in the absence of such a clause, a point expressly left open by Jenkins L.J.).

The true principle, then, is that a nuisance is permitted where to hold otherwise would substantially interfere with the apparent discretion given. It is only where there is a wide discretion which may reasonably be exercised without interfering with private rights that the *Hill* principle should apply. This is a matter of degree in each case, and the presence or absence of statutory compensation may be relevant in borderline cases, but clearly it is not conclusive.

Where a nuisance is authorised, this need not mean that the authority is immune from liability in the tort of negligence. It would seem that the usual principles relating to negligence liability, which were set out in chapter 6, are relevant to this question (see *Marriage*, above).

Finally, the defence of statutory authority applies only when a specific statutory power is conferred: in exercising its general powers as landowner a public authority is presumed not to be permitted to create a nuisance (*Page Motors v Epsom and Ewell B.C.* (1982) 80 LGR 337, discussed at 8.1.5).

8.1.4. Statutory provisions for compensation

In some cases where public works cause depreciation in the value of land there is now a right of compensation provided by statute, under the Land Compensation Act 1973 (see further 9.3.2.2 below). This and other rights to compensation for loss resulting from lawful administrative activity are generally justified on the basis that the public as a whole benefits from the activity, and therefore its cost should be borne by the public as a whole, rather than by the individual who happens to own the land affected, although another justification may be to reduce opposition to public works. Some judges had earlier tried to develop the common law to reach a similar result. It was argued by Bramwell B in his famous judgement in the Exchequer Chamber in *Hammersmith Railway Co. v Brand* ((1989) LR 4 HL 171), that private law rights to compensation should be retained unless the statute *expressly* authorised a nuisance, though an injunction might be refused if the activity was in the public interest (see p.194). This approach produces the same result as often applies today, whereby the activity is regarded as lawful because of the statutory authority defence, but compensation is payable for any damage. The problem with Bramwell's approach was that it was difficult to square with common law principles of tort, which assume some wrongful act which, where continuing, will normally be enjoined. Clearly in the cases before the court the activities could not be considered wrongful, and it would have been quite unacceptable to restrain them by injunction. As indicated, Bramwell's view was not adopted by the House of

Lords. The position thus remains that no compensation will be given for damage caused by authorised activities unless provided for by statute. The general issue of compensation for lawful administrative action is considered at 9.3 below.

8.1.5. *Nuisances naturally occurring or created by trespassers*

When a nuisance arises from natural causes or an act of a trespasser the occupier is only liable where he fails to take reasonable steps to abate it (*Leakey v National Trust for Places of Historic Interest or Natural Beauty* [1980] QB 485; *Sedleigh Denfield v O'Callaghan* [1940] AC 880; and see Jones at pp.207-209). In deciding what are reasonable steps the court will take into account the characteristics of the particular occupier such as his resources (*Leakey,* above; *Page Motors v Epsom and Ewell London Borough Council* (1982) 80 LGR 337). There has been some debate as to whether the action in this case is one based on nuisance, or whether it is the law of negligence which applies, modified by taking into account the characteristics of the particular occupier.

Where the nuisance is on local authority land, it is for the court to determine whether the authority has acted reasonably in abating it. This was made clear by the Court of Appeal in *Page Motors,* above (and see Cane [1983] PL 202). The authority was sued by the owner of a garage for a nuisance caused by trespassing gypsies encamped on land adjacent to his, which was owned by the authority. The garage owner claimed that the authority had acted unreasonably in waiting five years to enforce a possession order against the gypsies. The Council argued that it was within its discretion to decide whether and when to evict the gypsies, taking into account factors such as the pressure to delay until a political solution providing for alternative sites had been explored with the gypsies and the county council, and the fact that eviction would just lead the gypsies to camp elsewhere. The Court of Appeal rejected the argument that the authority could exercise its discretion so as to commit a nuisance. In other words, it is clear that an authority's decisions on how to exercise its powers as a landowner are generally regarded as justiciable and the authority will not be protected by the statutory authority defence, which applies only where a specific discretion is conferred in a specific statute (see 8.1.3.2).

In deciding what were reasonable steps it was held that the court itself could take into account the factors mentioned by the council. (Here it was held that these factors might have justified a delay of one year but not more). The court justified this on the basis that the individual circumstances of the defendant may be taken into account in determining what are reasonable steps in cases where the nuisance has not been created by the occupier (see, in particular, Ackner L J at 350-351; Fox L J at 354). This seems to suggest that such factors were only relevant because the defendant was a public authority. This is open to criticism: there is no reason why the factors which the court considers should depend on whether a public body or private individual happens to own the land. If the action is considered akin to nuisance, then arguably the only relevant factor is the financial cost of avoiding the nuisance, and concerns of public interest should not be taken into account once interference with the plaintiff's land reaches a certain level. If, on the other hand, the action is essentially one in negligence, then all costs and benefits of removing the nuisance should be weighed, as in any negligence action, and public interest factors will then be relevant whoever is the defendant. Whatever the nature of the action the public or private character of the defendant should make no difference. It may be, in fact, that the court was prepared to give more weight to these policy factors than it would have done in an action against a private individual, because it considered that it ought to defer to some degree to the views of the local authority. If the courts wish to do this, however, they should do it through the development of the public law immunity doctrine which they have applied in negligence cases (see 6.2 above), rather than through manipulation of the concept of unreasonableness when applied to public authorities (on this see further 6.2.3 above). Certainly, such an approach, if appropriate, should not be confined to the case of a nuisance not caused by the occupier - which seems to be suggested by the Court of Appeal in emphasising the relevance of individual circumstances to *this particular class of case.*

8.1.6. *Ultra vires exercise of discretion*

Since immunity from liability in nuisance is generally based on statutory authority and not justiciability, an authority will not have any immunity where it acts outside the terms of any discretion conferred on it by statute. Thus in *Edgington v Swindon Corporation* ([1939] 1 KB 86) it was held that the authority was entitled to interfere with private rights in exercising a power to build bus shelters; but it was the view of Finlay J that the court would intervene if the authority acted unreasonably by seriously interfering with private rights where other suitable sites were available. Presumably, liability could also arise in principle where the authority exceeds its powers by acting for an improper purpose or in breach of natural justice (see *Dormer v Newcastle-upon-Tyne Corporation* (1940) 2 All ER 421 at 423 per Slesser LJ). No damages should be awarded, however, where the authority would have exercised its discretion in the same way even if it had been acting lawfully (see 1.4.2 above).

8.1.7.   Public benefit

As noted in 8.1.1, the utility of the defendant's conduct is a factor in deciding whether a nuisance has been committed, up to a point; but where there is a substantial interference with the plaintiff's interests this will be a nuisance regardless of the benefit which results from the activity. This applies equally where the benefit alleged is a general public benefit (*Kennaway v Thompson* [1981] QB 88).

It is also a general principle of the law of nuisance that the fact that an activity is of public benefit does not provide grounds for refusing an injunction: a nuisance is regarded as a wrongful act and will normally be enjoined (*Kennaway v Thompson*, above). However, the courts are prepared to postpone an injunction to give a defendant, whether a public authority or a private party, a reasonable time to take steps to abate a nuisance, as in *Pride of Derby and Derby Angling Association v British Celanese* [1953] Ch.149, postponing for sixteen months an injunction against one of the defendants, Derby Corporation where a nuisance was caused by discharge from a sewer maintained by the authority. Probably time should always be allowed when the grant of an injunction would prevent the authority from performing a statutory *duty*.

8.2.   The Principle in Rylands V Fletcher

8.2.1.   Application to public authorities?

Under the principle established in *Rylands v Fletcher* ((1868) LR 3 HL 330) liability is imposed on a person who "for his own purposes brings on his lands and collects and keeps there anything likely to do mischief if it escapes", if the thing escapes and causes damage. There is only liability where there is some "non-natural user" of the land, and where the thing is "dangerous", though this may simply mean that it must be foreseeable that the thing may cause injury. The principle has been applied, *inter alia* to escapes of water, gas and electricity. (See generally Jones, at pp.232-243; Winfield and Jolowicz, ch.15).

The statement of the principle above suggests that there may be liability only where the defendant acts "for his own purposes". It has been suggested that public authorities cannot therefore be held liable since they do not collect things for their own purposes but for the benefit of the public. This view was expressed by Sellers L J giving the judgement of the Court of Appeal in *Dunne v North Western Gas Board* ([1964] 2 QB 806), where he commented (at 832 and see 836-837) that he did not think public utilities would be liable for escapes of gas etc.; and in *Pride of Derby and Derbyshire Angling Association v British Celanese* ([1953] Ch 149) Denning L J (at 189-190) stated that local authorities exercising statutory powers were outside the scope of the rule (and see also *Tock v St John's Area Motor Board* [1990] 64 DLR (4th) 620). A contrary view was, however, expressed by Evershed MR in *Pride of Derby* (at 176). The issue was also raised in *Smeaton v Ilford Corporation* ([1954] Ch 450) but Upjohn J found it unnecessary to decide the question (see p.478). Even if local authorities and similar bodies are not liable under the principle, however, it is arguable that liability will exist at common law for utilities which belong to the private sector in the sense that they aim to make profits for their shareholders.

In practice, even if there is *prima facie* liability for public bodies under *Rylands* the defence of statutory authority will often be available.

8.2.2. The defence of statutory authority

The defence of statutory authority applies to actions under *Rylands v Fletcher,* as to other actions in tort (see generally 5.2.4). Under this principle it has been held that where loss occurs from an activity authorised by statute, there will be no liability where the escape arose from carrying out that activity, unless the defendant has failed to use reasonable diligence to prevent any escape. It is sometimes said that the question is whether the damage is an inevitable result of the exercise of the statutory power, but it seems that the meaning of inevitable here, as with nuisance, is simply that the damage could not have been prevented by the exercise of reasonable care (see, for example, *Charing Cross Electricity Supply Co. v Hydraulic Power Co.* [1914] 3 KB 772 where the concepts of "inevitable" and "without reasonable diligence" are used interchangeably). Thus in *Green v Chelsea Waterworks* ((1894) 10 TLR 259) the defendant was held not to be liable for damage caused by a burst water main when acting under a statutory duty (and see *Department of Transport v North West Water Authority* ([1984] AC 336, where the principle was confirmed by the House of Lords and *Longhurst v Metropolitan Water Board* ([1948] 2 All ER 834). As with nuisance, this principle applies whether the defendant is acting in performance of a statutory duty, or under a permissive power (*Dunne v North Western Gas Board* ([1964] 2 QB 806, where one of the defendants, Liverpool Corporation, was held not to be liable for the escape of water which it supplied under a permissive statutory power). This principle can be seen as a parallel to the rule that there is no liability for a nuisance which results, without any lack of reasonable care, from the exercise of a power conferred by statute (see 8.1.3). The question of whether the authority acts under a duty or power is, however, relevant where there is a clause in the

statute expressly imposing liability for nuisance. The effect of such clauses
is considered in 8.3 below.

Where an authority is exempt from liability except in the absence of
reasonable diligence, it is not clear on whom the burden of proving diligence
lies. In nuisance cases, it rests on the party seeking to take advantage of the
statutory authority defence (see 8.1.2 above). However, in relation to
Rylands v Fletcher a bare majority of the High Court of Australia held in
Benning v Wong (1969) 122 CLR 249) that the burden is on the plaintiff to
prove that no reasonable care was taken. This view is open to criticism; it is
the defendant who will have possession of the relevant information, and the
burden of proof should be on him.

The restrictive approach of the courts in applying the *Rylands v
Fletcher* principle to activities carried on under statute has been criticised. As
with nuisance, the principles governing the operation of the statutory
authority defence have been deduced from the fact that something which is
authorised by the legislative authority cannot be wrongful: hence escapes
which cannot reasonably be avoided if the authority exercises the powers
conferred upon it cannot be tortious. However, as Craig (at p.447) argues:
"The activity, even if it should not be characterised as tortious, and is
regarded as lawful, should compensate a person who has suffered loss as a
result". The courts might perhaps have held that the statutory authority
defence does not apply to *Rylands v Fletcher*, on the basis that this form of
liability can be characterised as concerned with allocation of risk for lawful
activities rather than compensation for wrongs. However, this is not the
approach adopted and the operation of the defence is clearly established.

8.3. Express Nuisance Clauses

The question of liability under both nuisance and *Rylands v Fletcher* may be
affected by the fact that there is a clause in the statute which expressly states
that liability in nuisance is to be retained.

The effect of such a clause on liability under *Rylands v Fletcher* has
been considered in a number of cases. Where such a clause exists, it is in
this context necessary to draw a distinction between acts done under a
statutory duty - that is, where the authority is given a power which it *must*
exercise - and acts done under a permissive power. Where the authority acts
under a duty, the existence of a clause expressly imposing liability in
nuisance makes no difference where the escape was inevitable in the sense
that it could not have been prevented by reasonable diligence: there will be
no liability. Thus in *Smeaton v Ilford Corporation* ([1954] Ch 450) the
corporation was held not to liable under *Rylands v Fletcher* for an overflow

of sewage onto the plaintiff's land, where the sewage was collected by the authority in performance of its statutory duties. The fact that a clause in the statute expressly provided that there was to be liability for nuisance did not affect this principle (indeed, the court reasoned that the effect of the clause was positively to absolve the defendants from liability in cases where they did not actually create a nuisance). In *Department of Transport v North West Water Authority* [1984] AC 336 this principle was confirmed by the House of Lords.

Where, on the other hand, the authority acts under a permissive power, the position is different. Here, the fact that there is a clause imposing liability in nuisance has been held to mean that there will also be liability under the principle in *Rylands v Fletcher*. Thus in *Charing Cross Electricity and Supply Co. v Hydraulic Power Co.* ([1914] 3 KB 772) the defendants were held liable for damage caused by a burst water main where the mains had been laid under a permissive power rather than a duty, where a clause expressly imposed liability for nuisance. The decision was explained in *Dunne v North Western Gas Board* ([1964] 2 KB 806) as turning on the existence of the clause.

There is in fact no reason to draw such a distinction between permissive powers and duties in this context. A duty is imposed where the legislative authority has decided action must be taken; a permissive power is granted where the decision whether to act is for the authority itself. This rationale clearly has nothing to do with the question of damages for escapes - that is, with whether the actor should bear the cost of accidents resulting his activities himself, or whether their cost should be borne by those on whom they naturally fall. A possible explanation might be that where the damage results from the performance of a duty it cannot be considered a wrong since the authority has no choice whether to act; whereas in the case of a permissive power, the damage could be avoided by refraining from exercising the power. However, this is not satisfactory: powers are given to be exercised. This is recognised by the principles of statutory construction which apply where there is no nuisance clause. These principles state, in relation both to nuisance and *Rylands* (see 8.1.3 and 8.2.2 above) that there is no liability where damage arises from the exercise of a power which cannot reasonably be exercised without causing such damage: the fact that the authority could have chosen not to exercise it has no relevance. The application of the defence of statutory authority to *Rylands* liability at all was criticised above (see 8.2.2). If it is to be applied, however, logic suggests that no distinction should be drawn between duties and powers.

In *Department of Transport v North West Water*, above, the House of Lords purported to apply the above principles, developed in relation to actions based on the *Rylands* principle, to actions in nuisance also. The case concerned liability for damage caused by a burst water pipe laid under a statutory duty, and which it was conceded had not resulted from any lack of reasonable diligence. It was also conceded that in the absence of a defence of statutory authority there would be liability in nuisance (though this is doubtful: probably liability in nuisance will only arise if the defendant has not taken reasonable care to avoid the damage-causing occurrence: Winfield, at pp.383-385). The House held that there was no liability, despite an express clause stating that parties carrying on such works were not to be exonerated from liability in nuisance (confirming a statement in *Dunne v North Western Gas Board* ([1964] 2 QB 806). It was stated, however, that such a clause would mean the authority would be liable if acting under a permissive power.

The view that the authority was not liable has been criticised by Kodilnye ((1990) 19 Anglo Am L Rev 72, at 78): "With respect it seems odd that, where the declared purpose of the court is to discover the intention of the Legislature, the Court of Appeal and the House of Lords should have regarded an express nuisance clause as having been completely overridden by a mere inference based on the mandatory nature of the statute. A better approach would be to construe the nuisance clause as a restriction on the authority conferred by the statute, so that any acts which caused a nuisance would fall outside the statutory authority and thus give rise to civil liability". However, in many nuisance cases the activity complained of is ongoing and the plaintiff will be seeking an injunction. To hold that there is a nuisance would mean that the court would be asked to issue an injunction to prevent the duty's being performed, which clearly it ought not do. It seems a reasonable inference that a "no nuisance" clause is not to override a specific provision imposing a duty. This is particularly so where, as in the *North West Water* case, the "no nuisance" clause is a general one, applying to a range of works undertaken under various different statutory powers.

The House of Lords also stated that the principle applied to nuisance as to *Rylands v Fletcher* liability, that the authority *would* be liable in the presence of such a clause where acting under a permissive power. The principle is open to criticism in the context of nuisance as well as *Rylands*: there is no ground for distinguishing between permissive powers and duties, since powers are given to be exercised. In the context of nuisance the principle would mean that an act done in the exercise of a permissive power might be treated as a nuisance though the power could not be exercised without a nuisance being caused. The power would effectively be negatived by the clause if the court were to issue an injunction. Arguably, general "no nuisance" clauses should be interpreted so as to apply only to those powers which are capable of being exercised to some degree without causing any nuisance.

8.4. Statutory Liability

In many cases the legislature has now intervened to impose strict liability on bodies acting under statutory powers, which applies in situations where at common law the existence of statutory authority would provide a defence to an action based on nuisance or *Rylands v Fletcher*. The Land Compensation Act 1973 has already been mentioned (see further 9.3.2.2 below). Other examples include the Water Act 1981, section 6 (as amended by the Water Act 1989), which, with certain exceptions, imposes strict liability on water undertakers for the escape of water; and section 7 of the Nuclear Installations Act 1965, imposing strict liability for certain nuclear incidents, subject to a financial ceiling (see further Winfield, at pp.449-454; *Merlin v British Nuclear Fuels PLC* ([1990] 3 WLR 383), holding that the provisions do not impose liability for economic loss).

9

Compensation Outside the Private Law

The previous four chapters have examined the application of the private law torts to public authorities. This chapter considers the extent to which compensation is, and ought to be, given against public authorities under distinct doctrines of public law. The chapter first examines the public law tort of misfeasance in public office, and, second, considers whether further public law liability doctrines should be developed. Since the making of *ex gratia* payments is an important element in the public law compensation system, this area will also be dealt with briefly. Liability under European Community law is considered in the next chapter.

9.1. Misfeasance in Public Office

9.1.1. Introduction

Misfeasance in public office (sometimes called "malicious abuse of power") is probably the only tort of domestic law which can be described as a special tort of "public law". The case law on the tort is not well developed : as Wade points out (at p.777), there are "remarkably few reported English decisions on this form of malpractice". The origins of the tort may be found in the famous case of *Ashby v White* ((1703), best reported in 1 Smith's Leading Cases 253) where the plaintiff was wrongfully prevented from voting in an election, and sued for damages. The action failed in the Kings Bench, but Holt C.J. dissented, and the claim was upheld in the House of Lords. The decision was explained in later cases as turning on the fact that the public officers involved had acted with malice towards the plaintiff (see *Cullen v Morris* (1819) 171 ER 741; *Tozer v Child* (1857) 119 ER 1286). A principle of this kind was subsequently accepted in a number of other jurisdictions (*Farrington v Thomson* [1959] VR 286; *Roncarelli v Duplessis* ((1959) 16 DLR (2d) 689), a decision said by the judges to be based on the Civil Law of Quebec, but which would now probably be seen as based on the common law: see *Laurentide Motels v Beauport* [1989]). In *David v Abdul Cader* ([1963] 1 WLR 834) a case concerned with the Roman Dutch law of Ceylon, the Privy Council suggested such a tort might exist in the common law. More recently, Lord Diplock stated in the Privy

Council in *Dunlop v Woollahra Municipal Council* ([1982] AC 158]) that this tort formed part of the common law, and *dicta* of the House of Lords in *Smith v East Elloe Rural District Council* ([1956] AC 736) suggested that there could be an action in damages against a local authority clerk if it were shown that he had procured an order for the compulsory purchase of the plaintiff's property in bad faith (though the action failed for other reasons). However, the existence of any such tort had been rejected by the Court of Appeal in an earlier decision, *Davis v Bromley Corporation* ([1908] 1 KB 170), and, though the general authority of the case was called into question in *Abdul Cader*, above, the existence of the tort in English law was until recently not entirely beyond doubt. These doubts were put to rest, however, when its existence was unequivocally affirmed by the Court of Appeal in *Bourgoin SA v Minister of Agriculture, Food and Fisheries* ([1986] QB 716).

The dearth of English case law has meant that the scope of the tort has not been carefully examined and defined, and it is still in the process of development. It is submitted that there are two main requirements - that there is an exercise of "public power" and that the exercise is "wrongful".

9.1.2.   *"Wrongful" conduct*

Conduct may be characterised as wrongful for the purpose of this tort either (i) where the defendant acts with malice - that is, with intent to inflict harm on the plaintiff; or (ii) where he acts unlawfully, with knowledge that his conduct is unlawful.

It has often been said that an intent to injure the plaintiff - or "malice" - gives rise to liability. *Roncarelli v Duplessis* ((1959) 16 DLR (2d) 689) is often cited as an illustration of liability based on malice. Duplessis, the Prime Minister of Quebec, instructed government officials to revoke the restaurant liquor licence of the plaintiff, a prominent Jehovah's Witness. It was found that the order was motivated by the Prime Minister's hostility to the plaintiff as a Jehovah's Witness. The Supreme Court of Canada held the Prime Minister liable in damages for loss to the defendant resulting from the revocation.

It is now clear that liability is not confined to cases where an act is done with "malice" in the sense of spite towards the plaintiff, but may arise where an official (a) does an act which he knows to be in breach of public law; and (b) knows (or, possibly, should know) that this this conduct may inflict harm on the plaintiff. This was established by the Court of Appeal in *Bourgoin S.A. v Minister of Agriculture, Fisheries and Food* ([1986] QB 716). The plaintiffs were companies operating in France selling turkeys. A government Order permitted turkeys to be imported into the United Kingdom only when covered by a licence. The government had refused to licence the importation of turkeys from France, allegedly for public health reasons. It was held by the European Court of Justice that this policy was contrary to the Treaty of Rome (case 40/82 *Commission v UK* [1982] ECR 2793). The plaintiffs then sought damages for loss suffered from their exclusion from the UK market alleging, *inter alia,* misfeasance in public office. The claim was based on allegations that the government knew that it was acting unlawfully, firstly, in that it knew the measure contravened the Treaty of Rome and, secondly, in that the motive of the government was to protect English turkey producers, a motive argued to be irrelevant under the domestic legislation, and known to the government to be irrelevant. The Court was required to determine whether these allegations disclosed any cause of action. The government argued that they did not, since it was not contended that the government had acted with the "purpose" of inflicting harm on the plaintiffs. This argument was rejected, the Court holding that it was sufficient that the government did something which it knew it had no power to do.

It is not clear whether knowledge of illegality is required or whether it is sufficient that the authority is reckless as to the validity of its action. The latter should probably be sufficient. Lord Bridge in *Calveley v Chief Constable of Merseyside* ([1989] AC 1228) suggested, in relation to a power to dismiss a police officer, that there may be liability where such a power is exercised "in bad faith or, *(possibly) without reasonable cause"* (at 632; emphasis added). This may indicate the possibility of liability for misfeasance for conduct which is negligent or at least grossly negligent. However, other important recent authorities, notably *Bourgoin and Dunlop,* contain no hint of liability for mere inadvertence. It is preferable that any liability on an objective standard should be left to the tort of negligence, with its attendant restrictions - for example, on the recovery of economic loss (see 6.7 below).

Another issue is whether actual knowledge that the plaintiff will or may suffer damage is required, or whether recklessness as to, or perhaps even reasonable foresight of, harm is sufficient. Oliver L J in *Bourgoin* spoke of "knowledge"; whilst Mann J, at first instance in *Bourgoin,* spoke of harm being the "foreseeable" consequence of the act. However, neither really addressed his mind to this question.

It was explained above (see 6.3) that an authority is probably under a duty to take reasonable care not to act unlawfully, and in some cases it may be easier to rely on this doctrine than misfeasance. However, misfeasance remains important because of the many restrictions which limit potential liability for negligence: for example, on liability for economic loss (see 6.7), or for failure to confer a benefit (see 6.4). Many of the leading misfeasance cases, including *Roncarelli v Duplessis* ((1959) 16 DLR (2d) 689) and Bourgoin, above, concerned economic loss, and it was not suggested that there are any restrictions on its recovery (though the imposition of such liability based on mere knowledge of illegality has been criticised as potentially too wide: Steiner, T*extbook on EEC* Law (2nd ed. 1990), at p.113). The tort also applies to cases of failure to confer a benefit (*R v HM Treasury ex parte Petch* Feb. 28, 1989; Lexis; *R v Deputy Governor of Parkhurst prison, ex parte Hague* [1990] 3 WLR 1210, at 1245 per Ralph Gibson L J (Div. Ct.)). There may also be more favourable rules on damages where an action is brought for misfeasance rather than negligence (see 9.1.5 below).

There is a substantial overlap between the two categories of wrongfulness - that is, malice, and knowingly acting in an unlawful manner. In particular, infliction of harm is obviously a purpose for which a public official may not lawfully use his powers, and he is likely to know that this is so, so that here there will often be liability under both heads. It may perhaps be argued that there is one general principle, that of liability for conduct known to be unlawful, of which acting out of spite is one example. This appears to be the view taken by Rand J in *Roncarelli v Duplessis* ((1959) 16 DLR (2d) 689 at 706), who used the term malice to refer to this general category, rather than in any narrower sense of spiteful conduct. Such a view was also stated by the Divisional Court in *R v Deputy Governor of Parkhurst Prison, ex parte Hague* (above, at 1247). However, the better view is that the two should be regarded as separate categories. First, where the defendant's purpose of injuring the plaintiff makes his act unlawful in a public law sense, this should suffice to establish liability though the defendant might claim he did not know his act is outside his legal powers. Second, and more important, there may be some cases where an act is done with "malice" towards the plaintiff but is not unlawful because the act, whilst amounting to the exercise of a public power, is not the type of act to which the public law principles of judicial review apply, and is not otherwise unlawful. For example, misfeasance may arguably apply to acts done by officials of public utilities, though such acts would probably not be subject to review on administrative law principles.

If malice is a separate head it will be necessary for the courts to consider more precisely what constitutes malice. It should include not only personal dislike, but should be applied also where there is a desire to inflict harm on the plaintiff to achieve some further goal which is regarded as illegitimate or improper : this was the case in *Roncarelli v Duplessis,* above, where an object of revoking the plaintiff's licence was to curtail his ability to promote and assist the Jehovah's Witnesses group in Quebec. Such an approach requires the courts to decide what is a "legitimate" object of the right or power exercised, and what is not. For example, a power to terminate a utility supply could (quite apart from any relevant statutory safeguards or duties) be regarded as conferred solely for the protection of the economic interests of the supplier. This is similar to the problem of determining the purpose of a power for the purposes of judicial review under the "improper purposes" doctrine. A similar approach to the definition of malice is adopted in, for example, defamation actions (*Horrocks v Lowe* [1975] AC 135), and the tort of malicious prosecution (see the definition of Winfield and Jolowicz, at p.550).

9.1.3.   The exercise of a public power

Misfeasance in public office is, as its name suggests, a tort applicable only to the exercise of public powers. There has been no comprehensive attempt to define "public" in this context, but some recent cases have touched on the issue.

We may consider first the activities of bodies - such as government departments and local authorities - which are clearly recognised as "public" to the extent that certain of their functions, at least, are amenable to judicial review under the Order 53 procedure. The question which has arisen is whether all their activities are "public" for the purpose of the tort of misfeasance, or whether a distinction is to be made between their "governmental" and "non governmental" functions in this context (see generally 1.1 above). A generous approach to the scope of the tort in this regard was taken by the Court of Appeal in *Jones v Swansea City Council* ([1990] 1 WLR 54). The case concerned the council's decision as a lessor of commercial property to refuse its tenant permission for a change of user of the property, a power which derived from the terms of the lease. It was alleged that the refusal was made maliciously. The council contended that the tort applies only to decisions subject to judicial review; and that the exercise of a contractual right, was a "private" power, and not subject to review. The Court of Appeal held that liability could arise, regardless of whether the power was susceptible to judicial review, thus finding it unnecessary to consider whether the power was reviewable. (On judicial review see further 2.9 above). According to Slade L J (at p.71):

"All powers possessed by a public authority, whether conferred by statute or by contract, are possessed "solely in order that it may use them for the public good" (see *Wade's Administrative Law* (6th ed., 1988 p.400). In the present context, in my judgement, it is not the judicial nature of the relevant power but the nature of the council's office which is the important consideration. It is the abuse of a public office which gives rise to the tort."

Nourse L J agreed with Slade L J that there would be a good cause of action if there were malice, whilst Stuart-Smith L J agreed generally with the judgement of Slade L J. The case went to the House of Lords ([1990] 1 WLR 1453), but argument on this issue was deferred until the House had determined whether malice was established, and since the House refused to interfere with the finding that malice was not proven, and refused a new trial, this argument was not heard at all. However, Lord Lowry, with whose speech Lord Oliver agreed, stated (at 1458) that he was "respectfully inclined to agree" with the reasons given by the Court of Appeal for rejecting the council's contention.

The passage of Slade L J cited above appears to suggest that certain bodies, like local authorities, may be classified as "public", such that all their actions are capable of giving rise to liability for misfeasance, regardless of whether or not they are subject to judicial review. It is submitted that this approach is correct: all acts done in the course of an authority's business should in principle be subject to the misfeasance principle.

A narrower view, however, was taken in the House of Lords in *Calveley v Chief Constable of Merseyside* ([1989] AC 1228), which suggests that not all decisions of such bodies are capable of giving rise to liability. This case concerned an action for damages by certain police officers who had been suspended and subjected to disciplinary proceedings, but later reinstated. One of the officers claimed damages for misfeasance, on the basis that the investigating officer "knew or believed that there were no proper grounds for suspending the plaintiff yet procured the imposition of and/or the continuation of the suspension by continuing the investigation and giving misleading and/or incomplete reports concerning the same" (particulars of claim). It was held that there could be no liability for misfeasance since "the mere making of a report is not a relevant exercise of power or authority by the investigating officer" (at 1241 per Lord Bridge, with whose judgement the other judges agreed). Unfortunately, no general test as to what is a "relevant exercise of power" was offered. It was simply stated, by way of contrast, that the wrongful exercise of a power actually to dismiss could give rise to liability (at 1241). It could be argued that on this basis preliminary reports or decisions are excluded from the scope of the tort, or perhaps that it should not apply to decisions of junior officials (cf. the approach of the Court of Appeal to the award of exemplary damages against public bodies: see 5.2.2). Neither suggestion is satisfactory in principle, and each is likely to give rise to uncertainty in practice. It would be better to adopt the approach implicit in *Jones,* and not to attempt to draw any distinction between governmental and non-governmental powers of such authorities.

So far the discussion has considered the scope of the tort in relation to bodies subject to judicial review. The tort should apply at the very least to all bodies subject to review under Order 53, including those which do not derive their authority from prerogative or statute but are within the special procedure because they exercise public functions (see, for example, *R v Panel on Takeovers and Mergers, ex parte Datafin* [1987] QB 815; *R v Advertising Standards Authority, ex parte Insurance Services PLC* [1989]

133 Sol Jo 1545; *R v Bar Council, ex parte Percival* [1991] 1 QB 212). It might also be argued that the courts should extend the tort to cover malicious acts, and acts which are knowingly done in breach of statutory obligations, by bodies outside the traditional sphere of public law review, such as nationalised   industries, and even the newly privatised   public utilities, such as the electricity companies, water authorities and British Telecom, which often have statutory obligations to supply, and to act in a non-discriminatory manner (see 2.2.2 above). Some of these bodies may be within the definition of "The State" for the purpose of determining the effect of European Community Directives on the basis that they are entrusted by the state with provision of a public service under the control of the state, and are given special powers for that purpose (see 1.1 above). Arguably, their actions should also be capable of attracting liability under the tort of misfeasance in public office, where they are carried out maliciously or in a manner which is known to be unlawful - for example, when contrary to their statutory obligations.

9.1.4.   Relationships with other torts

Where a public officer maliciously brings a prosecution, there may be liability for malicious prosecution. For liability the prosecution must not only be malicious, but also brought without reasonable and probable cause (see Winfield and Jolowicz, at pp. 547-550). Similar requirements apply to the tort of malicious process (where the defendant institutes some legal process short of prosecution, such as the issue of an arrest warrant : see Winfield and Jolowicz, at p.551). If a plaintiff could choose to sue for misfeasance instead he would succeed simply on proof of malice, though reasonable and probable cause did not exist. However, it was held in *McDonagh v Commissioner of Police of the Metropolis* (The Times, Dec. 28 1989) that this option is not available: the requirement cannot be avoided by suing in misfeasance. Likewise it would be expected that misfeasance cannot be used to circumvent other requirements of the more specific torts, such as the need for termination of the prosecution in the plaintiff's favour.

9.1.5.   Damages

In principle the ordinary measure of tort damages will apply : the successful plaintiff will be put into the position in which he would have been had the tort not occurred - that is, as if the power had been exercised taking into account only lawful considerations. Thus, for example, if the plaintiff's complaint is that he was improperly refused a licence to trade, the court is required to consider whether he would have been awarded a licence if the matter had been properly considered, and only if it is concluded that he would have been will he be entitled to any profits which he has lost through being unable to trade. This principle was applied, for example, in *Roncarelli v Duplessis* ((1959) 16 DLR (2d) 689), where damages were awarded for lost profits.

The application of the principle requires the court to consider how the authority would have exercised its discretion if it had acted lawfully, a question which can present difficulties (see 1.4.2 above). It presents no problems in some cases - as in *Roncarelli* itself, where it was assumed that the licence would have been awarded but for the defendant's malice, in view of the history of the restaurant, and of past renewals. In others there is more difficulty - for example, where circumstances have altered so that a rehearing does not give any indication of what the original decision would have been; or where the application was for a single benefit or one of a limited number - for example, a particular government contract - which has already been awarded, so that reconsideration does not arise. The problem may arise in other contexts - for example, in an action for negligent excess of power or breach of statutory duty, and it has been suggested that it should normally be resolved by applying ordinary causation principles (see further 1.4.2 above). The best approach with misfeasance, however, since it rests on culpable wrongdoing, is probably to place on the authority the burden of proving that the discretion would not have been exercised in the plaintiff's favour, so that the benefit of any doubt goes to the plaintiff. Support for this view may be found indirectly in *Roncarelli v Duplessis,* above, and *Farrington v Thomas* ([1958] VR 286) where the courts expressly adopted an approach generous to the plaintiff in assessing other uncertainties, such as the future profitability of the plaintiff's business.

Misfeasance is probably a tort which is actionable *per se (Ashby v White*, best reported in 1 Smith's Leading Cases 253). Thus even where no substantial damage has been suffered an action may be brought, and the nominal damages recoverable may serve as a peg on which to hang an award of exemplary damages.

9.1.6.   Personal liability

A public official who knowingly acts unlawfully, or who acts with malice in exercising a public power, is personally liable for the tort of misfeasance - as shown by *Roncarelli v Duplessis,* discussed at 9.1.2, where the Premier of Quebec was sued personally. The employing authority will be vicariously liable where the employee acts in the course of his employment. The fact that the employee acts with malice does not take him out of the course of his employment, where the malicious act occurs in relation to the activity which he was employed to do (Atiyah, *Vicarious Liability in the Law of Torts (1967); Petterson v Royal Oak Hotel* [1948] NZLR 136). In the recent case of *Hague v Deputy Governor of Parkhurst Prison* ([1991] 1 All ER 733) Lord Bridge (at 745) stated that the Governor of a prison would not be vicariously liable in misfeasance or false imprisonment for an act of a prison officer which the officer knew to be unlawful. However, this statement is contrary to the general principle just stated. It was an *obiter* dictum - indeed this question was not even addressed in argument before the House of Lords - and should be disregarded.

9.1.7.   Direct liability of the authority

There may also be direct liability where the authority itself has acted maliciously or with knowledge that its conduct is unlawful. This was made clear by the House of Lords in *Jones v Swansea City Council* ([1990] 1 WLR 1453, discussed at 9.1.3) where it was the council itself which was sued. It was held in *Jones* that where there is a decision of a multi-member authority, malice will be established where it is shown that a majority of the members present at the vote were acting with malice. It ought, however, to be enough that those whose votes were sufficient to turn the decision were malicious, even if the majority of those voting were not. Thus, for example, if the decision was made by a majority of two, it should be sufficient that two members of the majority were activated by malice.

In *Jones* the malice was alleged to originate from two particular members of the council, including the leader of the majority group. It was held in these circumstances that malice would be established on the part of the council itself if the majority voting for the resolution knew of that malice and "acquiesced" in it, or voted according to the instructions of the person affected by malice, in obedience to a party whip (though malice was found not to be proven in the particular case).

9.2.   Damages for Unlawful Administrative Action

9.2.1.   The current law

There are a number of grounds on which a person may succeed, under the common law, in claiming damages for loss which is consequent upon unlawful administrative action. First, damages may be recovered for misfeasance in public office where it is known that the action is unlawful, or where there is malice (see 9.1). Second, it is arguable that damages may be recovered for negligence where the administration fails to take reasonable care to ensure that it keeps within its powers; though any such action is subject to important restrictions (see 6.3). Third, even where the case is not within the scope of one of these general torts, damages may be recovered where the interest affected by the unlawful action is protected by some specific tort. Thus, for example, there may be a battery where there is interference with the plaintiff's person; false imprisonment where he is deprived of his liberty; and trespass to goods where there is   direct interference with or damage to his property. If the administration has authority under statute to interfere with these interests, then this authority protects it from suit (see 5.2.4); but if it is mistaken in the view that it has such authority and is in fact acting unlawfully, it will be liable under the ordinary principles of private law. Fourth, there will be liability where the unlawful act consists of failure to carry out a statutory duty in those cases where a right to damages is implicitly created by the statute imposing the duty (see ch.7). Finally, damages may be recovered in certain circumstances for damage caused by unlawful conduct which is in breach of Community law, a matter considered in Chapter 10.

Not all cases where damage is caused by unlawful administrative action, however, fall within one of these categories. In these cases what is the position of the individual who has suffered damage? There are some cases in which the courts have seemed to suggest that there may be a right to recovery even when the case does not fall within the categories outlined above. Thus in *Ashby v White* (discussed at 9.1 above) Holt C J did not seem to require malice as an ingredient of the action, though the case was later explained on this basis. Similarly no special ingredient beyond invalidity seemed to be required in *Brayser v McLean* ((1875) LR 6 PC 398) or in the Canadian Supreme Court case of *McGillivray v Kimber* ((1915) 26 DLR 164; and see also *Wood v Blair* The Times, 3,4,5 July 1957; though in this case the issue of liability seemed to have been considered). However, the cases on liability for misfeasance and breach of statutory duty have proceeded on the basis that there is no cause of action based on invalidity *per se;* and in *Dunlop v Woollahra Municipal Council* ([1982] AC 158) Lord Diplock stated in the Privy Council that there is no right to damages in English law based simply on the fact of unlawful administrative action. The English courts have also denied the existence of any general private law doctrine that a person causing harm to another by an illegal act must pay compensation: such a principle was proposed by the High Court of Australia in *Beaudesert Shire Council v Smith* ((1966) 120 CLR 145) and clearly might have been used in a public law context to impose liability for acts which are *ultra vires.* However, its application in English law was rejected by the House of Lords in *Lonrho v Shell Petroleum Co. No.2* ([1982] AC 173 at 188), and it was also rejected in *Dunlop* (and indeed has now been denied application to Australia also). Thus, it is clearly established that a person who suffers loss from unlawful administrative action may only recover if he can bring himself within one of the categories which were outlined above, or has some specific statutory right to compensation.

The result of these principles is that many citizens who suffer serious loss as a result of unlawful administrative conduct will go uncompensated. Thus a person unlawfully refused a licence to trade or carry on a profession - for example, because the authority is operating a policy based on irrelevant considerations - will not generally be able to recover for wasted expenses or loss of his profits during the period when he was unable to trade. Similarly, a person wrongfully refused planning permission or denied a grant or contract from the government is generally unable, under the common law, to recover for losses suffered. These are all interests which are not protected by the private law of torts, and unless there is negligence or misfeasance, or - which is unlikely - a compensable breach of statutory duty, there is no basis on which a claim can succeed.

9.2.2. *Reform*

It has frequently been debated whether there should be a wider right to damages for unlawful administrative action, which could be invoked in at least some of these cases which are not within the scope of the existing law of tort (see, in particular, Gould (1972) 5 NZULR 105; McBride, (1979) 38 CLJ 323; Evans, (1982) 31 ICLQ 640; Craig, (1980) 96 LQR 413 at pp.435-455; Harlow, *Compensation and Government Torts* (1982) pp.58-61; Hogg pp.113-115; Aronson and Whitmore, ch.3; *Administrative Justice: Some Necessary Reforms,* Report of the Committee of the Justice - All Souls Review of Administrative Law in the United Kingdom (1988) ("the Justice All Souls Report"), pp.360-364; Public and Administrative Law Reform Committee (N.Z.), *Damages in Administrative Law* (fourteenth report, 1980); Ontario Law Reform Commission, *Report on the Liability of the Crown* (1989), pp.24-25; Committee of Ministers of the Council of Europe, Recommendation No.R (84) 15 ("Public Liability")).

The main argument in favour a general obligation to compensate for unlawful action, a kind of strict liability, has been put by Hogg as follows (at p.114): "The unfortunate individual who happens to be directly injured by an invalid governmental decision should not have to bear the cost. The entire tax-paying community should share the cost of its government's occasional errors". It is clear that this argument has some force, and that there is a case for recognising a right to compensation for unlawful action, in some situations at least. On the basis of such arguments, the recent Justice - All Souls Report, cited above, has gone so far as to recommend that a general right to damages of this kind should be introduced by legislation into English law (see pp.360-365). It suggested for consideration a draft provision stating that "compensation shall be recoverable by any person who sustains loss as a result of ... (a) any act, decision, determination, instrument or order of a public body which materially affects him and which is for any reason wrongful or contrary to law".

Others have been more cautious, however, about the desirability of reform of this kind. A number of objections have been raised to the recognition of a right to damages as a general principle, and there are clearly a number of difficulties which might arise in applying it.

One important problem, which has often been raised in this context is that proof of loss may often depend on showing that the authority would have exercised a discretion which it possesses in favour of the plaintiff. Thus, for example, a plaintiff wishing to recover for losses alleged to be suffered from the wrongful denial of a licence - say, for breach of natural justice - will have to show that he would have been granted the licence by the authority if his case had been properly considered. This is a difficulty which can arise in liability claims in many contexts and was considered at 1.4.2 above. It is true that this difficulty might cause some claims to fail. However, as suggested at 1.4.2 there is no reason why this problem should mean that liability should be precluded in principle, whatever the context in which the issue arises: in many cases the question will be adequately dealt with by the courts. The Justice-All Souls Report considered that the courts could draw on their experience of causation generally to resolve these kind of problems, though they did not attempt to analyse possible solutions (see pp.362-363). However, it should be stressed that the contexts in which a claim based on invalidity might arise, and the solutions which might be appropriate for each different case, are so varied that it would be much preferable that these kind of questions should be dealt with by legislation in each case than be left to the common law.

Another difficulty in granting a more general right to damages for invalidity is that most claims would be for economic loss. The courts have restricted recovery for economic loss caused by negligence to narrow and well defined categories (see 6.7), and it would create an anomaly to allow recovery for economic loss as a general principle where this is caused by invalid administrative action. One of the reasons the courts have been anxious to limit liability for economic loss generally is the potential for heavy and/or widespread liability, and clearly this may be a problem with compensation for invalidity, particularly with legislative action - for example, a Ministerial regulation restricting the trading activities of a large group. If a further right to damages for unlawful action were developed, the limitations would have to be at least as stringent as those governing negligence claims (though it was argued at 6.7 above that the courts should not be so restrictive as they are at present in negligence actions). It may be noted that there are severe restrictions on the right to damages for unlawful administrative action against institutions of the European Community, and these seem largely to have been influenced by concern at imposing liability for widespread economic losses (see ch.10 below). The need to limit recovery for economic loss does not provide a conclusive argument against a principle of liability, rather than one for limiting its scope, but the uncertainties which this might entail are a factor to consider in deciding whether any general principle of liability should be recognised.

Another important concern is that fear of liability might induce undue caution by public officials (see, for example, Craig (1980) LQR 413 at 452, who discusses this problem in the context of licensing). It was explained at 6.3 and 6.8 that this argument has often been used by the courts in refusing to hold public authorities liable for a careless exercise of their powers. It was suggested that the argument is not convincing in relation to negligence, since the problem can be dealt with by setting the standard of care at an appropriate level. However, it has considerably more force in relation to liability for simple invalidity.

Another problem, which influenced the Public and Administrative Law Reform Committee of New Zealand in rejecting a general right to damages, is that the possibility of a damages claim may make the courts more cautious in striking down administrative decisions in the first place. This is particularly likely to apply where liability might be heavy and/or widespread. However, a limited right to recover in appropriate cases would not present a problem.

Finally, an important point, emphasised by Harlow in her book *Compensation and Government Torts* (1982), is that the courts may not be the appropriate institutions for dealing with claims, both because of the expense and length of proceedings and their lack of expertise in the relevant area of administration. In addition, to give such claims to the courts might contribute a further load to an already overloaded system. A specialised tribunal, or even more likely, tribunals, may be more appropriate for administering and developing any legal right to compensation in respect of particular administrative activities. Justice-All Souls, on the other hand, envisages that the courts would administer the general right to damages which it recommends. Clearly any right which did not depend on legislation would have to be fashioned and administered by the courts.

Clearly there would be serious difficulties with any general rights to damages. On the other hand, the case for compensation does have a strong appeal in certain cases. Since the contexts in which the problem arises vary so widely, the best solution would be for reform to be implemented through legislation dealing with specific areas. Thus compensation would only be given in those areas where it is clearly appropriate; schemes could be devised which are appropriate to the area - for example, in the way causation problems are dealt with; specialist authorities could be set up to deal with claims where desirable; and uncertainty would be avoided. Some existing legislation does specifically provide for compensation for unlawful administrative action: for example, the Local Government Act 1988 allows the recovery of tendering costs by disappointed bidders where a contract is deemed to be awarded on the basis of "non commercial considerations" (see 3.1.4), and a right to damages must also be available to affected contractors where there is a breach of Community legislation on procurement awards (see 3.2.4). However, in practice legislative attention is not usually directed to this issue, and the question still arises whether a general right, despite the difficulties it entails, would not be an improvement on the present position.

It is the author's view that it would not be desirable to introduce a general right to recovery. A better approach, if liability is to be extended, would be for the courts to develop a right to damages on an incremental basis, by analogy with the tort of breach of statutory duty. Thus the courts could examine the nature of the legislative scheme and of the affected interest, and determine whether compensation should be payable on a case by case basis where the citizen is prejudiced by an invalid exercise of discretion. Indeed the concept of breach of duty might be employed if the courts wished to develop such a right, since a failure to keep within its powers, and to make a valid determination of an issue, can be characterised as a breach of a public duty, no less than can a breach of an express statutory direction (see Harding, *Public Duties and Public Law* (1988), at pp.33-50). For example, there can be said to be a duty to comply with the common law principles of natural justice or with the proper purposes rule, and it could be argued that, in relation to certain types of discretionary administrative decision, a breach of these public law duties may give a right to damages. It is, indeed, illogical to distinguish for compensation purposes between public duties according to whether or not they are embodied in an express statutory direction (see further 7.4.2). On the other hand, the concept of breach of statutory duty itself has its critics because of the difficulties of applying it in practice. For this reason it can be argued that there is a good case for refusing to extend it into the field of the public law duty to make a valid decision, even though the distinction between express statutory duties and other public law duties may be illogical and anomalous.

9.3. Damages for Lawful Administrative Action

9.3.1. Introduction

Individuals frequently suffer loss from government activity which is lawful, in that it is neither tortious nor *ultra vires*. Sometimes this occurs where conduct which would otherwise be tortious is rendered lawful by the existence of some statutory or prerogative power. An example is where public works are built or operated in a manner which would be a nuisance at common law, but the activity is treated as lawful because the works have been authorised by statute : this area was discussed at 8.1.2 above. Another illustration is the loss which may be caused to innocent individuals in the administration of the criminal justice system. Innocent persons are often lawfully, but mistakenly, arrested, as where there is an arrest by a police officer based on a reasonable suspicion which turns out to be ill-founded. Such a deprivation of liberty would normally constitute false imprisonment but will not do so where there has been a valid exercise of the power to arrest. Sometimes, though less frequently, persons are even convicted and imprisoned for offences which they did not commit, or are wrongly imprisoned because of some error of law by the judge. Those prejudiced by the errors of the system will rarely have redress under the law of tort. Those who prosecute, or who arrest within the general limits of the arrest power, are liable only for malicious prosecution or malicious abuse of process, which requires both malice and the absence of reasonable and probable cause; and the torts are hedged with so many other restrictions that actions rarely succeed (see Winfield and Jolowicz, at pp.543-552). Judges have a wide immunity from suit to tort, which means they are rarely liable for their errors (see 5.2.2 above).

An individual may also suffer loss from government activity in circumstances where there is no question of liability in tort, because the conduct is not such as would normally be tortious. Examples are where accidental injured is caused in the course of a properly conducted police chase, or an attempt to end a siege which is carried out without negligence (see Williams, (1991) 141 NLJ 231). Business and financial interests are also of course frequently adversely affected by government action; and many other illustrations could be given.

It can be argued that, in some circumstances at least, individuals who suffer loss from government action should   be compensated, even though the action was lawful. As it has been explained by Hogg (pp.115-116), "The rationale for this form of strict liability is risk theory: the risks of governmental activity should be borne by the whole community rather than by the individual who has been fortuitously harmed by the activity." In some cases, at least, it is also an argument in favour of compensation that this will facilitate the government activity in question, by removing or reducing opposition from those affected. This has often been put forward as one important justification for providing adequate compensation for the compulsory purchase of land for public purposes, or for those affected by the operation of public works.

Ideas of imposing the burden on those who take the benefit feature in the development of - or attempt to develop - certain private law principles of strict liability, such as the vicarious liability of employers for the torts of their employees, and the principle in *Rylands v Fletcher* (see 8.2 above). Where strict liability is imposed in private law for an individual's own actions, the conduct causing damage tends to be characterised as "wrongful" since our common law compensation system - the system of "tort", which means "wrong" - developed as a system of compensation for "wrongs", and the common law is still reluctant to acknowledge any role in redistributing legitimately inflicted losses. However, it can be argued that in both public *and* private law any strict liability is generally better regarded as a mechanism for redistributing losses arising from lawful activity, rather than being concerned with "wrongdoing". The government is, of course, subject in principle to all the usual doctrines of private law which are based on strict liability. The question to consider in this section is the extent to which compensation is and should be available for damage inflicted by government activity, where there is no right to compensation available under ordinary private law principles.

For further discussion of the question of compensation for risk in public law see Craig, (1980) 96 LQR 413 at pp.441-443; Harlow, *Compensation and Government Torts* (1982) pp.102-115; Hogg, pp.115-117; Craig, pp.464-466; *Administrative Justice : Some Necessary Reforms,* Report of the Committee of the Justice-All Souls Review Report), pp.348-351 and 362; Committee of Ministers of the Council of Europe, Recommendation No.R (84) 15 ("Public Liability").

9.3.2. The current law

9.3.2.1. Common law principles

In English law the courts have to date played little role in imposing liability on the government based on a risk theory: generally speaking it may be said that no such doctrine of liability is recognised by the common law.

We may consider first the position where the action in question would be tortious were it not for the existence of some statutory or prerogative authority. The general principle (as explained at 5.2.4) is that damage inflicted under such authority cannot be considered wrongful, and therefore is not tortious, though it would be at common law. This is logical. It need not, on the other hand, follow that no compensation should be given at all. It would be possible for the courts to require that compensation be paid on the basis of a "risk theory", holding that the costs of certain types of losses lawfully inflicted on others should be borne by the party causing the loss. This might be achieved by developing a presumption of statutory interpretation to the effect that, with certain interests at least, Parliament does not intend to authorise an interference without compensation being given. This might contradict the usual "literal" approach to the interpretation of statutes which has been adopted in English law; but it could be justified by analogy with the public law principles of judicial review, which have been developed on the basis of strong presumptions of interpretation in the face of silence in the statute. The English courts have not attempted to develop such a theory, however, but, as illustrated at 8.1.2 in relation to nuisance, have generally held that no compensation at all is payable.

An exception to the usual approach is found in the famous decision in *Burmah Oil Co. Ltd v Lord Advocate* ([1965] AC 75). In this case the House of Lords held that the prerogative power to take or destroy the property of subjects in waging war can only be exercised on payment of compensation (though the requirement of compensation was said not to apply where property is destroyed in the course of fighting), by analogy with old cases which held the exercise of the old prerogative powers of purveyance and angary to be subject to the payment of compensation. This is a clear instance of the courts imposing liability for damage lawfully inflicted.

Might this be extended to the case where property is taken under a *statutory* power? The English courts have for many years applied a presumption against the taking of property without compensation to avoid interpreting a statute as having this consequence (see, for example, *Westminster Bank v Minister of Housing and Local Government* [1971] AC 508; *Sheffield C.C. v Yorkshire Water Services* (1991) 89 LGR 326). In Canada the presumption has now been applied to require a payment of compensation in a case where a statute has been interpreted as authorising an interference with the plaintiff's rights, though no such payment was provided for expressly (*Manitoba Fisheries v The Queen* ([1979] 1 SCR 101). However, a contrary decision in English law is that of Avory J in *Re a Petition of Right* ([1915] 3 KB 649), holding that no compensation was payable in respect of the government's occupation and use of the plaintiff's land in war time. In this case the occupation was authorised by Regulations, and if the courts are not willing to imply a right of compensation into delegated legislation, they are unlikely to imply it into an Act of Parliament. In practice, compensation is, not surprisingly, provided for in respect of existing powers of expropriation held by the government.

Since there is generally no duty to pay compensation where, apart from the statutory authority defence, the authority's conduct would be tortious, it is unlikely that the courts will impose an obligation to do so where the authorised conduct is of a kind which would not normally give rise to liability in tort; and there appear to be no illustrations of the courts applying a "risk theory" in this type of case.

9.3.2.2. Compensation under statute

Although the common law has not developed any general "risk theory" of compensation, compensation rights are given by statute in a number of cases where the lawful exercise of statutory powers causes loss. Thus, as mentioned above, when the government is given statutory powers to expropriate land provision is made for compensation to be paid. (For an outline of the law see Moore, "Compulsory Purchase in the United Kingdom" in erasmus ed. *Compensation for Expropriation* (1990) 1). Another example is found in Part 1 of the Land Compensation Act 1973, which provides for compensation in certain cases where the value of a person's land is reduced because of the operation of public works (defined in s.1(3)). Compensation is payable where depreciation in value is caused by noise, vibration, smell fumes, smoke or artificial lighting or the discharge on to the land of any solid or liquid substance (see 1.1(1) and (2)). These provisions provide compensation for the kind of activity which would often be a nuisance at common law, were it not for the fact that it is carried out under statutory authority. Another interesting illustration of compensation based on a risk theory is section 133 Criminal Justice Act 1988. This gives a legal right to compensation in certain circumstances to a convicted person whose conviction has subsequently been reversed or who has been pardoned on the grounds that a new or newly discovered fact shows beyond reasonable doubt that there has been a miscarriage of justice (s.133(1)). The provision covers, though, only a small fraction of those prejudiced in the administration of justice: they apply only where the reason for the miscarriage of justice is discovery of a new fact, and do not extend to those arrested and released without trial, or tried but not convicted. It seems intended that the section is to apply only where loss is shown to be suffered - that is, where the convicted party was innocent. It is the difficulty of establishing not just that guilt is not proven, but that the affected party is actually innocent, which has contributed to the unwillingness of the law to give compensation rights to those wrongly convicted, or indeed to those arrested and released. Whether there is a right to compensation under the section is determined by the Secretary of State. It is unclear whether his decision is subject to judicial review: on this, see further 9.4 below.

In addition to general provisions of this type it is common for rights to compensation to be given on an *ad hoc* basis in particular statutes - for example, for losses arising from individual public works.

As Craig has pointed out (at p.465) there is a   greater willingness to compensate in cases where the affected interest is of the type readily protected by private tort law - for example, liberty or property - with compensation being given much less readily for action which interferes with, for example, a trade or business, or where there is failure to exercise a discretion to confer a positive benefit. Most existing legal provisions on compensation, as well as existing *ex gratia* payment schemes (see 9.3.2.3), reflect this hierarchy of values. Thus, for example, the owner of a garage or a café which is bypassed by a new road cannot generally expect compensation for the loss of business, though the person whose property is physically affected by the work generally can, either under the Land Compensation Act or the specific authorising statute. However, occasionally compensation for business losses is provided. A rare example is found in the Conwy Tunnel (Supplementary Powers) Act 1983, given powers for the construction of major road tunnel under the Conwy estuary. The construction work threatened the livelihood of a number of local people, and provisions were included to safeguard their interests. Section 11, for example, gives to the Secretary of State a power to compensate for business losses suffered by those whose business related to the waters of Conwy Harbour (such as those taking fish and shell fish from the harbour itself) or who used the harbour facilities, and those who were involved in taking mussels from the Conwy mussel fishery. The provision applies only to persons deriving a significant part of their income from the business in question and who had been engaged in it for at least three years. It must be emphasised that provisions of this kind are most exceptional, and have tended to be found only in private or hybrid Acts of Parliament (the Conwy Tunnel Act was a hybrid Act), where it is feared that local petitions might disrupt the passage of the Act.

9.3.2.3. *Ex gratia payments*

Though they have no legal right to any payment, those suffering loss from lawful action sometimes receive compensation on an *ex gratia* basis, either under a general scheme, or on an *ad hoc* basis. (General questions relating to *ex gratia* payments are considered at 9.4 below). An example is an *ex gratia* scheme which exists for compensating persons who suffer damage from the activities of military aircraft: for example, property damage resulting from "sonic booms" (see Parliamentary Commissioner for Administration, 2nd Report Session 1989-90, Selected Cases 1990, Vol.1, p.10). Another area where *ex gratia* payments have been made is in relation to persons wrongly convicted. As explained at 9.3.1.3 a statutory right to compensation now exists in some cases. Before, the government had sometimes made *ad hoc ex gratia* payments to persons now covered by the statute, and also occasionally to other individuals, such as those imprisoned on remand and subsequently acquitted (see Harlow and Rawlings, *Law and Administration* (1984) at pp.411-418; Ashman, (1986) NLJ 497; Zander, *Cases and Materials on the English Legal System* (5th ed. 1988), at pp.569-573). Many other examples of similar schemes or practices could be given.

9.3.3. Reform

Should the courts become involved in fashioning a right to recover which is based on more general principles? This could either be a general legislative right, the judiciary being left to work out its implications, or one developed by the judiciary itself. The courts have in some other European countries granted compensation on the basis of a risk theory (see generally Bronkhorst, "The Valid Legislative Act as a Cause of Liability of the Communities", Ch.2 in *Non Contractual Liability of the European Communities* (1988) eds. Schermers, Heukels and Mead). In France, for example, the highest administrative court, the Conseil d'Etat, has awarded compensation in a number of cases for losses caused by lawful government action. A leading case is Couiteas (Nov. 30th, 1923, S 1923.3.57). The applicant had obtained a court order for possession of land which he owned in Tunisia, but the authorities were reluctant to enforce the order, for political reasons. The Conseil d'Etat held that the conduct of the authorities was lawful but that the landowner should be compensated for the loss which had fallen on him in the pursuance of the public interest by the authority. Compensation was later given also for loss resulting from legislative action in *Fleurette* (C.E. Jan. 14, R.D.P. 1938, p.87, concl. Roujou, n, Jeze). In this case a manufacturer of artificial cream was awarded compensation when, in order to protect the dairy industry, its manufacture was banned by legislation. There are also decisions of the European Court which, drawing on the laws of the different member states as required by Article 215 Treaty of Rome, suggest that the Court may recognise a right to recover against the Community for damage lawfully inflicted in some cases (for discussion see Bronkhurst, above; though not all writers would agree that the court may be said to have recognised such a principle: see, for example, Steiner, *Textbook on EEC Law* (2nd ed., 1990) p.318).

   There would be many uncertainties and difficulties in developing any general liability doctrine, since clearly it must be subject to important limitations. Thus there should obviously be no right to compensation where a person suffers from a ban on an activity which is regarded as illegal or immoral. Nor should there be compensation where the infliction of loss is essential to the purpose of the legislation. For example, where the government gives grants to promote industry in one region at the expense of others, firms in regions which are not eligible for grants should not be compensated for losses resulting from the assistance given to their competitors. It will also be necessary to impose restrictions to prevent widespread and heavy claims : to the extent that such claims are likely to be for economic losses this is in line with the restrictions on recovery of economic loss in the law of negligence (see 6.7). Significant restrictions of this kind exist in other European jurisdictions (see Bronkhurst, above). It also needs to be recognised - and this has been done elsewhere - that regulatory legislation - on matters such as health, the environment and consumer protection - is often intended to have a redistributive effect, imposing the costs of regulatory measures on those engaged in the regulated activity. In the French courts few actions on the basis of risk theory have succeeded, because of the restrictive conditions imposed: in particular, special and abnormal damage must be suffered (for discussed see Harlow, *Compensation and Government Torts* (1982), at pp.102-106). The decisions are unpredictable and not entirely consistent, and there is such difficulty in extracting any clear rules of liability that it can be argued that the alleged "principle" cannot be formulated at the level of a general principle at all: rather the courts simply have a discretion to give relief in exceptional cases. In the case of European Community Law the European Court has indicated (case 59/83 *Biovilac v EEC* [1984] ECR 4057) that if liability is recognised at all it is likely to be subject at least to the restrictive conditions which have already been developed to govern recovery for damage unlawfully inflicted (see ch.10), and successful cases are likely to be rare.

Apart from the difficulties of developing a suitable principle, the same objections can be made to judicial development as in the area of compensation for invalid administrative action (see 9.2.2 above). For example, it may be doubted whether the courts are the appropriate institutions to deal with such claims.

Street has argued that the courts should provide a right to recovery for damage lawfully inflicted in cases of "exceptional loss" (*Governmental Liability* (1953) at p.78). However, few have agreed with him that such a task should be given to the courts. It is difficult to disagree with Hogg who concludes that "..... a single regime of compensation for harm caused by government, based on a risk theory, is not only impossible to design, but it would inappropriately convert a major field of political discretion into a set of legal rights" (p.117). It should generally be left to the legislature or Executive to provide compensation in specific cases where this is felt appropriate.

A more cautious approach to reform might be to require compensation where the action of the government would have been a tort but for the defence of statutory authority. This would mean that compensation would be available, for example, where public works involve interference to property which would constitute a nuisance at common law, or where a person is lawfully arrested but found to be innocent. It is doubtful, however, whether even such limited reform would be desirable - probably this would impose too great a burden, and could involve compensation for large numbers of relatively minor losses which are better left to lie where they fall.

9.4. Ex Gratia Payments

The State often pays compensation to those to whom it causes loss because it believes there may be legal liability to do so, either under statute or the common law, but it may also wish to pay in some cases where there is clearly no legal liability.

The Crown has a general power under the common law to make *ex gratia* payments of this kind, by virtue of the rule that the Crown has the powers of a private individual, though the funds to be expended must be voted by Parliament, as with any other expenditure by the Crown. It is the normal practice of the Crown to rely on the general headings of expenditure under the Appropriation Acts for *ex gratia* payments, rather than seeking authority in more specific statutes. The Treasury exercises a control over payments made by departments in connection with their own activities, requiring Treasury approval for all *ex gratia* payments above set thresholds (which vary according to the department and activity in question). Approval is not required where the payment is made by way of settlement of a legal claim which is disputed, since these are not regarded as payments made *ex gratia*.

The Crown sometimes makes payments on an *ad hoc* basis to a particular person or group. Often where this occurs it is a result of investigations by the Parliamentary Commissioner for Administration, who frequently recommends the payment of compensation on a finding of maladministration (see Harlow, *Compensation and Government Torts* (1982), at pp.119-143; *Administrative Justice: Some Necessary Reforms*, Report of the Committee of the Justice-All Souls Review of Administrative Law in the United Kingdom (1988), at pp.331-333; Mowbray, [1990] PL 68 (on compensation for misleading advice)). An interesting recent example of compensation was that which followed the Commissioner's investigation into the "Barlow Clowes Affair" (see Parliamentary Commissioner for Administration, First Report - Session 1989-90, "The Barlow Clowes

Affair"; and Gregory and Drewry, [1991] PL 192 and 409). Many members of the public had suffered losses after investing in the Barlow Clowes group of companies, which collapsed. The Commissioner found some maladministration by the Department of Trade and Industry in its surveillance and licensing of the group, and also found that had this maladministration not occurred losses to the public could have been prevented. Even if the Department's conduct could have been characterised as careless, it probably would not have been held liable to investors, on the basis that it owed them no duty of care (see 6.7 above). However, the Commissioner recommended that compensation should be paid, and the government compensated investors in part, with small investors (the vast majority) recovering ninety per cent of their capital and full compensation for interest lost. Although this did not entirely meet his recommendations, the Commissioner considered this a "fair" remedy (see p.168 of his report).

It may be questioned whether the Commissioner should be involved in areas where the principle and policy of compensation has been considered by the courts and rejected. Barlow Clowes was exactly the kind of case which the judiciary has determined to be inappropriate for compensation. If the legislature disagrees with this choice, the appropriate course of action is to change the law - or at least set up a formal scheme for compensation - rather than make an *ex gratia* payment in a one-off case. Arguably, the Commissioner should recommend, and the government grant, one-off payments, only where the case is of a type where a legal right is precluded because of the difficulty of formulating general principles (as with compensation for deliberate lawful administrative action, for example), or where the general legal rule has given rise to a "hard case".

As well as giving compensation on an ad hoc basis, the government has also set up a number of more permanent *ex gratia* schemes. An example already mentioned is the scheme for compensating losses caused by low flying military aircraft (see 9.3.2.3 above). An *ex gratia* scheme may be preferred to one based on legal rules in order to give flexibility in the initial stage of experimentation (in which case it would be expected that the scheme would be placed on a legal footing at later stage); or it may be appropriate because of the difficulty in devising suitable general principles, so that the matter is best left to a discretion. Alternatively, such a scheme may be preferred because it is not clear that the funding for it will always be available. The difficulties with such schemes are those which generally arise when the government chooses to act through informal rules, notably the problems of ensuring accountability and consistency in decision making, and the absence of an adequate legal remedy to those whose interests are at stake (see Ganz, *Quasi Legislation* (1987), *passim*). Of course, as in some other areas the government may deliberately choose an informal method of proceeding, to *avoid* accountability, particularly where difficult and sensitive issues are involved. In the case of compensation for a conviction which is legally unsound, one of the main difficulties is that it appears unjust to compensate if the convicted person is actually guilty; and it seems that a desire to avoid the Crown's openly making a determination of this question has been a factor in the "secretive" approach which has been adopted to making *ex gratia* payments in the past in this area (as to which see the works cited at 9.3.2.3 above).

Is the making of *ex gratia* payments by the Crown an activity subject to judicial review? It was held that the Criminal Injuries Compensation Board (providing compensation for the victims of crime, rather than for loss caused by government action) was subject to review, even when the scheme was run on a purely *ex gratia* basis (*R v Criminal Injuries Compensation Board, ex parte Lain* ([1967] 2 QB 864; *R v Criminal Injuries Compensation Board, ex parte Ince* ([1973] 1 WLR 1334). However, it was held in *R v Secretary of State for the Home Office, ex parte Chubb* ([1986] Crim LR 809) and in *R v Secretary of State for the Home Department, ex parte Harrison* ([1988] 3 All ER 86) that the Secretary of State's decision not to pay compensation to a person whose conviction had been overturned could not be reviewed by the courts. In *Chubb* the decisions relating to the C.I.C.B. were distinguished on the basis that that body administered a formal *ex gratia* scheme, whilst in the case of wrongful convictions payments were made on an *ad hoc* basis. This should not, however, be crucial to the principle of review, though it might affect the grounds on which the decision can be challenged (for example, if there is a practice under the rules of giving a hearing, it may be a breach of natural justice not to give a hearing in any particular case). In *Harrison* the non-statutory and *ex gratia* nature of the payments were both emphasised; but this was also true of the C.I.C.B. at the time of the *Lain* decision in which it was held reviewable.

The court was also, however, influenced by the difficulty of determining whether the applicant had been guilty of the offence for which he was convicted - something which the Minister regarded as a prerequisite for an *ex gratia* payment to be made. In the case before the court the applicant sought disclosure of the Secretary of State's reasons for refusing the claim, to enable him to make representations; but the judge did not think it desirable that this should be allowed, since this would involve a "retrial" of the charge originally brought. If a hearing is warranted by virtue of the nature of interest, then the difficult nature of this question should not, however, preclude a hearing of the kind normally appropriate: it certainly need not extend to a full "trial". The best explanation of *Harrison* is that the applicant's interest was not sufficiently important for a hearing, by analogy with *McInnes v Onslow Fane* ([1978] 1 WLR 1520 (no hearing on an application for a licence)), which was relied on by the judge. It is submitted, then, that judicial review of the making of *ex gratia* payments is available in principle, but will generally not extend to allowing a right to be heard. This view is supported by cases concerning the judicial review of decision not to make an *ex gratia* payment of the amount of overpaid taxes, where there is no legal right to recovery, which suggest that review is generally available. These decisions are discussed at 11.2.4 below.

Unlike the Crown, it is generally considered that bodies of limited statutory authority do not have the power to make *ex gratia* payments as incidental to their authorised functions: special authority must be conferred. Thus local authorities, for example, cannot generally make *ex gratia* payments of compensation. However, there is provision for such a payment to be made where a local authority feels it is appropriate following consideration of a report laid by one of the Commissioners of Local Administration (s.31(1) Local Government Act 1974, as inserted by s.1(1) Local Government Act 1978). In other cases such payments are generally unlawful. There is a power implicit in section 19(1) Local Government Finance Act 1982 which allows such an unlawful payment to be sanctioned by the Secretary of State. The effect of this is that an auditor may not obtain a declaration that the payment is unlawful. However, this does not affect the legality of the payment itself (*A.G. v Merthyr Tydfil Union* ([1900] 1 Ch 516; *R v Grain ex parte Wandsworth Guardians* [1927] 2 KB 205 at pp.213-214).

10

Compensation for Breach of European Community Law

10.1. Introduction

This chapter considers the question of compensation for loss resulting from a breach by the United Kingdom government of directly effective rules of European Community law. The principles governing liability were explained at 1.6 above. Briefly, any claim must be brought in the domestic courts and domestic law will apply; but this principle is generally subject to the important qualifications that remedies must be no less favourable than those applying to similar domestic claims, and that remedies must be effective.

Claims against domestic authorities may arise where authorities on their own initiative implement policies or make decisions which contravene Community law. This is what occurred in the *Bourgoin, Garden Cottage* and *Irish Dairy Board* cases, discussed in 9.2 below, and this situation will be considered first. As a result of the recent European court decisions in *Francovich* (jointed cases C-6/90 and C-9/90, judgement November 19 1991) it appears that domestic courts may often be compelled to give a damages remedy in such a situation.

In addition, liability may also arise out of action which the government takes on behalf of the Community or in applying Community provisions.

10.2. Liability for Domestic Administration

10.2.1. Non-discrimination

The principle of non-discrimination requires that all rules under which damages may be claimed for a breach of domestic law must also be applied where there is a breach of Community law. There is in English law no general right to damages for loss caused by invalid administrative action, but a number of specific torts provide redress in limited situations (see further 10.2.1 below).

First, the tort of misfeasance in public office (see 9.1) will apply where the government knows that it acts contrary to Community law. The important Court of Appeal decision in *Bourgoin v Minister of Agriculture* ([1986] QB 716, discussed at 9.1.2), which established that there may be liability for knowingly acting unlawfully though there is no malice, arose out of a breach of Community law by the United Kingdom government. Liability is obviously likely to be found where a decision that the action in question constitutes a breach has previously been made by the Commission or the European Court, and it has been suggested it might also arise where the Commission has proffered "strongly worded" advice to the effect that the action is illegal (see Ward, (1990) 19 Anglo Am L Rev 1 at p.34).

It is not certain whether there may be liability in negligence when the government carelessly exceeds its powers (see 6.3.1). Even if this is possible, however, successful claims for negligent breach of Community law will be rare, because of the serious restrictions on the recovery of economic losses (see 6.7). To succeed it would also be necessary to show that one of the purposes of the Community provision breached was to protect the plaintiff (see 6.6 above).

Another relevant tort is breach of statutory duty (see Ch.7). In *Garden Cottage Foods v Milk Marketing Board* ([1984] AC 130), the House of Lords appeared to take the view that a damages action would be available for a breach of any duty imposed by Community law, holding it to be unarguable that a breach of Article 86 of the Treaty of Rome, forbidding the abuse of a dominant market position within the Community, did not give rise to liability in damages. However, the existing English law cases concerning damages for breach of statutory duty generally were not discussed. In the later case of *Bourgoin v Minister of Agriculture* ([1986] QB 716) the majority of the Court of Appeal (Oliver L J dissenting) held that damages were not automatically payable for a breach of Article 30 forbidding quantitive restrictions on imports, and measures of equivalent effect. The court distinguished the *Garden Cottage* case on the basis that it concerned a different Article of the Treaty. A point emphasised by the court was that Article 86 imposes obligations not only on public bodies but also on private whilst this was not the case with Article 30 created a public duty enforceable by means of judicial review. Strangely, the court seemed to assume that a purely "public" duty is enforceable *only* in an action for judicial review in domestic law, and to give damages would be simply compensation for an *ultra vires* act. This is not in fact the case as was explained at 7.3 above. In appropriate cases the courts will grant damages for breach of a public duty under the tort of breach of statutory duty, and it is unfortunate that the court in *Bourgoin* did not examine the previous decisions to determine whether Article 30 was a case of this type. Had they done so, however, it seems clear that a right to damages would not, on prior authority, have been recognised, because of the possibility of widespread liability. It is unlikely in fact that liability would ever be found for legislative measures causing economic damage.

Oliver L J in his dissent disagreed over, *inter alia*, how the domestic tort of breach of statutory duty should be applied. In his view, domestic law requires a damages remedy whenever the statute has conferred a "right" on individuals, in the sense that it is intended to promote the interests of those individuals (as distinct from providing an opportunity for individuals to bring an action to safeguard the public interest). In contrast with the majority, he considered that it was not for the English courts to determine when such a "right" had been conferred, using domestic rules of interpretation, but for the European Court. Once it had been determined that such a right had been created, he reasoned, the English courts are bound to protect it by an award of damages because of the principle of non-discrimination. (He also considered that protection was required by the principle of effectiveness: this issue is examined separately at 10.2.2 below).

In applying the principle of non-discrimination, the approach of the majority in *Bourgoin* is to be preferred. (As to the position under the principle of effectiveness see 10.2.2). It does not follow, under the non-discrimination principle, that just because the applicant is prejudiced by an unlawful act he has a right to damages, even if he is entitled to bring an action for judicial review, so that in this sense he may be said to have a "right" rising out of the breach of Community law. What is essential for the tort of breach of statutory duty in domestic law is that the legislature intended to create a right to obtain a specific remedy - that of damages. The "right" created by the legislation, and the remedy given to enforce it cannot be separated. If the European legislation itself is intended to create a right to damages, the action would be based directly on the right created at European level : the European legislative authorities may prescribe a remedy, and it is only to the extent that no remedy is prescribed that the matter is one for national law (see 1.6 above). Thus, if Oliver's approach to the application of the domestic tort of breach of statutory duty were adopted the tort would become irrelevant: if the legislation created a right to damages the domestic tort would be rendered inapplicable, and if the legislation did not create such a right, then no right would arise under the domestic tort, which is said to depend on the intention of the legislature. In fact, it is submitted that the tort is not irrelevant. This is because, in most cases the question of damages is simply not dealt with, and by implication is left to the national courts. This creates a theoretical difficulty in so far as national law does seem to say that the question of damages depends on the intention of the legislature in enacting the duty! In these circumstances, it is submitted that the requirement that a remedy be given where it would be given in a "comparable" situation in domestic law should be held to require damages where they would be given for a breach of a domestic provision which is comparable *in substance,* according to the principles set out at 7.3 above. This interpretation gives effect to the policy of non-discrimination, and was the one adopted by the majority in *Bourgoin.*

Finally, in addition to misfeasance and negligence, and breach of statutory duty, the nominate torts of English law may sometimes enable an individual to obtain a remedy for a breach of Community. Since most complaints concern an impact on economic interests, the emerging economic torts are perhaps likely to be the most significant in this context, particularly in the area of competition law. (See Steiner (1987) 12 EL Rev 102 at pp.110-113).

10.2.2. *Effectiveness*

If remedies for breach of Community law are confined to those available for breach of domestic law, there will be many cases where a person adversely affected by a breach of Community law is unable to obtain compensation though he may be able to bring an action for judicial review. The majority of the Court of Appeal in *Bourgoin* (discussed at 10.2.1) took the position that damages should be confined to situations where damages are given in domestic law.

It appears now, however, that this approach is incorrect and that, in some circumstances, at least, national courts must give damages for breach of community law, whatever the domestic position (although it still may be correct that no damages would be required on the facts of *Bourgoin*). This appears to be the position of the European Court in the important recent case of *Francovich* (joined Cases C-6/90 and C-9/90, judgement Nov 19 1991). In that case former employees of certain firms which had become insolvent sought compensation for unpaid wages from the Italian government, suing in the Italian national courts. The government was obliged by an EC Directive(Directive 80/987 EEC) to provide for the payment of such sums to employees on the insolvency of their employer, but had not yet taken implementation measures, though the date for implementation had passed. The European Court, in answer to questions submitted under the Article 177 ruling procedure, ruled first that the Directivedid not have direct effect, so that it could not be relied upon in the national courts to allow the applicants to recover the sums provided for by the legislation. However, the court also ruled that the firms were entitled to claim compensation for the Italian government's breach of its obligation under Article 189 of the Treaty of Rome to implement the Directive. According to the court, compensation for failure to implement a Directive must be provided in the national courts whenever a) the Directive involves rights conferred upon individuals, b) the rights in question can be identified and, c) there is a causal link between failure to implement the Directive and damage is suffered by an affected party (para. 40 of the judgement).

This case clearly indicates that in at least some circumstances member states are obliged to provide damages as a remedy for breach of community law. No doubt this will be applied to breaches of other Treaty obligations as well as the obligation under Article 189, and may also require damages to be paid for a breach of Regulations or the provisions of directly effective Directives. This clearly seems to have been the view of the court, which stated as a general principle that protection of Community rights may require a damages remedy (see paras. 32-37), and regarded a breach of Article 189 as one specific situation in which such a remedy might be required. It may be argued that this shows that Community law may require the creation of new remedies, where necessary, to protect Community rights, a question doubted in some previous cases (see 1.6 above); or it might be argued that it is merely the adaptation of a remedy found already in all states. The theoretical basis for the position of the court is probably unimportant.

The question which *is* important is - in what circumstances must damages be given as a remedy?

The most extreme position would be that those adversely affected by a breach of community law are generally entitled to damages : everyone so affected may be said to have his rights infringed, and to protect these rights effectively damages must be given. This was the view of Oliver L J in his dissent in *Bourgoin*. He considered that damages remedy was required not only by the principle of non-discrimination, but also by the effectiveness principle *simply because* the plaintiff was affected by a breach of Community law.

However, there are strong arguments against such a wide view. They parallel the concerns which have militated against a general principle of liability for invalid government action in domestic law (see 9.2 above) and have led to a limited scope in domestic law for the tort of breach of statutory duty in the public context (see Ch.7). First, there are policy arguments against general liability on a strict basis, since the operation of Community provisions is uncertain and strict liability may induce caution in the exercise of government powers; and a general rule of liability will often result in wide and heavy liability. Second, it is significant that the Community itself is not generally liable for damages for breach of Community law: with respect to a legislative measure of economic policy (which effectively means most general Community measures) there is liability only where there has been breach of a manifest and grave nature, of a superior rule of law designed for the protection of individuals (case 5/71, *Zuckerfabrik Schoppenstedt v Council* [1971] ECR 975; see Steiner, *Textbook on EEC Law* (2nd ed. 1990) pp.321-325; *Non Contractual Liability of the European Communities* (1988), eds. Schermers, Henkels, Mead, ch.1, 2, 3 and 8;

Harding, "The Legal Accountability of Community Institutions: A Study of Illegality and Non-Contractual Liability under European Community Law" in *Current Issues in European and International Law* (1990), eds. White and Smythe, ch.4). There have been few successful cases; although there may be wider liability for individual as opposed to legislative acts (Steiner, above, p.324). This limited principle at the Community level has itself developed in response to the kind of concerns just mentioned. The fact that there is no automatic liability on the Community itself when it breaches principles of Community law suggests such liability should not always be imposed on the member states.

It is suggested that probably damages are not required to be made available as a remedy for breach of Community law in every case, but only in more limited circumstances. Thus it may be that the Court will develop some more limited concept of "Community rights", in the sense of individual interests which must be protected by the national courts, and will hold that damages must be available as a method of protection. Such rights might be based simply on the nature of the interest infringed : for example, certain Community provisions might be held to create a "right" in those whose interests they are intended to protect, and/or who are affected in a serious or special way; and/or they might depend on the nature of the conduct of the government - for example, there might be held to be right not to be prejudiced by a knowing or careless breach of Community law. It might be argued at least that there is a "right" to damages in the kind of circumstances where damages would be available against the Community itself for a comparable breach (though this view was not taken by the Court of Appeal in *An Bord Bainne Co-operative v Irish Dairy Board* [1988] 1 CMLR 605, holding that the *Bourgoin* ruling against liability for breach of Article 30 applied equally to administrative as well as to legislative or quasi legislative acts). Alternatively, and this is perhaps indicated by *Francovich* itself, it may be that the European Court will start with a presumption that damages are payable, but use appropriate limiting devices to preclude recovery for - for example - indeterminate economic losses. No doubt there will soon be questions put under the Article 177 ruling procedure in relation to these important issues.

Where European law does require that damages be payable in principle it is still for the national courts to determine questions such as time limits and interest. This will, of course, be subject to limits on their freedom of action in these areas (such as the need for time limits to be reasonable), in order to protect the effectiveness of the substantive right to recover.

A party adversely affected by a breach of Community law may also be able to obtain a remedy by way of judicial review to prevent or quash a breach of Community rules, and so minimise his damage, as is also, of course, the case with a breach of domestic law. Domestic remedies by way of judicial review must under the principle of non-discrimination be made available for breach of Community law; and under the principle of effectiveness any limitations on existing national remedies must be disregarded to the extent that is necessary to make those remedies effective for the protection of Community law rights. This is illustrated by the litigation in *Factortame* as a result of which the House of Lords has now held that interim relief by way of injunction is available against the Crown in an action for breach of Community law, though an injunction cannot be granted at all against the Crown in a case concerned solely with domestic law. (see 1.6.2.2 above). As mentioned above, the principles on which the discretion to award an injunction are exercised are those applied in domestic cases concerned with interim injunctions, as discussed by the House of Lords in *American Cyanamid Co. v Ethicon Ltd.* ([1975] AC 361) and *R. v Secretary of State for Transport ex parte Factortame Ltd (No 2)* ([1990] 3 WLR 856, and for discussion of these principles see Oliver, (1991) 54 MLR 442; Gravells, [1991] PL 180).

10.3. Liability for the Administration of Community Provisions

As was noted above (see 1.6.1) Community policies, including the agricultural policy and provisions on the collection of customs duties, are administered by the domestic authorities of the member states, since the Community does not have its own administrative machinery. The question of a damages remedy can also arise where loss occurs from an unlawful act or omission of a domestic authority in the course of administering Community measures. The issue may arise because the domestic authority has wrongly applied a Community measure, hence acting unlawfully; or because the Community measure which the authority implements is itself unlawful. Chapter 11 examines the position where an individual seeks to recover an invalid charge which has been levied by the member state in the course of administering Community policy (see 11.2.7), and chapter 12 the case where he seeks to recover a payment which is due under Community law but is wrongfully withheld by the domestic authority (see 12.3). It will be explained that the amount of any invalid charge, and (where the amount has been fixed) the amount of any payment due, must be recovered from the national authorities administering the scheme, in an action in the national courts, even though the amount of the payment must ultimately come from Community funds. The position where the affected party wishes to recover consequential losses (such as for damage to his competitive position) or where loss arises in other ways than through refusal of subsidies or the making of a levy, is considered next.

10.3.1. Wrongful application of valid measures

'Vhen a national authority wrongly applies a Community provision the unlawful act is attributable to the member authority for the purpose of damages liability. There is no basis on which the Community itself could be sued for damages in the European Court, since it is not the act of the Community which has caused the loss. This principle has been applied even where the Community led the authority to do the unlawful act by suggesting that the measure be interpreted in that way (case 133/78 *Sucrimex v The Commission* [1980] ECR 1269; *Interagra S A v The Commission* case 217/81 [1982] ECR 3657). Hence any action to recover damages must be brought in the national courts. Probably the usual principles of non-discrimination, effectiveness and, possibly, deterrence would apply in this situation (see 1.6.2.2 above), in order that a remedy is available in some forum to redress the breach of Community law which has occurred. If so, the position will be as explained at 10.2 above.

Where damages are recoverable against the member state and the Community is wholly or partly at fault, as claimed in *Sucrimex* and *Interagra*, it seems that the member state should have a right under Community law to be reimbursed for any damages paid out, or that the Community should bear the costs in the clearance of accounts, as appropriate (see further Oliver, "Joint Liability of the Community and the Member States", in *Non-Contractual Liability of the European Communities* (1988), eds. Schermers, Heukels, Mead, ch.10, at pp.142-143).

10.3.2. Application of invalid measures

When the Community itself is author of an invalid measure which causes loss, a damages action may be brought against the Community in the European Court under Article 215(2) of the Treaty of Rome. However, as explained at 10.2.2, with a legislative measure damages will be awarded only in a limited circumstances - that is, where there is serious breach of a superior rule designed for the protection of individuals, a formula which has been so restrictively interpreted that there have been few successful claims.

In some cases damage to an individual may occur where the invalid Community measure is implemented through the instrumentality of a member state. This arose, for example, in *Krohn* (case 175/84 *Krohn v The Commission* [1986] ECR 753), where a licence was unlawfully refused by a member state, but this was done on the binding direction of the

Commission. In this case, as well as the issue of a damages claim against the Community itself in the European Court, there may be raised the possibility of an action against the member state in the domestic courts in respect of the same loss. It is not entirely clear whether, in a case where the member state acts pursuant to a binding Community measure, the usual principles of non-discrimination and effectiveness would apply to require any existing domestic remedies to be made available. It could be argued that in this case the protection of Community rights is for the European Court alone in an action brought directly in that court against the Community. It does seem to be assumed that there is no *requirement* for national law to provide a damages remedy to compensate an affected party. This assumption has been made in cases in which actions against the Community itself for such damage have been admitted without requiring a party to exhaust remedies before the national court, on the basis that national law does not provide effective protection through a damages remedy (see further below). This could be explained, however, either on the basis that the effectiveness and non-discrimination principles do not apply, or that they do not require any damages remedy to be given (a matter discussed at 10.2.3 above).

Even if the non-discrimination and effectiveness principles do not apply, however, it may be that national law would choose to give a remedy.

It may be noted that it was assumed by Parker L J in *Bourgoin v Minister of Agriculture, Food and Fisheries* ([1986] QB 716) that the United Kingdom could incur liability for implementing an unlawful Community measure. The possibility that the domestic government may be liable where the Community itself cannot be sued in the European Court was in fact one reason for rejecting the argument that breach of Article 30 gave rise automatically to a right to damages in English law - though it would, of course, be possible for different principles to apply in the case of liability for implementing invalid Community acts to those applicable where the breach of Community law is purely the responsibility of the member state. Presumably the court considered that misfeasance liability would apply where the United Kingdom acts under a Community measure which it believes to be invalid. It seems theoretically possible that the national law right to damages against the member state might be wider than that given by the European Court against the Community, though this situation does not seem likely to arise in the United Kingdom, given the approach of the court in *Bourgoin.*

The relationship between the two possible actions - one in the European Court against the Community and the other in the national court against the member state - is not clear (see Durand, (1975-6) E L Rev 431, Hartley, (1977) 16 E L Rev 249; Harding, (1979) 16 CML Rev 389; Oliver, "Joint Liability of the Community and the Member States" in *Non-Contractual Liability of the European Communities* (1988) eds. Schermers,

Henkels and Mead, Ch.10). In the early case of *Kampfmeyer* (cases 5, 7 & 13-24/66, [1967] ECR 245) the European Court stayed an action for damages in the European Court and indicated that possible remedies in the national court, which would include an action for annulment, should first be exhausted. However, this alleged principle has been criticised and has generally been regarded as incorrect. In a number of cases brought before the European Court it has been argued that the affected party should have first brought an action in the national courts before proceeding against the Community, but the court has admitted the claims against the Community under Article 215 without requiring any action in the national courts (for example, case 126/76 Firma Gebruder Dietz v Commission; case 74/74, *CNTA v Commission* [1975] ECR 533; [1976] ECR 597, which concerned damages for consequential losses for sums wrongly withheld). The claim for damages for consequential losses from the unlawful refusal of the licence was also admitted in *Krohn*, above.

In *Krohn* the European Court indicated that the relevant principle is that an individual will be required to proceed before the national courts only where those courts can provide effective protection for his interests, which would include a right to damages. The same view seems also to be endorsed in the more recent case of *Rocquette Freres S.A. v The Commission* (case 20/80, [1991] 60 CMLR 6). Here Rocquette had paid to the French national authorities monetary compensation amounts, which were purportedly required under Council Regulations. The Regulations were subsequently held invalid (see case 145/79, [1980] ECR 2917). However, the overpayments could not be recovered from the national authorities because the European Court had ruled that the invalidity was not to affect payments charged or made before the date of its judgement. Rocquette then brought an action under Article 215 to recover from the Community itself both for the amount of the charges paid and for other losses consequential upon payment of the charges. The claim was held to be admissible. The Court considered, at least in certain cases, that where national law provides an effective remedy this must be used, as indicated also in *Krohn*. It was held, however, that the principle was not applicable on the facts, because the European Court itself had ruled that national law *could* not give a remedy in this case.

The problem with this is that it will generally be difficult for the European Court to know whether, in any given case, national law will in fact provide a right to damages for acts and omissions of member states in the administration of Community measures; and the European Court itself certainly cannot make authoritative rulings on what is required by domestic law. This is particularly problematic in view of the fact that there have been few cases in member states which address this question. This presented no problem in *Rocquette* because of the exceptional circumstances of that case, but normally it will do so. A better principle would be simply to admit an action in the European Court in all cases. The possibility of an action in both forums leads, of course, to the theoretical possibility of double recovery. No doubt, however, any court adjudicating the question would take into account damages awarded elsewhere in making its own award. Alternatively it may be argued that an action in the European Court should be stayed where an individual has *actually* brought a claim in the national courts, as in *Kampfmeyer* so that the national court can make its decision first.

An alternative approach to the whole problem would be to require member states to provide a damages remedy in certain circumstances through the principle of effectiveness in all cases where the damage can be said to be attributable to the act or omission of the administering authority, and to require the action for recovery to be brought in the national courts. There appears generally to be the position with the recovery of a specific sum in restitution and the recovery of charges wrongly withheld (see 11.2.7 and 12.3 below). Following the decision in *Francovich,* which was discussed at 10.2.2 above, it seems that a damages remedy may well also be required in such circumstances by the operation of the principle of effectiveness.

It was explained above (see 10.3.1) that where the damage caused is due to the fault of the Community in, for example, advising a member state to act in a particular way, the Community must bear the financial consequences. A *fortiori* this must apply where the damage-causing act is carried out by the member state pursuant to a binding measure of the Community. This should apply even where, in an action for damages in the national courts, the national government is subject to a greater liability in damages than is the Community itself in the European Court: the Community should still have to bear the cost.

11

Restitution

The law of restitution which applies to public authorities is in principle the ordinary private law. However, there are some modifications in the way this law applies, and the law also has to grapple with some problems which are special to the public sphere.

11.1. Crown Proceedings

The former immunity of the Crown from suit (see 1.2) applied to claims in restitution as well as other liability claims. It was established, however, that the petition of right procedure applied to some restitutionary claims (see 1.2.1.3 above). Today the Crown may be sued in the ordinary manner in respect of all claims which could previously have been brought by way of petition of right, under section 1 of the Crown Proceedings Act 1947 (see 1.2.1.3 above). The Crown's liability in restitution, as in contract, thus depends on the scope of the old petition of right.

It was established clearly that certain restitutionary claims were within its scope - namely those in respect of money or property in the hands of the Crown (*Feather v The Queen* (1865) 122 ER 1191 at 1204-5). Many restitutionary claims do not, however, fall within these categories - for example, claims for the value of services rendered, or expenditure saved. An argument that such claims could be adjudicated through a petition of right has been based on an *obiter dictum* of Cockburn C J in *Feather v The Queen*, above (at 1204-5):

"... the only cases in which the petition of right is open to the subject are, where the land or goods or money of a subject have found their way into the possession of the Crown, and the purpose of the petition was to obtain restitution, or, if restitution cannot be obtained, compensation in money, or where the claim arises out of a contract. It is in such cases only that instances of petitions of right having been entertained are found in our books."

This dictum was quoted by Cockburn C J in *Anglo Saxon Petroleum Company v Lord Commissioners of the Admiralty* ([1947] Ch 794), for the view that if a claim were not in contract or tort, a petition would lie only in respect of a claim for goods or services received by the Crown. However, this statement was *obiter*, since it was held that the action in the case was one in tort. In addition, it seems to be based on a misinterpretation of the *Feather* dictum, which is taken out of context. It seems clear that Cockburn C J in *Feather* did not have in contemplation other types of restitutionary claims, but was concerned solely to emphasise that a petition of right did not lie for an alleged wrong by the Crown, for he adds immediately after the words quoted above: "No case has been brought or adduced ... in which a petition of right had been brought in respect of a wrong properly so called." At the time of *Feather* the availability of restitutionary claims for services and other non-tangible benefits was not clearly recognised, and the judge obviously did not address himself to the availability of such claims against the Crown.

Against the view expressed in *Anglo Saxon Petroleum* Lord Dunedin in the House of Lords in *Attorney General v de Keysers Royal Hotel* suggests that a petition was generally available where no wrong was alleged ([1920] AC 508 at 530-531). Clearly it would be anomalous if certain types of claim could not be made against the Crown. The better view is that the petition of right was available for all restitutionary claims, and that an action in restitution may today be brought against the Crown whatever the nature of the claim (see, for example, Hogg, at p.180, note 2; Mewett, (1959) 13 U of TLJ 46; Street, at pp.125-127; and see also Crown Proceedings Act s.8, on salvage claims).

11.2. Recovery of Invalid Charges

11.2.1. Introduction

An important problem largely confined to the sphere of public law is that of the recovery of charges invalidly levied. This often arises in connection with taxes and duties - such as income tax or excise duties - when the government makes a demand for which it has no authority. It may also occur where a payment is made in return for something - for example, for the issue of a trade licence, or for the use of services provided by a public body. Often statute restricts the amount of the charge and the question of recovery may arise where this amount is exceeded.

To a large extent recovery of unlawful levies is now dealt with by legislative provisions, which are considered at 11.2.3. However, the common law is still important and will be examined first. It must be emphasised at the outset that the whole law relating to the recovery of unlawful levies is in a very unsatisfactory state. It has recently been the subject of critical examination in a Law Commission Consultation Paper, and the tentative proposals for reform which were mooted are considered at 11.2.5 below.

11.2.2. The common law

11.2.2.1. The traditional approach

The traditional approach to recovery has been to apply the private law. Thus, it has generally been necessary for the plaintiff to prove that one of the distinct private law grounds of recovery applies. The fact that he paid in response to an *ultra vires* demand has not been seen by itself to provide a basis for recovery. However, in *Woolwich Equitable Building Society v I.R.C.* ([1991] 3 WLR 790), a majority of the Court of Appeal (Ralph Gibson L.J. dissenting) chose to depart from the traditional approach, and held that a special "public law" rule of restitution allows recovery of invalid levies without need to show one of the private law grounds of restitution. In principle, such an approach is to be welcomed. Unfortunately, however, the reasoning in *Woolwich* itself is very unsatisfactory, as is explained at 11.2.2.2 below. At the time of writing an appeal to the House of Lords looks likely and it is not adequate to explain the current law solely in terms of the *Woolwich* decision. First, the decision may well be overruled by the House of Lords, or "reinterpreted" by later courts. Second, there may still be scope for the operation of the private law alongside the rule in Woolwich. Finally, *Woolwich* cannot in any case be understood without some knowledge of the previous case law. It is thus proposed first to examine the traditional approach, and then to examine the impact of the *Woolwich* case.

Under the traditional "private law" approach the grounds of recovery most relevant are duress and mistake of fact. There may also be a right to recover by virtue of an implied contract to repay.

A payment is made under duress when it is made in response to an illegitimate threat (*Universe Tankships v I.T.W.F.* [1983] AC 366, and see Goff and Jones, *The Law of Restitution* (3rd ed. 1986), ch.9). One established category is duress of goods, where payment is made in response to a threat of unlawful interference with goods. Thus there will often be duress where a threat is made to levy distress on the plaintiff's goods under an alleged statutory power of distress for non-payment. Such a power will normally exist only when the payment is lawfully due - if it is not due such action becomes unlawful. It appears that there is also an illegitimate threat where the authority threatens to act in a manner which is *ultra vires*, even though its conduct is not tortious - for example, by withholding a benefit to which the plaintiff is entitled (see Goff and Jones, at pp.216-222). There is no duress, however, if the payment is made in response simply to a threat to sue for the amount alleged to be due : a threat to sue in support of an *ultra vires* demand is not considered to constitute an illegitimate threat (*William Whiteley Ltd. v R* (1909) 101 LT 741; *Woolwich Equitable Building Society v I.R.C.*, above). There may, of course, be great pressure in practice to comply with a tax demand, quite apart from the difficulties of becoming involved in litigation with the Revenue; statutory penalties for non-payment may be incurred if the taxpayer's view is incorrect, and a business may fear damage to its reputation if it does not pay (as in *Woolwich*). Again, however, there is no duress, since the pressure does not derive from any illegitimate threat.

There may be some difficulty in determining when a threat exists, when no express threat is made. It seems that the test ought to be whether the conduct of the authority would have been perceived by a reasonable man as constituting an illegitimate threat (see Burrows, "Restitution, Public Authorities and Ultra Vires", in Burrows ed. *Essays on the Law of Restitution* (1991), p.39). When a payment is demanded in return for the provision of a benefit it might be argued that this carries with it a threat to withhold that benefit. Similarly, where there is a statutory power to levy distress for non-payment of particular type of charge it might be argued that a threat of distress for its non payment is reasonably perceived as inherent in any demand. The existence of a threat must always depend on the precise facts of each case - for example, the extent to which it has been the previous practice of the authority to use its distress powers. In *Woolwich* where the distress powers of the Revenue were in practice never exercised in the kind of circumstances which had arisen, it was held that no threat could be implied (though cf. *Mason v New South Wales* (1959) 102 CLR 108). This decision seems correct on the point; but in some other cases the courts have been too reluctant to find that a threat exists and the decisions seem hard to square with the general test of reasonable apprehension (see *Twyford v Manchester Corporation* [1946] Ch 236 and *Slater v Burnley Corporation* (1888) 58 LT 636; and for criticism Burrows, above; Marsh, (1946) 62 LQR; Birks, *Introduction to the Law of Restitution* (2nd paperback ed. 1989) at pp.294-299; Goff and Jones, at pp.243-244). Of course if the plaintiff himself did not perceive a threat, even though a reasonable man might have done so, his claim will fail on the basis that the illegitimate threat could not have been the cause of the payment.

Recovery of an invalid charge is also allowed, in accordance with general restitutionary principles, where it is paid because of a mistake of fact (*Meadows v Grand Junction Waterworks Co.* (1905) 21 TLR 538; and on mistake of fact generally see Goff and Jones, above, ch.3). Whether a party can be said to have made a mistake where he has doubts as to relevant state of affairs - and hence the validity of the charge - is not clear, but may not be important since, even if he is mistaken, he may often be considered to have made a "submission to an honest claim", which provides a defence to recovery, or to have waived his rights (see Arrowsmith, "Mistake and the Concept of Submission to an Honest Claim" in Burrows ed., *Essays on the Law of Restitution* (1991), p.17; Andrews, [1989] LMCLQ 431).

The fact that a payment is made because of a mistake of law, on the other hand, does not generally provide a basis for restitution under the private law (*Bilbie v Lumley* (1802) 102 ER 448; *Kelly v Solari* (1841) 152 ER 24). This is frequently the reason for the levy of invalid charges and for their payment by the citizen, and such payments have, under the general rule, been treated as irrecoverable (*National Pari-Mutuel Association ltd. v R.* (1930) 47 TLR 110; *R. v Richmond upon Thames L.B.C., ex parte Stubbs* (1989) 87 LGR 637).

A party may recover an overpaid tax where there is an agreement that it shall be recoverable if found not to be due. Such an agreement may sometimes be implied by the court. It seems that an agreement will normally be implied where the payment is made in circumstances where proceedings to challenge the levy are being taken and the payer makes it clear that his payment is conditional on the money's being found to be owed. An implied contract to repay was found in such circumstances in *Sebel Products Ltd. v Commissioners of Customs and Excise* [1949] Ch 409 and *Woolwich*, both at first instance and in the Court of Appeal. It was held in *Woolwich*, however, (again at both stages), that the courts will not generally imply a term that interest will be paid. This makes the implied contract a less favourable basis for recovery than restitution, since with restitution interest is normally available (section 35A Supreme Court Act 1981). No contract to repay should be implied where legal proceedings are not on foot: a payer who purports to make a conditional payment in such circumstances reasonably appears to be waiving his right of recovery, whatever he may say expressly. It seems also that a contract should not be considered to arise when the Revenue makes it clear that it is not prepared to accept a conditional payment, even when legal proceedings are on foot.

Where a payer cannot show that one of the above grounds applies, it has traditionally been considered - subject to exceptions outlined below - that there is no right of recovery. Thus payments made under mistake of law are considered irrecoverable. Payments made in the absence of any mistake but in the firm belief that they are not owed, have also been treated as irrecoverable in the absence of any duress, or an implied contract, as in *William Whiteley*, above. The suppliants had paid a licence fee for certain of their canteen workers, licences being required for "male servants". They contended their workers were not within this class but nevertheless paid the fee for several years. Eventually they successfully challenged the Revenue. Their subsequent claim for money already paid was denied, however, on the basis that none of the private law grounds of recovery was applicable (and see also *Slater v Burnley Corporation,* above; *Glasgow Corporation v Lord*

Advocate 1959 SC 203). Thus is the traditional approach; but it should be noted here that the authority of the *William Whiteley* decision has now been challenged by the Court of appeal in *Woolwich*. This is considered further at 11.2.2.2.

Before considering *Woolwich*, however, it is necessary to note some cases which had already been argued to create an important exception to the "private law" approach. These, often called the *colore offici* cases, concern the situation where a public body unlawfully demands a payment in return for the performance of a public duty. They have been suggested to support a principle that a payment made in response to such a demand is automatically recoverable. Although these cases sometimes refer to the existence of "compulsion" or "extortion" this does not appear to refer to a need for any duress in the modern sense, since there was in many of these cases no investigation of whether any threat to withhold performance was actually made (see *Morgan v Palmer* (1824) 107 ER 554; *Dew v Parsons* (1819) 106 ER 471; *Campbell v Hall* (1774) 98 ER 1045; *Steele v Williams* (1853) 155 ER 1502, which it seems cannot turn on duress, since, on the view of Martin and Platt BB, the sum was paid after the duty was performed; and *South of Scotland Electricity Board v British Oxygen Co. (No.2)*, [1959] 1 WLR 587). In *Mason v New South Wales*, above, Windeyer J (at pp.140-141) considered these cases to establish a right to recover any payment made to secure performance of a public duty. However, some writers have explained these as duress cases (for example, Craig, at p.46; Goff and Jones, above, at pp.216-22). The alleged special recovery rule also appeared inconsistent with *Twyford v Manchester Corporation*, above, and *Slater v Burnley Corporation*, above; and its existence always remained uncertain.

It has also been suggested that an exception to the private law approach applies to the extent of allowing overpayments to be set off against future sums due to the same authority, though they may not be recoverable. This stems from *Blackpool and Fleetwood Tramroad Co. v Bispham with Norbreck UDC* ([1910] KB 592) in which the court held that the council could not enforce a rate demand without allowing a set off for previous overpayments resulting from a mistake of law. Lord Bridge commented in *R v Tower Hamlets L.B.C., ex parte Chetnik Developments Ltd.* ([1988] AC 858) that the exception was an "anomaly", though he did not express a firm opinion on its existence.

11.2.2.2. The approach in Woolwich v IRC

The traditional restrictive approach was much criticised, but was until recently generally considered to represent the law. However, in the recent decision in *Woolwich Equitable Building Society v I.R.C.* ([1991] 3 WLR 790) a majority of the Court of Appeal, Ralph Gibson LJ dissenting, rejected this approach. Instead the Court adopted a special rule of public law which gives a *prima facie* right to recover money paid pursuant to an invalid government demand. The rule is, however, subject to two very important exceptions : money may not be recovered (at least in some cases) if paid under a mistake of law; nor may it be recovered if paid "to close the transaction".

Woolwich involved a claim for payments made by the Society under invalid regulations (successfully challenged in *R v I.R.C., ex parte Woolwich Equitable Building Society* [1990] 1 WLR 1400). The Society had always contended that they were *ultra vires* and challenged them immediately; but it paid the sums demanded through fear of damage to its reputation if it refused, and because of the interest which would be payable if its view that the regulations were invalid was erroneous. Once it was determined that the regulations were unlawful, the Revenue returned the capital sum paid, but refused to pay interest. Woolwich brought an action claiming interest. This was payable only if there was a right in restitution to recover the capital sum. On the private law approach there would have been no such right (there was an implied contract to repay, but this did not give Woolwich a right to claim interest: see 11.2.2.1 above). However, the majority of the Court of Appeal held that it was unnecessary to recover to show the existence of one of the private law grounds of restitution: it took the view that there is a special rule of "public law" allowing the recover of invalid charges, and on the basis of this rule Woolwich had a right to recover the sum paid.

The majority in *Woolwich* chose to depart from the traditional approach for policy reasons: the traditional narrow approach had been criticised and it has frequently been argued that there should be a general right to recover overpaid charges (see further 11.2.5). Support for the new rule was found in a number of cases which did not sit easily with the traditional approach, and which reflected the law's discontent with it. These included the *colore offici* cases (see 11.2.2.1), and the House of Lords decision in *R v Tower Hamlets L.B.C., ex parte Chetnik* ([1988] AC 858), where it was recognised that the courts may sometimes effectively compel repayment in a judicial review action, though there is no right to recover in restitution (see further 11.2.4). As regards the decisions in *William Whiteley, Slater and Twyford* (see 11.2.2.1), Butler Sloss LJ considered that they were wrongly decided and, as first instance decisions, need not be followed; whilst the other member of the majority, Glidewell LJ, thought they were either wrong or, possibly, could be explained as within one of the exceptions to the public law recovery rule, in that the payments there were made to "close the transaction" (see further below).

As indicated, however, the court recognised two exceptions to the rule. The first is where the payment is made under a mistake of law. It is clear that the court accepted this limit only because it felt compelled to do so by the prior authority of the Court of Appeal in *National Pari-Mutuel Association v R.* ((1930) 47 TLR 110), which was binding on the Woolwich court (and see also *R v Richmond upon Thames L.B.C., ex parte Stubbs* ((1989) 87 LGR 637, which also seems binding in this respect). Butler Sloss LJ thought this limitation would apply wherever a payment is made under a mistake of law. Glidewell LJ, on the other hand, suggested it might apply only where the payment was made because of a mistaken construction of valid legislation (as had occurred in *National Pari-Mutuel*), and might have no application to payments made pursuant to invalid legislation.

In practice, most overpayments to public bodies are made as a result of a mistake and recognition of the mistake of law exception very significantly narrows the "general" public law rule of recovery. How narrow the recovery rule is depends on the meaning given to mistake. Certainly there is no mistake where the validity of the payment is firmly denied at the time, as in *Woolwich* or *William Whiteley*. It is less clear if a mistake exists where the payer has some doubts but believes that the payment is, or may be, owed (see further 11.2.2.1). Whatever the scope of the exception, it is unsatisfactory, since there are stronger grounds for granting restitution to a payer who has no knowledge of possible invalidity, than one who had this knowledge but nevertheless chose to pay. This is recognised by the private law, which allows recovery where a payment is made under a mistake of fact, but not where it is made in response to a claim based on a fact which is denied by the payer. It is also recognised by some of the statutory provisions giving a right to recovery of overpaid charges, which allow recovery where the payment has been made under a mistake (whether of fact or law), but not where the charge was disputed at the time (on these provisions see further 11.2.3 below). The authority for the "mistake of law" rule by which the Court of Appeal in *Woolwich* felt itself bound did not regard the existence of mistake of law as a *bar* to recovery; rather, they proceeded on the basis that payments to public bodies are not irrecoverable in the absence of some positive ground for recovery, and their significance is in their refusal to recognise mistake of law as such a ground. Certainly it would have been assumed that if mistaken payments are not recoverable then, a *fortiori*, a payments made in the absence of a mistake (or duress) will not be. It is thus a distortion to treat these cases as authority only for the limited proposition that payments made under mistake of law cannot be recovered.

The second exception is where the payment is made to "close the transaction". Unfortunately it was not explained when this exception will apply. Arguably, it might apply wherever the payer does not make it clear that the payment is conditional - for example, where he disputes the validity of the demand but does not tell the authority of his view, or where he tells them but appears to accept the matter as finalised by failing to assert that the payment is without prejudice to his rights. It may even preclude recovery where as in *William Whiteley*, the payment is made "under protest" but the payer does not also indicate that he will be taking steps to challenge the decision: Glidewell LJ suggested that the decision in *William Whiteley* (and *Slater and Twyford*) might still stand, as an example of this exception to the general recovery rule. If so, it seems the so-called general rule is confined to those cases where there would anyway be an implied contract to repay (as in *Woolwich* itself); or possibly also where such a contract is precluded solely because the payee refuses to accept the payment as conditional (see 11.2.2.1 above). However, if a *prima facie* case to recover is recognised on the basis of the special position of public authorities, it is difficult to see why recovery should be permitted only to those who firmly maintain a "protest", and possibly, only to those who are in a position to litigate.

However interpreted, the exceptions to the recovery rule in *Woolwich* may render the rule of little importance in practice, and it is one which is anomalous as well as uncertain in scope. There are good grounds to believe that this approach would not be accepted by the House of Lords. The options for future development of the law are considered at 11.2.5 below. Certainly the need for reform is highlighted and rendered more urgent by the unsatisfactory decision in *Woolwich*.

11.2.3. *Legislative rights to recovery*

In many cases a right to recover overpaid charges is now expressly given by statute or in regulations. There are a large number of different legislative provisions, each dealing with a different charge, or group of charges, and most of the major taxes are now dealt with. (See Law Commission of England and Wales, *Restitution of Payments made under a Mistake of Law*, Law Com. Consultation Paper No.120 (1991) paras. 320-336). The various measures have been enacted in an *ad hoc* fashion and there are differences between them which are largely a product of historical accident, rather than considered policy.

Some of the provisions give a *prima facie* right to recover whenever an overpayment is made, regardless of the cause of payment. In the case of Value Added Tax, for example, section 24 of the Finance Act 1989 provides for recovery whenever a person pays an amount to the Customs and Excise Commissioners "by way of value added tax which was not tax due to them" (s.24(1)). There is also a general right to recover overpayments of community charge or non-domestic rates (for the main provisions see The Community Charges (Administration and Enforcement) Regulations 1989,

S.I. No.438/1989 Reg.26; The Non-Domestic Rating (Collection and Enforcement) (Local Lists) 1989, S.I. No.1058/1989 Reg.9; The Non-Domestic Rating (Collection and Enforcement) (Central Lists) Regulations 1989, S.I. No.2260/1989). An example of a regulation allowing for the general recovery of an overpayment of a fee, as opposed to a tax, is The Land Registration Fees (No.2) Order 1990, Article 9(1), providing for a refund of certain land registration fees "where an amount exceeding the prescribed fee has been paid". Provisions relating to some other types of tax or charge, on the other hand, have conferred a right to recover overpayments only if the payment was made by mistake (whether a mistake of fact or law). This is the case with car tax and excise duty, under section 29 of the Finance Act 1989, and with overpaid National Insurance contributions, under Regulation 32 of the Social Security (Contributions) Regulations 1979 (S.I. No.591/79, as amended; though see also Regulation 34, providing for recovery of certain voluntary contributions without proof of error).

With a number of taxes a legislative right to recover is given which is much narrower, being confined to the situation where the error causing the overpayment affects only one person or a small group. This is, effectively, the result of the provisions on overpaid inheritance tax under the Inheritance Tax Act 1984. Under section 241 there is a generally stated right to recover an overpayment (without the need for any mistake), but this does not apply where the payment is made and accepted "on a view of the law then generally received and adopted in practice" (s.255). A similar limitation also applies to another very important group of taxes - Income Tax, Corporation Tax, Capital Gains Tax and Petroleum Revenue tax, which are dealt with by section 33 of the Taxes Management Act 1970 (see further Law Commission *Restitution of Payments Made under Mistake of Law*, above, at para 325; and Stopforth, (1989) 5 BTR 151). The purpose of these limitations is to ensure that a right to recover does not generally arise where there have been overpayments by a large group, because of the disruption to the business of the Revenue, or even to financial planning and expenditure, which this might cause.

In addition to these wide variations in recovery rights, there are differences between the provisions relating to ancillary matters such as the payment of interest and limitation periods. (For details see the Law Commission Consultation Paper, above).

The relationship between the legislative rights to recover and restitutionary rights under the common law is unclear. With respect to overpayments of V.A.T., the problem is expressly dealt with in section 24 of the Finance Act 1989, it being provided that recovery is permitted only under section 24. Other provisions however, are generally silent on this.

One argument might be that where recovery of a particular type of charge is dealt with by legislation, that legislation by implication excludes any right to recover under the common law. However, this seems inconsistent with the approach of Butler Sloss LJ in *Woolwich Equitable Building Society v I.R.C.* She considered that the relevant legislative provisions in this case did not confer a right to recover payments made under invalid regulations, as opposed to payments made pursuant to a demand based on a misinterpretation of valid provisions; and considered thus that the common law applied. This is odd, since the difficulties in allowing recovery are likely to be greater in the case of invalid regulations, where large numbers of people may be affected, so that it might have been more logical to hold that recovery is precluded by implication where the situation does not fall within the statute. Given that *Woolwich* seems to accept that there may be a common law right to recover though the tax in question is dealt with in legislation, it is also arguable that it is possible to rely on other common law grounds, including the principle in *Woolwich*, where a statutory right is given on the limited basis of mistake.

Another question is whether it is possible to rely on the common law even where there is a *prima facie* statutory right to recover, in order to avoid limitations on the statutory right - for example, on the recovery of interest, or the effect of passing on a tax to customers (on the latter see below at 11.2.6.1), which may not apply under the common law. The relationship between statute and the common law is an issue which, particularly given the approach in *Woolwich*, considerably complicates this area of law.

11.2.4. Ex gratia repayments

Where there is no legal right to repayment a public authority may have a discretion to return an overpaid charge on an *ex gratia* basis. The Crown has a general common law power to make ex gratia payments (see 9.4), and it was suggested by Ralph Gibson LJ in *Woolwich Equitable Building Society v I.R.C.* ([1991] 3 WLR 790) that a power to refund in its discretion is implicit in the statutory powers of tax management given to the Revenue. Statutory authorities, on the other hand, have a power to make *ex gratia* payments only to the extent that such a power is conferred by specific provisions, and cannot otherwise give a refund, though this may be permitted if done on the recommendation of the Commissioners for Local Administration (see also 9.4 below). Sometimes a discretionary power of repayment has been given by statute, as under section 9 of the General Rating Act 1967, in respect of overpayments of rates.

Where an *ex gratia* repayment is refused an action may be brought for judicial review of the refusal. Such an action was successful before the House of Lords in *R. v London Borough of Tower Hamlets, ex parte*

Chetnik ([1988] AC 858), where the applicant sought review of a decision made in the exercise of the express discretion under the General Rating Act, a refund having been denied. Lord Bridge considered the fact the payment was made under mistake of law was an irrelevant consideration in deciding to deny the refund, as were the financial difficulties of the authority, though a claim might be refused where it had been compromised by the payer. Lord Goff went so far as to say that the section created a "statutory remedy in restitution" which, it seems, required restitution to be made where this would be required by the common law for payments made as a result of a mistake of fact. Their Lordships placed considerable emphasis, however, on the wording of the express statutory discretion. There was also a right to appeal to the courts, showing that the legislative intention was that the courts should have the final say on the refund. However, in *Woolwich Equitable Building Society v I.R.C.*, (above), the majority of the Court of Appeal stated that the principles in *Chetnik* were applicable to the review of any discretion to repay. If this is so, then wherever a power to repay exists there will be a *prima facie* right to recover, subject to the usual discretion of the court in a review action, as well as the short time limits (see 1.3 above). This will enable the payer to recover even when the *Woolwich* rule does not apply, including where a payment has been made under a mistake of law.

11.2.5. Reform

The current law is obviously unsatisfactory, not least in that the various rules do not reflect any consistent policy. Under the common law recovery is allowed where a payment results from a mistake of fact and where there is no mistake, but not where it is caused by a mistake of law - an illogical position since there is a stronger case for recovery where a payment is made by mistake than where it is not. It is possible that the mistake of law limit may not apply where it is sought to recover an invalid fee paid to obtain the performance of a public duty, or where a tax is paid under invalid regulations - though there is no particular justification for treating these cases differently from any other case of mistake of law. Under legislation a much wider right of recovery is given for some charges and taxes. This is also the case where a charge is levied in breach of European Community law (see 11.2.7) - a further difference in treatment of what appear to be like cases. Problems also arise from the fact that the relationship between legislative and common law rights of recovery is unclear (see 11.2.3).

Most of those who have examined this area have taken the view that there should be a much wider right to recover invalid taxes and charges (see Burrows, "Restitution, *Ultra Vires* and Public Authorities", in *Essays on the Law of Restitution* ed. Burrows, (1991) at p.39; Birks, "Restitution from the Executive: a Tercentenary Footnote to the Bill of Rights" in

Essays on Restitution ed. Finn (1990), ch.6 - where the author disowns the narrower view which he took formerly in [1980] 33 CLP 91; Cornish, [1987] J Mal & Comp L 41; Collins, (1984) McGill L J 407; Pannam, (1964) 42 Texas L R 777; and see McKenna, (1979) 37 U of T Fac L Rev 223). In particular, it has been argued that the constitutional principle of "no taxation without the consent of Parliament", enshrined in the Bill of Rights of 1689, requires such a right (see Birks, above). This would both provide a remedy for individuals and discourage unlawful taxation, it is argued (although the possibility of recovery for misfeasance in public office where an unlawful levy is made knowingly is perhaps a sufficient deterrent). A wide rule of recovery may also encourage prompt payment, and increase confidence in government. It has also been pointed out that the present position favours those who are well advised and have the resources to litigate and who are less likely to respect government authority.

The main argument against widening the right to recovery is that it would be disruptive of government business and general planning. Expenditure will have been made on the basis of believed revenues, and if these are upset the burden of these expenditures will have to be placed on current taxpayers - who may not have benefited from the original spending - either through increased taxation or a reduction in services. These arguments explain the earlier reluctance of the common law to expand the right to recovery, and also the restrictive approach taken in a number of statutes which do not allow recovery where there has been an error of "general practice" (see 11.2.3). They were relied on by Ralph Gibson L J in his dissenting judgement in *Woolwich* as justification for upholding the traditional approach of the common law. However, although these arguments have some force, particularly in relation to local authorities, they appear to be outweighed by the arguments in favour of a general recovery right, and this has been the view of Parliament in enacting many of the legislative provisions which give a right to restitution. The majority of the Court of Appeal in *Woolwich* also expressed the view that overpaid taxes should generally be recoverable, though they felt compelled by prior authority to accept the severe restrictions which had been adopted. It has never been suggested that any serious problems of disruption to public finance have arisen in applying existing provisions and should they do so in particular cases it is always possible for Parliament to pass legislation precluding recovery.

One approach to reform might be to provide for recovery of payments made under mistake of law in the same way as payments made under a mistake of fact. This has been advocated by many writers and it is generally considered that it should not be confined to the public sphere but should also apply to payments made to private persons. A provisional proposal for a reform of the general mistake of law rule has been put forward recently by the Law Commission of England and Wales (*Restitution of Payments Made under Mistake of Law,* Law Comm Consultation Paper No.120 (1991) Pt.II). Such a reform has already been achieved by legislation in some other jurisdictions (see the Law Commission paper, above, at para 2.46) and by judicial development in Canada (*Air Canada v British Columbia* [1989] 1 SCR 1161; though an exception was made for unconstitutional - as opposed to merely *ultra vires* - taxation: see Arrowsmith, (1990) 106 LQR 28).

Another possibility is to provide a *prima facie* right to recover unlawfully levied charges which does not depend at all on the reason for the payment, along the lines of section 29 of the Finance Act 1989 on V.A.T. This would mean recovery is *prima facie* allowed where the payer is not sure whether it is due (it is not clear whether or not this should be a "mistake"). It would also permit recovery where the payer is quite clearly of the view that the payment is not owed - a case which would certainly not be covered if recovery were to be based on mistake. The majority in *Woolwich* favoured recovery even in the absence of mistake (and indeed, because of prior authority felt compelled to allow recovery *only* in the absence of mistake) and the preferred view of the Law Commission in its Consultation Paper, was that "what is needed is a general right against public authority payees, rather than, as in the case of private law, one based on the circumstances of the payer" (para 3.61). The Commission considered that the right should not be subject to any limitation based on the idea of "voluntary submission to a claim" or "waiver of rights", even where the payer has doubts about whether the payment is due, or positively disputes this: the payment should only be irrecoverable where there is a payment made under a contractual compromise of the public authority's claim, or an estoppel (see 3.64). It also considered that a defence should probably be available where the payer has suffered no loss - for example, because the amount of the charge has been passed on to the payer's customers, or the invalidity was purely technical (on these problems see 11.2.6 below). It is submitted that these tentative proposals represent the best solution to the problem of overpaid taxes and charges.

The main area of difficulty with such a reform is determining the scope of the special public law rule of recovery. Certainly it would apply to bodies such as government departments and local authorities, but arguably it ought to cover also unlawful charges demanded by public utilities under the colour of statute, including those newly privatised, which are treated as "public" for the purpose of certain other rules. (For a discussion of the problems of defining the scope of the special rule see the Law Commission Consultation Paper, paras 387-389; and on the scope of "public law" liability rules more generally 1.1 above). The same problem arises, of course, in delineating the scope of the special common law rule recognised in *Woolwich*.

11.2.6. Some specific problems

11.2.6.1. "Passing on"

One important problem is that often referred to as "passing on" - that is, where the payer of an unlawful charge has passed on all or part of it to his customers in the form of higher prices. This situation is not confined to public law - it may arise in any case where a business enterprise pays out a sum to another and then seeks to recover it, since payment of any sum represents an increase in overheads, which is taken into account in calculating prices. In practice, however, the problem has been raised only with charges on specific goods or services, since only then is it normally possible to identify a link between the charge and the price of the product. It must be appreciated that even if the whole amount of the charge is passed on, the payer may still suffer loss, since increased prices may lead to decreased sales and consequently decreased profits. However, often this will not represent the whole amount of the charges paid, and if the payer is always allowed to recover the whole amount he may thus gain a "windfall" benefit (on this see Rudden and Bishop, [1986] E L Rev 243).

The statutory provisions on recovery of V.A.T., car tax and excise duty provide that there is to be no recovery to the extent that this would "unjustly enrich" the payer - that is, where he would receive a windfall (Finance Act 1989, s.24(5), s.29(3)). There are no cases in English law dealing with the position at common law. In *Air Canada v British Columbia* ([1989] SCR 116) it was accepted by La Forest J, with whom Lamer and L'Heureux Dube J J agreed, that there could be no recovery to the extent that the fact of passing on would produce a windfall benefit for the payer. The contrary view was taken, however, by Wilson J, and also by the High Court of Australia in *Mason v New South Wales* ((1959) 102 CLR 108, where the point was discussed by Windeyer J at 146)). It is submitted that the approach of La Forest J in *Air Canada* is correct: in principle the fact that the plaintiff has suffered no loss should preclude a restitutionary action, and to the extent loss has been avoided by passing on the charge there should be no claim. *Mason* is explicable on the basis that the claim there was based on wrongful conduct by the payee, namely duress. In practice, it may be difficult to determine whether any loss has actually been suffered, because of the difficulties of showing the effect of any increased prices on sales (see Bishop and Rudden, above), and probably the burden of proving loss should be on the government; but if the burden can be met then the claim should be denied. This is the provisional view adopted by the Law Commission in its consultation paper on *Restitution of Payments Made under Mistake of Law* (1991) (Law Com 120, para 3.85).

The rules relating to "passing on" in actions to recover charges which infringe European Community Law are considered at 11.2.7.1 below.

11.2.6.2. Technical invalidity

A charge may be regarded as "technically" invalid to the extent that it would still have been imposed had the decision in question been taken lawfully - for example, where it is only unlawful because of a breach of some procedural requirement which would not have made any difference to the outcome. In practice, of course, it will be difficult for the court to know how the authority would have exercised its discretion if it had acted in a lawful manner. This problem of "second guessing" the exercise of discretion potentially the courts in many different contexts in adjudicating liability claims (see 1.4.2 above). It has been suggested already in discussing the problem of "passing on" that the payer should not normally recover where he has lost nothing, at least in the absence of wrongful conduct by the payee. This principle should be applied where there is no loss because the charge would have been made anyway. However, the burden of proving this should be placed on the government. It may be noted that Ralph Gibson L J in his dissenting judgement in *Woolwich Equitable Building Society v IRC* refers to this as a "difficult question", in the context of deciding whether a decision to refuse discretion repayments should be subject to judicial review (as to which see 11.2.4). He does not, however, suggest what the answer should be.

11.2.7. European Community law

Special rules may apply to the recovery of fees or taxes which are invalid under European Community Law. Two types of case must be considered. The first is where the charge is levied in pursuance of measures brought in by the United Kingdom which breach Community rules. The second is where the charge is levied pursuant to a measure promulgated by Community institutions, which is collected by the United Kingdom government on behalf of the Community.

11.2.7.1. Charges levied under domestic measures

There are many circumstances in which a tax or fee levied by a member state might be held invalid as infringing Community law. In practice, the cases which have given rise to restitutionary problems have largely concerned measures which are invalid for infringing Article 95 of the Treaty of Rome, which prohibits internal taxation having discriminatory effect, or Article 12, prohibiting the levy of new customs duties, or charges having equivalent effect (see Steiner, *Textbook on EEC Law* (2nd ed. 1989), chs.7 and 6). Both provisions have direct effect - that is, they are capable of creating legal rights in individuals, which must be upheld in the national courts of member states (see further 1.6.1). The issue might also arise, however, in a variety of other contexts. For example, a recent case involved an action to recover fees paid to a Belgian institution for vocational training, held discriminatory under Article 7 of the Treaty, which prohibits discrimination on the grounds of nationality, since the amounts were not charged to Belgian nationals (case 24/86, *Blaizot v University of Liege* [1989] 1 CMLR 67).

An individual seeking a remedy for breach of Community law against the United Kingdom government must sue in the national courts, and, to the extent that the matter is not governed by express Community legislation, national law and procedure will apply (see 1.6.2). There is no Community legislation in this area: Council Regulation 1430/79 (see 1.2.7.2 below), which regulates the recovery of certain charges levied on behalf of the Community, has no application in the present context (case 199/82, *Amministrazione delle Finanze dello Stato v SpA San Giorgio* [1983] ECR 3595). The application of national law is subject to the principles of effectiveness and of non-discrimination (see 1.6.2).

The principle of non-discrimination simply requires that the remedy for recovery of a charge is at least as favourable as that available to redress a "comparable" breach of domestic law. This should cause no problems in United Kingdom law, since all statutory rights and common law recovery rights are formulated to apply equally where a charge is invalid under Community law, as where it is invalid under domestic law.

What is required by the principle of effectiveness in this context? It was explained at 1.6.2.2 that it is not clear whether Community law requires national law to provide new remedies where this is necessary to give effective protection to Community rights, or simply requires that any existing remedy be made available to protect those rights, in a manner which makes that remedy "effective". It is at least clear that where the law provides a right to restitution of a particular charge, limitations, such as time limits, which prevent it from being effective must be disregarded (see further below). Less clear, however, is the position where national law rules do not provide for recovery. An example would be where income tax is paid under a belief that it is due, when the provision under which it is levied is invalid as discriminatory under Community law. Where the error is one of "general practice" there would be no right to recover under statute (see 11.2.3); nor would the common law normally allow recovery where the mistake is one of law (see 11.2.2). Even if there is no rule that Community law may require new remedies to protect Community rights, it might be argued that English law does provide a remedy for recovery of invalidly by levied income tax, but with a limit for errors of "general practice", and that this limit must be disregarded. Alternatively, it might be suggested that the existing "remedy" is found under the common law principle expounded in *Woolwich* (see 11.2.2) that taxes unlawfully levied must be repaid, and that the "mistake of law" rule is a limit which must be disregarded. A narrow approach, on the other hand, would be to say that no remedy is generally provided by English law for recovery of income tax paid under a mistake of law, and hence no remedy is available even where the mistake relates to a matter of Community law. In practice it seems inconceivable that the courts would not adopt an approach which would compel the return of charges levied in breach of Community law.

In any event, as was suggested at 1.6, it may be that the European Court has now moved to the position that national courts must create new remedies where necessary effectively to protect Community rights, and if this is so there is no doubt that national law must give a remedy for the recovery of overpaid charges. Where there is a right to recover the question arises as to what limitations on this right it is permissible for national law to impose.

One matter which has been considered is the effect of national provisions which disallow a claim to the extent the payer would be unjustly enriched by recovery because the burden of the charge has been passed on to others, as provided for in English law in the statutory provisions relating to VAT, car tax and excise duty, and possibly under the common law (on this issue generally see 11.2.6.1). In a number of cases the European Court has ruled that such a limit is permissible (for example, case 61/79, *Hans Just I/S v Danish Ministry for Fiscal Affairs* [1980] ECR 501; case 61/79 *Amminstrazione delle Finanze dello Stato v Denkavit Italiana* S.r.1. [1980] ECR 1205; case 811/79, *Amminstrazione delle Finanze dello Stato v Ariete Sp.A.* [1980] ECR 2545). This has been criticised as detrimental to the policy of the invalidating provisions, since where provisions are concerned to prevent the distortion of competition, to allow recovery of the full amount of the charge minimises the distorting effect (see, for example, Hubreau, [1987] CMLR 87). (No such consideration arises with most charges which are invalid under domestic law, though it has been argued that such charges should still be recoverable: see 11.2.6.1). Although the "unjust enrichment" defence is allowed in principle, however, the European Court ruled in *San Giorgio*, above, that it is not permitted to put onto the payer the burden of proving that the charge was not passed on. This is so difficult that such a requirement infringes the principle of effectiveness, which requires that remedies not be unduly difficult or impossible to exercise. Thus in practice the defence may rarely apply, since the burden of proof will be equally difficult for the government to satisfy. It may be noted that the provisions on this matter in the English statutes relating to VAT, car tax and excise duty (see 11.2.6.1) provide for the "unjust enrichment" of the payer to operate as a defence, and thus seem acceptable in their application to charges which are in breach of Community law.

The court also stated in *San Giorgio* that other rules of evidence making it unduly difficult to recover would not be permissible. Specifically, the court ruled that a provision excluding all but documentary evidence of the passing on of the charge could not be upheld.

Another important question is the recovery of interest for the period prior to repayment. The European Court has ruled that whether interest is payable and the amount is for the national courts (case 26/74, *Rocquette v Commission* [1976] 677, a case concerned with invalid charges imposed by the Community). This can be criticised on the basis that repayment without interest does not give "effective" protection of rights, and also in that it permits too great a variation in the remedies provided by different member states.

Where national law requires any claim to be brought, or at least protest made, within a specified time, the time period stipulated must be reasonable, as laid down in *Rewe v Landvirtschaftskammer Saarland* (case 33/76, [1976]) and *Comet v Produkschap voor Siergerwassen* (case 45/76, [1976] ECR 2043). In *Bessin,* the European Court ruled that a three year recovery period was reasonable, and this applied even though during that period the payer was unable to prove his claim through no fault of his own, being unable to get the relevant documents from the Moroccan authorities (case 386/87, *Bessin et Salson SA v Administrations des Douanes et Droits Indirectes* [1991] 60 CMLR 855). The limitation periods set out in UK legislation are normally generous - usually six years from the time the claim arose, with the possibility of extension, as is also the case under the common law (see Law Commission, Consultation Paper *Restitution of Payments Made under a Mistake of Law*, Law Comm 120 (1991), para 3.20-3.26). One view is that where the claim is based on the invalidity of the levy *per se* and not some other ground, such as mistake, the decision must be challenged first under Order 53, normally within three months, but it was suggested earlier that this is incorrect (see 1.3).

It has not been specifically considered in this context whether defences such as estoppel and change of position, designed to protect security of receipt, are permissible. Such defences have been allowed in some cases where the government seeks to recover charges paid out in breach of Community law, and indeed may be required in order to protect the legitimate expectations of payees (see 11.3.2). However, the same principles will not necessarily apply to protect the government itself.

National law may not enact provisions which retrospectively prevent recovery for persons who, but for those measures, have a right of recovery (case 240/87, *Christian Deville v Administration des Impots* [1989] 2

CMLR 611). However, to prevent undue disruption of public authority finances the European Court itself, when it rules that a charge contravenes Community law, may limit the temporal effect of its ruling by providing that charges collected prior to the ruling under the offending measures shall be irrecoverable. Important factors in deciding what should be done will be whether the levying authority had good cause to believe that the levy was valid, and the nature and scope of likely disruption (see *Blaizot*, above 11.2.7.2).

11.2.7.2. *Administration of Community levies*

The European Community itself is responsible for many measures imposing charges on individuals. In particular, levies on imports are all set by the Community, and various levies are made by the Community for the purpose of the Common Agricultural Policy (CAP). Since the Community itself has no machinery for the administration and collection of charges, this is carried out by the individual member states. Formerly the amounts of these levies were retained by the member states and the Community was financed through general contributions paid by each state. As from 1 January 1971, however, charges collected have normally been payable directly to the Community to form part of the Community's own resources, after deducting a sum for administration costs.

Charges levied in the purported application of Community provisions may be unlawful either (i) because the provision itself is in breach of Community law or (ii) because the levying authority has misinterpreted the provision and levied a charge which is beyond its scope.

Invalid Community provisions:
In most cases where a payment is made under an unlawful Community provision, a right to recover from the collecting state is given by Council Regulation 1430/79 (Similar provisions will be contained in a planned new Community Customs Code). This requires a collecting authority to repay all import and export duties when no debt has arisen in respect of the goods in question, or the amount exceeds that which is lawfully payable (Article 2). "Import and export duties" are defined to include all the most important types of charges: the phrase effectively includes agricultural levies and monetary compensation amounts as well as customs duties and charges of equivalent effect (Article 1). Repayment is required where an application is submitted (or the error discovered by the authority itself) within three years from the date the duties were entered in the accounts (Article 2; though the period may be extended where the payer was prevented by unforeseen circumstances or *force majeure* from submitting his claim). All claims under

the legislation must be brought in the national courts since there is no provision for any action in the European Court.

Ancillary matters not dealt with by the regulation are governed by national law and procedure (case 130/79, *Express Dairy Foods v Intervention Board for Agricultural Produce* [1980] ECR 1887). There may be some debate whether a particular matter can be said to have been dealt with by implication. Attorney General Mancini in *San Giorgio* suggested that the Regulation does not prevent states restricting recovery where the amount of the charge has been passed on, implying that this is a matter left to national law and not dealt with by implication by the grant of the apparently unrestricted right of recovery (case 199/82, [1983] ECR 3595 at 3622). Any applicable provisions of national law must, of course, conform with the principle of effectiveness and non-discrimination (see 1.6.2 above).

For any case outside the legislation, recovery will be determined by national law and procedure in accordance with the usual principles. The application of the principles of non-discrimination and effectiveness in relation to restitutionary claims were considered at 11.2.7.1 above.

It appears to be no defence to a claim against a member state that the Community itself is ultimately liable to pay the amount of the judgement to the member state, but refuses or is unable to do so (case 99/74, *Grands Moulins des Antilles v Commission* [1975] ECR 1531, a case on recovery of subsidies, discussed below at 12.3.2).

Since charges collected by member states are ultimately paid to the Community, it might be thought that an action for recovery would be available against the Community itself. However, it is generally accepted that it is not. In the cases which have addressed this point litigants have attempted to recover the amount of the unlawful levy in an action for damages under Article 215(3) of the Treaty of Rome. This provides for the possibility of damages to be awarded against Community institutions in the European Court for "fault" by the Community, and it has been alleged that the amount of unlawful levies are a loss caused by the fault of the Community in enacting the unlawful measure. Such a claim appears, however, to be inadmissible.

The first important case was *Kampffmeyer* (cases 5,7,13-24/66, [1967] ECR 245). Importers of maize into Germany sought to recover damages for, *inter alia,* levies paid on certain imports. The applicants had earlier been refused a licence to import at a zero rate of levy. This constituted a breach of Community law by the German authorities. The measure had been approved by the Council of the Community, which was thus alleged to be at fault for the purposes of a damages action. (Although the case concerned approval rather than enactment of an unlawful measure it has been assumed in later cases that the same principles apply to both types of "fault"). The applicants had also instituted recovery proceedings against the national authority. The

European Court held that the action for recovery of the sum should be stayed until judgement was given in the German courts on the liability of the national authorities.

Kampffmeyer was decided at a time when levies were retained by member states. Surprisingly, however, a similar principle has been established for cases where funds collected are required to be paid into Community resources (which, as explained, is now generally the position). The first decision was Haegemann (case 96/71, *R & V Haegemann Sprl.v Commission* [1972] ECR 1005), in which the Court based its conclusion on the fact that the legislation entrusted to the member states the collection of the amounts and should be considered to impose by implication the duty to reimburse also. It was also held that any claim before the European Court under Article 215 should be held inadmissible, and not merely stayed pending determination of the claim in the national courts, a slightly different approach from that in *Kampffmeyer*. The Court ruled that since the charges were administered by the national authorities it was for the national courts "to decide what to do" about refunds (although, as has been explained the European Court may potentially have a considerable degree of control over what they must do through the principle of effectiveness). Some later cases did appear to retreat from the view that a claim for the charges cannot be brought against the Community in the European Court, but the most recent have followed the *Haegemann* line and this is generally regarded as representing the law. (For further discussion, see Durand (1975-6) 1 E L Rev; Hartley, (1977) 16 E L Rev 249; Harding (1979) 16 CML Rev 389; Lewis (1980) 33 CLP 99; Oliver, "Joint Liability of the Community and the Member States", in *Non-Contractual Liability of the European Communities* (1988) eds. Schermers, Heukels and Mead (Ch.10)). Arguably, the principle in *Haegemann* rests on the premise that a remedy for recovery *must* be provided in the national courts for at least the amount of the sum paid over, under the principle of effectiveness. This, in fact, seems the best explanation of the decision.

The alternative explanations of *Haegemann* seem to be either that the litigant will go without redress at all if it is not provided for in national law, or that the admissibility of the claim depends on whether or not national law gives a remedy. It has been suggested by Hartley (above at p.264) that the latter might be the case - that the admissibility of a claim in the European Court might be linked to the availability of a remedy in the national courts, so that a claim could be brought in the European Court if no national remedy exists for the amount claimed. However, as he admits, this is problematic, since the European Court cannot readily ascertain what is the national law. This view is also inconsistent with the decision in *Rocquette,* where it was held that a claim before the European Court under Article 215 for interest on an overpayment was not available, even though it had been established no interest was payable under national law (case 26/74 *Rocquette v Commission* [1976] ECR 677). If the European Court wishes to ensure a remedy is available in any particular case - for example, for interest - this should be done through the way in which the principle of effectiveness is applied to control the remedies available in the national courts, and no remedy should be given at European level. There is, however, one exception to this, which appears to be justified. This applies where the European Court itself has ruled that its finding of invalidity is not to affect charges paid prior to the date of judgement (on this see 11.2.7.1 above). In such a case no remedy for recovery at all *can* be brought before the national court. In such circumstances the European Court has held that an action for damages in respect of the amount paid is admissible in the European Court under Article 215 (case 20/80, *Rocquette Freres S A v E C Commission* [1991] 2 CMLR 6).

The above cases have considered the argument that the amount of an invalid levy paid is a loss caused by the fault of the Community. An alternative legal basis for recovery against the Community itself where it has actually received the levy might be that the Community has been unjustly enriched. Prevention of unjust enrichment has been recognised by the European Court as one of the general principles of Community law. Where one party has been unjustly enriched at the expense of another in national law the matter normally comes before the courts by way of an action in restitution to recover the benefit conferred or its value. There is no specific provision in any of the Treaties for a restitutionary action against the Community, however, and in the Community law cases so far in which it has been alleged that the Community has been unjustly enriched the matter has arisen only indirectly. It is arguable that it is culpable conduct such as to give rise to a damages claim in the European Court under Article 215 to refuse to disgorge on request the amount of an unjust enrichment. This seems the most likely basis of any unjust enrichment claim. If this is the correct basis of any claim, its use for the recovery of invalid charges would seem to be precluded by the *Haegemann* line of decisions, which has denied the admissibility of an action under Article 215: this line of authority would seem to apply equally where the alleged fault is refusal to disgorge a benefit, as where the fault claimed is the enactment of the unlawful measure. Other possible bases for a claim might be an action for judicial review for the refusal to disgorge the benefit, or an action against the Community in the national courts, but both seem unlikely.

Consequential losses from payment of an unlawful Community levy will generally be recovered in a damages action against the Community itself in the European Court, though it is possible national law might provide a remedy (see Ch.10). Thus a litigant may have to bring two separate sets of proceedings - one in the national courts for the recovery of the sum, where appropriate, and one in the European Court for the recovery of the additional loss.

Since charges levied by member states under Community provisions are generally paid into Community resources a member state should be entitled to be reimbursed from Community resources where the charge is recovered from it by the payer on the basis that it was unlawful. Such a right is specifically given by Article 24 of Council Regulation 1430/79 which provides that where duties are remitted in accordance with the Regulation a member state may deduct the sum from the Community's own resources.

Misinterpretation of Community provisions:
A second case arising from the administration of Community levies is where the domestic government misinterprets the relevant provision and raises a charge which is not within its scope. It seems that such charges, like those which are invalid because the provision under which they are levied is invalid, are covered by Council Regulation 1430/79.

Critique:
The principle that requires a party to sue a member state in the national courts for a sum unlawfully levied by that state on behalf of the Community has been criticised insofar as it may require two sets of proceedings to be taken by a litigant. This could be avoided if an action could be brought in the European Court against the Community for the amount of the payment as well as for consequential losses. It has been suggested that this would result in excessive litigation for the European Court, but this seems unlikely if this kind of action were used only when convenient for the litigant - which would probably be where a claim for additional losses would be brought before the European Court anyway. A more convincing objection is that given by the Court in *Kampffmeyer* for staying the action, which is the possibility of double recovery. It has been suggested by Hartley, above, that this can be met by allowing an action in the European Court only if the litigant assigns away his right to an action in the national courts. A possible problem, however, is that the European Court would have its own ancillary rules to govern a claim (for example, an interest and time limits), and in some cases these might be less favourable than those in national law. Would a litigant who sues in the European Court be required to assign away the whole right of action, or just assign it to the extent that he is able to recover before the European Court?

An alternative method of dealing with the double recovery problem would be to take away the right of action in the national court altogether. However, this might indeed substantially increase the case load of the European Court, and would also deprive the litigant of the convenience of suing in his own courts. Making available an action against the

Community on the basis of unjust enrichment in the national courts would not solve these difficulties: it would still often be necessary to bring an action in the European Court for consequential losses.

The problems which would arise in allowing all claims to be settled in a single action suggest that perhaps the current law is an acceptable solution to difficulties which are inevitable with a dual court system.

11.3. Invalid Payments Made by Public Authorities

11.3.1. Payments invalid under domestic law

It was explained above that until recently the courts applied the ordinary private law to the question of recovery of overpayments to public authorities, with the result that such payments have been recoverable only in limited circumstances; and that even though a special public law based on *ultra vires* is now recognised, recovery will generally be precluded because of wide exceptions. This has never been the approach, however, with *ultra vires* payments made by public authorities, for which a special, wide, rule of recovery was laid down by the Privy Council in *Auckland Harbour Board v R.* ([1924] AC 318). Viscount Haldane stated (at 327) that:

"Any payment out of the consolidated fund made without Parliamentary authority is simply illegal and *ultra vires* and may be recovered by the Government if it can be traced". Surprisingly the rule has not been further applied in the English case law (though for other Australian decisions see *Commonwealth v Burns* [1971] VR 825; *Commonwealth of Australia v Crothall Hospital Services (Aust) Ltd.* (1981) 36 ALR 567; *Sandvik Australia Pty. Ltd. v Commonwealth of Australia* (1989) 89 ALR 213; and see also *Attorney General v Great Southern and Western Railway Co of Ireland* [1925] AC 754, where no mention was made of the need for tracing). The rule is based on a public policy against the unlawful dissipation of public funds. As such it would probably be applied to all *ultra vires* payments, though it is stated by Viscount Haldane by reference to payments from the Consolidated Fund.

Since a person cannot be stopped from affirming or denying something when to do, or not to do, that thing would be contrary to statute the defence of estoppel probably cannot be applied to claims by a public authority under this principle. In the Australian case of *Commonwealth v Burns*, above, it was held that, for this reason, estoppel could not be invoked to prevent the recovery of an overpayment of a pension. This general limitation on the estoppel doctrine has been criticised in that it always gives priority to the public interest behind the *ultra vires* rule at the expense of the individual, when this is not always warranted (see further 2.3.2.1). The Law Commission in its Consultation Paper on *Restitution of Payments Made under Mistake of Law* (Law Comm Consultation Paper No 120 (1991)) said that it was inclined to the view that the defence should be made available; but it did not express any conclusive view (see para 4.20).

There is, on the other hand, no constitutional objection to a defence of change of position. Such a defence has recently been recognised by the House of Lords in *Lipkin Gorman v Karnpnale Ltd* ([1991] 3 WLR 10). Lord Goff said (at 35) that the defence would be available "to a person whose position has so changed that it would be inequitable in all the circumstances to require him to make restitution, or alternatively to make restitution in full". This defence ought to apply to restitutionary claims based on the *Auckland* principle: as a matter of policy priority over the interests protected by the *ultra vires* rule ought clearly be given to a recipient who has changed his position, and hence suffered loss, in reliance on the payment. This view was recently stated by the Law Commission in its Consultation Paper (para 4.18).

As with recovery of payments made to public authorities, the problem of payments by such authorities has sometimes been dealt with by statute. The recovery of most important welfare benefits is dealt with by section 53 of the Social Security Act 1986, and by regulations made under the Act. These provisions limit the right to recover payments made *ultra vires* to the case where the overpayment was caused by the claimant's own misrepresentation or failure to disclose a material fact (Social Security Act s.53(1), and Payments on Account (Overpayments and Recovery) Regulations 1988, S.I. 664/1988, reg 5). This applies even where the non-disclosure or misrepresentation was innocent (*Page v Chief Adjudication Officer*, The Times, July 5 1991). Payments which are not recoverable may still be set against future benefits payments (reg 5), so in practice the government may be able to recoup the amount of an overpayment even though the recipient was not in any way responsible for the overpayment.

11.3.2. Payments invalid under European Community law

Special rules apply under European Community law where public authorities make payments in breach of Community rules.

11.3.2.1. Unlawful state aids

The problem may arise where member states themselves take measures involving payments to third parties, which contravene Community provisions. In practice, this issue has arisen in the context of "state aids" - that is, economic aid given by states from their own resources. All such aids, since they may have the effect of distorting competition, must be notified to the Commission, which will then determine whether the aid is permissible in accordance with the principles on the grant of state aids laid down in Articles 92 and 93 of the Treaty of Rome (see Wyatt and Dashwood, *The Substantive Law of the EEC* (2nd ed (1987), ch.17). Any payment made without notification, or made during the period when the payment is under review, or - of course - after the proposed payment has been determined to be impermissible - is unlawful.

Any action to recover an unlawful payment must be brought in the national courts and will be governed by national law and procedure. In some cases concerning overpayments under Community schemes which are administered by the member states, the courts have held that severe restrictions on the government's right to recovery are permissible in order to protect the recipient of a payment who has a "legitimate expectation" of retaining a payment made to him (see 11.3.2 below). However, in relation to payment of a state aid it has been held in *Commission of the European Communities v Federal Republic of Germany* (case C-5/89, The Times Nov 8 1990) that there is no legitimate expectation of the retention of the unlawful aid (and see also case 142/87, *Belgium v The Commission* (21 March 1990)). This decision was made in the context of an action by the Commission in the European Court for a declaration that Germany was in breach of its obligation to recover certain unlawful aid as required by a Commission decision. However, it seems very likely that the same view would be taken should the question arise in the context of an action for recovery brought in the national courts. It seems that the recipient will generally have no legitimate expectation of retention where an unlawful state aid is received, since the Treaty provisions on aids are widely known to business, and any recipient ought to know of the conditions which must be complied with for aid lawfully to be paid. Such a strict rule ensures that any distortion of competition is corrected as far as possible, and, of course, acts as an important deterrent to the receipt of unlawful payments.

As explained at 11.3.1, there seems to be a general right to recover invalid payments under United Kingdom law in any case. Probably the change of position defence, which it was argued should normally operate in relation to this ground of recovery, could not be applied to bar recovery in a case of this type.

11.3.2.2. Invalid payments in the administration of Community measures

It has already been noted that many Community programmes are administered by the individual member states on behalf of the Community (see 1.6.1 above). The administration of these schemes often involves subsidies and grants being paid out by the member states, which will be met from Community resources. Payments made may sometimes be invalid, either because the measures which they implement infringe Community law principles, or because in making the payment there has been a misinterpretation of the authorising provision, and there is actually no authority to make the payment.

Any action for recovery of unlawful payments must be brought in the national courts and national law and procedure will apply (case 265/78, *H. Ferwarda B.V. v Produktschap voor Vee en Vlees* [1980] ECR 617; case 54/81, *Firma Wilhelm Fromme v Bundesanstalt* [1982] ECR 1449; cases 205-215/82, *Deutsche Milchknotor v Germany* [1983] ECR 2633). The question of recovery will normally be governed by Council Regulation 29/70 requiring a remedy to be given for the recovery of overpaid agricultural subsidies (Art 8(1)). Although this provision is concerned with remedies to be made available to a government, rather than individuals whose Community rights are affected, it was stated in *Ferwarda*, above that the principle of effectiveness applies, and thus the exercise of the right to recover must not be made unduly difficult or impossible to exercise. The principle of non-discrimination also applies so that in respect of ancillary matters not specifically dealt with in the legislation the remedy provided must be given on the same terms as any comparable remedy in national law (*Ferwarda; Deutsche Milchkonor; Firma Wilhelm Fromme*). It seems to have been considered by the court in *Ferwarda* that the principles of non-discrimination and effectiveness would also apply in relation to remedies given in the national court where no legislation governed the matter. Since United Kingdom law provides a general right to recover unlawful payments clearly the principle of non-discrimination requires that a right to recover payments which are invalid for breach of Community law should be given.

Whether any right to recover is based on Community legislation or national remedies, it is permissible to impose serious limitations upon the right, despite the application of the effectiveness principle, in order to protect the competing interest of the payee. This arises from the fact that it is a general principle of Community law that legitimate expectations should be protected, and this must be balanced against the need to provide an effective remedy to recover unlawful payments for the purpose of upholding Community policies. Thus, where those who receive unlawful payments have a legitimate expectation of retaining them it is permissible to impose short limitation periods on their recovery or to permit a "change of position" defence; and it is also permitted to provide that there shall be no recovery at all where the payee is not at fault (*Ferwarda; Firma Wilhelm Fromme;* and *Deutsche Milchkontor*). Thus if, as argued at 11.3.1, the change of position defence should be applied generally to the recovery of *ultra vires* payments, it would generally be permissible to apply the defence to payments which are made under Community measures. It is, indeed, arguable that the Community law principle of the protection of legitimate expectations goes so far as to require member states to provide for the protection of innocent payees (see the statement in *Netherlands v Commission* (case 11/76 [1979] ECR 245 at 278).

11.4. Benefits Conferred Under Ultra Vires Contracts

11.4.1. Introduction

It was suggested in chapter 2 (see 2.3.3 and 2.10) that agreements made by public authorities in breach of public law should be enforceable both by and against an authority. This is because the interests of the other party to the contract should be permitted to outweigh the general public or other interests protected by the *ultra vires* rule. Where an agreement has been made in breach of statutory procedural requirements it seems the agreement will indeed often be unaffected, and arguably this is so also where there is a breach of one of the general principles of administrative law (see 2.10 above). However, the balance of authority suggests that agreements made by statutory authorities which are not for authorised objects are not enforceable, at least against the public authority, and it may be that the courts would not uphold them (see 2.3.3). If so, it may be necessary for the courts to consider whether a restitutionary claim is available for any benefit which has been conferred under the invalid agreement.

It has already been explained that any property which is purportedly transferred under the agreement, whether by or to the public authority, will probably pass to the payee (see 2.3.3).

11.4.2. Claims against public authorities

A claim in restitution generally requires proof that the plaintiff conferred a benefit on the defendant, (in most cases) that the benefit was conferred at the plaintiff's expense, and that it would be unjust for the defendant to retain it (see generally Goff and Jones, *The Law of Restitution* (3rd ed. 1986) at pp.12-51). Where one party confers a benefit on another in performance of an agreement which turns out to be invalid, a claim in restitution is in principle available: it is considered to be unjust for the defendant to retain the benefit where it has been conferred in return for a consideration which has failed (see Goff and Jones, above, at pp.369-374; Arrowsmith, (1989) 9 LS 121). Where the contract is one which is void for *ultra vires* or some other type of incapacity, however, there may be a problem in allowing recovery, in that any action in restitution would be contrary to the very policy which caused the law to deny the existence of any contractual rights. Thus, for example, if a public authority has made an agreement for the purchase of goods for an unauthorised object, to require the authority to pay for those goods infringes the policy against permitting public funds to be used for unauthorised purposes, whether the claim for payment is based on contract or restitution. This type of case has caused some difficulty and will be considered below.

It may first be noted, however, that there are many cases where there is no objection to a restitutionary claim. Thus, a claim should be possible where goods purchased under an *ultra vires* agreement are still in existence, or can be traced into something else (see *Re Jon Beauforte (London) Ltd.* [1953] Ch 131 at 137). The same applies to the extent that money paid over can be traced into existing assets. A claim must also be allowed where money or goods, though obtained for an unlawful purpose, have actually been applied to a lawful purpose. There may also be cases where the nature of the rule breached is such that the policy behind it is not infringed by permitting at least some limited claim in restitution. For example, should a contract be invalidated by procedural breaches not concerned with the subject matter of the contract - for example, tendering requirements, which are concerned to open up the market to competition, or with obtaining best value for money - there is no objection to the authority's being required to pay for what it has received at least the sum it would have had to pay had these requirements been followed. (In practice, breach of such requirements will probably not even invalidate the contract: see 2.9 above). The same would not apply, on the other hand, to procedural requirements relating to the decision to make the purchase - for example, that it should be made or approved by a particular body - since it can be argued here that the purchase decision might not have been taken had the requirement been complied with.

What of those cases where there is some policy objection to restitutionary recovery? The current authority is rather unsatisfactory. The leading decision in public law is *Young v Royal Leamington* ((1883) 8 App Cas 517), which concerned a contract for the procurement of waterworks by the authority which was invalid for failure to comply with a statutory requirement to affix a seal. It was held here that there could be no action at all in respect of work completed under the contract. The purpose of the sealing requirements was to ensure proper consideration was given to entering the contract for the works in question, and to require the authority to pay for the works when such consideration had not been proven by the affixing of the seal infringed the policy behind the provision. Similarly in *Mackay v City of Toronto* ([1920] AC 208) the Privy Council held there could be no recovery against a municipality for work done on a contract which was not authorised by a municipal by law, as was required by statute. (Although there is a line of Canadian authority following this approach, however, there is also another line of authority concerning contracts with the Crown, holding that a claim is allowed : see Arrowsmith, *Government Procurement and Judicial Review* (1988) at pp.265-275). The leading English case on the position where there was failure to comply with the common law requirement, abolished in 1960, to fix the corporate seal to corporate authority contracts is *Lawford v Billericay R D C* ([1903] 1 KB 772), which is ambiguous on the point. It was held that the value of the work done could be recovered. However, it may be that the case is explicable on the basis that the work here - which consisted of services of an engineer in connection with the town's sewerage system - was necessary work, which the authority had a duty to ensure was carried out anyway. If so, the authority would have been required to pay for the work anyway: it could not be argued that the decision to procure the work could ever have been any different. This requirement of "necessity" as a condition for recovery had been mentioned in a number of earlier cases, and was the basis for the decision of Stirling L J in *Lawford*. It was not, however, mentioned by the other two judges.

Authority on the position under an *ultra vires* contract in private law is also relevant by analogy. This authority is, unfortunately, particularly unsatisfactory. In the nineteenth century it seems to have been assumed that restitution would generally have been available. This view was stated by Brice in his work *Ultra Vires* (3rd ed. 1893, at p.641 *et seq.*). It was adopted in *Re Phoenix Life Assurance Co.* ((1862) 70 ER 1131), holding that premiums paid to the company under a contract made in pursuance of an *ultra vires* insurance business were recoverable. However, a different view was taken by the House of Lords in *Sinclair v Brougham* ([1914] AC 398), concerning the winding up of a friendly society. The society had been carrying on an *ultra vires* banking business and the question which arose was whether the depositors could recover the amounts which they had deposited pursuant to the invalid banking contracts. The House of Lords held that there was no personal claim against the society for the value of the deposits. This was followed in *Re Jon Beauforte (London) Ltd* ([1953] Ch 131), holding that there could be no recovery for the value of coal supplied for and used in an *ultra vires* business of the company.

Prominent in the judgements in *Sinclair* was the reasoning that any claim to repayment would be based on an "implied contract" to repay the amount, and there could be no contract implied to this effect where the express contract to do so was invalid (see p.414, per Lord Haldane and p.440

per Lord Parker). At one time an implied contract to repay was in fact stated to be the basis of many restitutionary claims. However, this was a fiction developed for purely historical reasons, to enable restitutionary claims to be fitted within one of the forms of action (see Goff and Jones, *The Law of Restitution* (3rd ed. 1986) at pp.5-12 for the history of the "implied contract" theory). The fiction has long since been rejected, and it has been recognised that restitutionary obligations are not based on any implied promise but, like obligations in tort, are imposed by law (*Fibrosa Spolka Akyjna v Fairbairn Lawson Combe Barbour* [1943] AC 32). Insofar as *Sinclair* is based on this reasoning, allowing what was clearly recognised as a fiction to affect substantive principles, it is most unsatisfactory.

It was left open in *Sinclair v Brougham* whether the decision in Re Phoenix was correct. It was suggested in Sinclair that *Re Phoenix* might be distinguishable on the basis that in that case the court was not "indirectly" enforcing the invalid promise by allowing a restitutionary claim, since the latter type of claim simply meant return of the premiums, which was not what was promised under the contract. In *Sinclair v Brougham*, on the other hand, it was said, a restitutionary claim involved return of the moneys lent, which was also what was promised under the contract. Insofar as this alleged distinction is based on the argument that the court must not enforce an implied promise where an express one would be void, it is unsound for the reasons indicated above. In addition it does not reflect any distinction of policy. In both cases it is contrary to the policy of the *ultra vires* rule to some degree to give a remedy in restitution: in both cases the policy of the rule is to prevent the company risking its assets in an *ultra vires* business, and in each case a claim in restitution requires the return of assets received in the course of the company's carrying on such a business.

Although the House of Lords in *Sinclair* did not allow a claim for the value of the deposits, however, they did allow a claim to the extent that the moneys deposited could be traced into assets still held by the society. To this extent there is, as indicated above, no policy objection to recovery. However, the House held that this was a claim of a proprietary, rather than a personal nature (a claim which was held to rank *pari passu* with that of the shareholders). This holding has been much criticised (see Goff and Jones, above, at pp.69-71; Birks, *Introduction to the Law of Restitution* (2nd paperback ed. 1989) at pp.396-7; Maddaugh and McCamus, *The Law of Restitution* (1990) at pp.326). A proprietary claim will in principle give the claimant priority in an insolvency over unsecured creditors. There is no reason, however, why those who have made an *ultra vires* contract should be given such preference, unless, of course, they have obtained some security under their contract. (This priority question did not arise in *Sinclair*, since the other creditors had already been paid off, and the relationship between these creditors and the depositors was not raised as an issue). In addition, a proprietary claim will give a share in the value of assets conferred to the extent that the value has increased, and there is likewise no justification for this.

Both public and private law authority thus tends to suggest that no remedy is available in restitution where it would prejudice the policy of the *ultra vires* rule, though the decision in *Re Phoenix* does not really fit with this analysis. This position, it is submitted, should be reconsidered (a view taken also by Maddaugh and McCamus, above, at p.327). When the performance requested under a contract has been rendered there is a benefit conferred on the authority at the plaintiff's expense, which it is unjust to retain (see further Arrowsmith, (1989) 9 LS 307 at pp.310-311). The policy of preventing unjust enrichment should override the policy of the *ultra vires* rule, even if it is thought the latter policy should override the usual private law right to damages for breach of the agreement itself. Certainly, if some sanction to deter *ultra vires* agreements is felt necessary, making the agreement itself unenforceable should be sufficient.

11.4.3. Claims by public authorities

It was suggested at 2.3.3 that where the authority has executed its own part of the agreement it is arguable that it may be able to enforce the contract itself. If this is not permitted, then it is clear that a remedy in restitution is available (*Brougham v Dwyer* (1913) 108 LT 504). Such a claim could be based on failure of consideration, a ground which *prima facie* gives a right to restitution of all benefits conferred under unenforceable contracts (see 11.4.2 above).

Alternatively, it is arguable that a claim should be made available also on the grounds of "public policy" in many cases, since to refuse a remedy not only leads to unjust enrichment, but is contrary to the very policy which the *ultra vires* rule is designed to protect. Thus, if it is forbidden for the authority to risk its assets in an *ultra vires* manufacturing business, it is obviously contrary to that policy not to allow a claim for goods supplied to another by the authority in the course of carrying out that business, of, if it is forbidden to make loans, not to allow recovery of the amount of the loan.

11.4.4. Valuation of the claim

A question which may arise in a claim either for against a public authority is how it is to be valued. It seems clear that the greatest sum which can be obtained is a reasonable price for what has been conferred. The plaintiff may not claim a higher sum even though provided for under the contract, since the contract itself is unenforceable.

It was also suggested by the Court of Appeal in *Rover International Ltd v Cannon Film Sales Ltd* ([1989] 1 WLR 912) that the plaintiff is entitled to claim a reasonable sum even where the contract price is *lower*, so that he will to this extent gain from the fact that the contract is unenforceable. (The case concerned a contract which was void since it was purportedly made on behalf of a company which was not yet incorporated, but the same rules should apply, *prima facie*, to all types of ineffective transactions). This suggestion is open to criticism however. To claim in restitution it is necessary to show that the other party has received a benefit. Normally this is done by showing that the defendant requested what has been provided to him, knowing that payment was expected. Where a benefit is requested under a contract which provides that the price payable is lower than a reasonable price, the defendant can only be shown to have benefited to the extent of the price provided for in the contract, and thus cannot be required to pay more than that amount. This argument was not considered in *Cannon Films*. The view that the defendant should be required to pay the contract price only finds support in the older case of *Scarisbrook v Parkinson* ((1869) 20 LT 175), and it is submitted that it is this approach which should be followed (see further Arrowsmith, (1989) 9 LS 121).

11.4.5. Failure of consideration

In other contexts where restitutionary claims have been allowed for benefits conferred under ineffective transactions, it has been held that a condition of the claim is that there should be "total failure" of any consideration promised to the plaintiff (see, for example, *Steinberg v Scala* [1923] 2 Ch 452 (contract by minor); *Fibrosa Spolka Akyjna v Fairbairn Lawson Combe v Barbour* [1943] AC 32 (contract frustrated)). Generally this has been taken to mean that the plaintiff's claim will fail once he has received any part of the consideration which cannot be restored (see further Goff and Jones, *The Law of Restitution* (3rd ed. 1986) at pp.54-55). By analogy this would probably be applied to *ultra vires* contracts with public bodies.

This approach is open to criticism (see, for example, Goff and Jones, above; Arrowsmith, (1989) 9 LS 121 at 134-135). It is unfair to deny the plaintiff his claim simply because he has received some small benefit. Recovery should be allowed, in principle, but reduced by the amount of any benefit received. This may involve difficult calculations but is preferable to denying recovery altogether.

If the defendant has done something in performing his own part of the agreement which does not constitute a benefit to the plaintiff, then it may be fair to allow him to set his expenses off against any claim against him, but again the failure of consideration doctrine, by which the plaintiff's claim is denied altogether, is a drastic way of achieving this result. This may be achieved instead by allowing a defence of "change of position" where the defendant has changed his position in some way - for example, by commencing performance - in reliance on a belief that the agreement is valid. In *Lipkin Gorman v Karpnale Ltd* ([1991] 3 WLR 10) the House of Lords recognised a general defence of change of position in English law. Usually this will be applied in a case where there is reliance on *receipt* of a payment, but it should apply also where the defendant changes his position in reliance on the belief that a valid contract exists, to allow a defence to an action for recovery of a benefit conferred upon him.

12

Payments Due under Legislation

12.1. General Principles

Sometimes legislation provides for a sum to be paid by the government to a citizen - for example, a welfare benefit, a grant or subsidy, or compensation for expropriation of property or for other damage lawfully caused by government (on the last see 9.3 above). It is common for special tribunals to be set up to hear claims and to settle disputes over entitlement under the statute. Where no special procedure is provided for, a claim for the amount due may be brought to the High or County Court in an action begun by writ or summons (*Cato v Minister of Agriculture, Food and Fisheries* (1989) 1 CMLR 513). When payment is made later than due under the statute interest will be available under section 35A of the Supreme Court Act which allows interest to be awarded by the court in an action for recovery of a debt or damages: a sum due under statute is a "debt", even where the claim is for an unliquidated sum to be determined by the court (*B.P. Exploration Co. (Libya) v Hunt (No.2)* [1983] 2 AC 352).

With respect to a sum due from the Crown, it was formerly possible to bring an action for recovery by way of petition of right (*Attorney General v De Keyser s Royal Hotel* [1920] AC 508). Thus this type of case falls within section 1 of the Crown Proceedings Act 1947, which provides for an action against the Crown in accordance with the procedure laid down in the Act in all cases where, before the Act, a claim could have been brought by petition of right (see 1.2.1.3 above).

When there is an executive duty to make a payment, which can be said to be a public law duty (as opposed to a duty not confined to public authorities), it seems that an action for mandamus must be available to compel payment of the sum. In *R v Secretary of State for Transport, ex parte Sherriff & Sons Ltd.* (The Indep 12 Jan 1988: noted by Bradley in [1989] PL 197) it was held, however, that no interest may be awarded where it is sought to enforce payment by seeking an order of mandamus, on the basis that section 35A of the Supreme Court does not apply to proceedings in "public law". (On the meaning of public law in this context see further 1.3 above). Hence, an applicant will often prefer to proceed by writ. Another effective alternative when the government refuses interest on a sum due may be to complain to the Commissioners for Administration.

12.2.   Payments Which are Subject to Administrative Discretion

Sometimes legislation will provide for a payment which is conditional on the exercise of some administrative discretion. For example, it may be provided that a grant or benefit must be paid if a public authority is satisfied that certain conditions have been met. In such a case a party claiming a payment will be able to bring an action for judicial review to compel the authority to exercise its discretion - in the example given, to determine whether the conditions have been met. In *Cocks v Thanet D.C.* ([1983] 2 AC 286), discussed at 1.3 above, it was held that where there is a statutory duty which imposes an obligation to take action only following the exercise of some discretion, no private law right to enforce the duty (whether through an action for damages or otherwise) will arise until the discretion has been exercised in favour of the party seeking to enforce it. Until this is done, an action to compel the authority to exercise its discretion is the only remedy available.

This principle was held to apply in the case of a statutory duty to make a payment in *Cato v Minister of Agriculture, Food and Fisheries* ((1989) 1 CMLR 513). The case concerned regulations providing for payments to owners of fishing boats who withdrew their boats from the fishing fleet, as part of a European Community scheme to reduce the fishing fleet of the Community. The regulations provided that in specified circumstances a payment was required to be made by the Minister, provided he was satisfied that certain conditions had been met. The Court of Appeal held that no private law right to the grant arose until the Minister had satisfied himself as to the requisite conditions. Stocker L J expressly stated that this would be so even if there were no grounds on which the Minister could fail to be satisfied. In such a case, it will not be possible to bring an action by writ to recover the sum claimed. The claimant's only remedy will be an action for judicial review to compel the Minister to exercise his discretion. However, where the Minister has no ground for refusing to make a decision that the applicant is entitled, it can be argued that mandamus is available as a remedy to compel actual payment, by analogy with *Padfield v Minister of Agriculture, Fisheries and Food* (1968] AC 997). Here mandamus was given to compel the Minister to investigate a complaint which he had a discretion to investigate, where the court could see no grounds on which he could refuse to make the investigation. As explained at 12.1 above, however, no interest is available when it is sought to enforce payment through an application for mandamus.

It was explained earlier that where a public authority has exercised its discretion and made a decision that a grant should be paid, and has informed the applicant, the courts have held that no contractual agreement to pay generally arises, even where the payment is to be made in return for something done by the applicant (see 2.2.2 above).

The above discussion has been concerned with cases where legislation imposes a *duty* to make a payment in certain circumstances. In other cases there may simply be a permissive discretionary power to make a payment. In such a case it is submitted that where a decision is made to make the payment no private right to recover will arise. This seemed to be the view of Taylor J in *R v Secretary of State for Transport, ex parte Sherriff* (The Independent, Jan 12 1988: noted by Bradley in [1989] PL 197), where it was held that a decision to make a grant under a general discretionary power did not create a "debt" for the purposes of recovery of interest under section 35A of the Supreme Court Act. This implies that no private law right to recover the sum arose. An action for judicial review will, of course, be available, to require the relevant public authority to give proper consideration to whether to make an award. When there seem to be no grounds for lawful refusal of the payment, then arguably mandamus might issue to compel payment (see the discussion of *Padfield,* above).

12.3. Sums Due Under European Law

12.3.1. Introduction

Measures implemented by the European Community often provide for payments to be made to individuals by way of grant or subsidy - for example, for the purposes of encouraging, or, in many cases, discouraging, the production of certain products, or for facilitating competition with producers outside the Community. As explained at 1.6.1 above, Community schemes are generally administered by the national authorities on behalf of the Community. Thus it is the national authorities which are normally responsible for handing over these payments, though ultimately they will usually come from the resources of the Community itself.

In examining the rights of a party who is wrongfully refused a payment due under Community law, two situations must be considered. The first is where that party has a right to a payment under Community law but the national authority wrongfully refuses to make it - for example, because it wrongly believes the applicant is not entitled. The second is where the payment has been refused because of wrongful conduct by the Community, either in wrongly failing to provide for a payment at all, or in unlawfully reducing the amount of an existing grant or subsidy.

12.3.2. *Wrongful decisions of national authority*

Where a payment is wrongly refused by the national authorities, any action against the relevant authority to compel it to make the payment must, in accordance with the usual principles governing actions against national authorities to enforce Community law, be brought in the national courts. National law and procedure will govern the action, but this principle is subject to the Community law principles of non-discrimination and effectiveness (see 1.6.2).

The principle of non-discrimination requires that the remedies in domestic law for the recovery of sums due under statute generally should be made available for the recovery of charges due under Community law (on these remedies see 12.1 and 12.2 above). It is not clear whether the principle of effectiveness would require some new remedy to be made available if none existed already (see further 1.6.2.2), but this is academic since existing remedies are clearly generally effective to protect Community rights. (It is argued below that some remedy is in fact *required* to be provided, this being the basis of decisions not to admit claims against the Community itself). Whatever the position with the creation of new remedies, the principle of effectiveness will require in this context, as others, that remedies not be made unduly difficult or impossible to exercise. What this may require was discussed in the context of restitutionary claims (see 11.2.7 above). It was noted there that the provision of interest is a matter for national law.

Conversely, it seems clear that no claim for the amount withheld is available against the Community itself in the European Court, even though the payment will ultimately come from Community resources. It seems that this is the position even when the national authority's refusal is attributable to some fault by the Community. In such a case an action against the Community for damages under Article 215 will be declared inadmissible and the applicant will be bound to seek his remedy in the national courts. This was the view of the European Court in *Grand Moulin* (case 99/74, *Grand Moulin des Antilles v The Commission* [1975] ECR 1531). The applicants claimed to be entitled under Community law to certain grants payable by the French authorities. The French authorities refused to pay since no provision had been made for the Community to reimburse the national authorities in this type of case. An action for damages was brought by the claimant against the Community itself, it being alleged that the claimant's loss had been caused by the fault of the Community in failing to provide for reimbursement when it was under a duty to do so. The European Court, however, held the action inadmissible. If such an action is inadmissible where the Community is at fault in the sense alleged, then a *fortiori* it will be inadmissible where there is no such fault.

It is submitted that the basis for holding such a claim inadmissible is that the national courts *must* provide a remedy for recovery under the principle of effectiveness. The European Court knows that rights are effectively protected in the national court, and for this reason can leave the enforcement of Community law to that forum. It was argued above that the same applies with restitutionary claims for the recovery of sums levied by the national authorities in breach of Community law (see 11.2.7.2 above).

A party who is refused a payment may wish to recover not only the amount of the payment but also damages for consequential losses, either against the national authorities or, where the Community can be shown to be at fault, against the Community itself. The principles which govern such claims were examined in chapter 10.

12.3.3. Payments wrongfully refused by the Community

12.3.3.1. Where there is an executive duty to pay

A second class of cases to consider is where a payment is refused by the national authorities because of wrongful conduct by Community institutions. This may occur because the Community has wrongfully refused to provide for a payment when it should have done so, or because the Community has purported unlawfully to amend existing measures which provide for payments to be made, either by reducing the sum due or revoking the measures.

As will be explained, it seems necessary to distinguish between two situations. The first is where there is an executive duty on the national authorities to make payment, the second where no such duty exists. The first situation seems likely to occur only when the Community institutions have purported to reduce or revoke a payment already provided for, in such circumstances that the reduction or revocation is treated as ineffective, and hence the original measure remains in effect.

This first situation seems analogous to that where a national authority makes an unlawful levy in the purported application of Community measures, and the same principles should apply to the recovery of payments wrongly withheld, as to the recovery of unlawful levies. Thus the appropriate remedy will be to sue for the sum owed in the national courts, the action being governed by national law and procedure, subject to the principles of non-discrimination and effectiveness (see 1.6). Thus in English law the usual remedies for the recovery of a specific sum must be provided (see 12.1 and 12.2 above), and these remedies must not be made unduly difficult or impossible to exercise. As with the case considered at 12.3.2 above, it is unclear whether some remedy for recovery must be provided, but again this is immaterial since existing remedies in English law seem adequate to protect Community rights.

As explained at 11.2.7.2 there may generally be no action in the European Court against the Community to recover the amount of a sum wrongly levied - the appropriate remedy is to sue the responsible national authority in the national courts. There has been some debate, however, over whether there may be an action for damages against the Community for the amount which has been wrongly withheld (as opposed to a sum wrongly levied), as an alternative to an action against the national authorities, since the cases in this area are not entirely satisfactory and consistent (see Durand, (1975-6) 1 E L Rev 431; Hartley, (1977) 16 E L Rev 249; Harding, (1979) 16 CML Rev 389; Lewis, (1980) 33 CLP 99; Oliver, "Joint Liability of the Community and the Member States" in *Non-Contractual Liability of the European Communities* (1988) eds. Schermers, Heukels, Mead, ch.1).

In principle the position here clearly ought to be the same as with claims for the recovery of overpayments. Thus the court ought to hold that a remedy *must* be made available in the national court and refuse to allow any claim for this amount in the European Court. This was suggested above to be the position with overpayments (see 11.2.7.2). An alternative possibility is that a national remedy is not *required,* and whether an action is admissible in the European Court depends on the position in the national law of the member state concerned. In practice it makes little difference which approach is adopted since a national remedy will almost invariably be given.

The view that a claim for the amount of the sum is not generally admissible in the European Court is favoured by most commentators (see, for example, Harding, Durand and Hartley above: though cf. Steiner, *A Textbook on EEC Law* (2nd ed. 1990), at pp.326-327). In support of this view is the decision of the European Court in *Cotelle* (joined cases 65-85/75, *Lesieurs Cotelle v The Commission* [1976] ECR 391). Here the court admitted a number of claims which it appeared to regard as arising where there was an executive duty to make the payment in question. In this case it was considered there would be a remedy against the national authorities, and hence no action against the Community should be admissible. The conclusion that a claim should not be admissible in such circumstances is, as indicated, generally accepted, though it may be noted that the case has been criticised on the basis that the claims admitted did not in fact seem to arise from the type of case where national law would provide a remedy (see Durand, above, at pp.438-439; Lewis, above; and see also the opinion of Advocate General Warner in case 126/76, *Firmer Gebruder Dietz v The Commission* [1977] ECR 2431, suggesting the apparent difficulty is explained by the fact that the case was decided on earlier pleadings). The principle in *Cotelle* seems also to have been accepted in the later case of

IBC (case 46/75, *IBC Importazione Bestiame Carnis r.1. v The Commission* [1976] ECR 45).

A different view appears to have been adopted by the European Court in a case decided before *Cotelle*, that of *Merkur* (case 43/72, *Merkur v The Commission* [1973] ECR 1055). In this case the court suggested that it is not in keeping with the "proper administration of justice" and "procedural efficiency" to send a litigant back to the national courts to recover a subsidy where he has already commenced proceedings in the European Court, which might suggest that an action may always be brought against the Community in respect of non-payment of a Community subsidy. However, following *Cotelle*, and also the analogous decisions precluding an action in the European Court to recover the amount of overpaid charges, this principle is generally considered inapplicable (though the decision in *Merkur* itself is regarded as consistent with the principles currently accepted: see 12.3.3.2).

12.3.3.2. Where there is no executive duty to pay

The situation where there is an executive duty on the national authority to make a payment is likely to arise only rarely. More common will be cases where the Community has failed to make provision for payment where it ought to have done so. In such a case it does not seem that Community law will require any form of redress to be given in the national courts against the national authority for the recovery of the amount of payment which should have been provided. Such redress is not appropriate since the national authority is not under any Community law obligation to make a payment - the only obligation is on the Community itself to provide for payment to be made. It does not seem that English law would provide a remedy against the national authorities in such circumstances.

The appropriate remedy in such a case is a claim for damages in the European Court against Community institutions. In a number of cases the European Court has held admissible claims in respect of the Community's failure to provide for a payment (see case 43/72, *Merkur v The Commission* [1973] ECR 1055; case 153/73, *Holtz and Willemsen GmbH v The Council and The Commission* [1974] ECR 675; case 74/74, *CNTA SA v The Commission* [1975] ECR 533; case 126/76, *Firmer Gebruder Dietz v The Commission* [1977] ECR 2431). It was suggested at 12.3.3.1 above that the reason a claim for the amount of a payment not made is inadmissible where there is an executive duty on the national authority to pay is that there must be a remedy in the national courts. The fact that the claim is admissible where no such duty exists is because, it is submitted, there is no *requirement* for a remedy to be provided a national level.

It has often been suggested that the reason the remedy here is in the European Court is that the exact amount which would have been paid if the

Community had complied with its obligations to provide for payment will not always be clear, and it is not for the national authorities to fix this amount. Although this may be one reason for not requiring a national remedy and instead providing for one in the European Court, the fundamental reason, it is submitted, is that there is no Community law duty on the national authority to make the payment. The case where the payment remains to be calculated is simply one illustration of a case where no such duty exists.

When the action is admissible in the European Court the question then arises as to the conditions under which it will succeed. It was explained in chapter 10 that when damages are sought under Article 215 in respect of unlawful legislative action, a claim for damages will only succeed in very restricted circumstances - when there is a flagrant breach of a superior rule of law designed for the protection of the individual (see 10.2.2). The cases have said that these restrictions apply in actions under Article 215 for the amount of grants or subsidies wrongfully denied (see, for example, *Merkur*, above). This approach may be criticised. It seems that once the subsidy has been set there may be an action in the national courts to recover the amount without limitation, and there is no reason why more restrictive conditions should apply to an action in the European Court. The policy considerations, including fear of widespread liability, which have led to the restrictions on damages for consequential losses, do not apply in this type of case. It may be noted that in *Rocquette,* discussed at 10.3.2, the European Court denied a claim for the amount of overpaid charges which was admitted in the European Court because of the restrictions mentioned above (case 20/80, (1991) 2 CMLR 6). However, this case is not analogous. In *Rocquette* the very reason national courts were precluded from giving a remedy, and hence that the claim was admitted in the European Court itself, was that to grant a general right to recovery was considered to be unwarranted: for this reason the European Court had limited the temporal effect of its judgement holding the charges invalid. Hence it seems correct that damages in this case should have been recoverable only on a very restricted basis.

12.3.3.3. Damages for consequential loss

A claim for damages for consequential losses resulting from failure to make a payment will in all cases be admissible in the European Court. The principles applying here were considered in chapter 10.

Index

ACTS OF STATE
139-40
ARMED FORCES, LIABILITY AND CROWN IMMUNITIES 159-60
APPLICATION FOR JUDICIAL REVIEW. See also PREROGATIVE
ORDERS; INJUNCTION
  availability of 20-23
  damages in 20-21
  financial claims in 20-27
  interest on sums recovered in 21-22
  interim relief in 14-15
  obligation to use 23-27
  public-private distinction under 2, 4, 20, 20-27
  recovery of payments due under statute in 21, 297, 299

AUTHORITY. See CONTRACT

BREACH OF STATUTORY DUTY, TORT OF
  Crown liability for 157-158, 197
  omissions and 206-209
  scope of 197-209

CAPACITY. See also CONTRACT

CAUSATION
  ultra vires and 29-32, 33, 237

COMMISSIONERS FOR LOCAL ADMINISTRATION. See also
OMBUDSMEN

COMPULSORY PURCHASE
  compensation for 243

CONTRACT - See also EMPLOYMENT CONTRACTS;
PROCUREMENT CONTRACTS
  authority to contract 66-71
  between health service agencies 52-53
  between public agencies 52-53
  breach of warranty of authority 71
  capacity of Crown in 53-56
  capacity of Crown agents in 56-60